Texas High Sheriffs

Texas High Sheriffs

by Thad Sitton

★

TexasMonthlyPress

Texas Monthly Press
P.O. Box 1569
Austin, Texas 78767

ABCDEFGH

Library of Congress Cataloging-in-Publication Data

Sitton, Thad, 1941–
    Texas high Sheriffs.

    Includes index.
    1. Sheriffs—Texas—History—20th century. 2. Law enforcement—Texas—History—20th century. 3. Oral history. I. Title.
HV7979.S58   1988   363.2'82'09764   88-2260
ISBN 0-87719-079-8

Book design by David Timmons

To Bubba Sitton, 1912–1985, who told me tales of Sheriff A. J. Spradley.

Back in those days, the sheriff, he was law! They respected him, he was the law. And I couldn't be sheriff now, no. Nowhere in the world, nowhere in the world. 'Cause I'd want to do it the old way.

—Tom Brown

I had an old lady come in the office one day, said she wanted to see the high sheriff. Deputies wanted to know if they couldn't handle it. Says, "Naw, y'all too light, I want the high sheriff."

—Frank Brunt

CONTENTS

★

PREFACE

★

In small-town East Texas when I was growing up back in the '50s, the sheriff was still the "high sheriff"—master of the county courthouse, feudal lord of the county territory, manhunter, and keeper of bloodhounds—the person you least wanted to see while on teenage beer drinking excursions down obscure county roads. The city police stayed in the county seat, the Department of Public Safety troopers patrolled only the state highways, but the sheriff or his deputies might be anywhere, anytime, always on call, with a 24-hour patrol. No backwoods lane was so remote, no night so dark that you couldn't imagine the sheriff's patrol car appearing out of nowhere to strike terror into the teenage heart.

I saw my particular sheriff in parades, riding with his newly-formed sheriff's posse, or in newspaper photos standing beside the stars of the TV series *Bonanza*. His western-movie-star good looks were nonetheless associated with a nature both combative and controversial. I heard my father talk of the sheriff's latest public confrontations with jail bondsmen, county judges, and various "courthouse lawyers." Many voters liked our handsome sheriff's style, but others found him too feisty, abrasive, and overweeningly proud for their tastes. In a dry county, he was nervy enough to shut down such traditional oases as the VFW hall and the country club. He was a high-visibility, old-style sheriff in a new day of civil rights and the Miranda warning, and he still did things in the old way. He was nice to little children and old ladies, but was reputed to be very, very rude and irregular to the criminal element. He kept a friendly old bloodhound around his office for kids to pet, and on occasion to help locate lost children and old people who had wandered away from home, but his real pack was kenneled out on the edge of town. They were a mix of Bluetick and Walker hounds from the "Walls" pack at Huntsville, and they meant business. Like the sheriff himself, they had a taste for manhunting, and before they got to you, you had better climb a tree. Law enforcement in my county had teeth in it.

My sheriff is not present in this oral history of the old ways of law enforcement in rural Texas, though I think he would find his views well represented in some of the accounts that follow. Although the term is still used today, the rural sheriff is not the high sheriff anymore, at least not in the same way that he was in the 1950s. Some of the old awe and aura lingers on, attached to the persons of thirty-year incumbents like Rufe Jordan, H. F. Fenton, Truman Maddox, Nathan Tindell, and others; but the average sheriff today has his style far too cramped by the requirements of the new rules of evidence, the ever-present threat of civil rights litigation under the 14th Amendment, and the oversight activities of the Texas Commission on Jail Standards to operate in the old way. That was not the case even as late as the mid '60s. The persons interviewed for this book had their careers in whole or in part back in the days when, as one said, "the sheriff was really the sheriff." Some, like Jess Sweeten and the sheriff from my home county, left office directly or indirectly because of the new limitations on their powers to do the job. As Sweeten said, "I didn't want any part of it anymore. You were just screwed down too tight." Others stayed in office and adapted to change, not discarding any more of their old ways of doing things than they had to, keeping what Rufe Jordan called "the buggy" of old-time law enforcement because it still worked. The rules of close observation and common sense, the advantage derived from knowing one's county foot by foot and person by person, the ability to look into a man's eyes and see that he was lying, the use of a far-flung network of informants cross-cutting county social strata, these were part of what Jordan described as the buggy of traditional law enforcement in rural Texas, and its wheels still turned. It still did the job. Computers had not replaced it, and the expansion of state and federal law had not yet forbade it.

In any case, the focus of this book is on the old style of law enforcement as practiced by the rural Texas sheriff in the period before 1965, though several sheriffs comment on (and complain about) the great changes that came in the late '60s and early '70s. The book's substance is the personal stories of men who held office in the early years. Preserved in their voices, like fossils in amber, are historical fragments from the careers of even earlier sheriffs: of the legendary Bill Decker of Dallas, who had a line on every criminal in his county and could pull them in from the center of his spider's web at anytime; of Jim Scarborough, I, who may have killed over 30 men while enforcing the law in unruly Lee County at the turn of the century; and of Vail Ennis of Beeville, who replaced his car's hood ornament with a Thompson submachine gun and strafed evildoers like a fighter pilot.

A writer always has a choice to make in any work composed mainly of oral testimony. Shall he dissemble the personal accounts into a topical outline, gaining structure but lessening the impact of the individual personality? Or shall he edit and arrange the personal accounts, but leave them essentially intact, and organize his book by person? In *Texas High Sheriffs* I have chosen the second alternative. I have seldom met individuals like these, and they would not appreciate having their stories disassembled by me or anyone else. Furthermore, I would like to be able to travel through these sheriffs' counties in the future with a clear conscience! This organization by person is the most basic and potentially the most powerful approach to oral history—one in which the memoirists are left to tell their own stories in their own words without interruption. These sheriffs were interviewed and re-interviewed, their tapes selectively transcribed, and the transcribed elements edited into each man's personal account. In the process, topics were consolidated and the interviewer's words edited out; conversations became soliloquies. Considerable liberty was taken with the sequencing of the accounts, almost none with the sheriff's words themselves. Working with the raw materials of the interviews, I tried to be true first of all to the nature of the individual and his story. Each chapter is in a sense a created thing, a form of historiography, not a raw primary account. But in another sense each chapter is a distillation, a concentration, of each sheriff's spoken tale, an account that is more powerful than the original. The tapes, the unaltered primary documents, are preserved for future historians at Barker Texas History Center in Austin.

At its best, this form of history is compelling and unique. British poet A. E. Houseman once remarked that he could no more define poetry than a terrier could a rat, but they both knew it when they came upon it. The hair rose on the backs of their necks. The historian cannot define a person, either, but sometimes in forms of history derived from oral testimony the person is so fully present, so uncannily there in his individuality on the printed page, that the scalp prickles in that way. If these sheriffs had written their memoirs (and to my knowledge, no sheriff has—they were all much too busy), their experiences and their individual voices probably would have been translated and homogenized into some variations of standard English, and much would have been lost in the process. This was certainly true in the two accounts of Texas sheriffs written by others, the stories of A. J. Spradley of Nacogdoches and Jess Sweeten of Athens.[1] In this book each man's story is still as individualized and unique as the man who told it. I could not have created English prose like these men have spoken. I doubt if anyone else could have.

My greatest thanks for this book goes to the sheriffs, in office and retired, who were willing to tell me much, but doubtless not all, about how they did things back in the old days. Thanks also to the Texas Sheriffs Association for its advice and assistance, and to Barker Texas History Center of the University of Texas at Austin, where the original interview tapes will reside. Finally, deep gratitude is expressed to Dr. James G. Dickson of the political science department at Stephen F. Austin State University, whose pioneering research about Texas sheriffs enlightened the following Introduction,[2] and whose early interview with Sheriff Jess Sweeten rescued that particular voice from beyond the grave.

Thad Sitton
Austin, Texas

[1] Henry C. Fuller, *A Texas Sheriff,* Nacogdoches, Texas, 1931; Allan Sigvard Lindquist, *Jess Sweeten Texas Lawman,* San Antonio: Naylor, 1961.

[2] James G. Dickson, *The Politics of the Texas Sheriff: From Frontier to Bureaucracy,* Boston, Massachusetts: American Press, 1983.

INTRODUCTION

★

"High sheriff" is an archaic term of reference to an office that was already ancient at the time of the European settling of the New World. The origins of the sheriff go back more than a thousand years to a time of increasing royal power in Saxon England. Seventh century England was organized first for war, then later for administrative purposes. Ten families residing together in a *tun* (town) comprised a *tithing*. Each tithing chose a *tithingman* to lead them, and 10 tithings made up a *hundred,* which came to be led by a *gerefa,* or chief. Over the centuries, the word *gerefa* evolved in the Saxon language into that of *reeve,* although the previous title was retained as well. The gerefa and the reeve became elected officials of the hundred with both police and judicial powers.

This system of local government was greatly revised and extended under Alfred the Great (871–901 A.D.) in order to promote greater centralization of royal power. The existing hundreds were now gathered together into *scirs,* or shires, the direct ancestor of the county. Over each shire was placed a headman called the *scyre-reeve* (shire-reeve), the principal judicial and administrative official of the shire.

He played a multiple role as royal tax collector, law enforcement officer, judge, and the shire's military commander in time of war. This jack-of-all-trades and master of everything in the ancestral county became the *sheriff*.

The coming of Duke William and the Norman kings to the throne of England after 1066 only served to enhance and extend the powers of the sheriff. Now, the local sheriffs were even more the "king's men," playing a critical role in royal tax collection and the extension of kingly authority into every remote district of medieval England. The jobs paid for themselves for the great noblemen who usually held them. The king sold the offices to the highest bidders, who were free to pocket all tax revenues collected above the king's quotas. Later, the sheriff's police powers were greatly strengthened by the legal reforms of Henry I, who codified major crimes into a penal code centralizing criminal justice in the king's hands.

As dynasties and centuries passed, the sheriff's role changed and evolved, but he remained the chief administrative and judicial official of the county. His function as tax collector was reduced, and other local officials joined him to take away some of his multi-purpose power. Fiscal and judicial powers were gradually absorbed by the rise of other positions, but the sheriff was still important, the main link between central and local government and the chief law enforcement official of the shire.

With the settling of the American colonies, the office was easily adapted to its new context. It was at first appointive, rather than elective, and some symbolic and ceremonial trappings dropped away, but the sheriff was still the high sheriff, the central figure of county government. When colonial settlers moved west, the sheriff went with them. As in England, the American sheriff could make use of the *posse comitatus,* the ancient right to enlist the aid of all ablebodied persons in the county, their weapons, boats, and horses, in times of public emergency. This was the "sheriff's posse," like the sheriff himself, still functioning in twentieth century Texas, a direct link to Saxon England. In Anglo Texas at the time of the *empresarios,* the office met with a not-incompatible Spanish equivalent, the *alquacil,* whose duties of patrol, arrest and custody, execution of executive and judicial writs, etc., were very like those of the American sheriff. The constitution of the Texas Republic provided for sheriffs in each county, elected for two-year terms. Dave Rusk, San Jacinto veteran and later ferryboat operator, was the first Texas sheriff, commissioned for office in 1837. Not a great deal is known about the activities of Texas sheriffs under the Republic, but they were evidently drawn into their ancient duties of tax collection by the new government's efforts to exert its proper authority upon a reluctant citizenry. Disorderly Harrison County in the "Texas Badlands" had no less than 10 sheriffs during the decade of the Republic, including one who was killed by a mob in broad daylight and whose tax book was burned on the spot. Later in the nineteenth century, Harrison County sheriffs resumed their proper authority and ran the county for decades at a time. In 1876, despite recent unpleasant experiences with Republican authority, the resurgent Texas Democrats wrote a strong traditional sheriff into their constitution of that year. According to Article 5, Section 23, "There shall be elected by the qualified voters of each county a Sheriff, who shall hold his office for the term of two years, whose duties and prerequisites, and fees of office, shall be prescribed by the Legislature, and vacancies in whose office shall be filled by the Commissioners Court until the next general election." The pattern of the strong sheriff with multi-purpose powers would last for almost a hundred years, showing strong tendencies to expand in local circumstances to reassume almost medieval dimensions. Mild-mannered and self-effacing Brantley Barker of San Saba was nonetheless tax collector, truant officer, municipal police chief, and county sheriff, all at the same time, in the 1970s.

The social role of the old-time Texas sheriff stretched like a long shadow well beyond the dry statutory definitions of the office's duties, but the legal description was itself impressive. The sheriff was the chief law enforcement official of the county, with an authority that cut across all others, including municipal police, Department of Public Safety troopers, and even the local Texas Ranger. His duties included prevention of crime, the protection of lives and property, investigation of crimes committed, traffic control on county roads and highways, the arrest and custody of law breakers, and the enforcement of all state laws. This last duty points up one of the formal paradoxes of the office of sheriff. He was a democratically elected official of county government, his power base was local, but the laws he enforced were enacted by the legislative and judicial agencies of the State of Texas and were entirely state law. There is no such thing as county law, since county commissioners courts do not possess legislative powers. The sheriff enforces state law; hence, as James Dickson observed, "state laws are in a sense locally interpreted."

Beyond his direct law enforcement duties, the sheriff also served as formal administrator of the county courthouse and the county jail, the latter of which might contain at any given time persons apprehended and awaiting trial, persons convicted of a state crime and awaiting transfer to the Texas Department of Corrections, and persons sentenced to short terms by county courts. A final major duty of the sheriff was to act as executive officer for county and state (district) courts, serving all the writs, subpoenas, summonses, and processes that they issued. A designated deputy from the sheriff's department usually acted as bailiff for the courts in the daily processing of cases.

The Texas Constitution was, and still is, silent on the qualifications for county sheriff; hence, there were none. Deputies were appointed by the sheriff and paid from the sheriff's budget as established by the commissioner's court. In the old days deputies were just anyone the sheriff knew to be of good character, felt comfortable with, believed to possess the nerve to do the job, and (very often) knew to come from some politically strategic part of the county. If the sheriff himself had been born and raised a few blocks from the courthouse, obviously it made good political sense to choose a chief deputy from the rival town in the southern part of the county, where noses were permanently out of joint about not being designated the county seat. Today, unlike the sheriff, the deputies, jailers, and other members of the sheriff's staff must have attended formal courses of training to become certified peace officers.

Centered on the Texas county courthouse was, and is, an uneasy triumvirate of elected powers that were potential rivals for local political control: the county judge, the county sheriff, and the county commissioners court. The commissioners court controlled the sheriff's finances, but had no other say over his operations. The sheriff served the county judge and his court, as well as the district court, but whether the relationship between the two offices were close and functional or inefficient and combative depended on the two incumbents themselves. They tended to cooperate, since neither could do his job very well without the efficient functioning of the other.

At the center of county government, the office of sheriff still casts a long medieval shadow reaching far beyond its paper definitions. When Rufe Jordan goes to work Monday morning at the Gray County Courthouse, he knows there will be a line of people waiting to talk to him. There will probably be no such line on the doorstep of the county judge. Jordan knows that these people will want many things having nothing at all to do with law enforcement: help with counseling a rebellious son or daughter, legal advice over a will or property dispute, a chance to lodge an informal complaint about the trespasses of a neighbor's dogs or chickens, and many, many other things. Some just want conversation, as Jordan said, "just to talk to the old sheriff." This is part, but not all, of what Tom Brown meant when he spoke of the "old way" of the Texas sheriff. These supplicants at the citadel of county power have come to get their help and advice directly from "the man." The sheriff is an elected law enforcement official, who, as soon as he has taken office, begins to put some of his voters in jail, but the strangest thing about the office is how these voters feel about it. The sheriff is their man in the courthouse, and they feel free to call upon him for anything. Anything!

This unique aspect of the sheriff's social role that Jim Scarborough, II, called the "personal sheriff" is fading, but still persists in many rural Texas counties. The part of Tom Brown's "old way" that has changed the most has to do with the sheriff's procedures of law enforcement. The old-time sheriff operated with a style and directness that is denied his modern counterparts, even when they can well remember how they used to do it. For one thing, the old-time sheriff felt free to interpret the law, leavening its dry definitions with a generous dose of common sense. Sheriff Gaston Boykin of Comanche County spoke to me with some disdain of the game wardens, who enforced the law in a mechanical fashion, treating all lawbreakers just the same, and told me how the sheriff was different:

> There was a well-liked game warden here, and he would give his father a ticket, or you, or anybody else. Game wardens are high-class people, they're honest people, but they're taught to show no partiality. A sheriff never handles any two cases alike, a game warden handles 'em all alike. In other words, I got a guy drunk one time and I took him home. The next night I got him drunk again and put him in jail, the guy that was with him, I took him home. I treated 'em alike, but on different occasions.

Pointing out that all laws are made to be interpreted and that nobody ever arrests a man for going 56 miles an hour, though "that is more than the law says he is allowed to do," another experienced sheriff maintained that "All rules are made to be distributed to the people as the person sees fit."

> There's a law against a man using abusive language, but a man can do that up to a certain point. He might raise cain and cuss and cut up a little bit, but go give that man a chance to go on home. If he's got too much to drink, give him a chance, let him go on home.

In many ways, a sheriff's enforcement of the law showed the social sensitivity of an elected official engaged in the unpleasant task of arresting qualified voters. This is what political scientist James Dickson meant when he observed, "For the rural sheriff *everything* is political, even crimes." During National Prohibition, a good many Texas sheriffs' enforcement of the Volstead Act fell considerably short of absolute rigor. The sheriff of Cherokee County when Frank Brunt was growing up was widely believed to put out the word to local moonshiners and bootleggers whenever federal agents were going to enter the county. Just as an earlier sheriff had done for his father, Sheriff Corbett Akins of Panola County warned farmers the night before he had to serve them with bank foreclosures during the Great Depression, so that they could make a last desperate attempt to raise the money necessary to save their farms. As Boykin said, "A sheriff never handles any two cases alike." When one East Texas sheriff caught bootleggers on the county roads, his treatment of them was calibrated to the social circumstances. Sometimes he took them to jail and had rough conversations with them in the courthouse elevator. Sometimes he just took them to jail and notified their families. Sometimes he merely bade them stand and observe him while he took target practice on their gallon bottles of expensive bonded whiskey with his service revolver, then he let them go. The manner of enforcing the law was made to fit the crime, and took into consideration who they were, who their families were, who they were bootlegging for, how many times they had been caught in the past, and a variety of other things. Many old-time sheriffs were especially lenient with juvenile offenders, going well out of their way to keep the youths' records clean and to divise strategies of punishment and reform short of the full formalities of the law. In medieval England the sheriff had been both police officer and judge, and some of this ancient dual power seemed to persist in the early Texas sheriff's willingness to interpret the law and adjust it to local, personal, or political circumstances.

Given the large area of most Texas counties and the limited resources and manpower the early sheriffs had at their disposal, they compiled an impressive record of law enforcement. "Big Jim" Flournoy, Jess Sweeten, Frank Brunt, and others prided themselves on having no unsolved major felonies over long years of service. Some of the tactics by which this was accomplished are still available to the rural sheriff, some have been effectively curtailed by the rise of federal and state law—"federal and state interference," many sheriffs would say, though they might not say it to the tape recorder. One powerful weapon in the sheriff's arsenal was his detailed knowledge of place. He knew every road, cow track, and stream course in his county, he knew most of the families in his county by name, and could recognize most persons, at least to the extent of placing them by home community or family name. At one time, "Nig" Hoskins of Bastrop County also knew most of the telephone numbers in his territory "by heart." Leon Jones told me he once correctly identified the one nonresident at a political rally in Angelina County and did not bother to shake his hand.

Sheriffs were especially well acquainted with their resident criminal subclasses, often solving crimes by a detailed knowledge of their characteristic *modus operandi*. Sometimes these MOs even ran in families: "A Turkson (pseudonym) always breaks into a car by knocking out the wing window," one told me. In many counties, criminal behaviors persisted across the generations, only adapting to fit the changing times. In Kleberg County, members of one family were arrested by Jim Scarborough, I, for cattle rustling in the "teens," by Jim Scarborough, II, for auto theft in the 1940s, and by Jim Scarborough, III, for drug running in the 1980s. Sheriffs knew these personal and family tendencies very well. On more than one occasion, Gaston Boykin responded to word of a major felony in his county by sitting in his car in his driveway and thinking about who was most likely to have done it. In several notable cases this worked very well. Since sheriffs knew their counties in such incredible detail, they were likely to think that they could handle their own crimes and criminals without the need for outside assistance. According to Jess Sweeten:

> It's like I told the FBI agents that came in here on this kidnap thing, I said, "Gentlemen, maybe I'm over-rating myself, but I feel like that if I can't break a case in this county that other people can't break, I'm a damn poor sheriff. 'Cause, I'm supposed to know my people here, and I'm supposed to know the thugs."

Modern sheriffs still pride themselves on the way they know their personal territories, but populations have grown and shifted, the city has come to the countryside and the countryside to the city. As sheriff "Nig" Hoskins told me, when you went on a call in the old days, "You knowed where you was going 'fore you left here, and you knowed who you was gonna see. Now then, man, you don't know where you're going or where they live." Neither do you know who you will find when you get there. It may turn out to be a crew of speed lab technicians from Houston armed with Uzi machine pistols. The old-time knowledge of place still works, but only up to a point, since the human side of the county landscape is rapidly evolving into something very different than in the past.

Another law enforcement weapon of the early sheriff that persists into the present is his key position as coordinator of county law enforcement. The sheriff is the one county law enforcement official whose authority covers all crimes and every part of the county, crosscutting all jurisdictions. Now, as then, a wise sheriff works closely and tactfully with the municipal police departments, constabulary, DPS agents, game wardens, Liquor Control Board officers, Texas Rangers, and federal officers to weave together a net of cooperation and information exchange that greatly enhances his own abilities to enforce the law. Not surprisingly, the sheriffs like Truman Maddox and Jim Scarborough, III, have played a key role in the rise of county-wide law enforcement associations across the state, as well as in such multi-county organizations as the Coastal Bend Major Crimes Task Force.

But the old style of law enforcement has been most impacted by new constraints in the rules of arrest, interrogation, and prisoner custody. It was these changes that Jess Sweeten had in mind when he complained of getting "screwed down too tight." In the days before the Miranda warning, the rise of civil rights lawsuits under the 14th Amendment, and the Jail Standards Act, the county jail was still the sheriff's castle, and when he took a man into custody under suspicion of a crime, he really "had him" in a way that is not true today. In fact, many of the early Texas jails were even constructed to look like Gothic fortresses, and behind their walls the quality of the sheriffs' power was medieval as well. It was no idle threat when Tom Brown, exasperated at a prisoner's complaints and demands back in the 1930s, told him, "The first time you begin wanting to do something like that, I'm coming in there and stomp you through that damn floor!"

A sheriff rarely arrested someone until he was sure he was guilty, then he took advantage of the legalities and customs of an earlier day to get a swift confession. Usually this did not involve one finger being laid upon the suspect, but there was no "reading him his rights," and some sheriffs planned their arrests to have maximum impact. Frank Brunt, for example, liked to take a man in around two or three o'clock in the morning so that this experience might disorient and bewilder him and serve to loosen his tongue. The sheriff might also have long interrogations with the prisoner before he ever took him to jail, sometimes driving the prisoner around the county for hours. This sounds ominous, but consider one sheriff's explanation of his practices along these lines in the early days:

> I liked it a lot better in the old days, because my motto is "To free a man if he's innocent, prosecute him if he's guilty." I'd pick a man up and tell him, "If you've got a reason to show me that you're not guilty, you've got a chance to do it right now. I'll do this, I'll go with you anywhere and we'll check your story out. We'll check it out one end to the other and I'll not be prejudiced in any way. If you can prove to me that you're not guilty, that's what I want to do. Let's get in my car and take out and we'll do this and do that and I'll find out you're not guilty." I've cut a many a man loose thataway. The record does not show that he's been in jail or anything else.

With the rougher sheriffs in the older days, as the officer's degree of certainty in the subject's guilt went up, so did his impatience for a quick confession. Having identified to his satisfaction the butcher of someone else's Kleberg County cow by the technical details of the butchery, Jim Scarborough, I, might just go and get the man, take him somewhere in his car, and have a long conversation with him under a mesquite tree, emerging with a full confession. Likewise, one East Texas sheriff improved his information about county bootleggers by judicious application of a persimmon limb to one of their fellows before he took him in to jail. Many old-time sheriffs did not use these strong-arm methods, but many did, and they can be fairly judged only in the social contexts and expectancies of their own day.

In the times before federal court activism under the 14th Amendment and the Jail Standards Commission, the sound of a cell door closing seemed heavier and more final. Many a sheriff put an un-confessed suspect in jail and left him there for two or three days to "soften him up" before resuming the questioning about his presumed misdeeds. The jail was entirely the sheriff's turf in those days, his office and often his home as well. In the early decades of this century, many a county sheriff raised his family in an apartment on the first floor of the jail. Sheriffs' wives commonly cooked for the prisoners, preparing during their professional lives, as Loretta Fenton told me, "tons and tons of red beans." The sheriff's children grew up playing in and around the county courthouse and county jail, objects of wonder and envy to their plebian peers who only had houses to live in.

One's length of stay in the county jail was determined by the will of the sheriff to a much greater degree than today. Many former prisoners could sympathize with Sheriff Tom Brown's friend from Luling, who had requested his own incarceration because of drunkenness, and then could not get quickly released. As Brown reported it, "I kept him four or five days and he told my wife, 'I never am gonna call Tommy to get me again. He don't know when to turn me out!' " Many sheriffs spent a good bit of time conversing with their prisoners, playing the fatherly listener, getting them to repeat their stories over once again (if they still maintained their innocence), listening carefully for some tiny part of the oft-told tale to slip and change and turn vulnerable, waiting for any signs of weakening. Sheriffs really got to know their prisoners in the old days, those waiting trial in county or district courts and those serving time for minor offenses, and many of these acquaintances led to continued relationships once the former prisoners were back outside. Sheriffs had more chips to play with in past decades, and more power to deal, and the jail played a key role in recruitment of the informants so essential to rural law enforcement. The sheriff needed informants in all classes of society, needed to firmly establish a tradition of absolute trust with regards to confidential information, but most of all he needed informants among the community's under-class. The jail was often where these deals were struck, these relationships worked out. The outnumbered and understaffed rural sheriff needed the best information network he could fashion. Many a sheriff gave a few minor bootleggers or small-scale gamblers leeway to operate in exchange for information about what was going on out there in the darkness. The sheriff had to cultivate relationships of confidentiality with both bank presidents and thugs, but of these, the thugs were the most important. This use of "snitches" and informants is a significant part of the explanation of how the old-time sheriff did such an effective job. Very often, he didn't even tell his deputies where his information was coming from.

Perhaps no aspect of the role of county sheriff has changed so much as his right to use force, even deadly force, in the line of duty. Now his hands are effectively tied. One of the sheriffs in this book is involved in a lawsuit for striking a prisoner with a billyclub. The prisoner was trying to beat the life from one of the county jailers while in the county jail. Things were different for Sheriff "Nig" Hoskins when he first took office back in the '50s. As he tells it:

I'll be frank with you, back then I'd go over out here and just grab one, far as that goes, and just work him over. Everybody expected it and they respected the sheriff and that was all. But nowadays you can't do that. He's got to jump on you, now, and then you got to prove that he jumped on you.

It is important to understand that the sheriff was *expected* to react to many situations with an appropriate use of violence; it came with the job. Certain sheriffs, like Jess Sweeten in boom-time Henderson County, Jim Scarborough, I, in bandit-plagued Kleberg County, and H. F. Fenton in wide-open Coleman County after World War II, were chosen because (as Loretta Fenton told me) "the people needed a fighting sheriff." Rural Texas was a violent place, and people elected a sheriff that they thought could deal with that violence. If it turned out he could not, he didn't last. In the rough and ready oil boom town of Trinidad, as Jess Sweeten told it, two of the previous town constables had been run out of town.

They just couldn't handle 'em. One old boy there one night, an old drunk, the constable walked up to him and told him he was drunk. They had a few words and directly the constable rapped him on the head with the pistol and blood was flying. Then that

old boy said, "Now, hit me right there!" He whammed down on
him again. "Now, hit me over here!" Well, he hit again but he
still didn't go down, and that old constable just walked off and
resigned. He couldn't even bring him down with his pistol.

Jess Sweeten was just a youth of 24 when he was offered the job as
constable of Trinidad, but when he hit a man, the man went down.
   The mystique of legitimate violence hung over the old-time sheriff
and was a significant aspect of what set him apart from other men.
He had to be able to be effectively violent when the occasion demanded
it, and for the young and untried sheriff, many occasions seemed to
demand it. As H. F. Fenton said:

   About the first two years I was in office, I tell you what, I thought
   it wasn't nothing but fist fighting, 'cause there was lots of old tough
   boys here then who would try your boot on. I was just 23 or 24
   years old, and those first two years I had more damn trouble, more
   fights. They'd just start them old fists flying and you had to either
   run or stay there.

The young deputy or sheriff had a reputation to establish. He could
not afford to back down or lose a fight, neither could he *seem* to lose
or back down. He was given explicit advice to this effect by his su-
periors. When Tom Brown was recruited by Sheriff Walter Ellison of
Caldwell County as his one and only deputy, Ellison told him simply:

   "Now, they're gonna try to run over you." Says, "Now, if you
   give one inch, you might as well quit. Whatever you do, I'm behind you." And that was the only thing he ever said to me.

One lawman father of a young sheriff in East Texas gave him advice
that sounded as unequivocal as the Spartan mother's instructions to
her son about his shield ("Come home with your shield or bourne upon
it.").

   Don't attempt to arrest a man unless you are legally right. If you
   start to arrest him, arrest him or die. I'd rather walk by your casket
   and hear 'em say, "Well, old ____ stayed till the last," than to
   hear 'em say, "He's alive but we don't know where he is."

In the face-to-face world of the rural county, inexperienced sheriffs
were perpetually on the spot; whatever they did, whatever they didn't
do, was seen, talked about, and quickly became part of public

knowledge. Suddenly torn from peaceful labors at his meat market and launched into a high-noon gunfight on the streets of Sealy, young deputy Truman Maddox simply knew that he had to do what he had to do, with no conceivable retreat. The whole town was watching. When Tom Brown attempted to repossess a car and was threatened with a pistol by the car owner's mother, he just ignored the pistol pointing at his back and went ahead and hooked the car up to the tow truck. When they got back to town, the tow truck man asked him, "Tom, how come you to have enough guts to do that?" Brown said, "I'd have rather been shot and died right there than to have you come back here telling that that woman run me off." A sheriff could not lose and could not seem to lose. Maddox's predecessor as sheriff of Austin County lost a fight with three big men at a dance hall (*three* men), and he did not run for office again.

As the years went by, an experienced sheriff like Walter Ellison, or Tom Brown, or H. F. Fenton had to use force less and less. He was a known and perhaps feared presence in his county, and there was little stigma attached to backing down to him. A fighting drunk, giving hell to the DPS troopers trying to get him up the stairs of the Coleman County Jail, would still know enough to react to: "This is Fenton, what the hell's going on here?" The experienced sheriffs were like old Zenmasters of the martial arts, so feared and respected that they seldom if ever had to demonstrate their prowess anymore. Reputation was only part of it, however. They became so experienced in conflict situations that they could usually move into one, talk to the parties concerned, take their time, and diffuse the situation short of violence.

A reputation for the effective use of violence profited the old-time sheriff in another way. Just as cruel iron bars and fierce guard dogs prompted the house burglar to move on down the block, so did the reputation as a rough, perhaps even a "mean" sheriff cause the criminal to go ply his trade in another county. Some former sheriffs were totally unapologetic about these reputations, or how they were established. Said Corbett Akins, "I'm not boasting or bragging, but I was mean as hell." At the "Walls" in Huntsville, and at the other state prisons, word would be passed not to crack any safes in Frank Brunt's Cherokee County or to "go around" Sheriff Leon Jones' Angelina County. Several former sheriffs told a story that went something like this: A hardened thug is picked up in some other place and the sheriff goes down to get him and bring him back to the scene of the crime. The thug is Walls-tough, cocky, insolent, and uncooperative. Then, riding in the sheriff's car, at some point he realizes which county his crime was committed in (he has made a grave mistake, he had thought he was in another county) and just exactly who has him in his power.

He says, "Pull over right now. I've got something I want to confess."

While all successful sheriffs in the old days established their reputations for the effective use of violence, the use of deadly force—the pistol or the rifle—was another matter that was much more variable. A. J. Spradley in Nacogdoches County, Vail Ennis in Bee County, Jim Scarborough, I, in Lee County, Jess Sweeten in Henderson County, and many others found it necessary to shoot people to death in the line of duty—sometimes impressive numbers of people. By the time Scarborough and his nearby sheriffs had cleaned out the notorious "Yegua Notch Gang," Scarborough had perhaps a score of notches on his own guns. Decades later in Bee County, Vail Ennis (an accomplished sniper in the Great War) also found it necessary to use ultimate force on a number of occasions. Far from being repentant, he called the newly elected Sheriff Jim Scarborough, III, to his side while on his death bed in the early 1970s and gave Scarborough the following advice:

> He said, "Now, your dad won't agree with this at all, but I'm telling you, never get caught without your gun. When you go after a man, you get him and kill him. Don't bring him back to the hospital. When you bring him in, bring him in dead. Take him to the morgue. Now, that's the best advice I can give you." I said, "Mr. Vail, coming from you, I appreciate it from the bottom of my heart."

Scarborough was just being polite, and Ennis was quite correct that his father would not have agreed. Jim Scarborough, II, went to the other extreme from Vail Ennis and his own father on this issue of the use of deadly force. He emerged from World War I with the firm resolution never to kill another human being. As sheriff, he never carried a gun, and on several occasions he walked in unarmed to take guns away from people who had barricaded themselves into houses and were holding off the assembled law. The "sheriff who never carries a gun," like Scarborough and the incumbent Nathan Tindell of San Augustine County, is not just a modern phenomenon. Some nineteenth century sheriffs, like the highly respected J. P. Forsyth of Panola County, never carried guns either. Of the latter-day sheriffs included in this book, several have had to use deadly force on one or two occasions, and most professed to regret that necessity. Only the late Jess Sweeten was a real "shootist" in something of the old sense. Sweeten, like Vail Ennis, was a proponent of the gun. A skilled shot, he traveled about giving marksmanship demonstrations, shooting marbles out of the air, apples off of people's heads, and cigarettes from their lips. He also sent several unwise and well-armed felons to the cemetery.

Over decades of service as a peace officer, a kill-or-be-killed situation tended to come up—sometime, somewhere. Only a few resolved to go unarmed and take their chances. Most carried a pistol and hoped such circumstances would never happen. A few carried a pistol and found numerous occasions to make use of it. This was in part a function of each sheriff's particular place, time, and circumstances. It was in part a matter of personal taste.

Whereas the notion of the Texas sheriff as peace officer, lawman, and man with a pistol is part of the popular image of the office, the reality was both more complicated and more interesting. The sheriff was also everybody's personal man in the courthouse, on call 24 hours a day, always ready to help with matters having nothing to do with law enforcement. "Fighting sheriff" H. F. Fenton well remembers the first call he went on after taking office as sheriff. He took his gun with him, but he might just as well have left it back at the jail.

It was a fellow called me from Santa Anna down here. I had an old wore-out Ford car that didn't have no wipers on it, and it was icing in January and I had to ride with my cotton-picking head out that window to see. After I got down there to Santa Anna, this fellow turned out to have dogs under his house. His house was built up off the ground, and there was an old bitch dog under there with a bunch of dogs (that had) followed her under there, and he wanted me to get them dogs out from under his house! I laid down on one side of the house at a hole with a flashlight and everyone of 'em run out the other side. I got back in my car and drove home. Boy, it was cold, and I didn't have no defrosters on that thing, you know. I didn't realize the sheriff got those kind of calls.

In a questionnaire study conducted by James Dickson in the late '70s, sheriffs estimated that from one-tenth to two-thirds of their work day was taken up with personal requests from the citizenry that had nothing whatsoever to do with enforcement of the law. In *The Politics of the Texas Sheriff: From Frontier to Bureaucracy,* Dickson wrote:

A basic assumption of any appraisal of the politics of the Texas sheriff is that the office is uniquely affected by the imperatives of electoral democracy. The sheriff is the principal "good old boy" of the county, with an extensive knowledge of the voters' needs, priorities, and peculiarities; he is the number one "Mr. Fixit" and universal *pater familias* of the county. The personal service aspects of the sheriff's tasks intrude upon impartial and professional law enforcement with significant impact on getting elected and staying in office—shaping the sheriff as a social and professional institution.

Dickson's research established what all old-time sheriffs knew before they entered the office, or (like H. F. Fenton) found out soon after they went in: the rural sheriff was evaluated first and foremost by the voters not on the basis of his technical law enforcement standards, but by how well and frequently and cheerfully he performed this personal service aspect of his role. He was the "resident good old boy" of the county, the "Mr. Fixit," and as time went on the "Mr. Insider" as well, the master of everybody's secrets. The calls came in to the sheriff's office all day long, and very often, as for the old lady who called on Frank Brunt in Cherokee County, the deputies were "too light" and only the high sheriff would do. The personal phone calls pursued him to his home at night, where he learned (if he hadn't known before) that his job went on for 24 hours a day. Sometimes the phone did not provide close enough contact. There was usually a line of people at the sheriff's office in the mornings waiting to "talk to the old sheriff" face-to-face, as there is for Rufe Jordan of Pampa even today.

When asked what sorts of personal services they had been asked to perform, sheriffs invariably answered, "Anything, you name it." Besides removing sexually aroused dogs from under houses, sheriffs told of being asked to: evict polecats and armadillos; execute mad dogs; rescue cats from trees; investigate strange lights and noises; mediate neighborhood disputes over barking dogs, animal trespasses, fence lines, and rights-of-way; find lost children and runaway sons and daughters; deliver death notices; offer stern counsel (or even give a good thrashing) to rebellious youth; mediate marital squabbles; give business and legal advice, and many, many other things. Frank Brunt told how he once solved a young couple's marital problems right in the Cherokee County Jail. The wife came by to see him and he listened closely to "all of that, and she moaned and cried and give me her sad story," then he sent his deputy to get the lady's husband in off the Rusk street.

> And I sat 'em down there, and I let him tell his story, and she just rared and pitched over there, and cried. I listened to 'em a few minutes. I said, "Now, what you'll need to do—I know you're in love, you just both got married—you need to cool off. You ought to kiss her, make love to her, go on and sleep real close to her tonight, and love her." And directly, I got 'em to kiss and they left there arm in arm.

Other sheriffs report similar counseling interventions. Some even reported these experiences as the most satisfying part of their job. According to Brantley Barker, former sheriff of San Saba County:

> What makes me feel so good is to go to a family fuss, and they
> was ready to separate and divide up all the furniture, and I talk
> to 'em awhile. They'd go back together, and then I get a letter
> from 'em telling me how they appreciated me sitting there talk-
> ing to 'em that night.

This aspect of the sheriff's role had another side to it. Over the years,
as the numbers of citizens that had come to this public official with
their very private problems accumulated, the sheriff became a man who
knew too much, the county's Mr. Insider, the keeper of everyone's
darkest secrets. The man whose daughter finally had been located in
the motel just over the county line, the outstanding citizen who had
been saved from the embarassing consequences of his public drunkenness, the Kleberg County socialite who had once been on the staff of
the notorious Chicken Ranch near La Grange, all these became part
of that body of private knowledge that the sheriff could never divulge.
Jim Scarborough, II, carried the identity of the Chicken Ranch veteran to his grave, along with the rest of his secrets, but at times people
must have looked at him in the same manner described by his son,
the present sheriff of Kleberg County:

> Some of these personal calls are worse than that, especially about
> doper kids, pregnant girls that have to get sent off, things like that.
> They've come to me and said, "Where is a good place for my
> daughter to go to have this child?" I don't even tell my wife. I've
> been that way, my father was that way, my grandfather was that
> way. Some of those people now resent me because they know I
> know their family secrets, and I feel uncomfortable about it, be-
> cause when I say hello to 'em they give me that jaundiced look,
> like, "I wonder who he's told?" Yet, they call me knowing that
> I won't tell anybody.

The rural sheriff was often in office a long time, and over the decades he developed close, personal relationships to many voters with
whom he had repeated dealings. Over his 37 years in office, some supporters of Jim Scarborough, II, became so fixated upon him as their
personal sheriff that he would have to come out of retirement to deal
with their problems even after his son took over the office. As in the
following story from Rufe Jordan, on one side or the other these personal relationships often continued right up to the grave.

> I can remember a little lady here who lived to be 93 years old.

I don't care what was happening, she'd call me, bless her heart. Before she passed away she called and she talked to my wife and said, "I need to talk with Rufe right away." I got out there, it was in the evening, 8 o'clock or 8:30, she was very ill. She said, "Rufe." She had one of these little small, slick dogs, I think it was a Mexican Chihuahua. She said, "Rufe, I'm not long for this world, and I'm ready to go home. My people do not live here. Butch, that's the little dog, I want you to be responsible for this little dog. I'm not asking you to keep him, but you see that he has a good home, somewhere. I want to pass that on to you." I said, "That's fine. That is fine, my dear, and I'll surely do that."

However fast they were on the trigger, and however rude and roughly they came down on the persons of hardened criminals who wandered into their counties or were homegrown, the old-time sheriffs could not and did not neglect this personal service aspect of their role. If they did neglect it or answered these personal requests with ill grace, they would not remain in office long. Most gladly accepted it as an essential part of their job. Jim Scarborough, II, regarded himself as a "personal sheriff," a man who served and took care of his own. In his case, as in the case of Gaston Boykin and all the rest, this willingness to help voters solve their personal problems merged imperceptibly into a personal style of politics. Scarborough attended every family reunion within a two-county radius of Kingsville, and while he was present he danced with the little girls, their mothers, and their grandmothers, all of them. A common mode of politicking in rural Texas counties was simply to set out to meet every voter in the county face-to-face and give him or her your card. As "Nig" Hoskins said, "You just went and seen everybody that you could and give 'em a card. You had to see a whole lot of 'em or you wouldn't get no votes." One sheriff's mother, wise in the electoral politics of the county, told him, "Wherever three people gather, you got to be there, just like Jesus and his disciples." Gaston Boykin did this at family reunions, graveyard cleanings, political speechmakings, school closings, "rabbit drives," and at other occasions in the Comanche County countryside. Other personal sheriffs did the same. The county judge, the county tax collector, and the county commissioners were sessile officials, more or less permanently ensconced in the courthouse; but the sheriff went on the road everyday, meeting the voters in cafes and on street corners, always willing to attend a pie supper or to help an old lady who was hearing things go bump in the night. As Dickson aptly observed, "Of the constitutional officials of Texas county government, the sheriff best illustrates the grass roots, rurally oriented remnants of Jacksonian democracy . . . . The sheriff epitomizes government for rural folk."

As Dickson also emphasized, the institution of county sheriff goes on changing, evolving, and adjusting to circumstances in the urbanizing Texas countryside of the late twentieth century. The big city sheriff has already become something very different than the sheriffs who told their stories for this book. He is an administrator, a politician, and the personnel manager for a staff that may run into the thousands. But he is no one's personal sheriff anymore, he does not go out on calls, and many of his voters may forget his name from election to election.

The rural sheriff is changing, too, but such public forgetfulness is unthinkable in Rufe Jordan's Gray County, or Truman Maddox's Austin County, or H. F. Fenton's Coleman County, or even Frank Brunt's Cherokee County 20 years after he left office. These men made their mark on the public consciousness back in the days of the high sheriff, and they carry that mantle of authority into a present beset by federal courts and state agencies. The mark of the old days and the old ways is on all of these men, even those long out of office. In 1986 Corbett Akins was in his middle 90s and confined to his home, but people still called him "sheriff" and sought him out on an almost daily basis to hear him tell again of his exploits as moonshine hunter and master of hounds, and how "Dogs can talk, 'cause old Tuck would hit that trail, and you'd hear him at one or two o'clock at night say, 'How o-o-o-old is he?' And old Nip would say, '21, 22, 21, 22, 21, 22.' "

To accompany a retired sheriff on his daily rounds of coffee shops, country properties, and county cafes, and to watch how people look at him and the quality of their interactions with him, is to appreciate something of what it was like to be the old-time high sheriff, everybody's friend in the courthouse, the man with the power who had never lost a fight or run away. To interview a 30-year incumbent in his lair in the old courthouse or jail, surrounded by the trophies and momentoes of all those years, is even more impressive. It is like visiting some feudal lord in one of his fortified strongholds. Just as you had felt that you needed safe passage to enter, you feel as though you need it once again to go away.

Permission is always given. The 30-year men were strangely alike in their patience and courtesy to a visitor who, after all, carried a tape recorder and looked like a journalist, a person many long-term sheriffs do not particularly like to gaze upon. They were alike in other ways, the mark of the same medieval office was on them all. They were pleasant, affable, careful men, seemingly older than their years. They didn't seem like people who could be surprised by very much. As one old Navy chief once told me about himself, they looked like men who "had seen the tiger and heard the hoot owl." Finally, behind their surface differences, all of them seemed to have an assurance of power and authority that was built in, taken for granted, simply unshakable. James Dickson has well described his impressions of two Texas high sheriffs who were dead before my researches had begun. Thanks to Dickson's interviews, Jess Sweeten is in this book. The redoubtable "Big Jim" Flournoy of Fayette County must stand for all those for whom the oral historian came too late.

The late Jess Sweeten was sheriff of Henderson County (Athens) from 1933 to 1955, and the late T. J. (Big Jim) Flournoy was sheriff for thirty-four years in Fayette County (La Grange, 1947–1980).

Each of these men might physically have been created in Hollywood. Sweeten was six feet four inches tall, and Flournoy was six feet six inches tall, both exceeding two hundred pounds in their seventies. Each man began his career in the tough and turbulent 1920s, when sheriffs still operated partially out of their saddle bags. Flournoy served for thirteen years as a deputy in his county before being elected sheriff. After his initial election in 1946, he rarely had an opponent for reelection. Flournoy served as a Texas Ranger long enough to be inaugurated into the Texas Ranger Hall of Fame. Sweeten began his career as a constable in the early East Texas oil fields, a very tough apprenticeship.

The career of both men was sculpted in their immense hands, with knuckles gnarled by the innumerable contacts with the chins of men who had resisted arrest. On countless weekends as young officers, they would fight all weekend subduing oil field workers who did not want to sleep it off in the county cooler. Several unrepentant and unwise felons were forced by these two sheriffs to sleep forever in the county cemetery, and a number of miscreants bled for their sins from wounds inflicted by the two deadly marksmen. Sweeten's living room wall is festooned with awards and photographs resulting from his exhibitions of marksmanship, many of them coming after he was already retired. Flournoy was said to begin each deer hunting season by centering his rifle sight by knocking the center out of several dozen bottle caps. The center of several lawbreakers was much larger.

There is an "atmosphere" that surrounds each of these old officers, an aura of an eerie nature, which is only partly impressed upon a stranger by their reputation. The emanation of power, and, if necessary, meanness, still impressed strangers with these two men when they were nearly eighty years old. The aura is one of potential ruthlessness and utter fearlessness, augmented by the physical size of each man. A citizen of La Grange once recommended to an outsider that he look in Sheriff Flournoy's eyes. When contemplating anything threatening to his people, those eyes flowered with a hellish blackness and coldness that chilled one's blood, even when he was retired and approaching his eightieth birthday. The thought of federal judges and their favoring suits against sheriffs could precipitate this baleful countenance.

TOM
BROWN

★

I never will forget it. My brother and I worked about four-hundred
acres. We (also) had a store and meat market and grocery store in
Luling. He'd stay one week there, and I'd stay one week. During that
time, in the '30s when times was hard, I'd milk nine cows before daylight by the lantern. Milked them at night by a lantern. Then sell the
cream, about four, five dollars a week, and that's what we lived on.

But in '33, Papa drove out one morning and stopped and says, "Tommy, Walter Ellison needs a deputy, and he wants you to be his deputy
sheriff, chief deputy sheriff."

I told him, I said, "Papa, I just can't do it. I'd have to move to Lockhart." That went on about three weeks. Finally I told him, I said, "Papa,
I never done a thing in my life that you asked me to do that I didn't
do or try to do. Now, if you'd tell me to jump off that house, I'd jump
off of it. But," I said, "you're asking me to move to Lockhart." I said,
"I've always been taught all my life to love God and hate Lockhart."
And you know, he wanted me to move up there.

He said, "Well, he pays one-hundred dollars a month. You better
think about it." I said, "Well, I'll go up there and stay six months.

You keep my land here. I'll be back." Well, I've been in Lockhart ever since and never been able to leave.

I stayed deputy sheriff until 1940. I was elected sheriff in 1940. When I first went in as deputy, they only had one city policeman (in Lockhart), he didn't take care of the city much. And we had a constable in Luling. Now that's all the law enforcement we had in the county. Constable was just an old fellow that was night-watching and that's all. And Luling didn't have any city policemen.

And I come up here and (was) sworn in. Only thing Walter Ellison told me, says, "Now, they're gonna try to run over you." Says, "Now, if you give one inch, you might as well quit. Whatever you do, I'm behind you." And that was the only thing he ever said to me. But they never did run over me. I could take care of myself. I can say this, not bragging. I never went after a fellow that I didn't bring in, and I never did have to call on any help to bring him in. I never did, and I brought a many, a many a one in.

Many a night I put 35 or 40 in jail. We could hold them in them days as long as we wanted to. Weekends, you never went to bed on Fridays, Saturday, or Sunday. You might as well just stay up all night. In Luling, you couldn't hardly walk up the streets at night, and you couldn't hardly drive down that main street at night, there were so many people. And all kind of people in the world—it kept you busy. You'd get some information about some certain fellow, and you'd give him maybe 10 hours or five hours to get out of the country. And he'd leave.

One time Bonnie Parker and Clyde Barrow had some kinfolk down here at Delhi and stayed down there one night. I didn't find it out until two days later, and I'm glad I didn't.

I never did shoot anyone. I've shot to watch them run, jump through the fence or something, but not to hit them.

During the oil booms and things, I was the only deputy in the county. Had a sheriff and a deputy—we taken care of all of it. Lots of rough people were here in those days, lots of rough people. It was during prohibition times—'33 on up to I guess '36 or somewhere around there—and we used to catch these bootleggers and stills. You could watch certain ones that done a whole lot of drinking, just watch them a little bit, and they'd lead you to it.

We sent a whole bunch to the penitentiary for bootlegging and things. I caught one fellow one night. I found his still and his mash, but I couldn't find the coil. I sat there and talked to him. I told him, "Why don't you tell me where that coil is?" He says, "Haven't got one. Haven't got one." I said, "Well, I'm gonna sit here 'till in the morning, and I'm gonna carry you right through a little community out here and they're gonna see you. And I'm gonna have that still right on top of my car, and I'm gonna stop."

So he went up in a big oak tree, brought the coil down, laid it down, says (to the coil), "I'll tell you what. Me and Paw's run a many a gallon through you, but you've run your last."

A fellow called me from Luling one time, one I was raised with. Says, "Tommy?" I said, "Yup." Says, "I'm drunk, I need locking up." I says, "Well, where are you?" He told me. I says, "You just crawl up on that staircase and sit down. I'll be there in about 20 minutes." I went down there and got him and brought him up here and put him in jail. I kept him four or five days and he told my wife, "I never am gonna call Tommy to get me again. He don't know when to turn me out!"

The first case I had when I was deputy sheriff . . . my boss had a ranch in South Texas, and he went down there, and I hadn't been deputy but a few days. I felt like something lost. I was just a derned kid, 29 years old, here I was with a dern pistol on. Got a call over here at Martindale. They found a dead baby. So, I went over there. Baby laying up on the woodpile, head chewed off. The dogs had chewed it. It was a fresh-born baby—Fourth of July. This old Mexican woman—she looked old, long dress and things—she was out washing. She says, "The dogs drug it by." I got to talking to her and questioning her. I could talk Spanish before I could talk English, almost. I was raised with 'em on the farm. And it's right funny, people asked me, "How did I find out that that old Mexican woman, it was her baby?" I said, "Well, there was two young girls there, and I had them show me their breasts and tested it, and it didn't give no milk. So, I knew it wasn't them."

But I asked this old Mexican woman, and she said, "Yeah, that's my baby." What she'd done, her folks had left, and she had given birth to that baby, and she looked down and seen them coming, and she ran out and put it under a tub. Then she went ahead and cooked supper, fed the mules and the horses, and that night when everything got quiet she taken that baby from under the tub, and it was dead. She rolled it down the trail under the weeds and buried it. And two or three days later the dogs pulled it up—dug it up and drug it by.

So, we had her in jail. I did. On, she'd prayed and go on doing things. They would tell her they were going to kill her for doing that. So, I told the woman, I talked to her just before the trial, "Oh, you don't need to worry," I said, "I'll help you out." She was just an old ignorant Mexican woman, looked to be about 50, 60 years old, but she wasn't. I says, "I'll help you out." She says, "If you get me out . . . I've got a pig and a hen and some pecans. I'll give 'em to you." I says, "Well, OK." So they got ready to try her, and the district attorney says, "Tom, what you gonna give that old woman?" She'd been in jail about four months. I said, "Fred, give her a suspended sentence, five years suspended. She didn't know what she was doing. She's suffered enough." So, he did.

And I told her in Spanish that she was free, she could go. She jumped up and hugged and kissed me right there in that courtroom. That was Friday. Saturday at noon I drove up and here she come with that pig under her arm and that old hen in one arm and a little sack of pecans. And I told her, I said, "I don't want that." She said, "Oh, yeah, I promised God I'd give it to you. You've got to take it." So, I carried the hen down to Mama's at Luling, and I think I fattened the hog, and I guess I cracked the pecans.

I got a call one night, way in the night. It was cold and everything. Out six or eight miles out of town, had a killing—a mule had killed a man's wife. I went out there. He was telling me how bad this mule was, that he had come home, that he had found her laying out there by the rain barrel. "Out there by the water barrel, getting water," he said. "That mule kicked her, so I drug her in the house there." So I sat there a little bit, and I helped him put his wife up on the bed. I said, "Ennis, that mule sure did kick this woman. Yes sir, that mule is sure bad, but I bet he had an ax in his hand when he kicked her." And he said, "Oh, no, Mr. Brown, I didn't hit her. I didn't hit her." I said, "Well, there ain't no use disturbing the undertaker; I'll just wait. In the morning I'll get the ambulance out here and carry your wife into town." We sat there all night in front of that old fireplace. I said, "Why did you do it?" He said, "No sir, no sir, I didn't!"

So I brought him in, put him in jail. And about two nights after, I come in about midnight or one o'clock and went to the jail. Went to the cell. I had him to myself. And I began to kind of groan and squall. I said, "Ennis how come you kill me? My goodness, Ennis, you ain't ever gonna sleep or have no rest unless you tell Sheriff Brown that you knocked me in the head with the ax. You ain't never gonna have no rest. I'm gonna haunt you the rest of your life." I left the room and went back to bed. Went up the next morning and said, "Ennis, how did you sleep?" He said, "Mr. Brown, I didn't sleep at all. That woman come and talk to me. I'm ready to tell you all about it." So, we went and got the ax.

I had more friends than I guess any sheriff that went out of county office. And these old-timers, they're still my friends. I got a call one day at noon. There's a certain house here in town, there's some gunshots in it. And me, unknowing and not asking who it was, I just went down there and rushed in. And one of the fellows pulled a .45 on me and said, "Brownie, don't you come in here." I said, "I'm coming in." He said, "If you are, I'm gonna kill you." I said, "Naw, you ain't gonna kill me." He cocked that old .45, says, "If you get any closer I'm gonna kill you." I knew if I made a move for my gun he'd shoot. I grabbed him and we wrestled—I was a pretty good-sized batch of man then. I finally got the gun turned 'round and stuck it in his belly. And the old devil says, "Pull the trigger. Pull the trigger. Pull the trigger!"

But I didn't do it. Of course, I could have; I'd have said it was an accident. I finally got the gun away from him and threw it outside. In the meantime the others—they was all doped up—another one come running through with his little pistol and I kicked him, and his pistol went one way and he went the other one.

Then I got this first fellow outside and sat down on him. The district attorney, a friend of mine, happened to drive by and helped me carry him to jail.

And the next morning I talked to him there in jail. Says, "Now, you're sober." I said, "I'll never take that chance again. I'm gonna kill you." I said, "If I ever have to come get you again I'm gonna say, 'Come on.' And if you don't follow me, I'm gonna shoot." I had to put him in jail several times after that, but he always followed me. And I never had a better friend. I was pallbearer at his funeral.

Another time, I had to repossess a truck from a fellow. I had the papers, and I got a man here in town to go out there with his winch truck to pick it up. I went out there and the fellow wasn't at home, but his mother was there. I told her why I come and she says, "Well, you not a-gonna get it!" I says "Yessum, I'm gonna take it. I got to take the thing." So, I told that fellow to back up and hook onto it. (He) Did. She stepped out and she had a .45 under her apron. Says, "Don't you hook onto that truck. Don't you do it!"

I said, "Gramp, go ahead and hook onto it." He said, "What am I gonna do? A man with a gun telling me to do it and a woman with one telling me not to!" I says, "You just move and let me hook onto it. She ain't gonna shoot me." I bent over there and hooked onto it. I said, "Now, drive it on out of here." And man, she cussed me! I didn't know whether the old woman was gonna pull that trigger or not. When he got back to town he asked me, "Tom, how come you to have enough guts to do that?" I said, "I'd have rather been shot and died right there than to have you come back telling that that woman run me off."

While I was in the sheriff's office we sent four down to the electric chair. They electrocuted two of 'em. Two of 'em they sent to prison. One they transferred here, the sheriff (who) brought him up says, "You know, I sure feel sorry for you." And I says, "Why?" He says, "That's the meanest and the hardest to please man in the world." Says, "He'll give you the devil in the jail house." And I said, "Oh, well, maybe so." I went back there after they had locked him up, went back down there. And I put him in there with two or three other fellows, and he began to tell me what he had to have and what he wanted to do. And I said, "Well, that's all right. Now are you through talking?" He said, "Yeah, I'm through." I said, "All right, now I'm gonna talk and don't you say a word." I said, "The very first time you begin wanting to do something like that, I'm coming in there and stomp you through that damn floor. And if you don't believe I'll do it, you just ask some of these fellows here." And do you know, I didn't have any trouble out of him anymore.

He got the death penalty and I picked him up, left early Monday morning to carry him to the pen. Got down close to Brenham and I said, "We'll eat breakfast here." He said, "No. No. That's where that man lived I killed." He said, "They'll mob me out here." I said, "It makes no difference. I'm carrying you down there to be killed anyway." So, I turned him over to the warden, and he had a green necktie—I think I still have it somewhere around here—he took it off and he said, "I want you to remember me by this necktie." And he said, "Promise me one thing, that you'll come down here and watch them electrocute me." I said, "Oh, yeah, I'll be there. I'll be watching." He stayed in jail down there 18 months, then the night before they were gonna electrocute him the next morning at 12 or one, the warden called me, and he said, "That's still his last request, (that) you be here." I said, "Well, you tell him I'll be there looking right through that glass window." But I wasn't gonna be there—I wouldn't go.

They'll shave a little place in your head about that big. And then they've got a copper cap that fits around a copper spike—you put it right there. And they fasten your arms and your legs with a copper band. And they tell me that when they charge you that's to keep it from knocking you out of the chair.

I had two deputies sent down there to carry some prisoners, and they didn't come back and they didn't come back. The next morning, I asked them where they'd been. They said, "We stayed down there watching them execute a Mexican and a colored boy." And I said, "Well, you've got more guts than I have. I wouldn't want to watch an execution."

They electrocuted a nigger for killing his wife. And his last request, the warden said, was "to tell Mr. and Mrs. Brown he sure thanked them for being so nice to him while he was in jail."

I remember the first trip my wife went down to Huntsville with me. Warden down there asked me, "Do you want to show your wife around the penitentiary?'' I said, "Yeah," so we went through it. I always tried to get down there around 11:00 to 11:30, 'cause they fed them guards and wardens good. We went around and went down death row—little square windows and you could peep in and see 'em sitting in there and eating. Warden said, "Now, Mrs. Brown, we'll go down these 13 steps." He said, "Now, here's the 'lectric chair. Would you like to sit down in it, Mrs. Brown, to say you been in the 'lectric chair?'' She looked at me and I said, "Oh, go ahead and sit down in the chair." He sat her in there and throwed those straps around and fastened the thing. Says, "Now, right back here's where we shoot the 'lectricity to 'em." He stepped back there and hit the wall and she jumped up and said, "You son of a bitch!" I said, "Well, you been in the 'lectric chair."

When Joe Lewis was at his top heavyweight fight, this old—I guess I oughta call him colored—this nigger man told me, said they had a big party over at one of those beer joints in Cocklebur. Joe Lewis knocked his opponent out in the second round, and they said, "There ain't nobody in the world can whip that Joe Lewis." But he said to 'em, "Sheriff Brown can get him down on Plum Creek."

Right after World War II, this young boy come back and beat me. The commissioner's job is a retiring job. Being a sheriff was the hardest. Back in those days, the sheriff, he was law! They respected him! He was the law. And I couldn't be sheriff now, no. Nowhere in the world, nowhere in the world. 'Cause I'd want to do it the old way.

JESS
SWEETEN

★

When they offered me that constable's job at Trinidad, it was a rough son-of-a-gun down there. That (job) down there was being able and man enough to keep the drunks out of the street, the bullies. You had about 2,500 to 3,000 iron workers, steamfitters, and boilermakers that was concentrated down there, and there was no roads in but dirt roads, in and out. They couldn't get out of there in wet weather. And it was rough—drunks on the street, fighting.

I was coming across the street there one night and I saw them knock down an old night watchman, old man Joe Dyer. They knocked him down twice and disarmed him. The old man was helpless. He was a little bit foggy in his mental thinking, and it was pitiful. The crowd around there was just a laughing and having the biggest time, just making sport of it. I stepped up there and said, "Wait a minute." Old Jack _____ started to hit him and I said, "If you strike that old man, fellow, you're gonna answer to me. And I'm telling you, I mean you're gonna answer with your damn life." I said, "You give him his gun back, and if I ever see you running over this old man again I'm gonna tear up dirt!" I was wrong, too, but I was ready to take a hand.

So, the first thing I knew here they came wanting me to take that job. Well, I said, "Naw, I don't want it. I'm probably rougher than you'd want me to be." "No, no," they said, "We'll pay you well." When they made me an offer I decided to take it.

It was a knock-down-drag-out. The ordinary person couldn't have competed with 'em because he just wasn't man enough physically. They didn't want to kill you, they just wanted to beat you to death. It wasn't what you call cold-blooded criminals. They just wanted to whip you, they just wanted to whip the officers. And they just ran two out of town—they couldn't handle 'em. One old boy there one night, an old drunk, the constable walked up to him and told him he was drunk. They had a few words and directly the constable rapped him up aside the head with the pistol and blood was flying. Then that old boy said, "Now, hit me right there!" He whammed down on him again. "Now, hit me over here!" Well, he hit again but he still didn't go down, and that old constable just walked off and resigned. That was old Bates Bradley he was trying to bring down, but he couldn't even bring him down with his pistol.

I never did hit but one man with a pistol. I had on two, and I'd knocked him out of the house. I stepped over him, and when I did he grabbed my right-hand gun. Well, I went around and grabbed it, and the firing pin had me right in the hand, he'd pulled the trigger. I just reached over and got my left-hand gun and knocked him loose from it. But I usually just used my fists, and course, my fists will show that, they've been broke all to pieces. And I never did shoot a man without I thought I was supposed to do it. And I have had some pretty close calls.

I know one time I was called up here to a place where a fellow was shooting at everybody that passed up the street with a high-powered rifle. He had a couple of fellows pinned down behind a tree, knocking the bark off of it. Every time a car would pass he'd shoot at it. He was barricaded in a two-room shack there. I got there, and stood and looked at the place a minute trying to figure out the best way to take him, the safest and the best way. Didn't have a shotgun with me, or a rifle either. But it was just as well I didn't, 'cause he was barricaded in there with the blinds down. Had the windows broken out and he'd raise up that blind and *"Blam."*

Well, I stood there on that little old porch and listened. He didn't know I was on it. Directly, I thought, "That old house, I should be able to get him located. He's gonna be walking once and a while." Directly, I heard a board squeak. I thought, "He's right there." So, I pulled a .45 automatic, flipped the safety off, and when I kicked that door open he was just about as near as that desk there. He was coming up, but he was too slow. He got just about right there, and *"Bam, Bam, Bam,"* three hit him right in the belly.

When I was first elected sheriff, I had one outside deputy and a secretary and a jailer, and we had a population of 38,000 people to police, including all of Athens. In those days we had what they called the city marshall, but he never attempted to do anything. If he got a call, he'd probably call us. And we had to police all the smaller towns, the entire county. It just kept us going day and night. I don't believe you'd get an officer this day and time to work like we had to work. Now then they have a day off every week, but my gosh, we never thought about a day off! And very seldom did I ever go to bed that I wasn't called up from one to three or four times. If I hadn't of been young I couldn't have kept up with it. It was a terrible job.

And it was all crude. You had to train yourself. If you was dedicated, you was gonna be a good officer. If you wasn't dedicated, you better get out of it. You had to like it to have guts enough to stay with it.

The officer in those days had to fly by the seat of his britches. We didn't even have a crime lab in Texas. When I was working on the Patton case I had to have lab work—I had to. Well, I'd have to go to Dallas to a private lab to do the work for me, and I'd pay for it out of my own pocket. Course, I did a great deal of reading on gathering evidence and suchlike, and it did help me. I've always said that for any case the evidence is there if you can find it, but if you're not careful you'll overlook it. I've never seen a bad criminal case committed yet that the evidence wasn't there if you could just find it. And if you're not careful, a bunch of inexperienced officers will run over a bunch of evidence.

I broke 21 murder cases, and I went out without an unsolved highjacking, and I didn't have an unsolved rape case or an unsolved murder case. I was proud of my record. It did represent some hard work.

I know one time I needed a crime lab and needed it bad. A night watchman was shot at Malakoff, a little town just west of here, and I found a truck driver's cap. I took it to Dallas to this lab, and they gave me the approximate age of this fellow, the color of his hair, even his probable complexion. So, I did take the cap and catch the fellow. He was a truck driver out of Waco and he just decided he wanted to rob a place in Malakoff and shot the night watchman. But evidence is very tedious and very important, and if you're not careful you'll overlook something.

Let me tell you something. When I was sheriff . . . it's like I told the FBI agents that came in here on this kidnap thing. I said, "Gentlemen, maybe I'm over-rating myself, but I feel like that if I can't break a case in this county that other people can't break, I'm a damn poor sheriff.

'Cause, I'm supposed to know my people here, and I'm supposed to know the thugs." In your homeplace, you catch a man many, many times by knowing the manner he operates. Some burglars will drill holes in the ceiling (even) if every window and drawer is open, and there's other burglars that'll break in that window (even) if they didn't have no roof over it. They're crazy, there's just one way they see it.

When I first started, I made the reputation of being a man that was able to get a confession out of criminals. All the sheriffs were bringing their prisoners in here from over East Texas for me to question for 'em. Well, I had to quit that, because I found myself in court all the time. I'm not bragging. I've helped break a many, a many a case in other counties through questioning.

I did have a good informant structure, a system set up that was second to none. The criminals respected me and they trusted me, and they would talk to me. I'd get letters even from the penitentiary. There's one man that can help you, and that's an old criminal, 'cause he thinks like a criminal, and you better listen to him when he's talking to you. I'm not talking about an old cold-blooded killer or something like that, but just an ornery cuss. In those days our dopeheads were morphine heads—that's about the only thing you ever heard of. Well, they robbed me down there at Chandler right this side of Tyler of 10,000 dollars worth of morphine. I got the exact method of operation, and, by golly, I'd never heard of such-looking people. The description didn't mean nothing, not even their method of operation. I'd never heard of it. So, I drove over to Tyler. There was an old morphine-head that lived over there, and I pulled up in front of his house and called him out. I said, "Say, I had a big robbery this morning over at Chandler. There was two women and a man that came in there, and this fellow pretended he had a terrible bad shoulder on him, and nothing would help it but a mustard poultice. And while the druggist was upstairs putting this poultice on there, the women lifted about 10,000 dollars worth of morphine."

"Oh," he said, "I can tell you who you want there." Says, "You want old Helen _____, her daughter-in-law, and Charlie _____. That's the way they operate." Well, I called old Bill Baker who was sheriff, a good man. I said, "Bill, have you got a fellow up there named Charlie _____?" He said, "Yeah. Why, do you want him?" I said, "You dadgummed right I want him." Well, I could tell the way Bill was talking that Bill was using that son-of-a-gun for an informant. I couldn't help it. Bill was disappointed, but he said, "You come up here. I'll have him in jail when you get here." So, when I got there Bill had him sitting there in the office. He said, "Charlie, I've told you and I've told you, you better stay out of Henderson County. Now, this is Jess Sweeten, sheriff, and he'll get you." He said, "I haven't been in Henderson County." I said, "The heck you haven't. You was at Chandler." "Yes," he says, "I was at Chandler, but isn't that in Smith County? We got a pretty good haul down there, of morphine." But Bill had been using him and Bill was quite disappointed that I was getting his informant.

There was another one I caught driving a car. I found out he was a big dope over at Hot Spring. I called the county health officer. I says, "Can you prescribe some morphine for this old morphine head?" He says, "Sure. How much do you want?" I said, "Let me have about three grains." Well, I got three grains, cost me a quarter. I got the syringe and the spoon, they had it in the jail, and took him for a ride. I knew when I got him he was gonna be in a heck of a shape. He was about 65 years old and he had a chronic leg on him, from here down to here you could see the bone. He stunk so bad, that old leg, that I couldn't hardly ride in the car with him. I said, "Say, you're in bad shape, aren't you?" He says, "Oh, boy, you don't know the half of it." I said, "Well, would you like to have a little fix?" He looked at me and said, "What are you talking about? You're not about to give me a fix." I said, "It's right there in the drug box. Reach in there and get the spoon. How much do you take?" He said, "I take about a grain at a time." I said, "OK, there's three grains in there. Reach in there and get you a spoon, your syringe."

And you know, he says, "Stop the car!" There was a big mansion there and he run out there in that yard and got him a spoon of water out of that hydrant. I don't know if anybody saw him or not. He come back over there carrying that spoonfull of water, and he put his pill in there and he dissolved it, he sucked it up, shot himself. So, we were driving along and I said, "Say, you've really been on a lot of these robberies . . . ," and took it from there. In the time I had him I cleared up 375,000 dollars in highjacking, shoplifting—you never heard anything like it. I called Shreveport, New Orleans, said, "Did you have a real expensive fur coat lifted?" (They) Said, "Yeah." I said, "Well, I have him in jail over here." They said, "Well, by golly, hold him; we sure want him." But that old dopehead, he really told me everything I wanted—just for a quarter.

If we'd have had two-way radios I doubt very seriously that Bonnie and Clyde would have ran loose as long as they did. I had one run-in with 'em up here when they first started in 1931. I didn't know who they were, of course. That was before they got into the big time. They were stealing. They was right across the road in front of me and I was trying to pull a slick hill. They jumped over a fence right near a house, and there were a couple of old mules there. Well, they jumped on those mules and took off and they dropped a gunny sack, burlap sack, in the road. I picked it up and looked in there and there was a couple of pigs in it! It was about five minutes before dark when they jumped over that fence. You probably never rode a mule, but some of 'em will run and some of 'em won't. I don't care how much you spur him, he never gonna run, he'll trot. Anyway, their old mules run and mine just trot. They got over in the woods there and it was dark about that time, so I lost 'em.

I found out later he left her in an old abandoned schoolhouse there, and walked into town and stole a car. The sheriff at Kaufman called me the next morning and said, "We got that young couple you were looking for yesterday, the ones you called me about." I said, "What do you want 'em for?" "Well," he said, "theft and burglary." I said, "What's their names?" He said, "Just a minute, I got the old boy's name here on a pad. The old boy's named Clyde Barrow. The gal, she's Bonnie Parker." I said, "Well, you go ahead and file on 'em. I just won't do it."

But when they got out of that, they really cut loose. I missed 'em out here one morning (by) about 10 minutes. There was an old man, Wilbur, who was plowing corn with an old team in the early part of March. He came to the sheriff's office there about eight o'clock and says, "I believe Bonnie and Clyde are denned up out there in the road at the end of my corn rows. There's an old bridge there."

Well, I knew right where it was, and I knew him to be a man of good judgment, so I got my deputy and gave him the machine gun and I took the 30.06 armor-piercing. I told him, "We'll drive out the Tyler highway until we come to this old dirt road that leads out through there, and when we're up on a hill we can look down there, and if that car's there we're gonna come back on this road to the Tyler highway until we come to this creek. Then we'll walk up that creek and we'll be right on 'em before they know it."

I said, "You use that machine gun on him, 'cause he uses a 30.06 Browning Automatic and that thing's pretty hard to face in a gun battle. You take him with that machine gun." And so help me, maybe it's sinful to feel that way . . . but it had just been two weeks since Bonnie had shot two highway patrolmen off of their motorcycles. That Sunday afternoon Bonnie and Clyde had an appointment with Raymond Hamilton and they was waiting there for Raymond to show up. Well, these two youngsters, one of 'em was 21 and one was 22, come up, and she shot those boys off those motorcycles with buckshot. Then she went over there and took a foot to turn 'em over and shot each one of 'em right between the shoulders. I told my deputy, "You save her for me. Now, I'll disable the car. I'll shoot the motor out of the car. And we'll be at close range—just save her for me." There's two people while I was sheriff that I would have liked to kill, and she was one. Boy, she was so cold-blooded! I asked that lady in the house next to the bridge how long they'd been gone. She said, "About 10 minutes." I said, "Which way did they go?" She said, "When they hit the Tyler highway they turned left, towards Tyler." But if we'd had had a radio . . . !

Once, I had one of the Barrow gang in my jail. He had robbed a bank over in La Grange. I was a federal court witness in Beaumont in a slant hole drilling, and I'd been in the sheriff's office about two weeks. I took the stand and was there about 30 minutes. I left there with a bench warrant. I went from there to La Grange. I got in there about 10:30 at night and walked to the jail office. I had on a little snap-brim hat and double-breasted serge suit. You know, we had to go dressed up in those days. I said, "Sheriff, I've got a bench warrant here for one of your prisoners." He says, "Who is it?" He was gruff, a full-blood German, been sheriff 28 years. I said, "Gene O'Dair," and handed him the bench warrant. He never did look at it, just left it lie there on his desk. (He) Says, "You can't get him." I says, "What?" Says, "You can't get him."

"Well, now, sheriff," I says, "you've been in a long time, and you know that's a powerful piece of paper. I made a long drive down here. Sheriff, I tell you what I'm gonna do. I'm gonna put you or Gene O'Dair there, one (or the other), in my own jail. Now, I'll tell you what my plans are. I'm going from your office. I'm gonna spend the night in the Driscoll Hotel (in Austin), and I'm gonna be back in the morning with a telegraphic warrant for you, and I'm gonna put you in my jail, so help me God, for contempt, or I'm gonna have Gene O'Dair." I said, "One of the two! Now, the monkey's on your back and I'll be at the Driscoll."

Well, the next morning my phone was ringing early. He said, "This is the sheriff. I found out you was really sheriff. I didn't believe it last night. I thought you was somebody trying to break him out." I said, "Sheriff, it looks like if you had thought that you'd have arrested me." "Well," he said, "I just didn't know what to do. You just caught me cold turkey. Now, I'll tell you, that prisoner is right there in Austin. I took him up there for safe keeping."

See, Gene O'Dair was Raymond Hamilton's partner, and Bonnie Parker and Clyde Barrow was just like that with 'em. He and Raymond Hamilton had robbed this bank down in La Grange, so that's why the old man was being so careful.

So, I went up there and got Gene, and I was putting the handcuffs on him when he says sarcastically, "Do you really think you're gonna get back with me?" I said, "Sure." He said, "Bonnie and Clyde and

Raymond will have me before you hit halfway." "Well," I said, "Gene, you know, when you do something you gotta have a plan, and my plan is all set. When we get in the car and head toward Athens I'll tell you what my plan is."

So, I had a deputy drive the car and I sat in the back seat. Right there I had a sawed-off shotgun with buckshot and a 30.06 with armor-piercing ammunition with a machine gun in the back seat. We were going on down the road and he said, "If you'll take these cuffs off of me and let me get my hands in front of me, it would be more comfortable." I said, "I think it would, too." I told the deputy to stop the car and I uncuffed him and let him smoke a cigarette. I said, "Now, Gene, you know, I told you of my plan? I would really welcome (it) if Clyde and Bonnie and Raymond would try to take you. I'd like it. Now, I've got just as good arms as they've got, and I know that they can't handle their arms like I can handle mine. If they try to take you, they've got to come up from behind me." I said, "Now this is my plan, this is exactly what's gonna happen. I'm gonna take this sawed-off shotgun here and I'm gonna blow your head right through that windshield. You're the first one gonna die. Then I'm gonna turn my fire on Bonnie and Clyde." I said, "I know this, they won't have a chance." He said, "Oh, my God, I hope they don't do it!" He was in my jail about two months and when I sent him down there (to the state penitentiary) he had 410 years on him.

I believe there's more of 'em, more killers than we ever had, but I don't believe they've got the nerve they had in those days. I think they were more dangerous in those days than they are now. In other words, they would really stand up to you and face you. But I never did see a real criminal that wasn't a coward. When he looks at you and he knows that you've got an even break with him, 99 times out of a 100, he'll wilt. I've seen 'em wilt that really surprised me.

I never would put a deputy where I thought there might be a possibility of gun fighting or something like that. I always took the front of it myself. There was a fellow here one time by the name of Hood. He cut a young fellow with a pocket knife, ended him for life, cut all his tendons and he almost died. So, we tried him, and I swore that his reputation was bad. Well, he started gunning for me, and he always carried an old double-barreled shotgun. At close range, I never was too scared of a pistol, there's very few people that can really use that pistol, but most anybody can shoot a shotgun. I used a pistol, but I always thought I could sure hold my own to defend myself at close range.

I was watching him. I knew he was gunning for me, he was doing a little talking. But I couldn't get him right where I wanted him. You know, I wanted to kill him, but you just can't go out there and just shoot him. So, I kept watching him. He was trying to get me in the right place, too. Finally, one day, I had a call out east of Athens that a fellow had been killed out there. I went out there and he was driving a Ford touring car and he had tried to get out of the car on the opposite side from the driver and his head had hit the ground and his feet had hung up on this gear shift and emergency brake. His head was down, and blood, I guess, had rushed to his head. I looked at him, and I had a deputy with me and I said, "He's a damn nigger, isn't he?" He said, "No, don't you know who that is? That's old Hood." Nobody was around the car, but directly, I saw a fellow walking out of the woods. He came on down to the car and got through the fence. I looked at his belt and saw a gun sticking in it. He was walking right toward me and it was nice that I was able to watch him. And he walked up to me and stuck his hand out and shook hands and said, "My name's Johnson, and I'm the one that done the shooting. He'd been threatening me, and I decided the thing to do was just kill him." I said, "Well, that's a way to defend yourself." He handed me the gun, and I put him in jail and filed on him for murder, but I didn't think the grand jury would ever indict him, and they didn't.

You can imagine the unreasonable things, in those days, that was asked of you. Oh, boy! I was single when I was elected sheriff; my wife and I married five or six months after I took office. I made up my mind that I was married and wanted to stay married. I don't know why it is, but gals have a tendency to take after somebody carrying a darn pistol and wearing a uniform—why, I've never been able to understand. And sometimes we had the sorriest people in the world wearing a gun. I was married there when I was young, and I had many, many chances, but I just never did it.

A fellow, sure, would go out and help everybody you could and needs your help, even though it was beyond your duty. Go ahead and help 'em. In those days there was very few people had telephones, and you'd run your car thousands of miles delivering death messages. An important mess of people didn't have a telephone. And you didn't do it for politics, you was out there trying to help people, you was interested.

And you take the nigger, he was in pretty bad shape. The Negro couldn't vote, and he wasn't recognized. Over in the east part of the county there was a few fellows over there hiring 'em on as sharecroppers, and they'd let 'em get that crop laid by and then they'd try to run 'em off. Well, the niggers got to coming to me. They couldn't even vote. I'd go down there and say, "Look at his crop, what's the trouble with it?" He'd say, "Well, the sorry so-and-so, he won't work and

I just run him off." I'd say, "But what are you gonna do about the property he's got out there?" "Oh, he's half worked it," he'd say, "it's no good." I'd go over there and look at it, good clean tomatoes and watermelons and peas and corn and cotton. I'd say, "Now, you're not gonna run him off. If you run him off you're gonna pay, you're gonna pay him for this crop." Now, believe you me, you talk about politics, that was darn bad politics! But I wouldn't have gone against that nigger if they'd have beat me the next day. It was the principle of the thing. That nigger couldn't even go to the polls and vote, and he was getting a raw deal, and I just wasn't gonna stand for it.

I stepped on a lot of people's toes. We had a fellow who was a millionaire up there. Well, he was a good fellow. He was an educated man and he was a rancher and a farmer and an oilman, but he would get drunk. He wasn't a criminal, he was just a drunk. He had a fight up there with a fellow and I went up and got him, took him home, took him up to his big mansion there and put him to bed, walked out the front door and went back to the jail. I'd been there about 20 minutes when he came down to jail and said, "Why didn't you lock me up when you had the chance to? I'll tell you the reason, you didn't have guts enough to do it!"

I yanked him up and said, "I'm gonna throw you *under* the jail and forget you're in it." I put him in there and in about 30 minutes the president of the First National Bank was down there, Will Justice, Wayne Justice's daddy. Said he wanted to get him out. I says, "Can't." (He) Says, "Why can't?" I says, "Well, he's drunk. You can get him at two o'clock in the morning, he ought to be sober by then. That's one guy that's gonna stay in here till he gets sober. I give him a chance and he wouldn't take it." Well, that was bad politics, too!

You know, I'll tell you, there's very, very few counties where the sheriff and the commissioners court get along. We didn't get along too, too good. I thought of it many, many times, there could be a better way figured out. A sheriff is more or less at the mercy of the commissioners court, and if he's got enemies on that commissioners court, he's in trouble. Politics is a pretty nasty word, as far as I'm concerned. Somebody that will give away something that is good and right, and will fall into something that is not right to save him some votes . . . . Man, I can't stand that! I just get furious. I know one sheriff that will actually go to the lawyer and say to him, "I'm trying old John Doe out here for murder, can't you help me out just a little bit?" And he'll help him out.

The federals, the government, ought to leave the counties alone. There's nobody believes in police brutality, there's nobody believes in that. I may have a peculiar view on the real criminal. I'm not talking about the fellow who goes out here and commits a small crime, that you can take and straighten him out, I'm talking about the cold-blooded criminal that kills and highjacks and murders. I don't know why the state and the counties should be forced to give him a fine place to live, let him stay in a jail of luxury, and suchlike. And I'm a strong believer in capital punishment. You take a child murderer, he may live to kill again. And one child's life is worth more than every criminal that has ever been before.

You take this fellow up in Dallas about 20 years ago. He got 99 years. One of the worst punishments you can hand to a man is put him in there for the rest of his life. Now, you're really punishing that man. But he's not gonna stay there, he's either gonna break out or he's gonna be pardoned, he's gonna live to kill again. This Dallas man spent eight years in the penitentiary and they gave him a pardon. He came back to Dallas and put in a barbershop, and he saw this little girl, 10 years old, and her little brother going to the grocery store. Well, he kidnapped 'em, took 'em out there in a rural area, chopped the little boy in the head with a hatchet, thought he killed him, then raped the little girl and killed her. The little boy's still living and he's just a vegetable today, hasn't ever been out of bed; there he is. And the Dallas man is back down there with 99 years on him. Now, is it worth those little innocent things' lives to pamper, and protect, and take chances on that? We have a tendency to forget every 20 years. The next generation forgets what happened to this last generation. Somebody will feel sorry for that old devil, and if they're not careful he'll live to kill again.

This Miranda case in Phoenix, Arizona, was one of the most damnable things that ever happened to law enforcement. He violated a minor traffic law there, and the policemen stopped him to give him a ticket. He thought, naturally, that they were stopping him for this serious crime he had just committed, and he says, "I'm your man, I killed her." Well, they looked at each other, they didn't even know what he was talking about. "I killed her, you'll find her, she's dead." He had killed a housewife and raped her. They took him down there, and sure enough, there she was; she was dead. The Supreme Court, the Warren court, knocked that down because they didn't warn him that what he might say might be used against him.

That's one of the great problems they're facing now. I sometimes think I can see a little drifting back to a little common sense in law enforcement, but I don't know. But there's many, many problems, (because) the government's got their hand in it. These federal judges, you take this Judge Sarah Hughes, giving a county an ultimatum, a deadline, just shouldn't be. She does a jail inspection, goes down there and inspects a jail herself! That just shouldn't be. I didn't run in '54, I went with Mobil Oil Company as an investigator. I didn't want any part of it anymore. You were just screwed down too tight.

I don't think that anyone could've been harder on real criminals than I was, or more gentle with those who deserved it. But if a cold-blooded criminal decided he was gonna take things in his hand, well, he run into a saw. I've always had the opinion that a cold-blooded criminal was born. He's born, there's no doubt in my mind about it. The day he was born, he became a criminal. That's what I've said for 50 years. And if you take him and send him to school and teach him good, you'll just teach him how to be a smarter criminal. There's no cure for that guy. It'll always be a failure to try to straighten out a born criminal. Now, you can take the youngster out here that's grown up into a bad environment, yeah, he'll take that training and straighten up, but not that born criminal.

There's one place that if I was gonna be a little bit lax, it was (with) some youngster. Believe you me, I'd go to bat for him. This is one record I'm proud of, I served 20 years and I sent two to the reformatory in the whole 20 years.

We had juvenile delinquents. You know, I had 27 jailed down there one night, just is various cells, and them fellers run from eight years old up to 11. They'd been stealing bread and ice cream and hubcaps, anything they could get their hands on. They said, "We come to town and don't have no money, and we see other kids going to the show. We want to go to the show. We want to buy us a Coca Cola. And if we don't have any, we just got to steal it to get it."

I talked to those boys, I said, "There's not been a one of you boys here that's been up to the sheriff's office to visit me." They said, "Well, we're scared." And I said, "Why are you scared? You couldn't come to a safer, better place than the sheriff's office." Then I said, "I tell you what I'm gonna do. I'm gonna set a fund up at the First National Bank, and my office secretary is gonna be the banker. You can come in there and borrow. Now, two dollars is gonna be the limit, and you gonna pay this back, without interest. And if you steal to pay it back, that's gonna be the end of you, you're not eligible, and then on top of that, you're gonna be punished for it."

You know, I put that 250 dollars in there and set it up and they signed an oath. An eight-year-old would come in there and borrow two dollars and go to the show. That was there for five years, and when I went out of the sheriff's office I still had 150 dollars in that account, and I just didn't have any juvenile delinquency. Those little boys would come by there to visit with me, talk with me, borrow money. I don't know a one of 'em ever got in serious trouble.

Another time I arrested three youngsters here for robbing. They robbed three stores, wham, wham, wham. Well, it took me about an hour and a half for the deputy and I to catch 'em. Two of 'em was 18 and one was 19, and God knows, when I tell you this story you can see there's no politics in it. They lived in Van Zandt County, there was nobody knew 'em down here.

I talked to those youngsters, and they was all from broken homes. They'd been raised hard, and their mothers and daddies were all separated. I questioned those boys for about a week, and come to find out the two young ones, 18 years old, they had their application in for the Army. And the oldest one had his application in for the Navy. I talked to the Navy in Fort Worth and the Army in Tyler. I told 'em the predicament these boys was in. I said, "They've got their application in." He said, "Yeah, they do have. Here it is right here, we looked it up. But if you so much as give them a suspended sentence, we can't accept 'em."

I had all three of those boys in there to question 'em one night, and they said, "We've never even had nobody to take up for us like you have, we've never." I said, "Well, what I want to do is make good men out of you fellows, that's the main thing. You didn't hurt anyone. You got less than 10 dollars."

This fellow that ran the store out there, well, by golly, he could vote and he had some friends! Oh, he was mad. He wanted to hang 'em. I said to the district attorney, "John, why don't we dismiss those charges against those boys?" "No," he said, "I'm gonna prosecute 'em." I said, "John, I believe you're making a mistake, but since you're so hell-bent on prosecuting those boys, I'm gonna ask the jury to turn 'em loose."

They were tried together. I was the chief prosecuting witness. John Dowdy asked me the question and I answered it honestly, said, "Yeah, they robbed three stores, they'll tell you they robbed 'em. They didn't hurt anyone. They got less than 10 dollars."

He got through with his questioning and I looked at the judge and said, "Judge Hall, can I talk to the jury just one moment?" He said, "Yes, if you'll promise not to say anything that might cause a reversal." I said, "Your honor, I promise I will not." I said, "Gentlemen, we got three boys here, two of 'em are 18 and one 19. Now, we can send these boys to the penitentiary or you can give 'em a suspended sentence, but either one you give them, you tag them as criminals. Now, these boys are all from broken homes, and if there was anybody that needs help, you're looking at three boys right there that needs it. They've never had no help. Never. And believe you me, I'm gonna try to help these boys. The two young ones has got their application in to the Army, the other one to the Navy, and I'm gonna ask you gentlemen to turn 'em a-loose. If you give those boys a suspended sentence, they will not accept 'em.'' And by golly, they done turned 'em a-loose. They went to the Army, they went to the Navy, and they all came out and made good citizens. Sure, the store owner, he got mad as the devil, and believe you me, he votes, but I didn't care about that. That's not the point. The point is to try to help these boys to make good men. And they did, and I've been proud of it ever since. I never was scared to be in the right.

CORBETT
AKINS

★

I've given quite a bit of history about while I was sheriff, but now I'm in my latter days. It's wonderful to get old, but it's hell to be old. So, there's nothing I can do now but stay in a second childhood and sleep by myself like I ought to. There's so many things I could do in my early days that I can't do now. One was I could go barefooted and crack a walnut with my heel. But now if I pull off my socks and shoes and get out on the ground, I can't take it.

I never wore shoes till I was 13 years old, and the first shoes I ever had was a pair of brogans with a brass toe and brass buckle. My daddy bought them for me at J. R. Jones Store here in Carthage. That same day he bought me a pair of britches, first pair of britches I ever had, called knicker-bockers. You brought them up above your knee and snapped them together, and let them hang down over your knee. But all my shirts were homemade, Mama made my shirts, and one thing about the shirts she made, you couldn't tell which end the collar was on because one end was as big as the other. But I have enjoyed my 94 years on earth, trying to make that one hundred. I've gone six more years and a few months to go and I'll be at the hundred mark.

I wish I could still go to the cane patch and steal a few stalks of cane and chew them like I used to. In those days I had a full set of teeth, but now I ain't got nothing but my gums. I tried to chew some cane here awhile back but I never could mash the juice out, so I give up and give the stalk of cane to my boy.

Another thing I enjoyed doing while I was a kid on the farm was ride bull yearlings. A bunch of boys and me would get away from home on Sunday. We'd get out in the woods and run a steer down, tie a lariat rope on him, and one of us would get on him and ride. I was always a pretty good rider until one time one ran away with me and jumped in the creek. But I stayed with him. I never did give up in anything I started when I was a young man, and up to this day. That's the reason I never would quit. I've had hundreds of fights, but I'd win because I was always smart enough to get the first lick. It's that first lick that counts. Being raised in a family of four boys and six girls, if you don't take up for yourself you're in a mess, because when we'd all go to the table it was just like running a boarding house. There was 10 kids and a mama and daddy, which is 12 of us. But we had our groceries and didn't go to town to buy them. We had sweet potatoes in the bin, collards in the garden, turnip greens, and cane to make syrup out of.

I was born in Panola County, East Texas, seven miles west of Beckville, Texas, on Friday morning, October the twenty-first, 1892. When I was born, my mother and daddy named me Clifford. I went by the name of Clifford for six months, but after six months Jim Corbett and John L. Sullivan had a fight, and Jim Corbett whipped John L. Sullivan. My daddy came in from the field one day, saw me jumping and a-bouncing on the bed, and says, "We gonna call that boy Jim Corbett." And I been named Jim Corbett ever since. I was raised on a farm, lived with my mother and my daddy and plowed an old mule till I was 21 years of age. My daddy always told me, "Son, when you get to be 21 years old you can leave home."

I went a lots of places when I was a kid with my daddy, and we went to sacred harp conventions. He was a teacher of the sacred harp, and finally taught me to sing. I would get up and lead a song. I didn't have any shoes to wear to singings until my daddy finally bought me that pair of brogans. He tried to make me wear 'em, but we had to walk two or three miles to the school or church. I'd put 'em under my arm and when we got there I'd put 'em on.

I never knew what it was to ride to school. One school was about two miles, the other was about three. We'd walk every morning. We took our lunch in a tin bucket or syrup bucket. About all we'd have would be a baked sweet potato, a boiled egg, a piece of bacon or ham, and a biscuit. I recall one day we were all eating dinner and there was a young lady that had some syrup in a snuff bottle. She took that syrup around back of a boy and poured it on the top of his head. There was always something going on.

I went to school at Brooks Schoolhouse, which was just a country school. We didn't have no heaters, other than just old wooden heaters, and the schoolhouse was made out of one-by-twelve planks. I stayed in that school the biggest part of my school days, but my daddy wanted to educate me, so he sent me to Beckville. I went to school in Beckville and what you call graduated. Those days, they didn't have no diplomas or nothing, you just made a certain grade and you graduated. I made that grade, but the biggest trouble I had was algebra, and a fellow who takes algebra oughta be killed anyhow. Well, after staying in the school at Beckville, I graduated, and I thought I was a smart boy. I went back out there on the farm and begin to farm again.

In October Papa put me in the field, breaking land with an old mule by the name of Pat. Old Pat was a long-eared mule and every time she stepped forward her ears would go with her. I came in one evening 'most near dead. I looked at my daddy, and I says, "Well, Daddy, I'm gonna leave home tomorrow." He said, "Son, don't do that. I'll need you around the farm. Somebody's got to milk the cows and help your mama."

When I was a small boy, we'd kill our hogs in the fall of the year and hang the meat in the smokehouse. It was our job to see that the hickory fire was burning in the smokehouse to dry the meat. We also had to cook the lard. We would take the fat part of the hog, chop it up, and place it in a pot to boil it. After letting it cook, we'd dip the lard off. The part that was left was the cracklins. We put the cracklins in a tub and took it to the smokehouse. While they were warm, we would place 'em in a small jar. After placing the cracklins in the jar, we pressed 'em to get the lard that was left.

One time my brother and I were looking after the smokehouse to make sure the fire kept burning. My mother left that afternoon to help a neighbor quilt. She told us not to let the fire go out. My papa had gone to Carthage to be on the jury. Before he left that morning, I heard him tell my mother that it might be one or two o'clock that night before he got back. He had to ride the 13 miles on a mule.

Horace and I got all the cracklins squeezed into the cracklin jars. We had vented up the fire. We were sitting there like two little boys playing and having fun. I picked up this small, greasy churn that we had had the cracklins in. When he turned around I put that churn over his head. I wasn't thinking about any trouble. Naturally, he reached up and tried to get the churn off his head, but he couldn't. After he worked a good while, I tried to get it off. I pulled on that churn until I gave out.

About six o'clock my mother came in; she wanted to know where Horace was. "My brother," I says, "he's in the smokehouse with a churn on his head." She went out to the smokehouse and brought my brother Horace out. She worked with that (churn) till way in the night and stretched his neck as long as a crane, but never did get it off. So, after that, she brought Horace into the house and put us to bed. And I want to tell you, it is a job to sleep with a fellow with a churn on his head! He rolled and tumbled and beat the bed.

In the late hours, near two or three o'clock, my daddy came in. And my mother called my father, says, "Lee," which was my father's name, "Lee, Horace has got a churn on his head." But anyhow, we got him out of the bed and set him on the old bench. We didn't have many chairs those days; most all we had was benches, or stools, you might call 'em. Well, he worked and worked and he couldn't get it off. So, after a while he decided that there had to be something done. I remember quite well when he told my mother to go to the tool box and get his hammer to bust it off. She says, "Lee, don't do that, that will kill him." We lived so far in the country, we didn't, couldn't, get no doctor or nothing. But, after she told him that will kill Horace, he says, "Well, he's gonna die anyhow, so get me my hammer." I remember quite well he got the hammer, hit the side of that churn and busted it. And you know, my brother's ears looked like two bananas, they'd done turned blue and swollen. After that, Papa took him to town the next day to see if there's anything to be done for swollen ears. And Doctor Hornsburger, which was several miles from our home, said to take him on back, and said, "Nothing you can do except just feed him some peas and clabber and buttermilk and collards."

I was elected constable in 1937. I ran a garage and filling station, I voted each and every year, and on this particular year I got an idea to run for constable. So I decided I would go out and get votes. I ran a gristmill, and if I found somebody hungry I would give 'em a package of meal. I recall one time it was about three A.M., and this man woke me up and wanted me to ground some corn. So I got up and grounded it for him, and when we got through he asked me if I was going to take any toll. I said my toll was when he fed that meal to his babies. So that man, all the time I was running, he would vote for me.

Another way was, I had a portable light plant and I would carry it around in the old buggy I had, and (I) made it to all the box suppers. There was a box supper at least once or twice a week, then. I'd get there early, back my buggy up to the door, run some wires into the church, and when the people got there I had it lit up like the streets of New York. And that was quite a comment to me, because people were bragging about me. I heard two of my opponents as they came in the door. When they came in and saw those three-hundred-watt light bulbs a-burning, one said to the other, "Hell, we might as well go on home, Corbett's got this thing lit up to where we couldn't see anybody, much less get a vote." So they left.

I made a number of speeches during my years as constable. One time I was running against a man from out of town, and he would distribute pamphlets, etcetera, to every mailbox in the county. I found one of them and walked up to his car, and he slapped me in the face. When he slapped me, that made me nearly as mad as a possum. I pulled him out of the car and took my pistol and pistol-whipped him till he couldn't get up. They got a rumor started that Corbett Akins wouldn't do for constable anymore, he'd pistol-whipped a man till the blood run in his boots. When it came my time to speak that night, I got up there and told the people and said, "I am proud to tell you that if you fellers knew the history of that man, you'd have whipped him a little harder. The man that I whipped was carrying that filthy, funny stuff to each and every mailbox and home in the county." And I told the people there that this same man is the man that I arrested for stealing hogs, a man that was in jail shortly after he was living with another woman. I said, "If you want to vote against me because I hit the man, just go ahead."

And I made many votes by taking off warts; that's a gift to me. When I was eight years old, on Christmas Eve, my mother gave me and my brother a dogwood broom and told us to sweep the yard. And she said, "If you don't, Santa Claus ain't gonna come see you." So we swept a little bit. But then, me and my brother walked about two miles down to some hickory-nut trees. We knew there were lots of hickory nuts there. So we went into the woods picking them up. I recall quite well when I was bent over I saw an old man coming with whiskers down almost to his navel. Of course, the first thing I thought of was what Mama said: "If you don't sweep the yard, Santa ain't gonna come see you." So it scared me, and I started to run off. This old man got a-hold of me and said, "Son, don't be scared. I'm not gonna hurt you. I see you got a wart there on your thumb." I only had one wart on me, on my thumb. He rubbed that wart and looked at me and said, "Son, when you get to be 21 years old, you can take off warts." And from then on I could take a wart off anybody: man, mule, horse, cow, hog, or dog. I've been called from my home to take them off horses and cows. I've never failed, and I've tried everything except a toad frog. I never thought about taking them off of them. So that got me lots of votes.

I didn't have a car for those first elections, but a man by the name of Dixie Ross says, "Corbett, I got an old car. If you'll fix it up, you can use it campaigning." I had a little garage at home, and I took that old car and overhauled it. I didn't have any money to buy gasoline, but could still go out through the country, and not one time did I fail to get back home. I'd run out of gasoline and some fellow would come by and give me a little push, and when he'd find out I'd run out of gas, he'd draw a gallon or two out of his tank. I'd do that every day of the week except Saturdays. Anyway, I made the campaign for sheriff, and when the campaign was over, the first round of it, I won by 350 votes.

The second round of it, I beat my opponent by 358 votes, and in '42 was elected sheriff of Panola County. And the hour I was elected, my old daddy came by and sat down by me on the tail of an old bobtailed truck to talk to me. He said, "Son, you were elected sheriff of Panola County and I'm proud of you, but I want to tell you something. You've got two things you can be now, one the man, the other the monkey." And he said, "The dern monkey'll fit the cage." So, that advice came to me a number of times while I was in office.

During my 10 years as sheriff, I recall speeches I made. I had a voice like a bugle and a mouth like a dishpan, but I got the job done. One Saturday before the election day, my opponents were telling that the bootleggers and the gamblers were paying me. They knew it wasn't so. But in my speech I told the people that all the things they said weren't true. I said, "Even if it was true, there are two people who wouldn't vote against me just as sure as my name is Corbett Akins, and I want you to see those people." I said, "Mama, stand up!" She stood up with grey hair down to her shoulders. And I said, "That's one of 'em. Now I want the other one to stand up. Daddy, will you rise?" My daddy, about 80 years old, was there with tears in his eyes. He said, "What my son is telling you folks is true. He *did not* accept any money from the bootleggers or gamblers." It was my first (election), and I had five opponents, and I beat 'em every one the first round.

Before I was elected, I already knew I had to take care of my people. When I was a kid, Walter Anderson was sheriff of Panola County. My daddy bought a farm out there, 30 miles west of here, for five hundred dollars, and he had to pay a hundred dollars a year on it. One night, Mr. Walter Anderson rode from Carthage horseback to stay all night with us. I remember him telling my daddy, says, "Lee, you gonna pay that hundred dollars tomorrow or I'm gonna have to come out here and take your farm." The next morning we got in the wagon and went to an old man out here, and daddy got the money.

Well, that learned me this, all the time I was sheriff, that if you lived out there in the country, and if the bank had a note against you, a writ of sequestration, they'd bring me that writ, and it would read, "Without fail, you take into your protection immediately the land, chattels . . . ." Whenever I got one of 'em, I'd get my car at night and drive out to the old farmer just like Sheriff Anderson did. I know I drove out to Louis Williams one night at two o'clock. I said, "Mr. Williams, I've got papers to take what you got tomorrow if you don't pay that note off." But he got up the next morning and sold a bunch of stuff to pay it off. I wasn't supposed to do this, of course. When the case was called that morning by the district judge, he asked me, "Sheriff, what disposition did you make of Mr. William's property?" I said, "Your honor, he paid it off this morning and everything's in the clear." Well, then the bankers and the damn lawyers, everyone of 'em, said, "Corbett Akins is the sorriest damn sheriff, he wouldn't take that stuff out there." They wanted it for nothing, you see. But that's the way I stayed sheriff, I took care of the people. You can't be sheriff long if you don't help your fellow man. You won't be there long.

I'm the only sheriff in the county, you might say in the state, that fought parking meters; I wouldn't let 'em put 'em around the courthouse. We had lots of trouble with parking meters, and the parking meter company even got a man to run against me for sheriff. But I went down to Gary one night, it was a big voting box, and I told 'em, "I haven't got much to say, but I'll tell you this. My opponent is trying to get elected 'cause the parking meter company is trying to elect him." I said, "Now, if I'm elected sheriff, I want y'all to bring your tractors, mules, and grubbing hoes, and everything you got, and come up here and help Corbett Akins dig up them damn parking meters." I lost six votes out of that box. We did what I said, and they carried me to federal court in Tyler about that.

Being sheriff never did go to my head. I knew I had to do a job, and I would remember what my daddy told me, "You can be a man or a monkey." You can't be a sheriff and hold malice, you got to be over it, you got to be a man. You can't hold a grudge against nobody. Just 'cause you're a sheriff and got a gun, that don't mean you can go around and kill a man. Why, there's no telling how many I could have shot if I'd just wanted to.

You know the trouble with law enforcement today? Ninety-eight percent of the officers wearing a gun are not officers, they're damn pistol toters. That's all they are, pistol toters. Some of 'em had rather tote a pistol than eat a T-bone steak. A real officer will reason with you and talk to you and try to help you, a damn pistol toter will want to whip you or shoot you.

You had to use your pistol often enough, anyway. I was elected constable first of the year, I believe in 1938, and Carthage at that time was beginning to lease land and have a little oil boom. By the time I was sheriff it was pretty rough, and all I had was a deputy and a night watchman. I lived down here with my wife, but I come home lots of nights and she wouldn't know me, I was beat up so!

So, in February, after being in office six or seven weeks, they was having trouble at a cafe on the north side of the square. The owner had had some trouble with the law and run the law away. I passed by one day and he said, "Akins, don't you come over here. You won't last either." I says, "I'm elected by the people, and if you violate the law and I come after you I'm gonna get you or get part of you." He says, "Naw, you won't."

I never thought much more about it, but in a few days I was sitting in my office one night, and I heard an awful commotion over there. I saw this man pick up a broom and knock a waitress completely off the stool with it, hit her 'side the head. Well, she run out of there, came to my office. I made her stay in my office. I told her not to go back over there. After a while I said, "You go over there on that corner and you stay there. When the bus comes, you go back to San Augustine," and she went over there.

While she was waiting on the corner, I saw the cafe owner get in his automobile, go get his wife, and bring her back to the cafe. Well, when he brought her there, she saw this woman. She came out of that cafe with a six-inch butcher knife, and she went over and made a dive for this little waitress. And when she did, she finally caught her and they clinched. They was just standing in the street and the wife was hacking her over the head. I left the office, and by the time I got out there the cafe owner had come out of the cafe with a .44-40 pistol. As I walked up, he was standing there and telling everybody to stand back. I came up there to where he was guarding his wife and this woman with his pistol. I called him by name and I says, "Drop your pistol." Well, he didn't drop the pistol. I had my gun on him. Instead of dropping his pistol he backed back to his place of business, opened his door, screen door, with his left elbow, and when I stepped up on the sidewalk I saw him when he raised the pistol. I heard the click of it, single action, double action, but when it clicked the last time I was up on the sidewalk. My pistol fired four times and he went down in the door. When he did, his brother was sitting back on a stool at the back of the cafe. He placed his pistol up on his wrist, took dead aim, and when the gun fired he shot a hole right through the top of my cowboy hat. When he did that, I fired at him. He went down under a table, pulled hisself up on the door, and shot at the night watchman running down the street. I had shot four times at the cafe owner in the door, shot one time at the brother on the stool, and shot one time when he went under the table. My gun when it snapped, *"bling,"* I didn't know what the trouble was. But after it was all over, I knew I had an empty gun. The cafe owner was carried to Shreveport, and he died shortly after he got over there. He was one of the first. I wouldn't want to tell you how many men I've killed, 'cause I might have to count 'em before I went to hell.

With all the deals that I had while I was constable and sheriff, I never lost but one battle. That was with a damn nigger woman, six foot two, weighed 210 pounds. I come home here one noon and eat dinner, and when I left I carried my .45 setting in the seat. It rubbed my hip and I just laid it on the seat. I drove up to the sheriff's office and there this nigger woman was, a great big outfit. She said, "I want to get my boys out of the jail." They were in there for breaking into a home and she was their grandmother. I said, "Well, I can't turn 'em a-loose unless you get an order from the judge. My job is just arresting 'em and putting 'em in there."

She said, "Yeah, that's the way you white son-of-a-bitches do us poor niggers." I said, "You bitch, I'll put you in jail!" I had on a four-hand tie, and when I started to get out she grabbed this four-hand tie and jerked me and hit me over the head with her purse. And when she hit me I saw the moon and stars! I reached for my pistol but it was too far, I just tapped it and couldn't get hold of it. She hit me over the head again, and boy, she busted my head. It knocked me crazy there and I went to the ground. Then, when I went to the ground, she jerked me up again and knocked me over the head again. Well, I was fighting her, but I couldn't get loose of this tie.

But there was an old boy I was raised with name of Bob Jensen. He come by there and he had a hickory walking stick. Says, "Corbett, take this!" I grabbed it and popped her across the head. The first lick I knocked her down, and when I knocked her down, her bloomers fell off of her. She jumped up and run off, and the deputies caught her down at the depot. But she'd pretty near beat me to death. And you know what she had in the handbag? A damn Coca-Cola bottle! That old devil had it made up when she come up there. But if I'd have got my pistol she wouldn't have hit me, I'd have killed her.

They expected, in them days, for a sheriff to enforce the law. They don't do it now. They've got enough pistols, handcuffs, and tear gas for law enforcement in Carthage today to fill up a pickup truck, but all I had was a pistol and a pair of handcuffs and one deputy, who worked for 90 dollars a month, and the county stripped 30 percent off a dollar. He was a good one, though, Curtis "Cush" Reeves. He was just as tough as I was, but wasn't hardly as mean. Curtis wanted to whip 'em with his fists, he never thought of his gun much. He hit several over the head with his fist until one time he broke his fist. Then he learned to use his pistol more.

I was never scared in my life. I've been shot at 11 times, knocked down a number of times, but I always got up fine.

One time I got a call from across town at Davis's Store. They said to come over there quick. Well, when I got over there, there was a six-foot drunk standing in front of the counter with a switch-blade, a "Dallas special," and the woman clerk was trapped behind the counter and couldn't get out. He was having fun. He'd swing it at her, you know, and she'd scream.

I walked in and I didn't have no pistol. I told him to drop that knife, but he didn't drop it. I eased up close enough to where I could hit him in the belly, and when I did, I knocked him down. He got up, but when he got up he struck at me with that knife and caught me just below the navel. It cut through my shirt, but just made a red streak there across my stomach. Then I knocked him down and took it from him. I did get scared then; a scared man gets hurt.

In my days, before I ever expected to be an officer, I knew there was a number of stills in Panola County. I didn't know what whiskey looked like or tasted like, but I'd heard about it. The only thing I knew about, coming off the farm, was walking around a churn and dasher and churning and making butter, or going out to the cow pen and milking an old cow. But when I become of age I heard about corn liquor, I heard my daddy talk about people making it. So, after I became sheriff of Panola County, I knew that I had to do right, because I had a boy, and a wife, and the people throughout Panola County that voted for me. I was determined to do what was right or die, and I have done that from that day to this.

Stills are often located by smoke, but I also located them with my bloodhounds, which trail the party from their home to the place they make the whiskey. Most stills are hidden underground. This is done by digging a pit, covering the pit with logs and dirt and planting bushes on top of it, and leaving a place of entrance with a door with a bush nailed to it. You lift the bush and go down into the still, which is all camouflaged.

They're also found by tracks which you notice goes all in one direction. And there will be another (trail) leading from the still, they never walk back and forth in the same trail. When you find a trail like that, you can rest assured there is something. And after you get near the still, you'll notice the tree tops and brush in piles, and logs that have been moved. You can tell there's a still close-by by the way the leaves and grass are mashed down. If it looks like there's a lot of traffic in one spot, you can rest assured there's a still nearby. But they can be anywhere.

I was an old expert still-catcher and got 18 while I was sheriff and constable. Out here northwest of town, there was one that had been operating ever since I was a boy, and I knew it was there. So one evening I decided I'd go look for it. I took my .22 automatic rifle, got my car, got up here close to Rock Hill. I run into this young feller name of Gab Williams. He says, "Where you going?" I says, "I'm going squirrel hunting; come and go with me." Well, I knew I wasn't going a-squirrel hunting. I was a-going up there to search, walk around, and see if I could see it.

Well, when I got up there where I wanted to go, there was a field that had been plowed with a two-horse plow, and it was just as smooth as this floor except for the plow ridges. And right out in the middle of that field there was a pine bush. I never thought a thing about it, but I walked around and directly I seen a man come out from under that bush. So, I told this kid, I said, "Come on, let's go see what's over there." Went over there and it was this pine bush which was about four foot in diameter and maybe five foot high. And when I got there I could see tracks all around it. I got ahold of this bush, and when I did, I pulled the door open. I throwed this door back and I went down in it and it was a still, 12 foot square. I got down in it, and there was a 30-foot well, well rope, and a bucket! I believe there was five or seven barrels of mash and all kind of buckets and things down in there. After I got through checking, this old boy that went with me, he was scared to death after he found out what it was.

So, I decided to get out of that place. There was a five-gallon jug, a jug made like the old Texas water jug, little mouth with a handle on it, which was full of whiskey. Well, I got that thing and I started out with it. This old boy helped me up with it, but when I started out of that hole there was three men standing (with)in four foot of me, just standing there. Man, I didn't know what to do! I went back down in the still. I had read about stills being dynamited with people down in there, and being killed when you come out. There I was 20 miles away from home; didn't nobody know where me and this boy was, and it worried me. I sat there until the sun begin to make a yellow beam at the treetops, just about dark, then I figured I'd come out of there. I took my hat and put it on my rifle barrel and stuck that out first, 'cause I figured he'd shoot the hat and I'd be all right. Nothing happened, and I crawled on up. I told old Gab, I said, "Give me that five-gallon jug." Well, we came out of that thing and I walked about two hundred yards, and there was four men run up to me just like they were fixing to grab me. I didn't know what to do. It was my intention to shoot at 'em, but I didn't, just shot over 'em. I can hear that wire now as them four men were hitting the barbwire fence down there, that wire going *"wheep, whap, whap."* Well, that was the end of that. I got that five gallons of whiskey, got in my car, and came back to my office, got some deputies, went back out there. When we got there, (there) wasn't a well bucket, there wasn't a rope, wasn't a can, there wasn't a bit of mash, wasn't nothing in it. They had come back there and destroyed it while I was gone. But I had an idea who they were, so I called the revenue men the next day. We went out there and got their fingerprints off of some of those old cans and things and classified them, found out who they belonged to.

In 1939, me and the liquor control board had information that there was a man who was making whiskey on Dr. Daniels' farm on Brushy Creek below Gary. Me and a constable went down there one day and we located the still. After locating the still, we came back to Carthage and got in contact with the alcoholic unit in Tyler. They sent a man down here to help me apprehend the one that was making whiskey in the Gary community. We went in there about 11 o'clock at night, and it was cold, way below zero. We stayed in there and waited. We had already checked the still. There was a copper still with a big cooker and a number of feet of coil that went into a barrel of water used to condense the steam from the still to make whiskey. We knew that they would be there before the daylight hours, because there was five barrels of mash ready to run. We had checked it. You knew in checking mash that after the mash had settled and the water turned blue it had to be cooked soon, because if you didn't it would spoil.

Well, we stayed there for several hours until, as the sun broke through the treetops, we heard the crisp footsteps of someone coming. And you know, at that time of morning, when it was zero weather, you could really hear the leaves a-breaking. We knew that someone was coming and then we saw a husky man coming into the still. He went in and checked all the barrels of mash. After he checked those barrels of mash, he came out near me. I was almost snoring, I had been up all that night. After he didn't see anybody there, he went back to the five barrels of mash, checked the still, and saw that everything was all right. Then he looked down at the ground and walked around and walked over to a small bush, took his pocketknife out of his pocket, opened it up, and cut off a limb. When he cut the limb off, he took it and trimmed it up nicely. Then he raised it up on top of his shoe sole. He measured from the heel of his shoe to the end of his toe. He went down and took that stick he had made and measured the track he had seen around the still. When he did, he saw the measurements on that stick didn't suit the measurement of the track he had at the still. After measuring that track, he got up and stood and looked all around. He went back to the spring that was furnishing the water for the still. He knelt down upon his knees and took a big drink of that water and spit it out of his mouth.

Bob Regan, the revenue man, told me, "Corbett, I think we ought to watch that man because he's fixing to run." The man walked down near the still, which included a 55-gallon drum as the cooker. He had already went in the woods and picked up a bunch of limbs and started a fire under the cooker. So, he got the fire going and everything cooking well, then he took this limb he had measured his footsteps with and again went down near the still. He laid this switch on the track, and when he got up after measuring it he looked all around again. He still wasn't satisfied. He walked over to one barrel and raised the lid. There wasn't but this one barrel of the five that was closed. He reached down in the barrel and pulled out a possum that had gone down in that mash and drowned. Then he walked over to barrel number four, which was within 10 feet of me, and when he did, he reached in that barrel and stirred on top of that mash, and you could see very readily that something was wrong. He reached over in this barrel, which was within 10 feet of me, and pulled out a rat that had fallen in the mash. And I said to myself, "My God. How can a man drink that whiskey with a possum in it and a rat in it?" Well, he pitched that rat out and he stood up, and he still wasn't satisfied. He went back over near the big still which was the 55-gallon drum, and for a last time he measured that track. When he did, he raised straight up and shook his head. Mr. Reagan said, "Well, Corbett, he is fixing to leave." When he did, he took off through the woods and he was gone.

We both took off after him. We ran him about a half of a mile or better, we went around the hills chasing him. On the other hill we saw a shack which was on the bluff that crosses Brushy Creek. He went into this shack. When we got up to this shack, there was his wife and two kids. His wife said, "My gosh, what do you'll want?" We told her we was after the moonshiner. She said, "Don't bother that man, 'cause he's just trying to feed us chillins." I said, "Well, how does he feed you?" She said, "He takes the whiskey and sells it to the people around here."

We arrested him anyway and took him on up to Gary and then brought him to Carthage and put him in jail. He immediately made his bond and was released by the judge. After that, about 30 days, the court was called, and I went before the judge and told him this was a poor man with a little wife and two kids. I told him the whiskey he was making and selling in Gary was to feed his family. The judge told me he was going to turn this party back to me and let him go on back to Brushy Creek. He was not to make any more whiskey, but to get him a plow and a mule and plant him some corn and plant him some cotton and make him a living. And he did.

If you want to be a perfect moonshiner, you have got to know your stuff. The best is to take wooden barrels, not metallic barrels, and take those wooden barrels and be sure they are clean. It's best to build a fire in those barrels and clean 'em out. After you do that, if you want to make a good grade of whiskey: first, put about four or five gallons of water in this barrel; second, take a hundred pound of corn chops and pour it into this water and let it set about 24 hours, until that barrel of corn chop is swelled and fermented good. When you do that, go to your store and get about 50 pounds of sugar and pour into the chops. Mix it completely, and then finish filling your barrel, a 55-gallon barrel, up to the top about six inches from the rim. And when you do that, get you about eight or 10 yeast cakes and drop into this barrel, and then stir it all completely and forget about it. In about four days come back to this barrel and completely stir it and add about five pounds of sugar. In about three or four days this barrel will ferment on top. Dip that off and throw it out. If you ain't got no chickens, take that home to your hogs. In two or three weeks you will come back and you will see it has fermented perfectly. When you look into that barrel, you will see it looks exactly like the blue sky in Heaven. When it gets blue and hard, you take about a mouthful and rinse your mouth out with it. You don't have to swallow it. If it tastes bitter, wait just a few days and then come back and get your still ready. You take all that blue top and put it in this cooking barrel, and you start a fire under the cooking barrel. When it begins to get it to boil and go out through the copper coil, then you begin to make your whiskey. But, when you get down to the bottom, be sure you know what you're doing, because when you get to the bottom that's what the old whiskey maker calls white lightning. You save the bottom stuff, just cut your still off, pour into your 55-gallon drum a hundred pounds of chops and 50 pounds of sugar, and fill it up with water and let it ferment again. Then you get the second run of whiskey, and the second run is better than the first. I could take you boys down in the bottom and make whiskey and make a fortune.

When I was sheriff I didn't mind following a cold trail. In the 1920s, somewhere along there, when Mr. Henry Mathis was sheriff, a man had killed another man here in Carthage. The man killed was named Hoyt Rayburn and the killer was named King. When I became sheriff I decided I'd locate him, and I gathered up enough information so that I found him in Phoenix, Arizona, shining shoes for the Police Department. I sent a warrant out there and they placed him in jail. Me and

Mr. Reeves went after him and brought him to Carthage. He appeared in court and they called his case, but all the material witnesses had died, so they had to turn him loose. But, anyway, when I hit a man's trail I didn't bark much but I had a cold nose!

I was elected sheriff of Panola County in the summer of 1942, and I served as sheriff till '52, 10 years. At that time Panola County was a rough, tough place. Gas and oil boom, biggest gas-oil boom ever known in the world was at Henderson, 30 miles west of us. I was sheriff during those times, and I knew all the help I had was one deputy and one night watchman and nobody else.

But I had a pack of bloodhounds. I had 16 of the best bloodhounds that ever hit the earth. And many a night I heard them trailing a man; and when they hit a man, he's gonna have to take a tree, 'cause they'd kill him.

I've been a dog man all my life. Raised in the country, raised 12 miles west of here, and I always had coon dogs and hounds and squirrel dogs. I went to Nacogdoches one day to see Sheriff Montgomery down there about something. He had two bloodhounds that he'd trained, he was going out of office, and I bought 'em for 25 dollars each. They were two wonderful dogs; and I ordered a dog from England, a full-blood English bloodhound, that cost me 368 dollars when he landed over there in Shreveport. He could smell a track a hundred hours old. An old bloodhound will not leave a scent, it's wonderful how they do it. I trailed two men down there one night for 16 hours. When a real bloodhound hits a track, he can go through a crowd of a hundred or a thousand people, and he won't lose that scent. I run a nigger over there across the river four hours, and in the race he went through what the niggers call a convention—hundreds of niggers there just walking everywhere. That bloodhound trailed him right on through there and bayed him over in the church. A real bloodhound will not leave the track. They call 'em bloodhounds because they're blooded hounds. Lots of people got the idea they're dangerous, but a bloodhound is a peaceful dog. When a dog run up on him, if a man would sit down, or stand up, or not move, the old dog wouldn't do nothing but bay him like he was a hog or something, stand there and bark at him. But, brother, if he left there, that man went down, 'cause that dog would eat him up.

I had two hounds called Nip and Tuck, and (a) lot of people say, well, dogs can't talk. But dogs can talk, 'cause old Tuck would hit that trail and you'd hear him just as plain at one or two o'clock at night say, "How o-o-o-old is he?" And old Nip would say, "21, 22, 21, 22, 21, 22." This other old dog called Old Doc that had cost me 368 dollars when he was a puppy, he could trail any track one hundred to

120 hours old. Now, Old Doc, whenever he hit a man's trail out there, and he would bark for nothing but a man's trail, he was just like a big old gobbler. When you could hear him holler just as plain, you knew that he was fixing to get gone.

And I had one old dog named Rock, he was a wonderful dog. He'd trail with a pack all night, but when the party he was chasing crossed a foot log, Rock was the only dog that wouldn't cross. Old Rock would sit down on that log and beg just as pitiful as if you was whopping him with a limb, but when you got there old Rock would go on across. That was his instinct, he wanted to wait there and show the sheriff which way he'd gone.

I know one night we was up here at Kilgore. I had my pack of hounds, and a nigger had attacked a woman up there. She had rode the bus a mile west of Longview and then had to walk about as far as from here to the square. And this nigger attacked her before she got home. He cut her throat from ear to ear. Noble Crawford called me, and I went up there and put them hounds on that track. We ran that track, I guess, three hours, and we heard the dogs bay. We stayed pretty close, for some had horses, and when they bayed we all rushed up there and they were in a pen. A man had made a pen up there for some pet deer. High fence, had on top of it three bobwires. When he got there this man knew we was fixing to catch him and went over that fence, and when he did a barb caught a piece of the jumper and tore out a piece about two or three inches long. We got that off. Well, we got them dogs through that fence and went over there several miles and they bayed again. When we got there, there was a nigger woman sitting in there churning. We asked her where her husband was, because them deputies knew who it was when we got to this house. She said, "He's not here, hasn't been here tonight." The boys was a-shining lights under the house, and they had a brick chimney, and you know how a brick chimney is built—it's hollered out under there. Well, in the hollered place under this fireplace there was a tub. One of the deputies went under there and drug it out, and in this tub was a pair of striped overalls and a striped jumper. They was just as bloody as they could be. So, we took the clothes, and this man ran out of there into another deputy's hands and we caught him.

One time, we were called to Jasper County from Carthage. We were called there after two fugitives escaped from Jasper one night about eight o'clock. We went to Jasper and stayed all night. The next morning we ate breakfast and then got together with the sheriff and his posse. We turned the dogs loose about eight. The track was 20 hours old, and we ran that track from eight that morning to four that afternoon for a total distance of 16 miles. The dogs led us to the Neches

River where the suspects had throwed a gun into the water. One old dog went into the water and came back, then we went into the water and came out with the gun. We left there and in a short while jumped the two fugitives; that was about 2:30 in the afternoon. We run 'em until about 3:30, when I saw them come out of a river bottom into an old field. They crossed the field with the dogs close behind 'em, and ran into an old house or shack, and the dogs went in behind 'em. When the fugitives came out, one was carrying a pump shotgun. About that time I arrived at the house with some of the other officers, and so did a man riding a horse. I told him I wanted the horse, and I threw my gun on him and made him get down. I told my deputy, Acie Henigan, to get on it and stay with the dogs. He did, and the dogs crowded the fugitives so close that they throwed the box of shells away and the shotgun. But Henigan and the dogs stayed with 'em, and a little after four that afternoon the dogs bayed the two fugitives in a pond of water. They were standing in the water neck-deep. Old Doc, the old mean dog which was a full-blood bloodhound, had swam out into the pond. He put his front feet upon one man's shoulder with his hind feet on the man's legs, and was standing there baying in the man's face. Old Nip and Trouble, they were swimming around them, and I could hear them old dogs talking. I can hear 'em now. Old Trouble would say "H-o-o-o-ld it," and Nip would say, "21, 22, 21, 22."

Another troublesome race I had was on New Year's Eve. I got a report that two men were in the woods standing behind a tarpaulin formed in the shape of a tent. Also parked by the tarpaulin was a Chevrolet sedan. So after getting the report, I got in my car and drove out into those woods to investigate. When I did, they saw my car and took off. I radioed back to the office and told the deputies to bring the bloodhounds. They brought Old Nip and Tuck, Doc, Hitler, a mean dog, and Trouble. That was somewhere after the noon hour when we turned the dogs loose. We run them thugs all the evening through the woods near Keatchie, Louisiana. We never could catch 'em because of so many fences. The dogs tailed, but stayed on the men's trail. The men jumped from one net wire fence to another, and the dogs couldn't stay with 'em. But we run those dogs all that evening and all that night, a total of 16 hours. At seven o'clock the next morning it was awful cold, and I decided the best thing to do was to call off the hunt. But while we were standing there, some nigger boys come by with a book satchel and I asked 'em, "Have you seen two men down there in the woods, one with a red shirt on?" They said, "Yessah, captain, they over there in the woods about a mile and a half beside the trail."

I told my deputies to stay there, I would go over there and see what I could do. Well, I borrowed a horse from a man at this house and asked the old woman, did she have a stocking I could borrow? She went into the house an got an old-timey stocking and gave it to me. Well, I tied a knot in it and placed it over my head, placed my raincoat around my neck, and got astraddle of this old horse.

I rode that trail for about a mile and a half. I saw a log heap afire and two men laying on the ground near the fire. When I saw the men, I looked and saw five head of cattle grazing out on the edge of the trail. I got around these cattle, drove them to the trail, and began to holler and yell at them. And I drove those cattle right close by those two men, within 20 foot of 'em. When I got near to the men, I jumped off the horse and threw my gun on them and made them lay down. I walked in between 'em and handcuffed the inside hands. After I had done that, one of 'em looked at me and said, "If we knowed you was the sheriff you would be a dead SOB now. We thought you was some farmer driving his cows up." Both those thugs were escaped from the Huntsville pen where they were serving terms for murder.

I got behind those two men with my gun and marched them that mile or mile and a half to where the other officers were. We loaded them into cars and took them to town and placed 'em in jail. We called the sheriff in Rockwall County. He had warrants on 'em because they had burglarized a place in Rockwall. He took those two prisoners to Rockwall and placed 'em in jail, and that night they sawed out of their cell and got loose again. If they were ever apprehended, I never knowed about it.

Another time, I was called to Gilmer, Texas, by the sheriff there on a Thursday night. He asked me if I could be there the next morning at five o'clock with my bloodhounds to help catch a man suspected of cattle rustling. I told him I would, and the next morning, around five or six o'clock, I was in the woods with my dogs and the sheriff. He stated that a man had been coming in there every Thursday night for a number of Thursdays, and he had an automobile and a trailer that held three cows. He would get in that river bottom and catch his load.

When we got there that morning and turned the dogs loose, it wasn't long before they hit the trail. They stayed on that trail 30 minutes to an hour until they came to an old car body. That was where the cow thieves had cooked breakfast and slept under that old car body. We went on down the trail a little further, and I could hear that the dogs had treed something. I got within about a hundred yards of 'em, then I heard a terrible commotion, and I saw a man get up and start running. The dogs had tore all of his clothes off him. What had happened was that he had climbed a tree, and the wind was blowing awful hard. He had got so far up in the top, the top broke out, and when it broke he fell down in the middle of those dogs who'd got him. He ran about a mile, about four or five dogs on his heels. Well, after a while they treed him again down on the river bottom. This time they treed him up a tree about eight or 10 inches in diameter. This tree didn't have any limbs on it until about 20 feet up, but the dogs had cowed him so much that he had climbed up that tree about 25 feet. I could hear him a-hollering as I got nearer, "Come here! Come here!" When I came to the tree I seen him up there, and this tree was bending way over. I said, "Come down." He said, "Not until you tie them dogs and then I'll come down." Well, after he got on the ground I was a-talking to him. He was chewed up pretty bad because all my dogs loved meat. We directed that man up the trail to his car and trailer, and in there he had two head of cattle. He hadn't got the third one on yet.

I've had more fights than jaybirds had eggs, but I was always smart enough that when I was arguing with a man I'd get close enough to get in the first lick, and it's the first lick that counts. First thing he knew, I had him on the ground. I'd either hit him with my billy or my pistol or my fist, but, anyway, he went down. I'd wait until I had the advantage of him. To make an officer, always be sure that you're in the right and tell them to make it right. Make 'em do what you tell 'em, 'cause you can't back up one minute. If I'd have backed up a number of times, I'd have been dead now. You got to protect yourself and take advantage for yourself.

One thing I learned while being an officer. If you drive up behind a man's car to apprehend him or make him go with you, don't never drive up beside of him. Park behind him, and when you get out don't get out on the driver side, slide out and go on the opposite side and open the door. That door will give you protection. Open your door and come back around your car, then you have the door and the car for your protection. By using that method I know I've saved my life more than one time.

And another thing, if you're chasing a man and he's shooting at you, don't never stick your head out the door. If it gets too rough and tight for you, take your pistol and punch a hole through your windshield and shoot through that. That away you're protected. If you stick your head out the window, if you don't get it knocked off (then) you're liable to get it shot off.

I practiced all the time with my pistol while I was a law officer. When I was sheriff I carried a double-action .45, and when I missed a shot I kicked myself. Believe it or not, I have stood on my porch with a .22 pistol and killed English sparrows flying. I seldom ever missed a shot. I recall one time two FBI men came in my office and were making an investigation on a man, and they had information where he was working. They told me and Mr. Reeves that he worked at the ice plant here in Carthage. So, we went to the ice plant. When we drove up, there was an English sparrow jumped on that railroad track. I told those two FBI men that I bet you a dollar I can shoot his head off. They said they didn't have a dollar but had a quarter. When I shot his head off they looked at each other and said, "We've heard about you Texas SOBs, and we won't let you shoot at us."

It may be nothing to brag about, but I been tough all my life. I enjoyed fighting and enjoyed doing things I guess what you call mean. A preacher can't be a sheriff, 'cause he's going to hell if he don't watch out. Else, some guy will kill him! I'm not boasting or bragging, but I was mean as hell.

When I went after a man I was nice to him, said, "You better come on in." And in the last part of my time in office I never did go arrest a man, I'd just write him a letter and tell him to come in the office. I had a few that wouldn't, of course. I know out here eight or 10 miles there was a nigger deserter that I had papers to pick up. Well, I'd go out there and he'd hide, I couldn't find him. So, we walked up on him there one night, me and the deputies, at about 11 o'clock. Going to his house, they had broke some land with a two-horse middle-buster plow, and we like to never got across that stuff. When we got there we got him out and I made him take off his coat and give it to a deputy. Then I got astraddle of him and says, "Now, you son-of-a-bitch, I'm not gonna walk to the car, you're gonna tote me!" I rode him all the way across that field.

And there was another one who wouldn't come in. I was going to Fairplay one day and I saw this nigger. I turned around and says, "Why the hell didn't you come on in here when I sent for you?" He gave some kind of excuse. I said, "You get in that road and don't you stop. You do, I'm gonna run over you." He got in front of my car and commenced to run, and every so often I'd bump him about 18 foot. I brought him to town and put him in the office. I said, "Now, you son-of-a-bitch, you go down there and tell the jailer I said put you in jail."

You can't make a sheriff, and no other man can make a sheriff, by going with the written law. If you don't use some of that unwritten law, you ain't worth a damn. There was a nigger come in my office one night with a suit on during World War II. Said, "Sheriff, I want you to go with me and apologize to my mother. Y'all went up there today and just tore her house up looking for home brew." I said, "Well, I'm busy now, but if you'll wait a minute I'll apologize to you." When I got through I got in the car and he got in on the other side. I said, "I'm ready to apologize to you. Where your mother live?" He told me. I got down to the ice plant and I stopped the car, opened the door and walked around and pulled him out, and I apologized on his head with a six-shooter. I said, "Now, you get in that street and I'm gonna apologize to you some more." We got up there to the railroad and he slowed down, and I knocked him down with that car. I apologized again. I took him out to the Hilltop Cafe. We got to the Hilltop and he stopped, and I really bumped him then. I got out, kicked him and stomped him. I says, "Now, this is the last time I want to apologize to you. You hit that road, and if you come back to town I'm gonna kill you." I can hear that nigger running now, "*Clop, clop, clop, clop.*" But I apologized to him.

There's three old boys come to me one night. Says, "Corbett, we give a nigger awhile ago five dollars for a pint of whiskey, and he hasn't brought it to us. What can we do about it?" I said, "Go down there and beat hell out of him." They went down there and found that nigger and like to beat him to death.

After that, I was in the office one night and a nigger come in and says, "Mr. Corbett, there's a nigger stealing my plugwood." It was pulpwood, but he called it "plugwood." I was busy and just made the remark, "Go shoot the son-of-a-bitch." In about 30 minutes I got a call and went up there, and there was a nigger that had four bullet holes in him. He must have shot him when he bent over that plugwood, because he had four holes in the top of hs butthole. But he kept him from stealing plugwood.

And another time, a nigger run in my office, says, "Mr. Corbett, this nigger owes me a dollar and won't pay." I says, "Kill the son-of-a-bitch." In about 20 minutes I got a call to come to Niggertown, and there was a nigger laying on the ground with a butcher knife in his back, with the butcher knife clear through him, through his heart. The grand jury called me and asked me did I tell that nigger to kill that nigger. I said, "I did, but I was just joking with him." Well, they didn't indict him.

Along in the oil boom, the town filled up with whiskey heads and bums and winos and every other kind of thug you can imagine. Well, at night they didn't have no money to go to a hotel, but would sleep on the streets, on the side of a building, just any place out of the wind. I put numbers of 'em in jail till I found out they was just wanting a place to get out of the weather. So, I decided I'd do something about it. I went and bought me a can of lighter fluid, then, when I caught 'em asleep after 10 or 11 o'clock, I'd walk by 'em and squirt a squirt or two of that lighter fluid on the soles of their feet. As I left, I'd pitch a match in.

I lit the fire to that bunch. One night I come by there and put it on about four of 'em. Of course, you'd have to leave after you done it or they'd see you. I got to the sheriff's office and sat down when the phone started ringing. I answered it. They said, "Mr. Corbett, there's something going on at the cafe down here. Come down here quick. There's a man with his feet afire!" I went down there, I knew what had happened. I said, "Where's he at?" She said, "Mr. Corbett, he's back there in the bathroom with both feet in the washbasin." That was the unwritten law.

Another thing I done that probably wasn't according to the law . . . in them days we had lots of what they called "pocket bootleggers." The law allowed a man, in them days, one quart or two pints of whiskey. He could take a quart or two pints and walk all around town with it if he wanted. But these hip-pocket bootleggers would get them two pints and they'd make a haul to different places and sell it. Then they'd go back and get some more.

So, I made up my mind to break 'em. I got to where if I caught a man with a pint of whiskey, I'd make him sit down and drink it. I remember an old man named Wells. He said, "Mr. Corbett, that'll kill me if I drink all of that." I said, "Drink it, you're gonna die anyway." But I broke that peddling of whiskey. One night I made a man selling home brew drink nearly a gallon of it. I sat him down on the jailhouse steps, put my pistol on him, give him that gallon of home brew, and said, "Now, I want you to drink it." He drank about half of it, then he said, "I just can't drink no more." I made him get up and I said, "Now, you just get up and go on home. Don't you get no more home brew or I'm gonna make you drink all of it next time."

Next morning, it was Sunday morning, I got a call a man was in a ditch. I went up there, and there he was on the side of the street laying down in that ditch. His head was up towards us, and there was water running all over his head, all over his face, and down his body. I got some help and pulled him out of that ditch, and they took him up to where he lived. But he didn't sell no home brew. I was mean to 'em.

The sheriff had to be mean. Do you realize that the world started with 50 percent crime? Because, when the world started, Adam and Eve had two boys and one killed the other and that was 50 percent crime.

One man from Panola County came to Carthage every Saturday night and started a fuss or fight. I went to the Hilltop Cafe one night, and I saw a man standing up on the side of a deputy's car. He had reached in and got a half nelson on Mr. Reeves' neck and he was trying to get his pistol, but Mr. Reeves was a powerful man. When I walked up I saw what was happening, I stopped him and put my handcuffs on him. I swung his free arm around and handcuffed him to the center post of the car. I told him I was going to have to put him in jail, but he said, "No, by God, you're not!" I said, "You going to let me take you down to the jail peaceable?" He said, "Hell no, I'm not going!" So, I got in my car, me and Mr. Reeves, and said, "Let's take him to jail." We left from the Hilltop and he was swinging on the side of the car. When we hit the railroad, we bounced up and down and the hand-cuffs broke and he fell down. I asked him if he was ready to go peace-able, and he said, "Hell, no." I took a lariat rope I had and draped it over his neck, and me and Mr. Reeves tied him to the car. We went on a little while and he fell off again, but by the time I stopped I'd done drug him about 40 or 50 foot with that rope. "Well," he said, "I'm ready to go to jail now." So, we took him and put him in jail. Well, that broke up his roughness.

Right in front of my house one night there was a bunch of people in the road. I got up with a shotgun and went out there and asked 'em what they were up to? There were seven of 'em, I think two men and five women. They made some kind of excuse. I said, "I'll tell you what I'm gonna do, I'm gonna kill everyone of you." 'Bout that time, a neighbor of mine, Mr. Bingham, come up and said they'd been up be-side his house all night raising the devil. I said, "Well, they won't raise it anymore. I'm gonna kill everyone of 'em." I said, "All you line up so I won't have to use but one shot." I wanted to shoot every damn one of 'em with one shot. I asked 'em if they had anything to say be-fore they die(d). One of these women straightened up, says, "Yessir, Mr. Corbett, I'd like to talk." I said, "Well, go ahead, what is it?" She raised her head up and said in a loud voice, "O Lord, we need you now!" After she said this prayer I made them get in their car. It wouldn't crank, it was a Model A. I said, "If you don't get that car out of here I'm gonna have to kill you." Then they started pushing that car and you could hear the feet a-flopping on every crack. That's the last I heard of 'em.

The sheriff job was a hard job, but I was glad to be sheriff—I want-ed to be sheriff. I believe if I was sheriff today we wouldn't have near as many hippies and loafers as we've got. As I recall, I arrested one hippie, a fellow out of Dallas. He had on what they called a zoot suit. I had Mr. Reeves bring him over and put him in my office, and I sat down across the table and was talking to him. I told him, "I want you to get out of town, I don't allow anyone down here with zoot suits or feathers in their hats, such as that. We want people down here to do what's right." Then he gave me a little smart talk. I believe I pulled a chair up and sat down close to him. I believe I had a pair of pliers in my desk. I took those pliers and got a-hold of that Hitler moustache, and with about seven or eight jerks I had it all out. Then I got a-hold to his goatee, and I jerked it all out. Then I said, "Now, you go in the toilet and get that zoot suit off and that pretty shirt you got on and you hit the road back to Dallas." When he come out of there he didn't have nothing but his shorts on. I said, "You know the way to Dallas?" He said, "Yes sir," and he took off.

A lot of folks they cussed me because I took the feathers out of the man's hat. They never did know why. In those days we had what they called sabotage people come in and tear stuff up, and I got information through the federal government that those sabotagers had a way of identifying the partner they wanted to talk to. One was that he had a pencil in his pocket, another was a feather in his hat. After that information I got to protecting the state and country, if I saw anyone with a feather in his hat I took it out. Some of 'em wouldn't take 'em out, and I'd pull him up to the car and pop him over the head a time or two with a pistol, pull that feather out, and give it to him and make him eat it. I made a number of 'em eat those feathers, which made a lot of people in town cuss me for doing that, but I did it for the country. When one of those sabotagers come to Panola County and found a man with a feather in his hat, that was the way he recognized him.

I wish I could be sheriff again. Now they say you can't do this and do that, but did you know that in those days the sheriff could do any damn thing nearly that he wanted to? Now they take advantage of him, tell him the FBI will get him, this and that. Well, they didn't get me, and hell, I got the job done. You got to go by the unwritten law if you make a good sheriff. What do I mean by the unwritten law? Down here at Deadwood, that country, there was a 15 or 16-year-old nigger boy, a big old fat boy, that was molesting the women and girls down there. We'd go down there and he'd always be gone. But we got the hounds on him once and caught him and brought him to the jail. I always had a trustee or two in the jail, and I told this old trustee what he'd done, said, "I want you to work him over." Well, I didn't know what those damn niggers was gonna do. They took him in there and castrated him. Jailer called me down there and said, "Corbett, come down here, this nigger is dying."

I went down there and went over to Smith Hospital, told them what had happened, and they give me a box of salve about that big. (They) Said, "You put this on him about every four hours." Well, the trustee did, and he got well. I brought him down to the highway out south of town, and I said, "Now, by God, you're cut. You won't bother another woman." But I said, "You son-of-a-bitch, you come through town and I'm gonna kill you." And you know, I've never heard from him again.

But I'll tell you this, my law enforcement was something like a gift.

It was just there, just like me taking off warts. And if it ain't in you, you ain't no good. You got to have it in you. If it's not there, it's not there. I've done lots of things when I been in shooting scrapes, rough places, that how I done it, I don't know. 'Cause, when you've got a criminal right there in front of you, you haven't got time to do nothing but look out for yourself. By God, when you get in a tight, that Old Man Up Yonder will tell you what to do. Go by that unwritten law.

GASTON
BOYKIN

★

I grew up in Comanche County about five miles from the Eastland–
Brown County line. My father's father was a doctor, Doctor Starling Ray Boykin. When the war broke out between the states, he volun-
teered along with four of his brothers and his brother-in-law to fight
for the Confederacy. They had come from Mississippi to begin with,
and they went back to Mississippi in this war. They were all at Vicks-
burg, and his brother-in-law and his four brothers was killed and he
was the only survivor. He was captured and put in prison. He took
a fever and almost starved to death. When they sent him back on the
train, they let him off at Hempstead, Texas, and I think it was 30 miles
from there over to Buffalo where his folks lived. He walked across the
country barefooted, almost skin and bone. When he got there he rest-
ed up and took tutoring under a doctor. Later, he went off to medical
school in Fort Worth and got his diploma, then moved to Blooming
Grove in the 1880s and later to Comanche County, in the north end
of the county, and practiced medicine. He was buried there in 1902,
Starling Ray Boykin.

My father married when he was 18 years of age and came to

Comanche County. He had two racehorses, one was named Long Boy and one was White Beauty, and about 1890 he went over just in the edge of Brown County and traded this Long Boy for a section of land. Two of my sisters was born while he owned this little ranch in Brown County. He sold that and moved into Comanche County at Sipe Springs in 1906, and I was born four miles southwest of Sipe Springs on a little farm we had there. In 1920 they hit oil on that little place, and my dad leased it out and bought a ranch south of Comanche, about 1,500 acres in all, and we went into the cattle business.

When I was 13 I started breaking horses and got into the horse business. I owned hundreds of 'em myself—bought 'em in the West and drove 'em here—put on the first rodeo that was ever put on in Comanche County.

My dad run horses all (the) time, and he was a pretty good horse man. We had horses ever since I was just a kid. The first horse trade I ever made in my life, I was about 11. My dad didn't like geese, and I always wanted geese and he didn't want geese on the place. He went down to Greenville, Texas, on the train, and while he was gone I took an old poor horse out and traded it for two geese. He come back and I had two geese, but he just laughed and let me keep 'em. And then he was gone again and I took another horse, an old plug, and traded for three Spanish goats, but he didn't correct me that time either. Anyway, that's the way I started when I was just a little old kid in the horse business.

How come me to ever start breaking horses, Dad bought an old, old mare, 27 years old, and she had a yearling colt whose grandfather was Pid Hart, one of the famous racehorses of the past. I thought that was the prettiest animal. He gave him to my brother, and I turned around and bought him from him for 60 dollars. I was 13 years old and I decided to break it myself, so I broke that horse. I had a neighbor that was riding a few bucking horses, and first thing you know, I'd slip off and we'd ride steers, bucking horses. I got interested in horses more so all the time, I always did love 'em, and when I got to be 18 years old I just saddled my horse and a pack horse and took off for the Southwest.

I went to Ozona, Texas. They's a lot of people in Ozona who was raised here in Comanche. I got in with this fellow McCullom at Sonora and he had a horse he wanted broke, a big old grulla horse about 11 or 12 hundred pounds. I broke him for him, and then I worked there on his ranch. It was just 10 sections, but to the south Judge Davidson had 45 sections and I could look over there and see a lots of paint horses. They were the prettiest things I ever saw in my life, and I thought I'd just give anything in the world if I could get over there where all those paint horses were. So, one day the oldest of the Davidson boys came over to the ranch where I was working to buy lambs off of McCullom. And he saw me riding this grulla horse, and he asked me if I'd come over there and break a bunch of horses for them, which I did.

When I got through breaking 'em, I bought all of their surplus mares and brought 'em back to Comanche. Then I went back when I got through with that and went to breaking horses again for the Miller brothers. Finally, I was breaking 'em from Sonora to Fort Stockton, and was buying horses all along and driving 'em East. Sometimes I'd use a covered wagon and be on the road for as long as three months with a drove of horses. I was on the road when they closed the banks. I had carried 51 head over to Ballinger, and I sold those out and went back and bought another bunch. I'd go way on over close to Fort Stockton and I'd drive 'em into the south and east, and come back through the old Hoover ranch—cross the Pecos River at the Chandler Ranch and then into the Hoover—and I'd buy a few horses at nearly every ranch I'd pass by. I'd get back into Ozona and maybe I'd ridden a hundred miles before I started (back to Comanche). Then I'd get 'em together there in Ozona and take off again.

The first thing I would do in breaking a horse . . . . Here in Comanche County, one man would rope the horse, then they'd snub him up to another horse and lead him. But when I went out there to Ozona, I found that it was a different ballgame altogether. They never put a bit in a horse's mouth out there for six months after you started riding him; they'd use a hackamore. They'd cut the ones they wanted broke and turn 'em over to you, then that was your deal; they didn't help you.

But you'd rope the horse and choke him down, smother him. When he'd fall, you'd run up and slip a hackamore on him before he got time to come to. Then you'd go loosen the rope and give him air and get it off his head. You might ride him first. If you did, you'd tie a big rope, a loose-platted rope, around his neck, called a collar. Then you'd reach back and pick up one back foot, and tie that foot up. Then you'd pat him all over, take the blanket and slap the blanket around over him, then you'd saddle him, undo his foot, and get on him. He'd usually pitch a little. You'd ride him about 15 minutes, and then you'd take him out and tie him to a log or a burro. Whatever you tied him to, you'd have a swivel where the rope wouldn't twist up. You tie him out and you go back and get another one. It would usually take pretty well all day to go through eight or 10 of 'em. Then you would go back and get the first one and ride him again.

Then they'd get out their outlaw horses. Every ranch, nearly, had an outlaw that had thrown everybody, or had got to raring up and falling back, or had developed some other bad habits. They would throw those in with the young horses and you'd re-break them for 'em. And those you'd have to be pretty rough with, have to teach 'em who was boss. You might have to take a club and knock 'em in the head. The others you'd be good to, but those man killers you had to get rough with.

I broke horses and bought horses all at the same time in these years. I'd go back to Ozona, and by that time I knew everybody, and I'd go back over in Pecos County and Terrell County, and I'd stop at every ranch and add a few more to 'em. Then I'd bring 'em back on this mountain road. You couldn't get over it, lot of it, with nothing but a horse. And (by the) time I'd get in, I'd have anywhere from 30 to 50 head. One bunch I drove to Barnhart and shipped 'em to Crockett by train. Another I drove through the country to San Angelo and put 'em in a pen at Ballinger and peddled 'em out there. Then one time my brother and I and two hired hands bought lots of old horses in good shape and all, but a little too old for that rocky country. Horse gets about 12 or 14 out there and he's not very safe in those rocks. And we took this wagon and we'd break 'em to work. They'd already be saddle horses, and in just a few days they'd work perfect. Then, we'd go through little towns and camp for four, five days and peddle horses. Then we'd go to another one and another one and another one, finally into Brady and on down to San Saba. We had a lot of fun, and one time (we) were out three months.

You had to know what you were doing to make a living in horses. I learned how to tell how old a horse was when I was just a kid. I learned to study his mouth and the shape of his teeth till I could pretty well hit it within two (years), until he was 27 or 28 years old. First, if you don't know a horse's mouth, he's born with four teeth, and when he's a yearling he cuts two more. That makes him six (teeth). Then, when he's a three-year-old, he sheds the two front teeth and two big teeth come in, so he's got his four milk teeth and two big teeth. And the next year he'll shed two more teeth, and he'll have two little milk teeth and four big teeth. Then, when he's five, he'll cut two more big teeth, and if he's a horse he'll cut a tusk. If it's a mare, if she ever cuts a tusk it'll be at nine and sink at 11, a lot of times—disappear, you know. And then at seven years old they have black grooves in their teeth about one-eighth of an inch long and kind of down in there. These old crooked horse traders could take and drill those out and take caustic balsum and burn that tooth and put the groves back in 'em, then take a corncob and coffee and run their head if they was grey-headed to make 'em have their hair the same color. They had lots of tricks.

Those old horse men was a different breed. He's a little different than a cowman. If you ever looked at him, he's got a little meaner eye, you know, just a little different person. There're not that many left anymore. I liked those old horse men, but they were pretty rough.

I was always a little different from the others. There in Ballinger nobody could sell a horse for a while but me. I had 50 there, and there were about four hundred horses in town, and nobody moved a horse one month but myself. There was two fellows there who had come in with a big bunch from down at Junction. They just almost had one sold when the fellow said, "The only way I'll buy him is to go across the street and let that cowboy over there look at the horse's mouth. If you told me the truth about the horse's mouth, I'll buy it, but I'll take his word. I don't know how to tell."

I didn't even know the fellow. They come over and told me what the fellow said, and I said, "Now, you fellows realize, when I look I'm gonna tell what it is, not what you want me to tell." They roped it up and it was a year older than they said it was, they were honest about it. I think the fellow took their animal.

Then, another time, I had a big, black, beautiful horse, he ought to have been a work horse, he was too big for a saddle horse, weighed about 14-hundred. A druggest there named Weeks wanted to buy him and came over on Sunday. I told him I was sorry but I just couldn't trade on Sunday. If he could come back the next day I'd talk with him. And sure enough, he came back and bought him. He says, "The reason I bought him was 'cause you wouldn't sell him to me on Sunday." Says, "I was in business several different places, and the competition people wouldn't close on Sunday and I never could compete with 'em." I don't think its wrong to work if it's necessary on Sunday, but I think you should tend to the Lord's business first, and then if you have time do yours.

One time we stopped at a Bohemian's place, heard him holler out in the field. There was good grass there, and I told my brother I was gonna go out there and meet whoever that was and put our horses in there if I could. He bet me I couldn't. So, I went out there and visited with him. I suggested that it was too late to try to trade that evening. We'd pull inside there and stay till morning, then trade the next day. He said, "I guess that'll be all right." He was renting.

So, we did. That night he and his brother-in-law, supposed to be such a good trader, came down and stayed a couple of hours and told us who-all he'd out-traded and all about his trading career. The next day we met and I traded him three for two, and I got in this trade a two-hundred pound hog, 18-dozen eggs, a horse collar, a wagon brake, a curry comb, and a wagon load of corn and a wagon load of oats delivered to the next town. And I broke his butcher knife dressing this hog when we dressed him to put him in sausage! We had a tent with us that had a floor in it. Had a Dutch oven, and we'd cook beans and bake sweet potatoes and cook sausage, eat those 18-dozen eggs. We ate like kings and queens.

Once, we brought a drove of horses to Comanche, took us eight days. We'd have to find a place to put 'em every night. When we got to Fort McKavett—it was supposed to be the toughest town left in Texas—we left one guy to hold the horses in a pocket, and this Green Mankin and Ted Powers and myself went down to get groceries. When we went in, there was about 16 local cowboys in there, and I guess they were drinking. We had on cowhide coats with hair left on 'em about two inches long, and they got (to) trying to buy those coats. Well, it was just before Christmas, we'd already had one little snow, and we didn't want to sell 'em. Had to have 'em. They kept on trying to buy 'em and finally they said, "Well, we've offered you everything in reason for 'em and you won't take it. Only thing left for us to do is just take 'em." One of 'em grabbed me from the back and I slung him off. They meant business, but this Green Mankin walked out in the middle of the floor. He was the toughest guy I ever saw in my life, he was as tough as John Wesley Hardin. He stuck his fingers in his coat pockets, the coat unbuttoned, says, "Let me tell you fellows something. If you think you can take these coats, why in the hell don't you get started?" They begin to back off, you know, and we went on to the horses, but we forgot something and Powers had to go back. One of 'em walked up to him and says, "You think you're might smart in that coat. I think I'll just take it." He says, "Well, you SB (sic), you're not tied, why don't you just try to take it?" He had a German Luger with him and was just 18 years old, and he kind of wanted to use it. Those guys didn't know what they was fooling with.

This Green Mankin is my friend and I can tell you things about him. The more that's on the other side, the rougher he is. He can't help it, he'd rather die and win than wilt. He says, "I don't like any son-of-a-bitch that don't have the guts." I grew up with him, and he got whipped when he was just a kid. A fellow beat him nearly to death, beat him (till) both eyes shut. He was just a little old kid and the other fellow bigger and older, and I guess that's one thing made him so bad. He looked for this guy for years and years and years. Said, "I just want to see him one time." He always said, he'd tell the boys at Ozona— that was those old rough ones—"I never was whipped, I'm never gonna be, and I'm never going to any courthouse to settle anything."

The guys around Ozona sure did give him a wide path. One time he was in Arizona and this Ted Powers was with him, they was big old boys about 21 or 22 and feared nothing. They got out there and went into a boot shop in Globe, Arizona. Old Ted told me about it. The boot shop man was the biggest, best-built, stoutest-looking guy you ever saw in your life—about six-four, weighed about 230 and muscles all over, an Irishman. They pulled off their boots and asked him to put heels on 'em. He looked up and said, "What part of Texas is you guys from?" Old Green said, "We're from Ozona." Boot shop man says, "Must be a lot of good people in Ozona." Green says, "Why?" He says, "Well, there so many sorry son-of-a-bitches here from there, if there are any left they ought to be good ones." He was drinking. Old Green says, "Well, you big son-of-a-bitch. If you'll come out from under that counter I'll whip hell out of you!"

This old Irishman gets up. It was about 30 feet down there around the counter and he walks down to the end of it, pulls off his apron, hangs it up. And here come old Green who weighed about 165 pounds. The old boy hit him and Ted says he went end-over-end way out yonder. Said he got up, and here he come running, and the old boy hit him again and away he went. Here he come running again and away he went again, 20 feet out there. Then, the next time he come up he wasn't in any hurry. He started running circles around that guy, he'd run in an' out. Directly, he jumped and hit him right in the Adam's apple and whupped him with that one lick. Then he like to beat him to death.

Finally, two cops run in and got him (Green) off of him and got him out and going up the street. And it wasn't long until Ted Powers started to tell him (Green) what the Irishman had told him after they got Green out. (Powers) Said, "You know what, he even asked us to come back and see him. He said, 'You boys come back and see me.' " And when he told him that, Green says, "Yes, and that son-of-a-bitch thought I wasn't gonna do it. I'm gonna go back down there and finish him up!" Well, they all had to get ahold of him.

One time I came back with a bunch of horses from Ozona to Comanche County and my market was bad and slow. I had a friend that was sheriff here. He was about 32 years old and I was 24 or 25 I guess. He asked me if I'd come in and work the prisoners. They had so many prisoners in the jail laying out their fines, (that) they decided it'd be a good business if they'd work 'em and thin the population of 'em. I told 'em I'd work 'em if they'd let me do it like I wanted to.

They had balls and chains made for me to use to keep 'em from running and turned 'em over to me. I lived in the jail and worked the prisoners on the road. We left out at eight o'clock every morning and they did eight hours of good work, and I never did put a ball and chain on one. I didn't pay 'em much mind; I was nice to 'em, but fairly firm, and made friends out of practically every one of 'em. The locals, when

I ran for sheriff the first time, all but one supported me strong. We would put in culverts and cut out rights-of-way and dynamite rocks out of the rural roads. They made excellent hands, but it wasn't long until I run out of a job because I didn't have anymore prisoners.

It played out pretty quick, 'cause they'd use grubbing hoes and axes and there was quite a few rattlesnakes out where they was a-working south of town, and they didn't like that. They would kind of excite 'em. The same ones had been getting in jail over and over, but they didn't like that road job and we cleaned the jail out, nobody there left to work. But that's what gave me the idea of ever running for sheriff down the line.

I broke horses until I was about 30, then I went in the livestock business myself. I got a little too old to ride. The last one I rode, I had a Great Dane dog that was an eighth bloodhound, and I'd put two-thousand sheep out on the old Shanghai Pierce Ranch in Wharton County, and I decided to break one more horse. Jack Hutchins owned it and I was going to break it for accommodation. He was the manager of this 89-section ranch. I saddled this horse and it wouldn't pitch to the saddle and it would already lead. It was hot and I decided the horse was already broken and Jack didn't know it. But when I went to get in the saddle, the horse threw me. I seldom ever got thrown, but this one threw me and I carried my stirrup with me from the off side. I went on my head, but my stirrup held just before my head hit the ground. There was no way of escape, but my Great Dane dog jumped and grabbed the horse by the nose and he just stood there and trembled, and I got leather and pulled myself up and got back in the saddle. The dog saved my life. There was no one there and I had no way of ever getting away from him.

I called that dog Pretty Boy Floyd, Jr., and he was a cow dog, the best dog, I guess, in the world. He could smell a cow for several hundred yards through the air. I used to go out and gather cattle that a half-dozen cowboys couldn't gather. He was a freak. I traded a stallion for his mother, she was a Great Dane, and bred her to about a quarter bloodhound. He made a huge dog that weighed about 165 pounds. We had a lot of screw worms in that day and time, and the first time I started to rope a cow, when he saw me start roping he grabbed it, knocked it over, and held it. Then I got down and doctored it. Next time I started to rope one, he grabbed it again, he never got the wrong one in his life. He was as smart as he could be. I had some (cattle) stray one time, and took him over there and he caught all seven of 'em. I'd be tying one's legs and he'd have another one. When I got all seven, I put 'em in the pickup and brought 'em home. He was an amazing dog. Those things he learned, he did it watching me. I didn't teach him. I don't know myself, how did he know when I wanted goats, or hogs, or cattle? But he always did.

I didn't run for sheriff until I was 41 years old. When I came in out of the Army after World War II, I had decided that I wanted to get away from everybody and be by myself. I was tired of being hemmed in by so many people. I was in New York a while, Atlantic City, France; and there were people everywhere, you couldn't move for the people. So, I decided that when I got out of the Army I wanted to go back and farm and I didn't even want a tractor, I wanted horses. I wanted out where it was quiet. My dad had two blue horses that was part Percheron and I bought an extra one and borrowed one from a friend to make four. Then I started breaking land with an old sulky plow, like they used to do, to get away from people. And it was hot—old horses sweating, flies bothering 'em. I'd plow to 12 and go back and hook up again, and in a few days I'd got to thinking, "Well, this don't suit me near as well as I thought it was going to." There was a tractor setting out there, and I went out there and worked on it a little bit, for about a week. I got it running and got on there and run it just as fast as I could and still get the plow to stay in the ground, and got the land broke and sowed, and come into town and announced for sheriff. So, I just *thought* I wanted to get away from people.

At that time I had a friend as sheriff, and he told me that if I would run, he wouldn't. I didn't have but one opponent, but he was a good man out of a fine family and was well acquainted all over the county. He ran a wholesale gasoline business. So, I ran. I didn't buy a car. My dad had an old Model A and I campaigned in it, made all these rabbit drives and public speakings. In a rabbit drive, people would walk together in two directions. One bunch would get, say, north, and the other south, walk toward each other in two big lines until they'd meet each other, and that'd stir up all the rabbits. If they run one way, they'd get so close to one line that they could shoot 'em, or if they run the other way they'd get close to that line. Anyway, these communities would have rabbit drives, and they'd have cemetery workings and the candidates would go there and help work the cemeteries. Then they'd have little public speakings after the graveyard work, and you'd get a chance to say a few words.

I went down to one place, which once had a reputation as the toughest town in Texas. That was Joe Hardin's hometown for a while, John Wesley Hardin's brother. There was some old tough boys there, five of 'em, brothers. They was all ex-soldiers. They had bad reputations and were tough, but since they were all ex-soldiers and I was too, everywhere I went, they went. Where I hoed in the cemetery, they hoed too. I couldn't get away from them to visit anyone else, and I lost the box. I only lost two boxes in the county, and that was one of 'em. The sheriff had to keep clean company, you know.

When I ran that first time I had a famous horse, the best horse in the county. It was that first one I ever broke. She was fast and she was a cow pony and she knew all the tricks. She'd come to me, kneel, lie down, stand on her hind feet, stick her head between my legs and throw me on her back, dance. I used her in rodeos to perform and entertain the children. So, when I ran, everybody in Comanche County had seen that horse and everybody had seen that dog. Everybody knew the dog and the horse. I'd come to town in a pickup and the dog would always be with me. And he'd go to the North Side Cafe and lie down in front of the door where no one could get in or out till he was fed. His friend owned the cafe, Melvin Gore, and he'd feed him a good feed. That's the last visit he'd pay him, but (then) he'd go over to the south side where Jim Moody ran the cafe and the dog would cover both of his double doors. Then Jim would feed him, too, and he'd go back to my pickup. He was known all over the county. Really, my horse and my dog elected me sheriff. Every kid in the county was teaching their horse to lie down, you know. I won that race by 1,800 votes.

I was in from 1947 to 1952, then back in from 1965 to 1977. After '52 I run cattle and sheep. I was leasing, mostly; I had a number of places. I had 'em scattered 180 miles around, just anything I could get to run 'em on. Then it came a five-year drought and I got caught with all this stuff, and it like to wiped me out. That's how come me to run again.

Sheriff's race would get bitter 'cause the people would make it bitter. I was fairly strong, and the element that was against me was against me strong. The other fellow's friends and my enemies would make me have to run a pretty stiff race. I always had the lower element making up everything they could tell on me, you know. I always rejoiced that I didn't have to wonder if they would come up with anything dishonest; I was always too timid to do anything bad. I kept my skirts clean. But they'd make up stories about my opponent and tell 'em that I told 'em, say that I said this about his wife, that I said that he didn't have a restroom in his house, and so on.

I got beat for the fourth term, there had never been a fourth term won in the history of Comanche County. The newspaper took after me, the local newspaper. The fellow who owned the paper would write all of my opponent's speeches for him. He'd build up a straw man, and the straw man was me. He'd make up stories and get everybody to follering him, no I couldn't handle it at all. He was a real politician. The district judge, district attorney, everybody, would slip around and ask for his advice and what he expected. But I wouldn't ask him for it and don't yet; I didn't like him. You can't hardly beat one of those things.

When I came back in 1965 he fought me again, but I won that time. I had four opponents then, I always had three or four nearly every time I ran. But the way I got in the second time, I had a little courtesy card built like a sheriff's badge, a deputy card, with an emblem of an eagle on it. And I had printed on there: "This card will introduce so-and-so, and any courtesy extended to him will be greatly appreciated by me." When people traveled and went out of town, those was nice. Then I came up with the idea of putting on the back that "The bearer of this card is a law-abiding citizen of Comanche County. When he is driving on business trips to and from the county, according to Texas law he is permitted to carry a handgun in his automobile, and I endorse this privilege."

I didn't give those to everybody. I told 'em that this didn't give 'em any privilege they didn't have before they got 'em, but it just tells that arresting officer that you're a law-abiding citizen. My wife and I counted the votes before the election here in Comanche just to see. We took the phone directory and just counted 'em off, you know, and in the election we got five more than we counted. We pretty well knew that everyone that was carrying one of those cards was our voter.

But in 1965, I looked at the ones that was running, and there was one very popular man, a public relations man for REA (Rural Electrification Administration). He'd worked for the sheriff just ahead of me, and I knew that sheriff was through politically, but he didn't know it himself. I could beat this fellow if I could get the old sheriff to working for him. And I did. Everywhere I'd go the old sheriff would go and take digs at me. He'd get up and make a speech, just exactly what I wanted him to do. On election day he led nearly all the way. But I had figured up my votes and I said, "Now, Leon, that's just a bunch of Yankees voting"—I lived south, you see—"of course they're gonna vote for you, 'cause you're raised up there. These old Rebels are gonna come in after a while and I'm gonna catch you." Course, I always had the votes in my pocket; I knew exactly. It got up a little closer and a little closer and then I got ahead 165 votes. He says, "I just as well go home."

When I went in the first time as sheriff the salary was 75 dollars a month. That was over and above money you got to run the jail. Then, if you got a misdemeanor warrant for a man and arrested him and he paid off, you got four dollars. If you arrested him and he laid it out in jail, you got two dollars. You got 10 cents a mile for going after him if he paid off, and if you got a felony, you got your four dollars for arresting him and mileage for that, too, but you didn't get your pay till after he was tried and convicted. Then, if he was tried and convicted and you carried him to Huntsville, you got 10 cents a mile for the first prisoner, and so much for the next one, up to 45 cents a mile. All that was part of your pay, but you wasn't allowed to go over 3,750 dollars. If you went over 3,750 dollars you had to turn it back to the county.

The commissioners court would give 75 cents a day for each prisoner kept in the jail, and 15 cents a day for safekeeping. That went to the sheriff, but he bought the groceries out of his own pocket. If he made a profit or a loss on the jail, that was just on his management. I've bought can goods out of the Valley by the truckload, rejects, but good stuff, you know. If you were real careful you could run it to where you could break even or make a little money.

At first, if you had a deputy you had to pay him out of your own pocket. Well, that didn't sound right to me. I go to investigating and went to see Love Kimbrough, the sheriff over at Brady, and he had a good deputy and told me not to settle for anything but a good one. Said to get the commissioners to pay him a good salary and that it was legal. I got the county attorney to research it, and then I met with the commissioners court. They said it wasn't legal and I called the county attorney in. Then I told 'em if they didn't pay the deputy, then I couldn't run it by myself. The sheriff ahead of me was a good fellow, but he had 73 (people) selling liquor. One man couldn't touch that. I told 'em, "If you think you're not able financially, you hire me one, keep him six months, and if you don't think it'll pay instead of cost, you let him go and I'll never ask for another one." So, they hired one and paid him and let him have one end of the jail, him and his wife. And at the end of the year they had 10,000 dollars extra from the fines—that much profit.

When I went in the first time we had 73 (people) selling liquor for a living, and I thought they ought to pay for the privilege. They paid no taxes and most of 'em didn't have a job, were loafers. Anyway, I decided the only way to get rid of 'em was to let 'em pay for the privilege of selling it, and at the end of six years 72 of (the) 73 was out of business. The fines exceeded the costs by as much as 10,000 dollars and the county wasn't out anything. Sheriffs before me, there was some good ones, but they just caught enough to keep the people satisfied. I had a different idea. I had a lot of friends that drank a little, but I hadn't ever bought a pint in my life. I know some good men drink, but I didn't want for a deputy anybody that even smelled a stopper.

This one bootlegger, we was raised together, and I told him when I was first running that he couldn't sell if I went in, I'd break him one way or another. I said, "I have a list of all of 'em, there's 73, and I may let 72 go and center on you. You'll be one that won't sell, 'cause you're my friend." He said he was still gonna vote for me, but I said, "Now, don't forget."

I had this Liquor Control Board informant named Shorty, but he (my friend) knew him, so I had to work it a little bit different. I got me a friend, a prisoner, an ex-con, to buy a pint of liquor, then let the Liquor man give him (my friend) the 20 dollar bill, and they marked the 20 dollar bill, and then he watched the sale and arrested him (my friend) and recovered it.

My friend always took him (the undercover man) out to the cemetery to sell him a pint. This undercover man said to this bootlegger, "Someday you're gonna be sorry that you sold this liquor out of this cemetery, it just isn't right. Look at all those good people out there." Every time he'd buy a pint, they'd go out there around that cemetery and he'd (my friend would) get him a pint of liquor. This time that the bill was marked, he (my friend) had it (the liquor) in a prescription box with his mother's name on it.

But he was arrested, and the district attorney, who only had one aquittal and one hung jury in four years, came into county court to prosecute the guy. The bootlegger hired two real good lawyers from another county. Anyway, they got ready to try him, and these two defense lawyers tried to try me instead of him, and they made it awful rough on me. Mr. Cobb, the district attorney, had a wonderful voice, and when he got ready to argue he says, "These two gentlemen defending Mr. Welch in this case have put in two days trying to blow this up. It looks like a big liquor case, when in fact it was only one pint. And it depends on you as jurymen whether it be a big case or a small case—your citizenship, that's what counts." He says, "All I ask you in this case is to fine the man a thousand dollars or turn him a-loose and tell him you don't believe in law enforcement. Then will you please have the courage to walk over and tell the sheriff that you don't believe in law enforcement." Says, "I just ask you to do one of the two. But, gentlemen, should I ever stoop so low as to sell a pint of liquor, I'd never disgrace the name of my mother by placing it in a box with her name prescribed thereupon, and neither would it be by the cemetery where mine and your loved ones have gone to rest." So, they stuck him a thousand dollars, then tried him again and stuck him another thousand dollars, and he never did sell another pint.

I really broke up the bootleggers by using informants. The county was nice to me, they believed with me. I made a trade with the county to pay a prisoner four dollars a day to work in the jailyard; but at night, when I got the right one, I turned him a-loose and let him go out. The judge knew it. This prisoner would go out in the field and buy, and bring me what he bought, and the United Drys would pay for it. I wouldn't use that in court, but would put it away and later give it to the Liquor Board. Then, when I got everything set up, I'd call the Liquor Board and they'd send in a man. I'd let my prisoner go with 'em, and after he went with 'em a few days he'd drop out of the scene. Then the LCB man would go back and buy on his own. On one occasion the fellow came in, the fines ran 3,222 dollars for that one day. But I made friends out of all those bootleggers. They wasn't bad guys, they was just in the wrong business.

The county attorney at that time was Harris, a Catholic. He said, "There's some reason they're letting these bootleggers off on such light sentences, or turning 'em a-loose. The next time we try a case I want to cut the jury. I think we can get a nice conviction." He says, "The Baptists work harder on the liquor laws than anybody else, and contribute more to it, and most of the United Drys are Baptists. When I go to cut this jury, I'm gonna make every one of 'em a Missionary Baptist."

So, he cut the jury. We had a guy with 16 previous fines, a known bootlegger, but they was out about 30 minutes and then turned him a-loose. And I said, "Now, you let me cut the next one, and I think I can show you something."

There was an old lawyer back here, an infidel, a big ranchman and the strongest character; he could make a witness tell the truth and tear him all to pieces. He'd always said that the rougher element went to the brush and the rougher country, and the better citizens went to the prairie country and open country. I was raised in the open country south of town, and I got to thinking. There was three-hundred-and-twenty-two fines paid that first year I was in office, and only one of them that way from town. So, I cut the next jury in a bootlegger trial, I just cut everybody off that didn't live south of town in the open country, and that's when they fined the boy a thousand. Then they let me cut the next one and they fined him a thousand, too.

We didn't have as much moonshining as in some places. They was making it all over there at Glen Rose, and even killed a federal officer one time. It was pretty well wide open over there and the sheriff was making it, too. I knew the old sheriff pretty well. He went to the pen. He sold a bunch of his moonshine on credit and the fellow didn't pay him, so he went over and got enough of his cows to sell to make up for it, and they got him for stealing cattle. So, he went up for cattle stealing and served his hitch and came back and was elected again. He was a character.

I had a few moonshiners, myself. Had one man named Mark Willard up in the north end of the county who had moved in there from

Arkansas, and he was a moonshiner. While I was running, I overheard two men a-talking about a still. They didn't know I was listening, but I wrote down what they were saying. Then, when I got in office, I went to the courthouse and got abstract numbers and went up there and started to search. I went through one place and didn't find anything. Then, I got to the next one and met the old man. I had a search warrant for the first place, but didn't have one for his (place). I told him my purpose and asked his permission to search. He told me to go ahead, but instead of going out(side) like he thought I was, I went in the house and found some. Then he got mad and told me to stop the search.

Well, I didn't know at that time that I didn't have to stop, that once they give permission they can't take it back. I sent a deputy in to get another search warrant, and then he had to give me permission. I told you, I read people. I was watching him, I was trying to read him while he was talking to me. He gave me a lot of good advice about where I should look, and when he got through I went exactly opposite to where he'd told me. I hadn't gone very far until I come to a hog pen, and there was three 50-gallon barrels of mash. I examines 'em and found that one of 'em was whiskey mash and two of 'em was hog mash. Then I went to stobbing in the sand in the corral and dug up eight-and-one-half gallons of whiskey, his worm (coil) and his still. So, I got that.

Well, then he set up again. I was raised there in that area as a kid, and there was big timber, post oak timber, a tree every two foot. He set him up another one and I went out and found it. I watched it for two or three weeks, and when he never would come back to cook it off, I carried a gun and shot it up. Then he'd set it up somewhere else in another direction, about three or four-hundred yards from there, and I'd find that one. I had a friend that lived up there, an old man in that country, and he'd say, "Boykin, the bees are working again," and I'd go on up. Another time it was his partner who told me where it was. He said, "Now, Boykin, all I ask of you, if you ever do catch me, just let me off a little bit lighter than you would ordinarily."

Finally, this old Mark Willard tried to hire somebody to get me to come up there and to let him know when I left town. He claimed to be tough and was going to shoot me. He had shot at one fellow while he was plowing. So, one day he came up to town and looked me right in the eye, a mean-looking old devil, says, "Boykin, don't you ever, don't you ever take after my whiskey again." I just let him talk. I didn't have anything on me at all, but when he got even with my car I stepped out, says, "Mark, you think you're pretty tough, and I'll just call your damn hand. I'm just gonna see how damn tough you really are. If you got any guts, let's see 'em!'' Well, he like to shook out of his car and then went home and moved into another county.

If I'd gotten killed every time I had a threat made I'd have been dead lots of times. But one time a fellow threatened me to my face and he meant it. I got an order to take a truck in. They told me where the fellow was. He didn't live here, he was visiting up north of Comanche. I went up there with this writ of execution and there he was with the truck. I spoke a little quick. I introduced myself, told him I had papers to take his truck, and he says, "Mister, let me tell you something. Don't you take that truck. I mean every word of it, don't you even put your hand on it.'' And I could tell by the look in his eyes he meant just exactly what he said.

And I says, "Well, I'm not in any hurry and don't guess you are. Sit down here, I'd like to talk to you a little bit.'' So, we sat down and visited a little while. I says, "Now, you realize that I have papers for the truck. First of all, just supposing you got the drop on me and you shot me, do you think that would let you keep the truck? Don't you know in a few minutes every officer in Comanche County would be out here. First thing you know you'd be surrounded by the Texas Rangers and the Highway Patrol from all over the country. And just supposing you shot 'em all, you got by with it, just supposing that, you know what they'd do? They'd call the National Guard out. And supposing you shot all of them, well, they'd have the Army out. You don't have a chance to begin with.'' So he said, "Well, if you'll let me, I'll just drive the truck in for you.''

Years of service taught you a whole lot. That's why you don't want to put a greenhorn, people that don't have good judgment, in that place. If you use your head in your approach, if you can ever get to say the first word to the fellow, you can usually handle the situation very good.

When you stop a fellow for driving a red light, some little something, and you push him over, and he's killed somebody or robbed a bank, he knows it and he thinks you know it. He's ready for you and he's got the first shot. That's why so many officers are so careful how they approach a car. The highway patrol are so skilled at that and they still get killed. One will go up on one side and one the other, right behind the cab. You never see 'em go up beside the car, he's got to stick out backwards when he shoots. I was awful lax, way too lax. I kept a gun with me all the time, but I never wore one. My deputy, one of 'em, never wore one. I always figured like this, if they set out after me, they're gonna get me, 'cause they're gonna shoot me in the back. My gun is to protect the other fellow, and maybe I can protect him better without one, specially when serving civil papers, handling juveniles, witnessing in court. You take an old boy that goes to the witness stand with a big six-shooter on (and) in shirtsleeves, that's not very good for the jury.

One of the most dangerous things the sheriff has to do is put people out of their homes, to have to go out on the orders of the district judge and take a fellow's furniture out and stack it, relieve him of everything he has, he and his wife and children. One time the district judge down there at Beeville ordered Sheriff Vail Ennis to evict a bunch of people. He asked the judge to give him a little time to let him work it out, but he (the judge) said, "My orders says now." So, he went out there and they had barricaded themselves under their house and opened fire and he had to kill 'em to get 'em; he killed everyone of 'em. He killed a lot of men, anyhow. One time this neighbor sheriff called him. These guys had stole a car, and he (Ennis) arrested 'em and carried 'em into a store and picked up a phone to call back. One of 'em jerked a gun and shot him, and as he was falling he pulled his other gun and killed 'em both. He was a very dangerous sheriff.

Jess Sweeten of Henderson County was another one. Jess Sweeten played the piano and was real good at it, and he was a fistfighter and a crack shot. He could split a playing card 20 or 30 feet in front of him, and he could shoot between his legs and cut a pencil 20 or 30 feet behind him, and he could bust marbles in the air with his six-shooter. But what hurt him, what caused him to get beat—I had a niece that was there—he was raiding a place and there was an old colored man working there, a good nigger, but he's scared and he run to a closet. He had nothing to do with the crime, but when Jess Sweeten opened the door of the closet he shot the nigger. He was hid in there and he mistook him.

I guess I came close to getting shot a few times. This fellow Gifford was a speeder and a reckless driver. He was a car salesman and rebuilt cars, and he'd come through town here at one-hundred miles an hour just to aggravate the officers. It was a misdemeanor and there was nothing we could do about it. His car was way faster than anything we had, we didn't have anything to even get close to it. You'd have to kill him to catch him, anyhow. But I got tired of it. I went to the district attorney and told him that I had told all the officers not to shoot him, that it'd be a crime and they'd probably go to the penitentiary for it. So, none of 'em would shoot him when he come through. I says, "He thinks we're afraid of him, the public thinks we're afraid of him, and all we've been doing is chasing him and can't catch him." The district attorney just listened for about 45 minutes. Then he said, "Well, if I was the sheriff of the county, the next time that SOB comes by I'd just let him have it. And you won't be prosecuted, I'll guarantee you won't."

So, I went and got the guy and brought him in to the sheriff's office, sat him down, and I says, "You've been an awful brave man around here. I've kept all the officers from shooting you. They didn't shoot you on account of me; I told 'em not to. And now I'm gonna tell everyone of 'em to shoot you. And I'll dare you to come through one more time. You think you got guts. You never did have 'em, you just had the advantage, but you don't have it anymore." I said, "Now, you come through one more time and see what happens." That's when he left the county.

That old boy said he never would be taken alive. I went out of office and the next sheriff never did arrest him. Two or three years after I went out he came to the house. My wife happened to see him a-coming. She said, "Yonder comes Louis Gifford." He came to the back door, and I went to the door and he says, "Can I come in? I want to talk to you." I says, "Sure you can come in." He came in and I told him to have a seat. He said, "I came in in the first place to apologize to you for what I did. I'm sorry. But I've always been a-wondering. I started to shoot it out with you one time." He said, "I stopped where the library is now, and you stopped over by the First Comanche Bank. We was facing each other, you on the east side and me on the west side of the street, about 150 yards apart." And he said, "I had a high-powered .22 and I've always wondered—I figured you just had your six-shooter—I've always wondered what you had." I said, "I had a Springfield. I believe I could have out-distanced you." He said, "I run over every officer in the county but you, and I never did run over you." I says, "Well, there's one thing you know, don't you. If you had tried me, one of us would have went, wouldn't we. I'd have taken you if it had cost me my life." He said he realized that. And anyway, we were friends after that. I liked the old boy. He comes by to see me every once in a while.

One pretty close one I had, I had a place down there, my wife's grandfather was living on it. There was a fellow wanting to buy some cattle, a farmer here, and I carried him down to look at those cattle. That was about 10 miles southeast of Comanche. And when we started to leave, the chief of police from here in town and my deputy drove up. They said there was a man over on the highway that had run a man and his wife and children off a bridge, and got out and pulled a .45 six-shooter on them. They was following him and took it for granted he went that way. He headed for Comanche. So, me and this farmer headed north, instead of south, until we hit the pavement. Then we got on it and set it on a hundred. We went to Priddy in Mills County, went through the town and turned around and started back, then I saw him a-coming. I pulled off to the right of the road and got out. I went across the road and he slowed down. I stepped on the running board, and just as I stepped on it he shot the gas to it. I jumped off. He had got about 10 feet before I quit (left) him, but he was already going much faster than the speed that a man can ordinarily stand on his feet. I was a lot younger then, but I imagine my feet hit the ground about every 20 feet. But I did manage to stay on my feet.

Then I ran back and got in my car, and I could see over there about a mile or three-quarters of a mile south that he took a right hand turn west. I got in my car and we took off, and we got to that turn off and headed west like he did. We got about two miles and saw him coming back, driving probably one-hundred miles an hour toward us. He was a good ways from us, and there was a road turning north. Before we got to him, he slowed her down and made a left hand turn and headed north. Well, that thrilled me, 'cause I was out of my county. Only way you could follow a fellow is direct pursuit, and I hadn't been direct all the time, see? In other words, he had been out of our sight. I had made a lot of people mad in that county and they didn't think I had any business down there.

Well, when I turned and went after him, he started shooting. Then, every time he'd shoot, I'd shoot, too, but I'd shoot at his tires. I was trying to get him to shoot some more and empty his gun, but he wouldn't shoot but two or three times and I didn't know if he was out of shells, or what. Finally, I got him back in my county, then I crowded him and he turned this pickup over.

The glass door was down on the left and he was down in it, and I jumped out of my car and run up just as he come up, and I hit him on the nose. He went down and he come up again, and I hit him again. Course, he couldn't hit me; he never had gotten his arms out of there. Directly, he didn't come up, and I looked and I saw that .45 laying down on the other glass beside of him. I don't know why I pulled such a bonehead stunt, but I jumped in there on my head just a little bit ahead of him and got the pistol.

I didn't know how tough he really was! I brought him in and put him in jail and found out that a sheriff had killed his brother in another county because he couldn't stop him, and this guy was the same way. He was a lot tougher than I was. I was talking to some fellow that knew him and he says, "Boy, you couldn't whip one side of that fellow." And that's right, too. He could have whipped me if he'd been out where he had a chance.

Another time, there was a fellow named Gilbert Clarie, a resident of this county whom I didn't know, who had moved to Waco, he and his father and his mother, and they were all convicted of armed robbery down in McLennan County. They was all sentenced to the pen. I got a letter from Gilbert that he'd commited a burglary in Comanche

County and would like to clear it up. So, I went down and got him, but I knew why he wrote me. He thought he'd have a chance to get away.

I brought him back here and put him in jail, and he pled guilty to the case he had admitted. And I had a deputy working for me, raised on a farm, who was just awfully dumb in some ways. I kept this Clarie in a strong cell, and when he had any company I'd be back there while he was talking to 'em. But the day before I was to take him back, there was a bunch of thugs come over from Brownwood, and this deputy, unbeknowing to me, let 'em all go back to see this guy and didn't even go with them.

Next day I went up to get him and he was sick, trembling all over, but we took off for Huntsville and this little constable was driving. We got down the other side of Marlin and he kept getting sicker. I did first one thing and another to make him feel better. I'd let him vomit every once and awhile, and I'd stand beside of him and watch him. He finally told me if I'd get him a glass of buttermilk he believed it would be all right. So, we got him a glass of buttermilk, but he said it just made it worse. He was just getting so sick (that) I let him get on the back seat. We was driving pretty fast because we was afraid he was gonna die before we got there. And we let him lay down on the back seat.

He was sick like he was saying he was, all right, 'cause he'd got some Benzadene, that comes with an inhaler, to take to give him the guts to pull this stunt. He was smarter than I was, and I didn't know they'd visited him. But we got down to a little town the other side of Marlin and I was turned in the seat sort of facing him, and he said, "Sheriff, if you'll let me vomit one more time, if possible, turn off the road . . . ." And I looked off, and he said, "Hold it Sheriff!"

Well, I knew when he said "hold it" that he had a gun back of my head. I sat with my back to him for a few seconds, and when I turned, I turned as fast as I could. He had the gun about six inches from my head, and I hit the gun, and just as I hit it, it went off. He was a little bigger man than I was, and awful strong, but I used to have an awful strong grip in my hands and I grabbed him and got an awful good hold. The constable jumped over the seat, grabbed hands and all, and he (the prisoner) shot him through the finger. We thought he shot three times. But I kept the first grip that I got and I squeezed the gun out of his hands and he gave up. Then, we handcuffed him and carried him on down to Huntsville and delivered him.

But I just came within an inch of killing him, to tell you the truth. He hit me right here in my chest, and I thought he'd got me, and I thought probably I'd die. I thought he'd got me a direct hit, you know;

I felt a burning sensation. I'd hit that gun with such force when I turned that I'd tore my shirt all to pieces. Only one button was holding it. I reached down, and I sure was dreading it, and unbuttoned this button to see how bad I was shot, and it was just a little burned place. The bullet had went in the top of the car and come back and hit me. I wasn't mad until I saw that I wasn't gonna die, and when I saw I wasn't dying it just flew all over me. That's when I got my gun, and this poor devil sitting back there trembling.

He had had that gun, a Belgium .25, laced up in his boot, and he had it on safety, and he told 'em down at the pen that he thought he'd take the car without killing me, and he didn't pull the safety down. That was the only thing that saved me. I was a tenth of a second ahead of him.

I made friends with most of my prisoners, and I was good to 'em, honest with 'em. One time we overhauled the jail. It was sinking and we took the top off and we didn't have any doors on the jail for three months. We had prisoners like we always had, but with no doors, and we didn't lose any.

In fact, one of our greatest assets was making friends with prisoners. When I'd come to the right one, that would cooperate, I'd get the commissioners court to pay him a little salary. I'd keep him in jail in the daytime and turn him out at night—let him go 'round and mix in and gather information. You had to study 'em and pick the right one. And I hired a few informers that never did go to jail, that were extra good. I had one that was far better than I was. He could look at a tire track and he could identify it at the scene of a crime, just beat all I ever saw.

I'll give you one little example. We had a house burglary about 12 miles northwest. Fellow had left his house, had more or less moved, and somebody had burglarized it. I carried this informer out there, and he got out and looked the tracks over real good, says, "Take me over yonder about seven miles." So, we drove over southeast and drove up to a cattle guard on one side of a farm-to-market road. He got out and walked over to the cattle guard and looked, then motioned for me to come there. Says, "Now, this track here will be the track that was over yonder. The boy is named Martin. There's two of those boys, this will be the oldest." And sure enough it was. Years later I asked him how he did that. He said the guy made him mad one time and he looked at his tire and never forgot it.

He never did mislead me. Whenever he told me anything it would turn out to be that way. I couldn't understand it myself, how he could do it, his mind, how it operated that way. He was a law violator himself, a trespasser, an extra good shot and a deer hunter. He hunted on everybody and they couldn't stop him. And he'd illegal fish, too. He's still my friend and he'd do anything in the world for me.

I had one boy over here, an old ex-con about six feet four, mean-looking and deep scars all over his face. He was up here one day a-visiting and some company came just as he got ready to leave. He excused hisself, says, "Well, I'll be going. But listen, if y'all ever have anybody you want killed, be sure and call me." He left and those people said, "Does he mean that?" Those guys are still my friends yet.

I thought I had a natural ability, I thought I knew people. I've always studied people, and people interest me. I put everything I had into the sheriff's office, and I ran it as honest as any preacher ever ran his pulpit. I put myself into it to the extent that, if something happened, I could usually pretty well guess who did it, if it was local. I wasn't any smarter than anyone else, except that you get out of anything about what you put in it. We had some serious crime. I had a bank robbery here of 18,000 dollars one time. I was in Fort Worth and it came over the radio, and I came home one-hundred miles an hour and figured out who I thought did it before I got out of Fort Worth. When I came in, the Texas Ranger and the FBI was in my office. They hadn't got anything done. I asked 'em did they have anything going and they says, "No, not a thing." I went over the file and jerked out a picture of the fellow I thought it was. I ran it over to the Comanche National Bank and asked 'em all to look at it. Says, "Is that him?" They all said, "Naw." I said, "Well, why isn't it him? What about the hat?" "Well," they said, "the hat's all right." "How about the age?" "The age is all right, but this fellow had a moustache." So I ran it to a Mrs. Harlick, says, "Draw me a moustache on this fellow, right quick." Then I ran it back to the bank, and they said, "Now, that's still not him. This man's moustache turned down." So, I went back to the office and got another picture and had her turn the moustache down, and they said that was him. But he got killed in Waco later on, and by the time he got killed the first picture was right, his moustache was turning up.

The worst that happened during my years as sheriff was the murder of a druggest friend of mine. He run a drugstore and had gone to Fort Worth and come back to his drug store and called his wife that he'd be home in a few minutes. Then he didn't come, and when she sent someone down there to check on him, there he lay on the floor.

He was my personal friend and it was cold blood. This man had first made him go around and give him all the dope he wanted, then took his money, then tied his hands and pushed him on the floor. Then he started to walk off and says, "I've got too much to lose. He's got to die," and went back and cut his throat in three different directions.

My wife and I was out looking for tornadoes. We came back by the house, she decided to stay, and there was one that had hit the ground at Justin, 13 miles south. I started to run to go to it and she hollered that there had been a robbery and a murder at Durham Drug. That's all I knew, but I jumped in my car and started the motor, started backing out, and I guessed who did it. The Rangers come in and they said that it wouldn't be him, but I didn't pay that no mind. I worked the case just like I wanted to, and it was him, after all.

I knew this guy was tough. His mother worked at the post office and I'd gotten to know her fairly well. One day a long time before, when another man was killed, she had come up to me and says, "I'd like to ask you something." I said, "What do you want to ask me?" Says, "Do you think my son killed Woodruff?" I didn't know her son, I'd seen him one time. I said, "No, I don't think your son killed him. But I want to ask you a question, how come you to ask me that?" She says, "Well, I just know where he was and know that he didn't." I didn't forget that, and when this other one happened I put it together.

And cattle theft, I had a good bit of that, sometimes. Sometimes they'd just get one and then sometimes they'd get more. The most I ever lost at any one time, I believe, the first time I was in, was six that came from Ira Nichol's auction barn out there. I guessed who it was in the first guess that time, too. Nobody's gonna believe this, of course, but I had been standing on the street a month before and a boy named Harold Spivy walked up and says, "You see that guy standing over there with the black hat on? I went to a party last night, and he went along with my girl friend and I, and he got fresh with her." I said, "Well, you want to do anything about it?" He says, "Naw, just wanted to show him to you." When I looked him over, he was about 50 yards away, he looked like what I thought a cow thief would look like. I don't know why, I don't know what a cow thief looks like, but I followed him at a distance and wrote down his pickup number. It so happened I gave one of those numbers to Johnny McDonald and T. A. McDonald, two brothers; told 'em it was a fellow I thought was gonna steal some cattle and to help me watch him. It happened he stole 'em from their daddy. I started to checking on him and called Abilene, and he'd sold two of 'em there and one of 'em had gone to Tyler and two to Fort Worth and one to Goldthwaite. I went up there to Abilene, and on the way back I overtook he and his wife in a car. She had the money on her.

But how did I know it was him? It's something you can't describe. I don't believe the Lord appeared and told me, I think it's practice and working at it. The Lord helps you if you help yourself.

I had a good average of everything like that, but the further I went, the harder it was. It was getting harder when I went out because the government was gradually kind of taking over. For instance, when I left the jail cost about five-thousand dollars a year to run it. I'd hire some old gentleman on Social Security, give him about 125 dollars a month, let him draw his check, and he'd do an excellent job. Now, it costs 56,000 dollars to run it a year, because they all tell him exactly how to run it. He don't run it, he's just a tool unto them. He's a good boy, but he's just running it for the Jail Commission. I was the only sheriff I know of that fought it and tried to tell the other sheriffs they's getting their feet in the water. One of 'em told me awhile back, says, "Gaston, I just wanted to tell you how right you was about the Jail Commission." The man that comes by to inspect the jail also has the authority to close it. That chain link fence around the jail, he come here and told 'em where to put the posts!

There was a great justice up in New York named Learned Hand, and he was known as one of the greatest justices America's ever had, and he had this to say probably 65 years ago. He said, "Within 50 years of this date the Supreme Court will have interpreted the American people out of law enforcement." Well, we have come to the period he was talking about.

They sure went too far with the Miranda warning. When you arrest a fellow you can't even ask him what time it is till you say, "You don't have to make any statement at all, and I must tell you now that any statements you make may be used against you in a court of law. You have the right to have a lawyer, to have him with you while you're being interrogated, and if you wish one, one will be appointed to represent you. Now, do you want an attorney?"

Well, who's gonna say no? So, you've got to learn to handle that thing. But through psychology, I'll admit this, you learn to use the tone of your voice and the way you present the questions, so that in spite of giving 'em the warnings they'll still talk. You just got to be an artist with it. You got to be honest with 'em, but you got to be honest to your state. You're working for the state, you're not working for them. You're gonna do all in your power to learn how to question.

We had a guy from Dallas—he wasn't crazy, just went wild—out of a wealthy family. He'd been on a big burglary here, went over the top of a big building, took the skylight out and come down. Anyhow, I got him and he tore the commodes out everywhere we put him, just tore 'em out, never had nothing like that before. And he broke I don't know how much glass. That was when they was getting so strict, and what he was trying to do was to get me to give him a whipping, where he could sue me. That's what he was wanting, you know, and I didn't want to play in his hands. I was even afraid to handcuff him. If I handcuffed him he'd sue me. Well, all these sob sisters could never see through that, you know. It got where it wasn't worth being sheriff, really, with the law all changed for their favor.

I admit, it used to be the other extreme. I've been to places that had a little box just big enough for both of a man's feet. One would interrogate him till he give out, then he'd walk out of the room and another one would take over, till he was so tired from standing there. Most of the times he confessed, he was guilty—nearly always. They did get one guy that used a "hotshot" on 'em, and they sent that fellow that used the hotshot (electric cattle prod) to the pen. They ought to have. I never did that myself, but in questioning 'em, after you learn, you do try to get him in the right place, if you possibly can, that you believe in your mind is the best place. You sit him in a chair that's several inches lower than the one you're on, or either you stand while he sits. You put him on lower ground and you look him right in the eye while you're talking to him. It gives him a little bit of an inferiority. It's like selling real estate, when you take 'em to the closing room, you have the seat just a little bit lower for the buyer, and yours a little bit higher.

We had one case, a burglary. A boy over at May in Brown County was a suspect, a good-looking boy. I got him in the back office and interviewed him and almost got a confession, but I didn't. But I was real nice to him. Then I let him go on, but told him when he came back by to stop, I hadn't finished talking with him. He said he would. When he got back, he'd made up his mind definitely not to talk. So, I got the present sheriff here to go in and say, "You know what I'd do, Sheriff, if I was you? If that fellow started lying to me like he is to you . . . !" And he called him a thug and a little bit of everything, just anything he didn't want to hear, then he turned around and walked out. And then this boy said, "Sheriff, what that fellow said didn't help one bit—nothing, nothing he did. But you been so nice to me, you made me feel so little, so I'm gonna go ahead and tell you the truth."

I learned those kind of law enforcement tricks as I went along, and there were some good teachers around. I had an old deputy, dead now, who was kind of crippled up. I never did tell him what to do in my life, though he worked for me ten-and-a-half years. He served more papers than me and the sheriff we got now put together, but we drove 10 miles to his one, and walked 10 miles to his one. You'd see him culling those citations. He'd get the mail and he'd put one here and one here and one here and one here, that's where those fellows lived. Next day you'd see him switch 'em around a little bit and stack 'em all up, separate 'em, and put 'em in a drawer. You'd wonder what he was gonna do, he's getting so many on hand. One day you'd say, "Well, don't we have a bunch of citations?" He'd say, "Naw, we don't have any."

No farmer is at home anymore, he's off somewhere. Most of 'em work three or four places, can't make a living on one. You can't hardly catch him in the daytime. What this old deputy would do is go home at night and get on the phone and say, "Hey, Charlie, I got a little old citation of some kind for you. Now, I don't know what it is 'cause I never read 'em. That's your mail, and I don't believe I should ever look at a citation. But I just wondered if you would like to pick that up or if you'd like me to bring it out to you?" And nearly every one of 'em wanted to come get it! He thought and thought and thought, and when he's sitting around like you and I, he wasn't loafing. He was running these things through his head.

He'd wait on court, and one day the district judge was talking to a whole bunch of peace officers. He was telling 'em the authority that a district judge has, a lot of it he never enforces. If you're late for court they can put you in jail if they want to, and do sometimes. He's telling these officers, and all the officers, nearly, in the country were there. Says, "I wouldn't hesitate one moment to enforce these laws on anyone present except that old grey-headed devil sitting there. He can just do anything he wants to in this court, and I won't ever say a word."

You see, people really preferred to come to the courthouse. People don't like the sheriff to drive to the house very much, anyway. A lot of 'em resent it. My wife and I collect arrowheads, and during the drought we could find 'em. When we wasn't in office, we could go any place in the county and walked, but when I was in office I could never crawl over a fence unless I called that fellow and told him about it. They'd get extremely mad when they'd see the sheriff in their place, think you're trying to catch 'em, or something. And I've had two or three jump me for following 'em when I hadn't followed 'em at all.

One time before I married, when my mother and I lived in the jail, we went to Brownwood to a show. We drove back and there's a Cherokee Street turns off the main road a ways back of town. I was always taught that on ranches don't ever come back like you went, because you were being paid for what you see, so I came the old road and there was a car parked over on the right. I didn't pay it any mind and went on to the jail. Then, just as I stopped and my mother got out, these two guys walked up and stuck their heads in. One says, "What was you follering us for?" I says, "I don't think it's any of your damn business." It just irked me, I wasn't follering 'em at all. He says, "Well, I been a-hearing I was gonna be shook down." I says, "That's another damn lie you could've kept from telling. If I want to shake you down, I'll let you know." Then I said, "For your information I didn't follow you anywhere, and I don't appreciate your approach."

People are always ready to get mad at the sheriff about something, and they all vote. That's why, on the whole, the sheriff has as little to do with the game law as he possibly can. It's a little like speeding, nearly everybody violates 'em a little bit. The sheriff usually says, "Well, you're the game warden, I'm the sheriff. You run your business and I'll run mine." There was a well-liked game warden here and he would give his father a ticket, or you or me or anyone else. Game wardens are high-class people, they're honest people, but they're taught to show no partiality. A sheriff never handles any two cases alike, a game warden handles 'em all exactly alike. In other words, I got a guy drunk one time and I took him home. The next night I got him drunk again and put him in jail. The guy that was with him, I took him home. I treated 'em alike, but on different occasions.

Everyday they took every minute of your time. Lots of times there was more people than you could talk to, and most of 'em wanted to see the sheriff. Didn't want to talk to a deputy, wanted to see the sheriff. And lots of times the phone would ring more than you could answer, you'd just have to put 'em off until the next day. They'd be important calls, but you couldn't make it because you had others ahead of 'em. In fact, they kind of poured it on the sheriff, he was the busiest man in the county. The boys in the jail one time counted the times the phone rang in half a day when we were out of the office, and it was 104 or 105.

I was out all the time. I had a red light on the top of the jail, and if I was at a ball game or anywhere in the city—me, the deputy, the highway patrol, liquor control, whatever—we'd watch that jail and if it was blinking we'd run to see what it was. If I went to the ball game, I'd sit where I could see that blinking light, and I'd go from there.

There wasn't anything they didn't ask. A fellow gonna be a sheriff, he needs to be a super detective, he needs to be a prize fighter, he needs to be a foot-racer, he needs to be a preacher, he needs to be a lawyer, and a liar and everything else, I guess, 'cause it took every qualification to make one. They'd call me and ask, "Would it be all right to give my baby a certain kind of medicine?" And, "Gaston, I'm sorry, but I stepped all over my husband last night. I didn't do anything wrong, but I had to tell somebody." You get a lot of 'em like that, liable to be a cat on the top of the house, whatever. One fellow came in and said there was a dragon out on Lake Comanche, and it was about 80-foot long, and it was swimming in that water and was the darndest thing he ever saw. Man, he was excited. I got in my car and carried him out there, and we got in his boat and rowed out in the lake, and it was a bunch of ducks, swimming in formation.

When I was sheriff here the first time, they had one city policeman and he drew 75 dollars a month and furnished his own car. He would get the cows that got into somebody's yard, but he didn't have too much to do. It's not that way anymore. They have a good police department here now, a good many men that patrol all the time, and pretty well take care of the complaints in the city. But they won't average over one felony a year, the whole group; the sheriff is the one that makes all the felony cases. Not that they're not good men, the reason they don't make more cases is that they work by the hour. A good officer doesn't pay any attention to the hour of the day or day of the week, he goes, that's what he likes, like a bloodhound. These boys work eight hours and they're off. If they have a burglary and it comes five o'clock, they leave. Some of 'em don't even have their phones listed. But a good officer cares, you know; time doesn't mean nothing if you got it in you.

I guess what helped me more than anything in being sheriff, I always give credit for two things. One is that I was religious and a fairly good Bible student. I had a strong conviction and that helped me in my work. And the other was that I'd bought and sold hundreds and hundreds of horses. There's lots of old crooks in the horse business, you know, lots of old crooked horse traders, and trading horses you learn people. People would cheat you and tell you a lie, and you just learned people by dealing with 'em. You learn people by looking at 'em a whole lot—the ears going down the side of the head, different things. Never could tell a Mexican, though. A white man, you could pretty well learn what he was pretty quick. I think that you have to be born with a certain knack.

T.W. "BUCKSHOT" LANE

★

I didn't weigh but 145 pounds, but I had a good pistol. An old uncle of mine, when I was just a kid, he put me on a watermelon, and he says, "His eyes look like they're little buckshot." After I got to be an officer, I used "Buckshot" Lane. It was a good name to have. But I carried a pistol, only—a .45 automatic. I used one of those German Lugers one time and shot a Mexican three times with it, and the bullets went completely through him. They don't shock. The .45 shocks, and you got to have something to shock 'em and knock 'em down.

I was broke, was how I come to get in law enforcement. All I had was a big paper route. I was married and had to make a living, so I ran for constable and was elected. Then I burned that damn Kentleton Bridge out there because the state wouldn't do anything about it. This was in 1934 or 1935. When the highway was paved and designated U.S. 59 they didn't replace the old wooden bridge, they left it offset—I mean, it didn't line up with the highway. The bridge had killed 13 people. While I was constable, three boys from Texas A&M went off it one night and got killed, and one of their daddies said, "I'm gonna blow that damn thing up!'' A banker down here called the governor, said, ''We gonna blow it up, if you don't do nothing.'' Anyway, I was constable of Precinct One and I had taken an oath to protect the lives of the people. That bridge had killed 13 folks, so I decided to do something about it.

At this garage I got me a bunch of gunny sacks and some oily waste, and I filled a five-gallon Koto can with kerosene. I went out to the bridge one cold winter night and wadded those sacks up and wired them onto the bridge with baling wire in three places. Then I soaked them with my can of kerosene. After that I come on back to town and fooled around, so I'd be seen, and about 10 o'clock I went back out there. I took my waste rags and dipped 'em in my gas tank and stuck 'em onto the gunny sacks and lit 'em. Then I came on back and went to bed.

Well, I hadn't got to sleep yet when a Red Arrow truck driver called me—I knew all the truckers—says, ''Buck, do you know the Kentleton Bridge is on fire?'' I said, ''Naw!'' I got up and went back out there. The wind had come up and it was sure burning good. Only thing I worried about, I was afraid the railroad bridge alongside it would catch. When I saw that railroad bridge smoking it scared me.

Some truck drivers down in the Valley started taking up a collection to help defend whoever got charged with burning the bridge. The district attorney here then was Bob Bassett, and he announced he'd buy the finest suit of clothes that money could buy for the man who burned that bridge if we could find him, but that he'd still have to prosecute him.

The day after the bridge burned I was due to go to Austin, so I went on. I got up there and old Homer Garrison at the Texas Rangers said, ''What in the hell are you doing here? I just sent two Rangers to Wharton County to find out who burned that bridge last night. You ought to be there helping.''

So, I came on back, and for about a week around here we investigated the bridge burning. We never did find no leads. J. Edgar Hoover told me later that the statute of limitations on arson ran out after 10 years. I saw Bob Bassett then, and I told him, ''Bob, you owe me a new suit of clothes.'' And he said, ''You SOB. I *knew* you were the one burnt that bridge.''

In those days the candidates met on the courthouse square and they had talks. I told 'em all when I was running for constable that first time, ''Now, let me tell you people something. I know what it's like to be in jail and out of jail, 'cause I was in jail in Houston, and I know what it's like.'' And they all voted for me. I had been drunk, and Jim Shown and Bill Slack had caught me and put me in the city jail in

Houston. And old Bill, later on, he called me and says, "I want to get married, and I want you to get the license for me."

But they all voted for me. If you tell 'em the truth, people will understand you. If you lie to people, sooner or later they's gonna catch you. I've had people go into the real estate business here, and I told 'em, I said, "Now, fellows, keep your nose clean. Tell the truth. Because if you tell one lie you gotta tell 'em another to back it up." They wouldn't listen to me. But if you tell people the truth, people gonna stay with you.

One old fellow told me . . . I said, "Are you gonna vote for me?" He said, "Hell, no." I said, "Why? I thought you was my friend?" He said, "I am your friend. I don't want to see you made a two-bit politician."

The constable had as much authority as the sheriff, only he had a small precinct. You operated out of a precinct. But he's the only man who could arrest the sheriff. They had the same authority as the sheriff, but mainly they served papers, mostly. Some constables took it on themselves to enforce the law. I enforced the law in my precinct.

The county was wide open when I came into office. There was slot machines and there was whore houses. I had the biggest paper route in the county, and I knew 'em all. When I got in, I told 'em that these places had to stop. We just couldn't have these houses of ill repute, and we wasn't gonna have slot machines. I put a stop to all that stuff. I didn't want any of that going on in this county. We had four clean counties in here. Besides Wharton, Jackson County was clean, Matagorda was clean, and Calhoun was clean. The Highway Patrol would help me, too. We'd go over there and get those nigger whores, white whores, too, and we'd take 'em out on the road and put a strap to 'em and run 'em off. They knew that we didn't allow anything like that in this county.

During the bootleg days, I had bought a lot of whiskey, drank a lot of whiskey. But I told these fellows, I said, "Now, fellows, when I'm elected to be an officer, you gonna have to go out of business." They said, "We know that, but we still gonna support you." Good people was making whiskey, too. The sheriff over in Fort Bend County was selling it out of the jailhouse. But my people quit—they knew I meant business with 'em.

You can't be on the take and be a good sheriff. I had a friend ask me if I would talk to a fellow from Corpus Christi. I said, "Sure, I'll talk to anybody." He says, "You been elected for sheriff. Just let me put in a few slot machines over here on the county line and I'll give you a car and so much money." I said, "I better talk to my wife." She said, "Buck, our little boys might have patches on their britches, but they can go to any church they want to. Let's you and I stay straight." We did.

I was constable for eight years and sheriff 12 years, so that give me 20 years of police work. I could have been sheriff a long time before I was, but I was making more money than the sheriff. The sheriff was turning all the fees over to me. He was getting three-hundred dollars a month as sheriff and I was on four dollars a case. You see, he didn't want me to run agin him anyhow.

Finally I did run; I knew he was gonna get beat. His deputy was a drunk and had turned his car over several times. He was a German and the war was coming on, too, and the people was against Germany, as a rule. We'd have county meetings and he'd say, "What you gonna talk about tonight?" I'd say, "I ain't gonna say much." He'd say, "If you don't say nothing, I wouldn't either." He was a nice old fellow. He and I were friends all the way through, but I knew he was gonna get beat and I think he knew it, too.

I was sheriff here for 12 years. The only reason I quit was because I wanted to be the congressman. I wanted to beat Clark W. Thompson, who was a Moody, had married a Moody. They owned a 80-million-dollar hotel in Washington, D.C. I ran against Thompson and beat him, I thought. He called me and congratulated me, but on Sunday morning they found 138 votes in Galveston that had not been counted, and so with that he beat me. He beat me, and it was the best thing that ever happened to me. I went out on the road then, with the Knife and Fork Club, talking about my way of enforcing the law and demonstrating the lie detector.

I had my own way of enforcing the law. I believed in doing the right thing by all mankind. I believed there was "accidentals" and there was "habituals," and if an accidental gets in trouble, you should be happy to help. If it's a habitual, put him in jail.

I went out every night about four o'clock in the morning. I'd just take a car and drive, see what was going on. You'd catch lots of things, too, at that time of morning. They never knew where they'd find me, they never knew when I was coming. I was mostly after cow thieves at that time of day, and burglars. After they found out I was always on the move, they didn't bother me. I'd go different roads all the time.

"Lone Wolf" Gonzaullas, he was a noted Ranger. Lone Wolf told me a long time ago when this boy robbed a Luling bank—they called him the "Honeymoon Bandit," and he and I had a shooting scrape— Lone Wolf told me, says, "It's a hell of a lot better to be tried for killing some sorry son of a bitch than to have some sorry son of a bitch tried for killing you." He says, "When you travel, travel by yourself. Ain't nobody to tell the tale but you."

Well, I did. My wife would say. "Buck, you're going out by yourself?" I'd say, "Darned right, 'cause I can't do you any good if I'm dead. If I'm alive, ain't nobody gonna tell the tale but me." Lone Wolf was right about it, he sure was.

Vail Ennis felt that way, too. The last time I saw Vail he had a new Hudson car that he'd just bought in Houston. I said, "Vail, you done killed eight men in seven years, now, don't kill a ninth man." He just said, "You son of a bitch." Vail was a good sheriff. He was tough as a boot, he straightened out Bee County.

I was still constable when I had this shoot-out with the Honeymoon Bandit. They called him the Honeymoon Bandit because he married a preacher's daughter from Corpus Christi. He posed as a rich oilman's son out of Houston, he married her, and then he robbed the bank at Luling. I was with my wife, just sit down to dinner, when they called me from Victorio and said, "Harry Wells is coming your way. Would you head him off?" I called the deputy and told him to meet me at the river bridge. I said, "Bring your shotgun, sawed-off shotgun, and pistol," and he did. Then we went out and met Harry Wells over about Louise somewhere.

He had a '37 Ford and I had a '37 Ford. His was a sheriff's car from Bee County. He had shot them up and taken their car. See, he first shot the sheriff over there at Karnes City, then he shot up a liquor control man and the chief of police at Beeville. They got out and got behind trees and he shot 'em anyway. Then he took their car with a 30-30 rifle and everything else in it. He was loaded and I wasn't. All I had was a pistol, a .45 automatic, and the deputy's sawed-off shotgun and pistol.

Anyway, he took off and I took off. It was back before the days of radios, so I had the deputy throw off a message as we went through town to call ahead and have the Houston police meet us. We didn't do any shooting till we got stopped. His car blew up on him, and he was out shooting at me with the 30-30 before I could get stopped. I threw mine sideways, then I got behind the battery box, which was up in the front of the car, so that he wouldn't hit me in the chest. He put 54 bullet holes through my car and shot my hat off.

Then a fellow come by there in a brand-new Chrysler car, says, "Get out of the way, boys, I'm going through." Then this old boy threw down on him and made him get out of the car. And he took the car, and when he hit the ground his wheels were rolling! My car was shot-up and wouldn't run, but I had hit him in the foot. When they caught him later, he asked me, "What sort of machine gun were you using?" I says, "It wasn't a machine gun." He said, "It sounded to me like a machine gun."

Another time, I got shot myself. I had Pete Norris in my jail, the FBI's number one badman. Pete had a grey eye and a blue eye. He come from Dallas. It was on Christmas Eve, and his lawyer called from Houston, said, "I want to talk to my client." There was two law officers upstairs talking to him. I said, "All right, I'll go get him." At that time we didn't have telephones in the jail, only one down in the office. I went to get Pete and brought him down. Mr. Haines was there. He was a special guard hired by the FBI just to watch Pete. Mike Flournoy was sitting here at the radio station. Well, Pete got the phone upside down. I said, "Pete, you got the phone upside down." Then he pulled a little old pop-shooter out and says, "I mean, fellows, get 'em up, get 'em up!" Old Man Haines' and Mike's hands were going like that, but I said, "Pete, I'm coming. Don't you shoot me, I'm a-coming!"

So, I ran around the end of the counter and he shot and burnt this left cheek. Then Pete and I went to fighting. He was six feet tall and I was just a little man, but he had been in jail and I hadn't. He and I wrestled, and Old Man Haines was shooting a .44 with hollownose bullets, and I knew if he ever shot Pete he'd shoot me too. I said, "Mr. Haines, don't shoot, don't shoot!" I finally got my foot into Pete's stomach and kicked him loose, and then they both shot him. I said, "Don't shoot him anymore, fellows. Don't shoot him anymore." But Pete was taken off to the hospital and he got over it.

It's hard to say how we enforced the law in those days. You didn't have the officers then you have now. I think we had two here in Wharton and one in El Campo, that's all we had. You just didn't have much in those days, and the county wouldn't pay for much. Our cars were as cheap as they could buy. You see, the county fought me, the county commissioners fought me, 'cause I made 'em count the gravel trucks. You know, commissioners can rob the county quicker than anybody in the world and get by with it, but I stayed after 'em. They didn't like me. It's hard to get along with your commissioners if you count the gravel trucks.

You had so little, you just had to have the information, had to have "bird dogs." I had a bunch of niggers here that would keep me posted on things that went bad. And I had people like this Joe Yamada, this Jap. Joe was my friend, and boy, anything happen in Harris County, I'd know it 'fore the sheriff down there would know it. Joe would put me wise.

During the war, gasoline was rationed, tires was rationed, whiskey was rationed—everything was. So they started breaking in these filling stations, breaking in liquor stores, and I got to following them thieves. Finally, I found out Joe Yamada was one of 'em. Joe was a high-class Jap, his momma was Irish and his daddy was Jap, and he was highly educated. I called up Sheriff Henderson and told him to put Joe in jail. He called me later and said, "You better rush up here, because he has called Percy Foreman." Well, I knew Percy would get him out and I'd never get him back, so, two deputies and myself went up there and got Joe in the middle of the night.

We got Joe, and they sat in the back seat of my car and started hammering on him and he wouldn't tell 'em nothing. When we got over to Lufkin for breakfast, I said, "Joe, when my district attorney gets through with you, you damned Jap, he's gonna set you on fire." Joe said, "Can I go to your jail?" I said, "Yeah. Why?" He said, "I want to talk with you. You're all right. You ain't lying to me and you ain't beating on me."

Years later, the federal district judge from Corpus Christi called me. They was robbing post offices over there and they had caught Joe and some Irishman, and they wouldn't tell 'em nothing. But the judge said, "Joe says if he could go to your jail, he'd talk." So, I went and got him and he talked. The last time I saw Joe I wasn't sheriff then, I had done quit, but Joe told me, "You the only honest man I know that's a sheriff."

I had that reputation. The Maceo boys was running Galveston, and they'd call me when they wanted to hire a man. The gamblers from Houston, the gamblers from Galveston, everywhere, would call me to investigate 'em before they'd hire someone. I asked the Maceos, "Why do you people all call on me to investigate when you want to hire somebody?" They said, "If we can buy the sheriff of a county, so can the thugs. And we can't buy you."

The convicts down on the prison farm used to call me "the white sheriff," and I appreciated it. That was 'cause I wouldn't lie to them, I didn't have to lie to them. They'd lie to me, but I didn't have to lie to them.

I didn't have any dogs, I didn't believe in dogs. The only dogs I ever used was the state penitentiary dogs. I don't know, they were too much to keep and I just didn't never use 'em. I was clever enough I could catch 'em without that. I had men that was bird dogs for me. They helped me out a lot.

I had several other bird dogs that was good, too, but Pete Traxler was the best. He kept me posted on anything that come into this county that was bad. Pete Traxler was one of Pretty Boy Floyd's gang. Pete was raised in Oklahoma, and he had had a hard life. His mother separated from Pete's daddy, I don't think they were married, and his stepfather beat the tar out of Pete. Pete got to bootlegging some, got him an old car, then got in with the Pretty Boy Floyd Gang. He was in the train robbery up at Kansas City with Pretty Boy Floyd. Pete never did kill anybody, and Judge Bracewell saved him from the electric chair. He called me one day and said, "If you can, help Pete. Pete's had a hard life. If you treat Pete right, Pete will treat you right."

One day I was pumping gas down here and Pete came walking by, crippling, said, "Do you know me?" I said, "Hell, yes, I know you. Where you going?" Said, "I'm going in the hijacking business." I said, "Well, if you are, you gonna get caught." "No," he said, "mine's gonna be legalized. I'm gonna work for Cramer the plumber." He said, "Now, listen. I'm gonna talk to you, but I ain't gonna talk to no other officer. When you see me walk by that jail, you come on down to the river, 'cause I'm gonna tell you all about it. And there ain't gonna be no saferobbers, nothing like that, in this county long as I'm here."

He was on the level. If any convicts hit this county, any hard guy hit this county, he'd try to run 'em off hisself. He'd say, "You bastards, don't you work in this county." And if he couldn't, he'd put me on to 'em. And he'd tell me anything that was irregular, any police business. Pete was a bird dog, Pete kept me in touch. They caught Pete over here in Victoria County, one time. Pete said, "Just let me call Mr. Lane in Wharton." Bill Crawford, who was sheriff there, said, "All right, call him." Bill said to me, "Do you know him?" I said, "Yes, I know him. Turn him a-loose. He'll tell you the truth." So Bill turned him a-loose and Pete came barreling back to me.

Pete thought the world of me and my wife, and when he found out I was gonna leave office he come to see us and just cried. He said, "Well, if you're leaving, I better leave, too." And he did.

Nowdays, they prosecute the officers and don't prosecute the criminals, they turn the criminals loose. In those days, if a criminal got in a bad way with us, he got killed. And they knew it. Or he got whipped and they knew it. We were not tried. I'll tell you the truth, one reason I quit was because they was sending a bunch of sheriffs up for violating civil liberties, and I knew they were after me for whipping that nigger woman. I said, "I'm quitting before they get me," and I did.

I whipped on this nigger woman one time when *Life* magazine was down here doing a story on me. There was a deputy killed over at El Campo, and the highway patrol brought this woman in on a Sunday, dead drunk. She was a drunk driver. I asked 'em, "Did you shake this woman's purse down?" And they said, "No, we didn't." So I grabbed the purse and she kicked me, and when she did I knocked the tar out of her and threw her in jail. *Life* magazine photographed that and wrote it up, but they didn't tell the whole story. I told her husband I got her down here, and he said, "Keep her, Mr. Lane. That car was stolen she was driving. She been used to having these Houston police around, and they can't do nothing about it." He says, "You can. I sure do appreciate you catching her." Well, *Life* magazine didn't tell that!

Now, there's a Houston lawyer came over here one time and throwed his weight around, and I whupped him, too. He throwed his weight around telling me what he was gonna do, and I whipped him in the jailhouse, really wore him out, too. This fellow at the law firm he was with in Houston called up and said, "You know you whipped a lawyer?" I said, "Naw, I didn't know it was a lawyer." He said, "You sure did a good job. He needed it."

It used to be that you could really enforce the law. We had a cow thief one time that was stealing pretty good, and I caught him over in Hallettsville. He stole lots of cattle over around Hallettsville and Shiner. He'd drive down the road in the middle of the night, see what he wanted, shoot 'em with a .22 rifle, put 'em in the truck, and then take 'em into Shiner to butcher 'em. That sheriff there at Hallettsville said, "Naw, it couldn't have been him." I said, "It was, though." I got him and knocked him in the head one time, and he started spilling his guts. He went to the penitentiary, and when he came out, he came back to me and got a job driving a bus. I helped him get a job. But I broke up the cow thieving in this county, we didn't have any cow thefts around here after then.

During the war, when we had a lot of Border Patrolmen stationed here, they'd take these zoot-suiters off of trains and out of busses and say, "Sheriff, we're through with 'em," and the Rangers would do that, too. Your women were having to go out in the fields and harvest the crops, but the zoot-suiters, wearing long-tailed coats and no cuffs on their britches, the zoot-suiters were four-F'ers. Their pants were tight and their coat tails went down to their knees. I had a special knife that I used to cut the britches legs, make 'em look like sailors, and cut the tails off of them coats. The mayor told me, "You gonna wreck us." I said, "I don't give a damn if I do wreck you. These white women are having to go out in these fields, and these damn zoot-suiters are not fighting the war, and without cuffs on their pants. Goddamn four-F'er bastards! They ain't gonna come in this county and take over."

You had to be rough. One man lived in this house right yonder, and he was a bad guy, too. The former sheriff ahead of me, that I beat, he took his gun off of him. But he didn't get me, my men killed him. I gave orders, and his mama gave orders to kill me. But they didn't. There were lots of threats on me, and I've got lots of enemies, now. That's the reason I got a burglar alarm on this house.

I may have been rough, but I was more or less on the FBI side. I didn't wear the big hat or the boots, and the pistol I kept hid all the time, and then I introduced the radio. This was the only county-wide radio system in Texas at one time. The lie detector was bought by the people for me, the county did not buy it. The people bought the airplane for me, too. In other words, I tried to be modern.

I learned fingerprinting by book work. I stayed awake at night studying when I was constable. I could read a fingerprint backwards, too. When I went to Washington, D.C., I taught fingerprinting. J. Edgar Hoover told me, says, "You know more about it than our man does." I was asked to go to the F.B.I. Academy. They were gonna make a lie detector operator and fingerprint man out of me, but I said, "Uh uh! I'm still sheriff of Wharton County and I gotta go back there."

I kept a single fingerprint file here, and I studied it hard. That was before it got to be such a widely-known thing. If you don't know what a fingerprint is, you better leave it alone. You could take a fingerprint with a piece of silk, if it was in grease—if somebody had robbed a restaurant and had grease on their fingers. Only way you could do it was with a piece of silk and iodine crystals. And you could take a fingerprint by blowing a cigarette ash on it, if it was a good fingerprint. And a fingerprint on paper was another different situation. You had a powder that you brushed on there that made the fingerprints pop up, and then you had a plastic thing that would take the print off. I fingerprinted everybody that come in the jail. Everybody that was present was fingerprinted and pictured, it didn't make any difference who it was. I had a big file, a nice file, when I left there. That had a lot of effect on people, you bet your life!

We stopped all that mess around here. All them thieves, they dodged this county for a while, we had 'em dodging this county. They called me the white sheriff, and they'd dodge around me, too! I kept a file on all of 'em, I kept one fingerprint on file for all of 'em, and I took pictures, I kept pictures, of every man. They knew I could clear a case down here. And a thief is a funny thing. A man that will rob a bank, he won't break into a house. A man that will break into a house won't rob a bank. And a man that'll write a check, he won't highjack. And a man that'll steal a piece of wire, he won't steal a horse. They have their ways of operating. Just like the Good Lord has a way of making a white man out of you, and a black man out of a black man, and a hound dog out of a hound dog, and a greyhound out of a greyhound, and a racehorse out of a racehorse, you just don't change. I kept a file on all that, too, and they knew it. They knew I could clear a case down here, and they dodged this county.

The lie detector broke a lot of cases, too. You hook a man's fingers up to it, see, and put a thing across his chest. It reads the heartbeat and there's an electrical reading. Everything I caught that I didn't know,

I put on the lie detector. A fellow called me one day, says, "A smart-alec run me off the road down here on my own ranch." So I went down there and found this man stashed out in the woods. I thought he was a suspicious guy. He had a bunch of fine clothes, women's clothes, in his car. I brought him up here and the county attorney's office says, "I want you to turn him a-loose." I said, "I'm not gonna do it, 'cause he's killed somebody." He said, "How do you know? The lawyers are gonna make his bond." I says, "They're not gonna make his bond, I'm not gonna let 'em make his bond, because he killed somebody." I said, "You better start your *capulus, capulus* going, 'cause I'm damn sure going to hold him."

I called John Moore of the *Houston Post*. I said, "John, I've got a story and I want you to write it up," and he did. And the district attorney from Cape Girardeau, Missouri, called me up and said, "Boy, you've got our man." He flew down to get him. He had killed this newspaper woman. Everything that I caught that I didn't know, I put on the lie detector, and he had responded very muchly to it, to the question about murder.

Then, I had an airplane, though the county commissioners didn't buy it for me. When I called for one dollar for that airplane, one-dollar bills came from Russia, they came from everywhere. I talked it on the radio and I put it in the papers, about sending me the one dollars. I wouldn't take but one dollar from any person, and I put all their 6,500 names on the airplane. I had in big letters on the side of this airplane, "A Buck for Buck," and "The Spirit of the People."

I used it a lot, once I learned how to fly. If we had a car stolen, something like that, I'd get after it. Then, I'd go across country and pick up a lot of people in it, too. The penitentiary system would mark the areas around as (sectors) A, B, C, or D. If they broke, they'd call me to fly over, say, "They're over in A or they're in B," or so on. And I'd fly out, and those convicts didn't know if you could see 'em down in those woods or not. They'd start running again, and the dogs would pick the trail up.

The KULP radio station in El Campo run a straight line to my office and paid me to do a 15-minute broadcast every morning at 7:30, six days a week. I'd go on the air and I'd say, "I've got a warrant for you, Joe Doe. You gonna have to come in. If you don't, I'm coming after you." One time I had a drunk preacher in here, and I had him on the radio telling about the evils of drinking. Then I'd report on what had gone on in the county overnight. People sure did enjoy it, too.

People do not realize the power of the press. You see, I wrote a daily column for the *Houston Post,* and I didn't put any periods or commas, I didn't know that difference. A county judge said, "He didn't know a dot from a dash," and he was right. Then, I wrote a weekly column for seven or eight different local papers, including one that translated me into Czech. But people do not realize the power of the press, the press has got a powerful lot of power. Homer Garrison laughed at me when I told him, "I want you to keep the Highway Patrol out of my county." He said, "Why?" I said, "Because they don't know the difference between right and wrong," and he laughed. But in two weeks time, when I started writing for the *Post*, things changed up fast! I was writing stories about what the Highway Patrol was doing, and it wasn't long till they got out. I told 'em, "Now, when I need a Ranger, I'll send for him."

They were working up and down the highway, and I didn't like what they was doing. I called 'em all together at one time in the courthouse one New Year's Day. I said, "Now, fellows, let's have an understanding. I'm the predominant officer. The county judge has got a job, the JP's got a job, the constable's got a job, the sheriff's got a job, the Highway Patrol's got a job, the district attorney's got a job. You tend to your business and let them tend to theirs, and don't you try to tell them how to run their business, 'cause if you do, you're in trouble." All right, they didn't do that. They kept on telling the judges what to fine a man. I couldn't stand that, I run 'em out.

Jim Scarborough of Kleberg County came up here, says, "How'd you get them goddamn Highway Patrolmen out?" I told him. He says, "I got to get 'em out of my county!"

But that was a result of the power of the press. I believed in the power of the press. If you print this, you ought to print one of my columns from the Wharton newspaper. And if you do, print it just like I wrote it.

Thursday, October 8, 1953

Tradegy, struck hard in our county for early Saturday morning and late Saturday Afternoon—near Rancho Grande Road on Hy. 59, it was a head on, a group of young folks strangers in our County met head on with a local colored woman of our county—the woman probably had no idea as to what was taking place, she died instantly as the Officers report, the car loaded with young people were inroute home from a football game near Corpus, they glanced off the side of a truck after sideswiging it, and ran into the car the colored woman was driving—Officers report the young folks are in a most serious condition at the Hospital in Wharton at this time—late of the afternoon near Hungerford, for no apparent reason as the report goes, it was a Colored man in a pickup that didn't make the curve, and the pickup rolled, the man was thrown and the pickup rolled over him—he had no idea as to what it was hit him.

For years the officers have learned it, where there is one, you can look for a series of three very serious accidents or deaths—it was two and who knows among those now in the Hospital it may before all is done be the third—altho we pray not, one can never tell when people are inside seriously injured.

In Eagle Lake our neighbor, it was the Night Police Officer that made the call—the call to that man no doubt was nothing more than the regular nightly local disturbance call, no doubt the officer went as usual, thinging no more of making the call, than of hollering at the speeding car, he didn't have much chance the man he knew—before he had handled him—before in handling him it had been routine—such is always the case with any and all Police Officers, that man was crazed, he was mad, from reports his troubles were woman troubles—and with men, when in trouble with women, all ways it should by all officers be considered as serious troubles—that local well known colored man, likely completely off his rockers, caring not—and thinking not, grabbed the officer, before the officer had time to think, he was disarmed and then his brain penetrated by the bullet from his own gun. That man, as the column is being written is running, where likely few will ever know, before his troubles were little, now his troubles are great—his days of running now are few—for few indeed is there of the evil dooer that for long keeps running. Such is bad, such is the life of any man that is a pistol packer, never is it he is warned, each case regardless of how little or how big to the officer should be at all times classed as serious—such has happened, and such from now on until the end of time will again happen—I now am no officer, as I now see it, never gain will I be an Officer, but from now until the end, there will be in my heart a feeling for the Officer—the lot of the officer is not good, and indeed with the people, few indeed is there of them that realize the for ever chances the officer is daily for the benefit of you the people and a bare living taking. Each Officer daily takes new and many chances, the wrong doers, they know those that are the simbols of decent living, the officers at most times have an iota of an idea whom it is in the next car he will stop, or who the man is he will next be after to arrest. It has been by many said the Officers they are worth a dime a dozen—true in many instances there are people that can be hired as dime a dozen Officers—but never you should forget it, there are no Officers that are dime a dozen men.

——*Wharton Spectator*

FRANK
BRUNT

★

Cherokee County was a pretty rough place when I was growing up there. There was a fine man, a well-thought-of man, down there by the name of Miller Hoover, a schoolteacher. Back when I was just a big old kid about 15, me and my cousin Billy Boyd and I were knowing him, and there was a tent show out there across from the Ford place in Alto. We slipped in the back end of this tent show, and after a while we heard a shot outside and went back out the way we come in. We had a city marshall by the name of Jim Nelson, and a man that lived out there in the country by the name of Gully Landrum. He was drunk, and the city marshall got ahold of him and was trying to carry him over to the jailhouse. Then Mr. Hoover—a big fellow, wore a number 12 shoe—walked up there and said he wasn't gonna let him (Jim) take him (Gully) to jail. Jim pulled his pistol, and they got to wrestling and he shot Mr. Hoover in the stomach.

That's when we went out there. It was about half a block over to the doctor's office. We walked down that sidewalk, and I can still see them number 12 bloody tracks. Blood was running down his britches leg into his shoe and overflowed, and it made a track of blood every-

where he went across there. They later took him to the hospital and
he died the next day. They tried that city marshall on it, and he come
clear. Mr. Hoover was a fine man, but he was a little out of place trying to take a prisoner away from the city marshall.

I was born and reared near Alto in Cherokee County, born July 24,
1913. At that time we lived about five miles from Alto in what we called
the Central High community. When I was four my parents bought a
place closer in to Alto so we could go to the schoolhouse there. Father
had 120 acres. About 50 acres of it we farmed, the rest of it was pasture.
In those days we depended on cotton and tomatoes for a living. That's
what we did, we raised corn, cotton, and tomatoes; tomatoes was the
cash crop. At that time they didn't think they could grow tomatoes
anywhere much but East Texas.

I can look back on never thinking about going into law enforcement,
but when my brother Bill was a junior and senior in high school, the
principal, when he saw a little trouble a-brewing, called him in and
told him what to do to try to break it up. I guess he had a lot of natural
ability. He was captain of his football team, and after he graduated I
was captain of my football team two years. And the superintendent
(principal) kind of done me the same way he had Bill.

Bill graduated in '28 and I graduated in '33. He went to Houston
and went to work as a special officer on the Southern Pacific Railroad.
A real depression hit in '29 and '30, and he got laid off. He joined the
Navy and was in the Navy four years. Course, I was awful proud of
him, he was heavyweight champion of the *Saratoga* at that time. He
loved that old ship. When he had joined the Navy and doctors had
examined him—when he made application—Dr. Redman made the remark that he was the most perfect human being that he'd ever examined.

I went out there (San Diego, California) to visit him one time—
hitchhiked out there, me and a couple of other boys, hoboed on freight
trains. Went out to the base to see him, and Wallace Beery and Clark
Gable were out there making this picture, *Hell Divers*. They were using his squadron, and he carried me over to where they were making
this picture. Course, I recognized 'em soon as I saw 'em. Anyhow, I
visited him.

Well, about a year before he got discharged, my brother Bill came
in from the Navy on a furlough, and I was real proud of him. One afternoon we decided we'd walk uptown and visit at the corner drugstore, that's where all the people come in and hung out. While we was
standing outside the drugstore, here come four well-known thugs, the
toughs of the town, down the street. They had a gallon of whiskey
and was wobbling around drunk. There was nobody that would fool

with 'em then. The officers was about half afraid of 'em. They were mean! Well, down close to where we were, 'bout fifty feet I'd say, here come a young black man across the opposite side of the street. He didn't even come close to 'em, he walked out in the dirt street trying to avoid 'em, but he was happy and singing and he spoke to 'em there.

Well, this fellow, the main tough of the four, looked over there and said, "Hey, Nigger, come here." He went out there and hit him on the head several times, and my brother just walked out there and stopped it, got ahold of him and pulled him off this black fellow. Says, "What's the matter here?" "Oh," he says, "this black SB (sic) owes me for a pint of whiskey." My brother says, "Well, you whupped him enough, you leave him alone." Then he looked up at my brother and called him a nigger-loving SB (sic). When he did, Bill hit him with that left hand and knocked him about 20 feet, and the fight started. We kind of had a knock-down-and-drag-out down there, but Bill gave him all he wanted, right quick. I remember several people had run up there to watch the fight and were tickled to death to see this fellow get a whupping, or for somebody to even challenge him. I heard one of the men, I think it was the superintendent (principal), make the remark, "If he's got the courage to challenge that bunch, when he gets out of the Navy we ought to make him city marshall."

This bunch in Alto, people was actually scared to serve on a jury against 'em. They figured if they did and they convicted 'em, they might slip around and burn their barn or their house up, shoot 'em in the dark, or something else. They would jump on people and whup 'em and beat 'em nearly to death right in the middle of town, and nothing done about it.

When I was just in high school they had a man down there at Alto by the name of Grady Carlton, the city marshall, and this group around there was trying to get rid of him. One time this man was in town drunk on his horse, and these boys got ahold of him and ribbed him up. This city marshall was trying to get him to go on home, but he wouldn't do it. So, the city marshall wanted to arrest him and put him in jail, but those boys kind of ganged there and got with him. One of 'em got up behind him on the horse, I never will forget that, ribbing him up, you know. He was the type you could rib up, and when he was drinking he was mean and tough.

So, somebody went and called the sheriff, and Sheriff Richard Grey and his deputy, Spence Swan, came down there. Right in front of where Bud's Drugstore is now, they stopped their Model A and got out. The city marshall met 'em there. They was all ganged up and the drunk man out there on his horse. The sheriff must have encouraged the marshall or something, but he went off his rocker, lost control of himself, and started shooting at the drunk on his horse with his .44 right down through Main Street. The old drunk would kick that horse and he'd rare up, and he'd holler, "Shoot, you yellow bastard!" And *"BOOM! BOOM!,"* he emptied that pistol but didn't hit him. 'Bout (the) time the marshall fired the last shot, the drunk spurred that horse and took off. He went to the house and got his rifle and started back. Sheriff and his deputy started to Nacogdoches, went up there about four or five blocks. There was a street that turned and went up by the drunk's house, and they got out of their car and here come the drunk on that horse. They tried to stop him, the drunk cut down on them, he shot the sheriff in the arm, and then the drunk got away. They left their car there. I never will forget, it was a brand new A-Model sedan. There was a box of .38s laying on the back seat. They walked through fields and woods about three miles out there to a man by the name of Bloomer Florence's place, and got him to go down to Linwood, that's over toward Nacogdoches, and cut back and take 'em to Rusk. They carried the sheriff to a doctor and got his arm dressed and sent down there and got the car. They had that right there on the main street of Alto.

That's one of the first times I ever thought about being an officer. My brother and I both says, "Well, don't believe I'd let one run me out of town." But I actually saw that with my own eyes.

Another time, this gang I was telling you about, this older brother who didn't run with this main four, he had a business there, and he had a T-Model roadster. Two of these old boys wanted to go down in there to Dogtown and get 'em some whiskey and they wanted to use his car, and he wouldn't let 'em have it. They'd all been drinking. They was over there about where Mr. Hoover got shot. They went out there and got in his car and started down the road toward Nacogdoches. I can see him just as plain—he run out in the middle of the street with his pistol, *"BLOOM! BLOOM! BLOOM!"* They stopped, and directly here come old Buddy Joe down there holding his butt. It had gone through the car and hit him right in the butt and he was bleeding. Directly, they go over there to the doctor's office and the doctor dug that bullet out, and then they went to Dogtown and got 'em some whiskey.

Well, after a year and a half, Bill was discharged from the Navy, and soon as he got home, they offered him a job as city marshall. It only paid 60 dollars a month, but he didn't have anything else to do, so he took the job. That was 1935. He was city marshall of Alto and he knew what he was getting into.

He'd been working about two or three months when the night watchman there, by the name of Arthur Ross, wanted to take a little vacation, and my brother asked me if I would work in his place for a week. I decided I would, so, on Sunday afternoon about five o'clock I went up there. I had my pistol with me and a flashlight, and my brother looked over there and saw what I was wearing and says, "Here, take my pistol if you're gonna work tonight." I took his pistol, a nice .44 Smith and Wesson, pearl-handled, and put it on.

We were there right beside the back end of this drugstore, and just north of it was what we called "Chinatown" at that time. There was an old cafe and a pool hall, a gambling hall, and just above that was a barber shop, and by it a garage, all under one roof.

Anyhow, I was there fixing my flashlight when here come two of these main toughies, pretty drunk-looking. They passed in front of us and went over to a domino hall about a hundred yards down the street. When Bill saw 'em he told me, "I better go over there and tell 'em to get on out of town." Well, I was fooling with my flashlight, getting it ready, and when I looked down there where they were, they were in a fight. I ran down there and Bill was bleeding across the nose, one of 'em had cut him with a knife. He said, "Hand me my pistol." Then he whopped both of 'em up beside the head and kicked 'em in the seat of the britches, and marched 'em on down there and put 'em in that little old jail.

Well, that was against their dignity to be locked up in that thing, specially in their hometown. Anyhow, we put 'em in there and went on over to the doctor's office. Doctor McDonald had an office upstairs in the back of Allen's Drugstore. Bill wanted to get his nose patched up and cleaned up, but in the meantime some of 'em had called the ringleader of this little gang, and here he come running down there, sliding in on two wheels. He jumped out and just about that time my brother came downstairs from the doctor's office. The drugstore was full of people. He challenged my brother and commenced cussing and raising sand about how he was going to do so-and-so, and shaking his fist in his face, saying, "You get over there and turn 'em out!" He just kept on, and directly Bill hit him in the jaw and knocked him plum out of that thing. Then he kicked him in the seat of the britches and marched him over there and put *him* in jail. And that's something that's never been heard of in Alto.

Well, they decided they'd kill him, and set up a deal two weeks later. They owned this building back of where the garage set, there'd been two or three killings in that building already. It was really an old bootleg joint, at one time an old saloon. Anyhow, this ringleader put three of 'em in there with pistols. They got situated in certain spots. Had a screen door and then had big heavy plate glass on each side. Then the ringleader come out on the street and got in his car, and just gunned it and whupped and slid around, you know, just to attract my brother Bill's attention.

Bill blew his whistle at him and tried to stop him. He said, "Oh, go to hell," cussed him, and went around to this building and parked and went in. That was the decoy, you know. Bill didn't even have his pistol on, so he walked around there and got his .44 and put it on and walked up to that building. The ringleader was standing at the end of the counter, the old bar, with his pistol in his hand, sort of tucked away under the other arm. And the other three was scattered around in the building. That building just had a screen door, and when Bill started to get hold of that screen door to pull it, they started shooting. Course, Bill stepped back and started shooting through that heavy plate glass. He hit this man right on the heart and killed him, and they shot Bill in the leg. The constable over at the Chevrolet place was watching. When this fellow fell, the other three run out the back door and Bill hollered for the constable to go around and head 'em, but this man went the other way.

Well, they got the ambulance over there and carried this man to Nacogdoches, but he died before they got there. They got down there about the river and saw he was dead, so they turned around and come back.

I had a date with my wife and my cousin had a date with her sister. We drove into town and saw all that crowd of people, and when we heard what was going on we carried them home right quick and went and got us a pistol and come back. After he had had his leg dressed, Bill come down out of the doctor's office and we went with him and got the rest of 'em and put 'em in jail.

Course, from then on we began to have threats. They said, "We gonna kill you," meaning both of us. At that time Bill never had even bought a car. He was living out there with my sister and her husband, right at the city limits. It was about half a mile out of the main part of town, and we'd walk home at nights. We'd always walk at an angle. I was carrying a .45 too, I'd be on one side of the street and he'd be on the other, 'cause we figured they was gonna waylay us. If they did that, he said, "At the first shot fired, we'll drop, and maybe we'll get one of 'em."

We did that several nights, but they never did try to waylay us there. But one night he and I was standing there in front of a little old cafe and one of this main gang leader's brothers drove up. He was the most peaceful one of 'em, but he was mean, too. He called Bill out to the car, and before I knew it they drove off, 'cause Bill wasn't scared of him. But what he intended to do, we don't know. He got out of town and went down a country road, a side road. He stopped and made out like he was gonna have to use the bathroom. Bill just punched him with that .44, says, "If you stop, and if anything starts, I'm gonna get you first." Punched it pretty close up in his heart and he kept driving, but I think they was out there fixing to kill him (Bill).

By then, even the ambulance man, the undertaker, had got in his ambulance and started looking for him. And about that time was the first time I ever saw my father excited. Some of 'em got him up, and here my cousins come with some more guns. There was several relatives come in there bringing shotguns—on their side and our side, too. Oh, it was shaky there, I know! The sheriff was kind of a weakling, and he come down. They were standing there talking and I said, "Well, why the hell won't y'all go down there and see if you can find 'em?" They just looked at me and didn't say nothing. I wasn't but about 20 years old.

Anyhow, in a little while the ambulance driver come back and said, "I found 'em. They're going around all over, they're still moving." When they got back Bill told us what happened.

For a while there, people almost lost a crop coming to town to see the next killing. But the thing went on and settled down, and I went to Houston, then, and went to work as a special officer for Southern Pacific Railroad, the same place Bill used to work. They got after him to run for sheriff, and he was elected.

Englewoods Yard, where I started, was the biggest yard in the South other than New Orleans. There was 50-some-odd tracks in that one yard. Trains going and coming all the time, hauling whiskey, cigarettes, and all those kinds of things. And times wasn't so good, we had lots of people hoboing. Sometimes we'd put 30, 40, 50, 75 people out of that yard at night. The other thing was to keep 'em from breaking in those boxcars to get cigarettes and whiskey, and sometimes we'd have to ride those trains. We even had one thief, one time, that would catch that train, come down that ladder beside the door, break the seal, kick the door open and swing in, and throw out cases of cigarettes. Then he'd come back with a truck and pick 'em up. We caught two at Rosenberg one night that had gone to the penitentiary seven years before that, and had been out three days, then robbed the same train.

In certain circumstances we rode the trains. I know one time the chief called me in and says, "That special train is going out of here in the morning with that Rice football team and fans, going to Dallas to play SMU. And back in the baggage room they'll put down that big drum and they'll start shooting craps." And says, "We've got two or three professionals who've been getting on that train and beating those college boys out of their money. I want you to get on there and ride that train and put a stop to that."

Well, that just suited me. I was ready to go the next morning, and when that train pulled out, I was on it. I let 'em get about 50 miles out and I went back to the baggage room and here was that big crowd around that big old drum. I looked down there, and there was two old boys I knew from East Texas, professional gamblers. I just walked up to an old boy by the name of Patrick and says, "Come here, boys. Y'all got to get out of here. You boys are out of your class. You get out of here and stay out or I'll put you off of this train." They thanked me and got up and that's all there was to that. Then I enjoyed the game and the ride.

You know, on the refrigerator cars, on each end, they had a little door up on top. You can open it and close it, and there's a pretty big little area down in there. That's where they used to put ice when they shipped our tomatoes. I've got a many a hobo out of those things. And, of course, those gondolas, those open cars that haul coal, gravel, stuff like that, lots of times they'd be in there. And course, there's always some empty cars and they'd get in there, too. I'd open one of those things up and they'd be 15 or 20 in there.

Most of 'em was just some old boys trying to go somewhere and get a job, but then you had your professionals. I know one time I took an old boy off the train. Across the street from our office at the railroad yards was a little cafe. I had seen this old boy in there several times. He just made a habit of riding up and down the railroad, maybe come through there every month. He used a crutch and was supposed to be crippled. I got him off there one time, and got him outside, off the property, and said something to him, and he got smart and cussed me out good and proper. Well, he was off the company property and I just took it and went on, but it wasn't but about three weeks till one night I got up on top of one of them refrigerator cars and looked down in there and there he was. I said, "All right, get out of there." He got out and hit the ground, and when I got through with him he wasn't even using that crutch. He was just a natural bum; he wasn't any more crippled than I was.

After a while, my partner and I were working at what they called Clinton Docks—the Southern Pacific shipline, Morgan Shipline, at that time. We had to go down and police those ships when they were unloading. I'd just started on this daylight job. We drove up that morning and relieved the two men that had worked the night before. We were out in the driveway exchanging greetings and talking a few minutes when the telephone rang. A boy by the name of Codger run down there and answered the phone and hollered for me. "Brunt, it's for you. Your wife wants to talk to you." Well, I felt for my pistol and my billfold, the two things I had to have, 'cause I had my commission and my badge in that billfold. I knew there was something wrong by her calling. It scared me to death and I run down there, and she told me Bill was dead.

Bill knew the fellow that killed him and had said he was dangerous. Why he walked up a-side that car and didn't make him get out, I don't know. He always told me, "They'll get me someday, but I'll get the one that gets me." And he did. He didn't see no fear, that was his trouble.

Bill just had two deputies at that time, Leon Halbert and Burl Avra. They had a bootlegger that had been causing a lot of trouble, and they were trying to catch him. They figured this man was hauling a load out of Kilgore, so my brother sent his two deputies up to the Smith–Cherokee County line down at Bullard, south of Tyler, and he went by himself down (Highway) 69 to watch that way. That was at about four o'clock in the morning on August the third, 1939.

Bill hadn't been there but an hour when he met this car, and sure enough, it was driven by this man Isiah Creel. He had a woman with him that he just carried along as a blind. My brother turned around and turned his siren on, but Creel wouldn't pull over. He was trying to get to his house on 69 just north of Rusk about three miles. My brother shot left-handed, and he shot both left tires out on the car, and finally Creel stopped. According to the woman that was with Creel, he told her to look back and see if anyone else was with him, and she looked back and said, "No, he's alone." Creel took a .35 thumb-buster pistol and stuck it under his arm, and as my brother approached the side of the car, he just raised up and pulled the trigger. The bullet struck my brother just over the heart. I guess Creel tried to get out of the car as my brother was falling, because Creel had three .45 bullets in him and they were all ranging up. Creel and my brother died right there on 69 right on the center stripe.

After the funeral the next day, the county attorney asked me if I would consider coming back and working as a deputy under Bill's wife. The commissioners would appoint his wife to serve out his term, which was customary. So, after I considered it, I told 'em I would, and I took a six months leave of absence from Southern Pacific Railroad. And after working up there a while, people got me to run for sheriff, and I decided I would, and ran, and was elected, and never did go back to the railroad.

I was just the deputy sheriff at first, but being the brother of Bill Brunt, everybody come to me instead of going to a woman. That's just a courtesy that most commissioners do when a sheriff is killed, to appoint the widow to serve out that term. That's just a little insurance money. Some of 'em, you know, they take it to heart, but then they get up there and soon find out they're out-placed. I was more or less acting sheriff. If I hadn't of had two of the best deputies in the world, there would have been some jealousy; but fortunately, I had two of the best men, the best deputy sheriffs, I ever knew. I just took over and run it. Burl Avra told a friend of mine here awhile back, says, "The day Frank Brunt walked in that office he was sheriff."

Bill and his deputies had been working on the bootleggers pretty good, and he had the county in good shape. But after he got killed, I think they thought that I was a little young and soft, and they all started back. But I changed their mind(s), I went to work on 'em. You take, for instance, in the north end of the county, the Jacksonville area, they was most just what you call "hip-pocket bootleggers." And some of 'em was just regular bootleggers. The nearest wet area was Kilgore, so they'd go over there and get a pickup load of liquor and beer and bring it back and sell it out. They was making one-hundred percent on anything they could get in bottles, legal whiskey, "bond," they called it then. They'd pay $2.50 for a pint of whiskey when they bought that case, then they doubled their money on it. During that tomato season I was telling you about, when we had so many people to come in and everybody was working and making a little money, the boot-leggers would really bloom out.

So, I got some Texas Liquor Control Board undercover men in there one time, turned 'em a-loose and told 'em what I wanted 'em to do and where to go, and they made about 30 cases on different people for selling whiskey. We started around in there one Saturday, and we liked to filled the jail up with bootleggers. And with a few licks like that, well, I got 'em on the run.

They's (a) lot of fine people went down there and bought whiskey. Cherokee County, all the time I was sheriff, was one of the finest counties in the state of Texas. Fine people, the majority of 'em, but there was very few homes in our county didn't have some whiskey in 'em. They'd drink, but they kept to themselves, didn't get out in public. Course, you had a few that would get out and get drunk. But the majority of 'em like to drink, some of the finest people that was down there. After they legalized it, if you lived in a dry county the law was that you could go to a wet county and bring back one case of beer and one fifth of whiskey. I tried to educate 'em, told 'em that "If you want to drink it, don't go down there to Dogtown and buy this rotgut, go over here and buy legal whiskey. You just bring back a case of beer and one quart of whiskey and take it home and drink it, don't get out on the highway."

Well, a lot of 'em did that, but at football games they'd want a fifth, and they'd send a couple of old boys over to Kilgore to bring back liquor, five or six or a dozen quarts, and they'd get to drinking at the football game and I'd have trouble. I got to where on Friday afternoon I'd got out there on the highway, and I could spot 'em as soon as I saw 'em, them old boys coming back. I wouldn't arrest 'em. They'd have four or five quarts in there of pretty expensive liquor, maybe a case or two of beer, and I'd make 'em pour it out. Lots of times I done it, I feel kind of mean about it now. About 90 percent of it, somebody had given 'em the money to buy 'em some, so they'd be out of liquor and had lost their money. I'd say, "You boys can pour it out or go with me to the jailhouse." They'd get out there and open it up, and look back at me, and pour out a little, and look back again! I see people now, getting up in years, kids that I made do that. But they still treat me nice, I'm surprised at some of 'em. I used (to do) a little target practice on those 50-dollar bottles of Jack Daniels, sometimes. Looking back, I kind of hate that I did that, but it smelt so good!

Moonshining was another problem. Legal, what we called bonded whiskey, was a new thing, and a lot of people had been buying that old corn whiskey down there for years, and they just didn't want to give it up. We had some people down there that had the reputation of making some of the best that was. They had to go a good ways to get bonded whiskey, and take a chance of being caught, and it took a right smart of money. And at that time sugar and corn chops were so cheap, I think they said they could make a gallon of whiskey for about 30 cents. When I went to high school in 1930 you could buy a half a gallon for 75 cents. Later it was three dollars a gallon.

In earlier days in Cherokee County these moonshiners had the federals paid off, but before that, they had the sheriff's department taken care of. If the federals come in, usually it's customary to get with the sheriff to raid the still, if you both trusted one another. It got to where, when the federals come into the county, the sheriff would get on the telephone and call the main bootleggers and tell 'em, "You better bring your clothes off the line, it looks like it gonna rain." That was the signal. Everybody went and hid their whiskey and shut their stills down. That was true. I had heard that the biggest part of my life.

Down in the south end of Cherokee County, on that Buckshot Road, they's about 12 or 14 houses down there on that road to the river and everybody made whiskey except two people, and they'd come from far and near to buy that corn whiskey. That community was known as Dogtown. With what we called a pretty-good-sized still, they'd have 10 or 20 50-gallon barrels out there, with usually a little log cabin or something built around them and with hay down between 'em to keep 'em warm in cold weather to keep it fermenting. They'd keep that with chops and sugar and rye, sometimes. It would ferment for so long, and then they would start cooking it in that copper kit. It comes out of a little copper tube into a five-gallon demijohn. It looks like vapor to start with, just vapor, comes out just as white pretty crystal as you ever looked at. Then it settles down and has a little color to it. Sometimes they would color it a little. Course, if it was put in charcoal barrels, it colored itself. Some of the cheap ones, the fly-by-nights, got to cooking some in those iron oil barrels, and they'd sometime get poison out of that. I had a pretty good friend died there in Houston from drinking some rotgut white lightning.

On that Buckshot Road back in the moonshining days, most of the bridges then was built out of this heavy oak lumber. And they'd get a little loose anyhow, but they'd help 'em to get loose. I've driven over a many an old bridge, and it'd rattle, you know. You hit one of them old bridges and it'd make quite a noise. Well, that would cause the first neighbors close from that bridge to look and see who's coming. Maybe you wasn't gonna stop at their house at all, but they'd see you. And if they recognized you, when you passed they'd go out there and shoot a gun. And you'd go on down about a mile or so and maybe hear another gun. And that was just a signal that there was officers in the community.

So, they didn't think that could be broke up, but I went out one night and got three of 'em. I knew an old boy really considered to be a Negro, but he was white, a halfbreed. I picked him up and found some whiskey on him and tried to put a little pressure on him, and he told me where a local still was. So we went and got that. We'd bring those copper cookers in and sell 'em to scrap dealers to buy ammunition. I put a little more pressure on him, and he told me about two more old boys that was cooking whiskey down there in the Dogtown area. You ask anybody down south of here where Dogtown is and they'll tell you. That's where that Buckshot Road goes through.

Then I met two down there, and I got out and got me a persimmon limb and talked to 'em a little bit, and they told me where theirs were. So we went and got it, tore it up, poured out the liquor and stuff, and got the copper kit. I was looking for the king bee, he was a little related to me. I had been to him and asked him to quit when I went in as deputy sheriff, because I thought a lot of him. I stayed some at his house, and his boys used to stay with me. But he more-the-less made fun of me coming to him, and made some remarks that he had two black men cooking for him that I'd never get to talk. Well, this second pair we got that night told us where his still was.

Anyhow, we got in there just before daylight, back in the woods on the southwest side of Alto. Whiskey had always been made out east, but they had moved over there way back out of the way on the west

Tom Brown of Caldwell in the late 1930's. At this time he was Sheriff
Walter Ellison's chief deputy.

Jess Sweeten at
about the time he
became sheriff of
Henderson County
(1933).

Sheriff Corbett
Akins and father in
the Panola County
sheriff's office,
around 1943.

Sheriff Gaston
Boykin of
Comanche County
leading a parade
into Comanche,
Texas, around 1950.

"Buckshot" Lane of Wharton County in early 1940's.

Cherokee County sheriff Frank Brunt with drugstore burglers in the county jail, early 1940's.

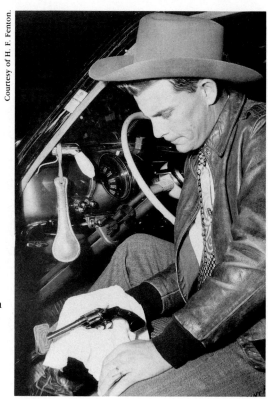

Sheriff H. F. Fenton examines a murder weapon, around 1950. The object dangling from the spotlight control is a ''slapper.''

H. F. and Loretta Fenton of Coleman County, around 1950.

Truman Maddox, sheriff of Austin County, 1953 to the present.

Sheriff I. R. "Nig" Hoskins in the 1930's. At this time he was "dog captain" with the Texas Department of Corrections, Harlem #1, Raymondville, Texas.

Jim Scarborough I, sheriff of Lee County (and later Kleberg County), sometime in the 1880's.

Jim Scarborough II,
sheriff of Kleberg
County for 37
years.

Jim Scarborough III,
sheriff of Kleberg
County.

"Rufe" Jordan, sheriff of Gray County, 1951 to the present.

side of the county, near a sawmill site way back in the pineywoods. I got up about as far as I figured we could drive without disturbing 'em before daylight. I got out and walked through those woods and got up on a little old hill, and down at the bottom of that hill I could see steam coming up, vapor from those copper cookers. I could see two black men sitting there, and two dogs sitting there, all four of 'em asleep. I knew if I woke 'em up, they'd take off through those woods. So I crawled down close as I could get, and when I got to a certain point I motioned for 'em (the deputies) to come on, and I broke and run just hard as I could right down there on 'em. And I got down there and had to tap 'em on the shoulder to wake 'em up. Those whiskey stills was just a-blubbering, and there was about a hundred gallons of whiskey and about five or six sacks of sugar and seven or eight sacks of chops. I had to send back to Alto to get a truck to haul it out.

But I had set this Mathis, the first one we caught, on this truck— (and) I saw him 20 years later. He went through the woods 10 miles to the highway and made it someway to California. Had a sister there. And when I resigned and come back to Alto one day and went into a colored barbecue, there he was. He like to fainted! He still gets nervous when he sees me.

But I brought 'em in and put 'em in jail. I got ahold of the investigators for the Alcohol Beverages Commission, the federals. One good investigator come out of New Orleans, and he made a conspiracy case against the owners of this still. He checked there where they'd been buying their sugar and chops and stuff for years, and made a case on it, a good case, one of the prettiest jobs I've seen for investigation of that type. They tried 'em here in Tyler at federal court. Judge Randolph Bryant was the federal judge, and he gave this white man two years in the penitentiary, the first time any of 'em got that punishment, and he gave those black men about a year suspended. I filed on 'em in county court, and they had to stay in jail down there a year or two. They didn't even want to leave that jail when they got out, my kids thought as much of 'em almost as they did of me.

Down in the Dogtown area where most of the colored bootleggers lived, there was a little old white man named John Woods. Course, he made a little outlaw whiskey. Sometimes his children would be sitting up at the dinner table with an old keg of whiskey for share. That's true. And if you'd go down there to buy a half gallon or a gallon, he'd pour you out a peanut butter glass about half-full, enough to make you drunk, a sample.

Anyhow, on Sunday, these old boys in the country would go up there and hang out—kind of congregate there, some of the old stragglers that lived around there. There were several there one Sunday when two deputy sheriffs drove up and were going to talk to Mr. Woods and search him. Naturally—and I've seen it happen a lot of times when I'd drive up—those stragglers started easing off soon as their backs were turned, 'fraid that they might want to pick them up. And this particular Sunday, Mr. Woods had a neighbor down there by the name of Mr. John Cruseturner, and he was sitting out on his (own) front porch rared back against the wall in a straight chair reading the *Alto Herald*. He lived two-hundred yards from John Woods, his neighbor, and you could see the house. This old boy walked up there and said, "Mr. Cruseturner, the law's down there at John Woods a-raiding him." Course, Mr. Cruseturner was a nervous type of old gentleman. He flew that paper right straight up and hollered. "Where in the hell does John Wood(s) live?" He'd been living in sight of him for 40 years. He run and grabbed his double-bitted axe and run back there in the smokehouse. And he had six five-gallon kegs and several five-gallon demijohns, and he broke a hundred gallons of whiskey and poured it out. But, when the officers got through (at John Woods), they just went on by and went on back to Rusk, never did stop at his house!

The bootleggers would come down there to Dogtown and buy it. They'd buy sometimes 25 or 40 gallons and haul it out of there. That's where we helped break it up, catching those big customers of theirs, running 'em down. When you'd catch one with a load of that corn whiskey, you'd bring him and turn him over to the federal authorities, and they'd take his automobile and all. We caught an old boy from Frankston that come over there and bought about 20 gallons of corn whiskey and started back and we caught him, and he was in a brand-new Ford. Had eight-hundred miles on it, a V-8. We brought him up here to federal court and they took his car, he had to pay a fine, and he lost his whiskey. That hits 'em a lick.

That was the way we really helped break it up in Dogtown, we'd block those roads. I like to get killed chasing 'em—get on those dirty roads in summertime and that dust fogging up, and you couldn't see where you was going. Had a bridge over there just as you cross to go over into Nacogdoches County. On that slough bridge there's a curve where we wrecked two or three. That was a good place to catch 'em—crowd 'em on that curve and wreck 'em. Most times we'd catch 'em before they got out of there to the highway. Some of 'em had their cars tuned up professional, but I had mine thataway, too. I was young and I'd give 'em a pretty good race, wonder I didn't get killed. If you got behind one and it was dry and dusty, you had a problem. It was worse than driving in the dark.

I didn't lose many, but I took a chance. I turned one over one night, I never will forget that, an old colored fellow. It threw him in the back seat, and he was laying down in the back seat with a five-gallon demijohn of whiskey on top of him and his hands over it like this. Well, I walked up there. He was waving those hands, "Don't shoot, Mr. Brunt! Don't shoot, Mr. Brunt! Don't shoot!" I said—his name was Watson—"Get out of there, Watson, I'm not gonna shoot you. I got you caught, now."

Finally, to break the whole thing up, I found an old boy that was just like an Indian in the woods. He knew every pigtrail back in that 40,000 acres of open range, and I knew that he knew who all was making whiskey. I didn't have any money to pay him, wasn't able to, but every time we'd catch one of 'em we'd bring him to Tyler, and (he) ended up getting 15 dollars out of making two or three trips up there and testifying. I (just) run across this old boy that I knew could inform, if he would. I already had 'em on the run, just about whupped down, but I knew that there was one or two that was still making a little back in there. I said to him, "Every time you find one of those stills, let me know and I'll give you 15 dollars."

Well, it wasn't a week till he knocked on my door one night, said, "I got one located." The next night I got one of my deputies and a Liquor Control man and drove in there and met him and let them out. They stayed in there the rest of the night. Right after daylight here come an old boy by the name of Wilmer French on his horse. He fired that one (still) up, had those coal oil burners under it, you know, and started cooking his whiskey. They walked out on him and got him and arrested him, and destroyed that old still. Then they called me and I sent and got 'em. We brought him up here to Tyler to federal court, then he made bond.

Three weeks later this same man came knocking on my door again. Said, "I got another one located." Well, I sent the same deputies down there, and about daylight here come a man in there on a horse—the same man. He fired her up (the still) and they walked out on him and got him again. We brought him up here and turned him over to federal authorities. Judge Randolph Bryant was the district court federal judge. When his trial came up, he was standing up before the judge, the judge was reviewing his case, says, "I see here where the officers just caught you back on June the second, and here on June the thirtieth they catch you again." He says, "Yessah, judge, I want to explain that to you." Says, "They caught me that first time cooking whiskey in my still. Now, I've decided it was a wrong thing to do, and I was riding through there that morning and found this other still. So, I fired it up and thought I would just burn it up and destroy it." The old judge had to turn his head. He was pretty lenient on him, says, "I'm gonna give you six months in the penitentiary."

Actually, that was the last one. I don't believe there's been one there since, and they had made whiskey there for many years, nearly everybody who lived down there. Times got hard and they thought they had to make it to make a living.

Stopping 'em was a hard thing to do. They didn't ever think they'd be stopped in Dogtown community, but we put the pressure on 'em and kept handling 'em and finally caught this last man that was cooking whiskey. Now it's one of the best communities we have. We stayed in there and finally broke it up; and the year I left, there was a piece in the paper that we had the cleanest county in the state of Texas, far as liquor violations were concerned.

Nineteen-forty was the time to run, though you didn't take office till '41, and I was elected sheriff on my twenty-seventh birthday. There was a man there at Rusk who was chief of police and he ran for sheriff, and I announced, and I beat him about two to one. The next time I didn't have an opponent. Then the third time a wild man got after me.

This bird had moved in there and nobody had ever heard of him. He put in a tire shop, a vulcanizing shop. Just to meet him the first time, you'd think he was great. He's one of these kind of people that push himself on you, be real nice. But a lot of these people are just trying to get to you. Anyhow, the constable's job came open. It didn't have a salary then, just got a commission, a fee for every arrest you made. But he just wanted to carry a gun. He made application for that thing and they appointed him constable. Before it was over he was out there taking money off of speeders, and had to quit that. Then he decided he'd run against me for sheriff.

I'd had some old thieves, part of 'em used to live in Cherokee County, and all had been in the penitentiary and had drifted off down there to Beaumont. One day I was over at Henderson and the sheriff told me that just the night before somebody had burglarized a store out there in the county and knocked the safe open. He told me several little items they got, like some of them gallon coal oil cans with the red top around them, and of all things, a bunch of BB shells. I said, "Sheriff, I might know who did that. I heard about these old Pearson boys doing that."

That night, me and one of the deputies drove out there to their house and run in on 'em. There was one of 'em there, and two women, and the first thing I noticed was a bunch of BB shells laying up on the mantleboard, and down at the side a brand-new gallon oil can. Well, I gathered 'em up and called Beaumont, and they gathered me up four more. And this ringleader, old Pearson, he wanted to kill me so bad he didn't know what to do. He had a little old gal he was living with, and he was training her. I thought I'd start and question her first.

Well, I never did like to slap women, and I never did do very much
of it; but I had her in there and I started questioning her, and she looked
up at me, says, "Why, you big SB (sic), that's what they're paying you
to find out." When she did (that), I slapped her plum out of that chair.
I said, "Now, you get up from there and you respect people around
here when they talk to you." She did from then on. Then I started
questioning one of the others, and I finally got a statement out of him.
Her man tried to get 'em to slip him a gun or a piece of iron in there
so he could knock me in the head. Well, we got that statement that
they had done that safe job over at Anahuac, that they had hit about
15 places, and they tried 'em in Lufkin and give 'em 35 years.

But this little gal, she made a written statement and swore to it that
I beat her and kicked her and she had a miscarriage (as a result), and
all five of those others made affidavit about me whupping 'em and
knocking 'em around. And that wild man that was running against me
had a lawyer backing him down there, and they took circulars about
that and put 'em in everybody's car and nearly every house in Cherokee
County. And for 24 hours people wanted to hang me! They'd have
impeached me if they could have, right quick. You'd look around on
the streets and you'd see 'em ganged up a-talking. Oh, they were hostile
when they'd read that. Well, it did look bad. It called me "Hitler,"
and that was during the war then!

Well, one of them old boys that had signed the affidavit was a son-
in-law of an old friend of mine, and he had never treated his wife right,
had half starved her. So, I just thought about that, and I got him over
there. You could buy a good lunch then for 35 or 40 cents, and get
a bus ticket to Jacksonville and Rusk for about four bits. I put him on
the bus and sent him to Jacksonville for several mornings. People were
ganged up talking about it, and he'd usually ease up there, you know,
and listen. When it kind of slowed down, he'd say, "Now, gentlemen,
you'll excuse me but I just want to tell you. One of 'em that signed
that affidavit is my son-in-law, and he's a sorry SB (sic). He starved
his wife to death. The rest of 'em is just like him." People would just
look, say, "Yeah, I thought that's about what it was."

And you know, the word got around. Then, in a week's time, the
tide changed and they come back to me stronger than ever. And I beat
that son-of-a-gun, and I sent him word that I had one of those circulars and if he stayed in Cherokee County he was gonna have to eat
it! He took me at my word and I haven't seen him since. And I meant
it, I intended for him to eat it.

I know there was some that wanted to kill me. In Wells there was
a man by the name of John Mason. He run a garage there in Wells.
After my brother got killed, I'll never forget, there was an ex-convict

hanging out down there by the name of Shannon Bothwell. When he got the word my brother was killed, he stretched his arms out and says, "I feel more like living today than I have in three years." That was how long my brother had been sheriff. And I heard about that and just thought to myself, "There might be another day."

And after Bill got killed, they begin to start up bootlegging again, and everything. They thought I was pretty young and soft, wasn't going to bother 'em too much. John Mason had a deal a-going, I believe he had rather make a dollar stealing than he had somebody give it to him, or earn it. He'd get these little old convicts that would get out of the penitentiary, and they'd come there and hang around. And say he wanted a '40 model Ford sedan, he'd tell 'em, "Here's 25 dollars, you go get me a '40 model Ford." And they'd go steal that Ford and bring it down there, and he had four men with his wrecking crew that would take that car over in Houston County in the Davy Crockett National Forest, and by daylight the next morning they'd have it completely dismantled. He'd take part of those parts to his place in Wells, part of 'em to Dayton, and part of 'em to Cleveland. He had those places, and he got to be wealthy handling car parts off of stolen automobiles.

I finally got an old boy up tight, and he told me about 'em fixing to go do it that night; and when we got over there the next day and located that car it was completely dismantled. I went back that night and called the sheriff at Crockett to meet me over there, but we jumped the gun a little too quick and messed that deal up. But I got him on several other things and begin to put pressure on 'em. Finally, I heard that he had four of 'em down there one night at a crossroads between Forrest and Alto, that old road where you cut to go across over into Houston County 'cross that Anderson Crossing on the Neches. Four of 'em was supposed to have been in there and shoot me when I come by that night, that was the information I got and I don't doubt it, but I went the wrong road.

That was the only time I ever told a man what I told him (John Mason). I'm not proud of it, but it had got so bad . . . . There was 21 ex-convicts living down there then, that hung out. I went down there to Wells one day with my shotgun and called him outside. I says, "John Mason, you're gonna kill me or I'm gonna kill you, or you're gonna get out of this county in two weeks and don't ever come back." Thank God, he gave me back a week of that. He moved to Lufkin.

I came even closer to getting killed another time. I was down in Wells one morning. I had a call down there on a barber shop that had been burglarized, of all things. Went down there and checked that out. Had a constable down there by the name of Pete Bailey, a friend of mine and a pretty good officer. There was a citizen there by the name of Hicks, Mr. Emmit Hicks, and he had quite a bit of land there and some land leased up as a hunting club out east of Wells back near the Angelina River.

They had hired an old fellow who come through the country, just a straggler they didn't know nothing about, and put him down there as a guard on this hunting lease to keep people out. They give him a 30-30 rifle. You wouldn't call him insane, he had plenty of sense in a lot of ways, but he was just overly mean. He got to even challenging the members when they'd come down there to the hunting club, and they got scared of him. So, they asked me if I'd go down there and get that rifle away from him.

Pete Bailey was with me that morning after we'd made this investigation of that barber shop. I drove in by the house and said, "Let's go down and check Mr. Hicks' lease out." He got in with me, and it was way back in the backwoods. We started down a little old dirt road (on) a hill, and just before we got to the gate going into his hunting lease, I saw this man coming up the road with this 30-30 rifle, about half-way up that hill. Well, we just went to the bottom of that hill, turned around, and come up beside him. Pete Bailey, big, thick-chested man, was sitting over to my right. I moved over there beside of him, says, "We're officers, want to talk to you a minute."

He just stepped back one step, it was so close, and *"BALOOM!"* The bullet hit that little ventilating window frame. You know, all cars used to have that little ventilating window, little steel rim around that glass. That 30-30 bullet grazed that and knocked that steel coat off, and the bullet come over and hit Pete right across his chest—took 36 stitches (to close)—just ripped him. I had bent over to talk to him and the bullet caught me right there in the chest and stopped right up close to my backbone. And we started shooting. I shot through the glass a couple of times, shattered glass and cut us all over. A little of it is still in me, I think. Anyhow, I looked at Pete and I saw the blood shooting everywhere. I looked to see if this guy was down, and he was. He was still trying to pull that trigger, but he didn't have no life in him. I looked in the rear view mirror at my face, and there was just a perfect size of a 30-30 bullet right there over my eyebrow. I felt back here at the back of my head to see where it come out, but I couldn't feel it.

I couldn't figure that out. But I looked at Pete and picked up the radio, said, "Attention all officers." Old Sam Drewry, police sergeant at Nacogdoches, heard me just like that. I said, "Get us an ambulance if you can. Meet us in Wells. I'm gonna try to get out of here. We're both shot, we gonna try to get to Wells." Course, when we got to Wells it looked like a peace officers' convention there. They carried us in

Dr. DuBose's office. He patched old Pete up a little and me too, and then sent us over to the Jacksonville hospital.

Anyhow, Pete had a terrible time getting that healed up; it looked terrible. Mine was mostly shattered glass and that bullet—I went over to Jacksonville and Dr. Ryan dug it out. It was right up next to my backbone, a 30-30 bullet. Two weeks later that thing over my eyebrow festered up and turned blue, so I went up to Jacksonville Hospital, got ahold of Dr. Ryan, and said, "Doc, must be something in there. It's throbbing and it looks like it's got corruption, or something." He took his little knife, split it open, and reached in there and pulled out that rim, part of that rim from around that bullet, enough of it to cut that round hole.

Another time I almost got shot, there was a report of cattle stolen in Cherokee County. I got to investigating it, and I went over to Palestine to a (livestock) sale. I got a little information and the description of a man by the name of Sullivan who had sold a cow. And a few days later I went to Houston and got ahold of a deputy by the name of Leon Chapman, and we got to checking the records for this O. C. Sullivan; and we found the record of him and where he lived, way out in south Harris County in kind of a low, flat country. It wasn't very thickly populated at that time.

Well, we looked and looked and finally found this old house where he lived about 10 o'clock that night. I had a warrant with me, and we went to the house and his wife let us in. We told her we wanted to see Mr. Sullivan, and went back in his bedroom and he was in bed. He weighed 311 pounds, he looked like a big bear laying up there in that bed. I told him I had a warrant for his arrest, and for him to get up, I wanted him to go with me. He told me he wasn't going nowhere, and reached under his pillow; and when he did I busted a .45 right by his ear, and I got his attention. He had a pistol under that pillow and he was fixing to shoot me. Then his wife run in there and grabbed a .22 rifle, and Deputy Chapman stopped her and took that rifle away from her. I thought I was gonna get killed before I got out of there, or have to kill him. But, anyhow, after I shot a hole in that pillow pretty close to his ear, he decided he'd better cooperate with us, and he did.

We brought him up to Houston there to the county jail and processed him and fingerprinted him, and I left there with him at about two o'clock in the morning and come on home. Soon as I brought him in, I sent a telegram to the Department of Public Safety, and they sent me back a telegram. I wasn't positive I had the right man, but sure enough, I had the right man and they wanted him in Kountz for cattle theft and hog theft.

Down in Kountz in Hardin County there was an open stock law.

The county judge had a lot of hogs running out there; I've been down there when hogs would be on the courthouse lawn. But anyway, Sullivan had a long trailer, and had it specially built, and had a thing on the back end for hogs to go up into that trailer. He'd go down to where these hogs would gang up there, pretty close to one of those roadside parks, and he'd take him a bunch of overripe watermelons and bust 'em and make a little trail up to that trailer, and he'd bust a bunch of 'em in that trailer. Then he'd hide off out there, and them old wild hogs would come up there and eat those watermelons and go on up in that trailer, and when he'd get a load in there he'd pull the trigger and close 'em up. He like to stole the old judge out of the hog business. He did it without any trouble, one man; and 40 men couldn't go out there in the woods and round up that many hogs.

I was more known amongst them safe crackers up there in Dallas than anybody beside Bill Decker, 'cause they used to come down here and knock safes off in Jacksonville regular. And I got on to 'em—I treated 'em pretty rough. I had some tough, rough hombres in my jail, the Lois Green gang. Green was shot down and murdered up there in a night club one night. And Nick Cassio, an old Dago, they all run together and they knocked safes all over this country. Had every officer in Texas and Louisiana looking for 'em. I had 'em down here several times and throwed a bunch of 'em in the penitentiary. Anytime I had a safe knocked in Cherokee County north of Rusk, you could bet they had come out of Dallas. Them old safe burglars, they're hard to catch, but I'll be honest with you, I treated 'em pretty rough. Treat a couple like that and they'd go around you. They were rough and tough criminals, they killed each other. There was a gang of 'em, and Dallas was full of 'em. Bill Decker, the sheriff up there, and I got to be good friends. They wouldn't bother him, he had an understanding; they housed up up there. He told 'em, "You can live here, but don't you bother anything here." I'd go up there and I'd want somebody and he'd send after 'em, he'd pick up a telephone and call 'em, just say, "Come in."

One of my tricks, if I had an old boy out here that I thought was guilty of a murder or a bunch of burglaries, some pretty serious crime, I'd wait until about 2:30 or 3:00 in the morning, go out there and run in on him while he was asleep and arrest him. I'd pull him out and take him to jail and start questioning him. See, that's to kind of flusterate 'em. That's just one of my tactics that I used, and it worked pretty good a lot of times. It really shakes 'em up.

When I was sheriff, there wasn't a highway patrolman in the county, and I had all of (Highway) 69 from Bullard to Wells, which was about

60 miles long. And every time it come a little rain you could just look out for some wrecks. We had to work our wrecks, we had to serve all the civil papers, we had to wait on court, we had to make the investigations of any burglaries, thefts, cow thefts, hog thefts, murder, what have you. Hell, we did it and liked it and enjoyed it. And I've told a lot of people, the only thing I regret was that I lived on the job day and night. Only time I went home was to eat and sleep. I didn't treat my family very good, I didn't take them out much; I lived on the job. But people got where they expected that. That's the reason I wouldn't want to be sheriff in Cherokee County if they give it to me. They'd want me to do like I used to do, and I couldn't do it.

If somebody got killed overseas, or otherwise got killed in a wreck or accident, first thing they did was call us. We had to go deliver the message. Some of the hardest things I ever did, some old boy getting killed in a wreck, and we'd go wake his mother and dad up and tell 'em about it.

I had an old lady come in the office one day, deputies still laughing about it, said she wanted to see the high sheriff. They wanted to know if they couldn't handle it. Says, "Naw, y'all too light, I want the high sheriff." She waited till I come in. Somebody had stolen two little old chickens from her. I had to go out and check it out.

The teachers would say, "Now, you better behave or I'm gonna get Frank Brunt," that kind of stuff, you know. And if a kid run away . . . I've had people come up there and ask me if I'd come out and whup their kid and get him straightened out. You get pretty close to people. An old kid comes to town in the family car and goes whupping around the streets and acting a fool, I wouldn't call his parents or put him in jail. I'd just get him in the car over there, and pull his car back home and put it in the garage, then he'd ride back to town with me. I wouldn't tell his parents. But that'll break 'em pretty quick—he'd be careful about sliding around the corners on the square from then on.

My opponents used to say I spoilt all them old people down there, but they could call us on most anything, you know, and we'd try to help 'em. If somebody come through town that was stranded, or in trouble, or needed to get somewhere, broke down, ran out of money—well, they'd call on us and we'd do something to help 'em get going. Or, if somebody died off somewhere else, and they wanted to get somebody a message that lived way out in the country, didn't have a telephone, they'd call us and we'd go out there and deliver the message. Just anything like that. If their child hadn't come home when they thought it was due home, they'd tell us. Lot of it was unnecessary, but lot of it wasn't. We tried to render a service. I think that's what made me as strong in that county. I was proud of the fact that I was elected eight times, the last time without an opponent.

People would come to me wanting nearly everything. I even had them call me from a lawyer's office wanting me to come over and witness a will. Then, when they got ready to settle the estate, his widow and the lawyer called me to be there when they settled this up, and verify that I signed this will, which I did. Just things like that, you know. And mad dogs, I killed a many a one! One old constable was an old shade-tree veterinarian. I bet he's cut off more dog heads and sent 'em to Austin than anybody in East Texas.

But I think I earned the respect of the people, and I could go out in most cases and talk with those people and get 'em straightened up. I know Burl Avra, one of the deputies at that time, still remembers this and laughs about it and razzes me about it to this day. Back in 1940, the year I was elected sheriff, we had an office upstairs in the old jail. My wife and I lived there at the old jail. One day a lady come up there squalling, about 35 years old, crying and taking on, her nose was running, about how bad her husband was, what a sorry thing he was, and about how he mistreated her.

I sat there and listened to all of that, and she moaned and cried and give me the sad story. I said, "Where is your husband now?" She said, "He's over yonder on the street." I said, "Well, I thought he was off somewhere else here in some other county." So, I sent Burl Avra, deputy, over there to see if he could find him. Directly, here he come marching him up there. And I sat 'em down there, and I let him tell his story, and she just rared and pitched over there, and cried. I listened to 'em a few minutes. I said, "Now, what y'all need to do—I know you're in love, you just both got married—you need to cool off. You ought to kiss her, make love to her, go on and sleep real close to her tonight, and love her." And directly, I got 'em to kiss and they left there arm in arm. Never had another word out of 'em.

When I was having an opponent, I had two or three accuse me of being the sheriff, the judge, and the jury. You know, lot of times when you got a good case, a safecracker, burglar, or something like that, he's gonna plead guilty. He'll try to get out of it as light as he can when he knows you got him. A lot of our cases, when we went to court, they pled guilty. I've never had a case that I remember that the district attorney and the judge didn't call me in and ask me what I recommended. Well, I don't think you can have any better confidence and backing than that, and I tried to be reasonable in what I did. One thing I put in my campaign announcement, I didn't leave an unsolved murder in 14 years in Cherokee County.

I want this clear, my brother Bill paved the way for me. He bulldozed the right-of-way off. They hadn't been used to real law enforcement in Cherokee County for a long time until he went in. He lost his life, and people then just rallied around me and give me wonderful support. There wasn't any way for me to keep from doing some good, if I tried, because the people was backing me up. So I give him credit. I think he was one of the best sheriffs I ever knew. I tried to carry it on like I thought he wanted it carried on.

You know what I did when I went to the sheriff's office? I could hardly drive a car and I didn't know anything about law. I just used what common sense the Lord give me, and studied it a little as I went along, and listened to the lawyers in court, and the judges—that's where I learned what little I did. The Lord give me a little common sense. I don't have any formal education, but I do believe I had a little common sense about handling people. If a sheriff hadn't got a little judgment, common sense, about him, he can make the biggest monkey out of himself—them (people) hating him and cussing him before the sun goes down.

People still say I'm campaigning. I was blessed, I guess, with a gift of getting around to people, though I don't stay very long. I'd heard so many complaints about former sheriffs from different counties, that they never did go out and see people, that I made it a point to go to every community. Every time they had a graveyard cleaning, or a memorial service, I'd go out there and visit with those people. I'd go down to Wells one Saturday and visit with the people who had come to town. And I'd go to Jacksonville and Rusk and get out on the street and shake hands with people.

One of the biggest compliments I ever had was from Mr. W. H. Brown, a fine old Christian gentleman, a very highly respected man who owned Brown's Department Store there in Jacksonville. I was up there shaking hands and visiting with people on the street one Saturday, and he made the remark that "If they were to rob that First National Bank over there, and Frank Brunt was over here at my store just across the street on (a) Saturday afternoon, he'd never get over there." They said, "Why, Mr. Brown?" He said, "Because they'd all stop him and want to shake his hand."

I kind of electioneered the year 'round. People liked what I was doing, and I tell you, I went day and night. About the only time I went home was to eat and sleep, and when I'd go home and eat lunch, the phone would ring two or three times. The operators knew where to call me at noon, they'd catch up with me there. Down in Dogtown, one of the citizens said one time, "I've seen the sheriff come by here more this year than I have all my life." And anytime when a campaign was on and everybody had an opponent, they'd have little box suppers, little rallies, different communities would invite you out.

Being sheriff of Cherokee County was the biggest honor that I ever had. People were great to me, good to my family and good to me. I'm still welcomed down there when I go back. I know I have some enemies, but a lot of people that I arrested and put in jail walk up to me today like they're really glad to see me, and some of 'em even thank me for what I did. I had men up in years come to shake hands with me with tears in their eyes when I left there, and that made it that much harder on me. It was hard to get away from there myself without shedding a few tears. The day I left Cherokee County I was 20,000 dollars in debt and nothing to show for it.

In those rural areas in Cherokee County, Nacogdoches County, and all the rest, the sheriff was the man. Back when I was making my first race, W. Lee O'Daniel was running for governor. There was an old gentleman at the Maydelle community out west of Rusk, Mr. Roach, a one-legged man. And he was walking to town on that wooden leg, he lived out there a couple of miles in Maydelle. Fellow come along and picked him up, says, "Where are you going, Mr. Roach?" Says, "Going up here to vote for Frank Brunt and W. Lee O'Daniel." That was all he was interested in. Wasn't no use anybody running for anything else.

H.F. and LORETTA FENTON

★

My father was a farmer. We lived out there on a little old farm about 10 or 12 miles west of Coleman in the New Central community. New Central was just our school, where we went to grammar school, and our church; we had a little tabernacle there. I had two brothers and three sisters. We raised cotton, maize, small grains, and had a few cattle, just a small place. Back in those days they were raising lots of cotton and picking that cotton and pulling it. I remember one time my dad and mother kept all us kids out of school for a week. We went over to Talco, which is in Coleman County, and we worked over there, camped out in a house, and picked cotton for a week and made one-hundred dollars. We used that one-hundred dollars for groceries for quite some time. I remember that mighty well. My sis and I would get trying to out-pick each other, out-pull each other, and dad gum, she was hard to beat, too.

I mobilized with Company B of the 36th Division back during World War II. I signed up for the National Guard when I was 16 years old; I lied a couple of years about my age and signed up in 1939. When war was declared and we mobilized, we was down there in Camp

Brownwood for 18 months, then we shipped on out. We were in Africa, but didn't do no fighting there. Our first fighting was in Italy at Salerno. We came on up through Italy and made a couple of invasions in Italy, and come in through southern France on an invasion, and went on across the Rhine River. I stayed with 'em all this time up until just before we crossed the Rhine.

Salerno was the roughest, toughest battle that I believe I was ever in. We went in on the first wave. We had got word just before we left the ship that they'd pulled off of the beach, that the Germans had all pulled out. We got in those landing boats and started in to land, and we found out that they hadn't pulled out. They didn't even give us any artillery support from the ships going in, or any air support, or nothing. They just throwed us in there. And boy, they hadn't pulled out, and they was blowing them landing barges ever way in the world but loose. We finally got in on land and got in far enough to take a little old town, Alta Villa, and we got kicked out of that thing twice and took it three times. We went back the third time 'cause we didn't have no place to go, the ocean was back there. Salerno was the roughest of all. Course, we had lots of mountain fighting, and that mountain fighting was awful rough, but it wasn't anything like coming in there to land and facing all that artillery and machine guns and everything shooting direct into you.

I saw lots of action, all right. I was lucky. When we landed over there in Salerno I was platoon leader, and I got a battlefield commission during the deals over there and just got wounded one time. When I left Company B there was one other man in there from the original bunch I went over with, one other man. We had lots of replacements and lots of casualties, sure did, but the Good Lord was with me all the way through. I was in a lot of tough places and He always helped me through it.

I received quite a few medals over there: the DSC, the Silver Star and Cluster, the Bronze Star, the Purple Heart, and all that kind of stuff. But all of that was just getting in a tight, and your men in a tight, and having to get out. There wasn't nobody any scarder than I was. After a while they made me a second lieutenant, then they tried to make me a captain and give me a company, and I told 'em I didn't want to leave my platoon. When I joined up in National Guard in 1939 I went into Second Platoon, B Company. I stayed with it all the way over, landed with it, and when they commissioned me I stayed in the same platoon. I was everything in that platoon, every rank, and when I left B Company I was still Second Platoon.

We was sitting right north of Monte Cassino on a hill that we went around and took when they (the Allies) bombed it. The first bomb dropped didn't hit Cassino, it hit to the east of it about half a mile or so. We were sitting there and them planes come right over, and the next one, boy, they lowered the boom on her then. That was what was giving us so much trouble. They (the Germans) had tunnels built in under that son-of-a-gun, and they were bringing their supplies and troops in that way. They (the Allies) wouldn't let 'em bomb Monte Cassino for the longest. We had one heck of a battle up there on that hill, then they had a truce for the Germans to get their men out of our foxholes and our lines. I come off of that hill with eight men in the Second Platoon out of maybe 20-some-odd.

This boy was in my platoon all the way over there. His name was Forest Kimble, but we called him "Booger Red." He was a red-headed kid, not too large of a fellow; but when we were overseas, if I had to take somebody out and find out something about the enemy, I'd usually take Booger Red. He didn't never have to look back, you know. He was a real good little soldier, a real good soldier. We were up behind Cassino one time before they dropped the bombs on it, we were sitting up behind that thing, and they attacked us one cold morning and our machine guns and rifles were froze up. They wouldn't fire. And old Booger Red, he carried hand grenades from the CP (Command Post) for an hour or so.

We were in lots of places like that, and when he got hit we was having a bayonet charge. We took a hill, and another troop had come up behind and they got in trouble, and they sent my platoon back there to get 'em out of trouble. We had one tank with us. The Germans started to charging us with bayonets, and we lined up a-side of this tank and fixed our bayonets. The tank crew wouldn't get out of that dang tank and man their machine gun, but Booger Red did, and he got shot off that tank. He got hit in the neck and wounded bad.

Then he come on back home to Coleman County, and after a while he wrote me a letter. He told me to hurry up and get on back, he wanted to run me for sheriff. I never dreamed of running for sheriff of Coleman County till then, and I didn't pay no attention to that.

I worked seven months with the Pampa Police after I got out of the service. They had me enforcing traffic and checking parking meters. They put me on one of these three-wheel motorcycles up there, and then they decided they'd make a two-wheel motor cop out of me and put me on one of them big old Harley Davidson things. An old boy took me out to a ball diamond, gonna learn me to ride that thing. I got to running those bases on it, and I come in from third base to home; and instead of cutting that gas off, I was cutting it on; and instead of turning my wheels, I was leaning. I hit the backstop and broke that thing through. Course, it throwed me, and the motorcycle went on through and hit the ground and started spinning. This old boy that was training me, he finally run in and got that motorcycle stopped. I went back down and told 'em that they could have that motorcycle. That was one of them big son-of-a-guns. I had been riding that three-wheel motorcycle all right, but that two-wheel rascal got me.

Up there at Pampa, at that time, it was an oil boom and pretty rough. We got a lot of fight calls from all them old night clubs. When I started working there, they put me with an old man who had 15 years service. He says—he called me son—"Son, any time you're dealing with a man, change boots with him and deal accordingly." That's what that old man told me, and I've always thought of that and always tried to do that, "deal accordingly." If he'll let you treat him right, deal right down the line with him. And if he don't want it that way, then deal accordingly.

This old policeman I told you about, I never saw him hit a man with a fist or a nightstick. He'd always use the palm of his hand. And boy, he could knock one on his bottom quicker than you could turn around. They'd have some pretty good fights in those places up there.

I went to work there on the Pampa Police in the early part of '46, and while I was there Booger Red wrote me another letter. He wanted me to come on down to Coleman and run for sheriff, he was still after me. I came back to Coleman and there was an old judge here at that time, J. K. Baker. He was a real old-timey judge, an old man at that time. I went up to his office upstairs there in a building in Coleman and talked to him and told him who I was. He knew my family. I never will forget, the old man says, "Son, come on down here and run. I think you'll win." He's the only man I talked to. I went back to Pampa and resigned, then I come down in '46 and run for county sheriff.

Back then we had more pie suppers and ice cream suppers. We had 28 voting boxes in the county, and ever doggone one of them boxes would have a pie supper or ice cream supper sometime during the campaign. All the people in the community would meet there, and you'd have to get up and make a stump speech, tell 'em what you planned to do and this, that, and the other. Ten minutes, 15, would be plenty. You didn't want to get up there and jabber too long about it.

Then, course, you had your cards, and you tried to give every person in the county at least one card and maybe two or three during the campaign. You'd get out on the streets. Back then the old town would fill up on Saturdays, and you could hand out lots of cards there on the street. Then the rest of the time you'd be making business places, and going door to door to houses and asking 'em for their help.

Course, I was 23 years old when I was running, and there were lots of 'em saying I was too young and too high-tempered, just coming back from the war and all. But I had lots of good old supporters that said, "Well, if he's old enough to go over there and fight, he's old enough to be our sheriff."

I was out putting posters all around town, asking all these business-es if I could put 'em in their windows. There was a barbershop there, and I knew that George Robey, the party I was running against, that all of 'em was his friends in this barbershop. There wasn't but three chairs in there, three barbers. Anyway, I went in there one day and asked these barbers if I could post this poster in their big plate glass window. They said, "You bet," so I pasted it there with Scotch tape and went on about my business. When I come back by there the next day, somebody had took this poster down and took a knife and had picked that face all over, and then had put it back up there. I stopped and looked at it, and it made me pretty hot when I was standing there and looking at it. But I had enough thought, thank goodness, to think, "I know that's what they're wanting me to do, to come in there and raise a bunch of hell about them picking that picture up." There was a bunch of people in that barber shop, and I was standing right there and they was all watching me. I thought, "Best thing I can do now is get me a handful of cards and go in there and give 'em all a card and ask 'em for their vote." That's what I done. I walked in there and went to everybody, chairs, barbers, and all. Didn't say a word about the poster, just gave 'em cards, turned around and walked out. And boy, that got 'em worse than if I'd come in there and raised hell with 'em! It was a set-up deal, 'cause them three old barbers in there, they were George Robey men. They had set that deal up hoping I would come in there and kick the snot out of 'em. And that really would have hurt me, 'cause I was supposed to be high-tempered.

When I went in in January of 1947 I had one deputy, and we had the whole shebang, the whole county. I moved my deputy into the jail, we didn't have a jailer, and we didn't have nothing but two old wore-out automobiles. We didn't have no two-way radios. They didn't have no police department down here in Coleman, only a night watch-man and a chief. We had to take calls from everything—city, county, everywhere. That was a different ballgame back then. You'd take off in a car and wouldn't know what was happening anywhere, 'cause you didn't have a radio.

I'll never forget the first call that I made after I went in. It was a fellow called me from Santa Anna down there. I had an old wore-out Ford car that didn't have no wipers on it, and it was icing in January, and I had to ride with my cotton-picking head out of that window to see. After I got down there to Santa Anna, this fellow turned out to have dogs under his house. His house was built up off the ground, and there was an old bitch dog under there with a bunch of dogs (that had) followed her in, and he wanted me to get them dogs out from under his house! I laid down on one side of this house at a hole with a flashlight, and every one of 'em run out the other side. I got back in the car and drove home. Boy, it was cold, and I didn't have no defrosters on that thing, you know. I didn't realize the sheriff got those kind of calls.

I've gotten lots more, over the years. We've had calls about coons and possums up in trees, to come get 'em out, and lots of calls were animals and chickens was getting across the fence on the next lot, such calls as that. I guess we've had about everything in the world. I've had people to call me out in the country that had seen these lights, these flying saucers. They'd try to describe 'em to me.

And we've had calls on things that happened that I've never been able to figure out. I've been out on a number of calls about these dead animals that had been found out in the pastures. Big old cow be laying out there dead, and maybe her right eye is gone or tongue cut out or udder cut off, and there wouldn't be a sign of nothing nowhere around this cow. I worked a number of cases in the county like that. Sometimes a steer would be killed, or a bull, and his penis be gone. In past years it run plum up on into the northern states. They always thought it was some cult outfit that would send these people out to get these parts of these animals, I suppose that was what it was. But what always griped me was that I never was able to catch the son-of-a-guns, or come up with any information that would lead me to 'em. No tire tracks, no foot tracks—I've started at the dead cow and walked just in a circle till I got on out for three-hundred yards or so, and I just didn't come up with nothing. That happened in other counties and other states, it was a pretty big thing.

And what killed 'em, that's another thing I didn't never figure out. They'd just be laying there dead, and you couldn't see no cause of death. I've had 'em skint, skinned 'em trying to find bullet holes in 'em. I always had my thought that it was some kind of needle that was shot into 'em, that's what I always figured. I've even had veterinarians come out on a number of 'em and try to find something that caused the death. It was just unbelievable to go out there and see these things and not be able to come up with nothing.

Raymond Greaves was my first deputy. He was an old boy that had been with Company B since it mobilized. We went overseas together, we fought together over there. He made it back and so did I, and when I went in office he's the one I got to be my deputy. We knew each other for a long many years, and back then we could more or less read each other's minds for what the other one was gonna do. He stayed my deputy for 14 years. He was a good officer, a good, solid boy. Lots of times he'd take the south part of the county and I'd take the north part, we'd split it down through the middle. We'd just take off and patrol here, there, and yonder. We'd check in by telephone every once and awhile with each other. If we needed any help we'd have to get to a telephone.

The first radios we ever got . . . I never will forget that. There were some old boys down here at Brownwood who were license and weight men. I was pretty good friends to 'em, and they told me that they would work up here in this county more than they had been if the commissioners court would give me the fines to buy radios with. So, I went to the commissioners court and told 'em, and that suited 'em fine, 'cause it wasn't costing 'em no money. It took a little better than a year to get enough money to buy two radios. Just after that I got a call from Brownwood on an old bootlegger that was coming across the end of the county. I went down there, I had my radios, you know, and a radio is what helped me catch this old boy. He had a pickup with sideboards on it and a tarp over it, and had that son-of-a-gun loaded down with beer. He was coming back from Angelo right across the end of the county and going to Brownwood. I took him before the judge and he fined him a thousand dollars for transporting that load of beer. The old boy paid it in cash. It happened that the commissioners court was meeting the next day. I took that one-thousand dollars cash and walked in there and throwed it down on the table, and I said, "Now, there's your radio, paid for." Those radios made a world of difference.

About the first two years I was in office, I tell you what, I thought it wasn't nothing but fist fighting, 'cause there was lots of old tough boys here then who would try your boot on. I was just 23 or 24 years old, and those first two years I had more damn trouble, more fights. Most of the time you'd just start to arrest somebody and they just wasn't gonna be arrested. They'd just start them old fists flying, and you had to either run or stay there. But back then I was in good shape. I wasn't tough or nothing like that, but fighting never did bother me too much.

And I always had pretty good luck, I never did try to do no more than I had to. I did have an old boy one night down there at Santa Anna at a dance . . . that's the closest I ever come to getting killed while I was in the sheriff's office. He was drunk right in the back of the dance floor, and I went back there and told him, "Let's go." We got out in front of the building, and I just placed my hand on his shoulder and told him to get in my car. It was setting right over on the sidewalk. At that time I wore an old .44 on my left side, a cross-draw deal, and the old boy reached and grabbed my gun and got it out of my holster and jobbed it in my gut. He was trying to pull the trigger on it, but it happened that I grabbed it and stuck my thumb right there behind the hammer. We went down, and he still had ahold of it and had it in my gut trying to pull the trigger. I finally got my other hand around and twisted it loose from him. Then I used it two or three times, after I got it loose from him, on his head. There was a place there on my hand a long time after that. A lot of officers have got hurt with their own guns. I changed my position of carrying it after that, too.

I've found out that a lot of those that's fighting, they really don't want to fight, and if an officer shows up, a percentage of 'em will quit. But some of 'em won't, either, and then you've got to use force to get 'em to stop, either with nightsticks or tear gas or something of that nature. But a percentage of 'em, they'll quit when officers arrive.

I remember back in the good old days we'd get a couple of punks wanting to fight and we'd just draw 'em a circle and tell 'em to get in it and get after it. I remember one instance where two old boys really wanted to fight. I told 'em, ''Let's just get in the country where they won't be nobody bothered.'' We went to the country and it was at night. I drew me a circle in front of my car, and boy, I seen a good fistfight. When it was over with they was both satisfied. I guess the federals would hang you if you was to take a couple of men out and let 'em fight now, standing there and watching it. But they don't even fistfight today like they used to. They use weapons or knives or something. Shoot, I've had old boys to fight and get up and shake hands, and I mean have a fight, too. Just a good old fistfight.

This was a dry county back then, and we had what we called hip-pocket bootleggers. They'd be down on the street there in Coleman. We used to have a place, Fatty Thames' Cafe, hamburger joint right on Main Street, that was where the biggest part of your gamblers and bootleggers hung out. They had an old domino hall in the back of it. Those bootleggers, after they'd sold a pint, they'd go back to their house or their car and get another pint.

Then after we got to bearing down on 'em, a number of 'em later on would hide it out in the country. We had one bootlegger I remember very well, 'cause I handled him a number of times. He was liable to drive three or four miles out in the country and just have one pint hid right where he didn't even have to get out of his car. He'd just have it in the soft dirt right beside of the road. He'd drive and pick it up and bring it in and sell it whenever he got a sale thataway.

One particular case, we knew these people was selling whiskey, and we was raiding 'em but couldn't find their stash. I started out of the house there one time, and there was a little baby laying in a crib. They had this little mattress on this bed, the crib come up on the side, and for some reason or another I told this woman to move that baby. She picked that baby up, and I jerked that mattress up and that son-of-a-gun was lined with whiskey!

Most of these bootleggers were just old boys too lazy to work, making some easy money. I remember one particular case. There was an old boy here bootlegging, and I had an undercover man come in and make several buys off of him. Whenever he got ready to make a pick up on this one particular bootlegger, I told him this bootlegger was a fisherman, liked to fish, and I told him I wanted to get in the turtle of his car, him shut the turtle, and drive up in front of his house and make a buy off of him. After he'd made his buy, I wanted him to tell him he had some fishing tackle out there in his car that he wanted to give him. We did it just like that. I was close enough that I could hear the conversation. The old boy come out on the porch and they made their deal. This old Shorty was a good little undercover feller that talked like a damn colored man. He says, "I got something out here I want to give you." They walked out there and he plopped that thing up, and man, there I am in that turtle! That old bootlegger started running backwards and like to fell down before I come crawling out of that thing. And old Shorty, man, he got all over this old boy then. "Now, I want you to show me where your stash is, right now. You're in lots of trouble." And dern if that old boy didn't take us and show us his stash there behind the house. That boy, he was a pretty good old fellow. He still lives there. He talked about that to me hasn't been a year ago. He's a good friend of mine today.

Them rascals, they kept it stashed just about anywhere and everywhere. There was all kind of stashes they had. There was one old boy that we had trouble finding his stash. Right at his back door he had a sandpile, I guess a six-by-six-foot sandpile with boards around it, that was for his little boy to play in. Sand was up there two foot or so deep. We finally got a little information and got to digging in that sandpile, and right in the middle of the damn thing we hit a barrel of whiskey. The barrel was laying on its side, with about a four-inch piece of pipe welded into it that come up about a foot to a spout with a lid on it. That's where he kept his whiskey, in that barrel. Whenever somebody would come there wanting some, he knew right where to run out there, and kick this sand back, and reach down and unscrew that lid to get him some. That was a 30-gallon barrel. Later on, where he drove into his driveway and on into his garage, right up between the tracks where his car went, we dug up a 50-gallon barrel. He was a pretty big operator.

The biggest thing back then was to find bootleggers. Back then, you could set up roadblocks anywhere you wanted to and stop everything you wanted to, and we caught lots of bootleggers that way. We used to go out there to Talpa, out in the west part of the county, and set up a roadblock and stop everything that come in. And we picked up lots of bootleggers that way, not only coming into Coleman but going to other places. They'd be traveling from Angelo going to Brownwood or Eastland or other places. It's 75 miles from Coleman to San Angelo, but that was the closest wet area at that time. They'd bring it in and stash it everywhere.

We had a lot of colored people bootleg back then. They'd keep it stashed under the house and up on the eaves of the house, or in lots of rough places. I used to get a lot of kick in getting them crap games of the colored people, too. Most of 'em would be in somebody's house over there on the Hill. I remember one night I went over on the Hill by myself. I stopped my car about a block from a place I heard they were having a big game. I sneaked up to the front door and kicked it open, and that thing was full of colored people. I lined 'em up and took a pistol off of one old boy. There was 21 of 'em in there. That was too damn many to put in a car, and there wasn't any way of calling anybody, so I just put 'em in a column of twos and marched 'em all of the way from the Hill to the courthouse with a flashlight. I took 'em in the office there, had a little old small office at that time. I had them 21 colored people in there and I took this little old gun, it was a .380 automatic, and pulled it back and jacked it off like that, you know; I thought it was empty. I pointed it down at a corner and pulled the trigger and that thing went off, and them boys fell all over that floor! Then there's one raised up and says, "Mr. Fenton, you better jack that thing off again."

Back in the good old days, you might put some of your suspects over there in the jail and let 'em sweat for a while. Most of the time you can get a man in a small room, and one officer get in there—I'd like to just get in there with him by myself—and not have no listeners, nobody around, and interrogate him that way. Some of them old hard things, I've had five or six officers lined up and we'd interrogate them for a good many hours, swapping out. If I knew in my own mind that a man was guilty, I've done that. I never did like to do that if I wasn't certain that a man was guilty. But that was back when you could do things like that, now it's different. You can't even question a man many hours, now.

What you can do there, when you're working on a subject, a suspect, is to put him up there in that jailhouse and just have somebody else feed and water him, not go back up for about three days. Lots of times them old boys get a lot softer after they stay up in that jail awhile. And another thing, you can get you lots of information out of that jail if you get somebody up there that you can halfway trust. It may not be information you can go to court with, but it's information you can use to go ahead and solve your crime. That old jail, you can use it a lot of ways. You can put you receivers in it. There's just lots of ways you can use that old jail to get information.

Without informers you're not gonna get no big lot done, far as that goes. You got to have about every walk of life of informers, but an old thug that's been to the penitentiary, he can be your best informer. A preacher can't give you much information about what's going on out here in the old underworld. An old thug can get around and find out more, if he trusts you. And an officer has got to be trusted by his informer. If you ever divulge his information to anybody, these other informers they find that out pretty quick. You better not go tell that other officer, 'cause he's gonna let somebody know it. I've had informers, and I've got informers, and don't nobody ever know who my informers are. They never will know. An officer has got to build confidence with his people to do his job, because without these people's help, an officer has got trouble. If he don't build his confidence with his people as he goes along, well, he's not gonna make no officer. That's my feeling about that.

Another main thing that I always told an officer that he better do, if he gonna be an officer, is to go right down the middle of the line with every one of 'em. I don't care who he is; if he's a preacher, if he's the president of the bank, or if he's an old boy picking up garbage out here, he better go down that line with 'em. Thataway they'll all know, after a while, that you're going down that line, that you're not gonna vary. Law is about 75 or 80 percent horse sense; that's all it is, it's horse sense. They can have all those law books and send you to all the schools, all this crap they want to, and give you all the education, but if you haven't got that horse sense you ain't gonna be no officer. I think these schools are good, but I'm afraid that they're gonna get too much school. If they ever get it to where a deputy sheriff or a sheriff got to have two years in college to be a deputy sheriff, I think they gone too far. I'm afraid they're working it toward that point.

If you've been there long enough you know just about all of these old thugs in the county, just how they break into a place, their MOs. Lots of old things will come in through the ceiling, lot of 'em come in through the door, lot of 'em through the window, and lot of 'em use certain tools doing that with. If you learn these old things, their MOs, well, you kind of know who to go to looking for whenever you have one of them jobs. I had one old boy that would break into things and always take a crap on the floor before he'd leave. He'd do it just

ever time he'd break into a place. Most of the time he'd break into
grocery stores. He'd drink some milk and eat something 'fore he'd take
out, and he'd always take a crap 'fore he'd leave. All them old thugs
got their own traits and the way they do things. Course, it would really throw you a curve when one came through the county that was not
a local man.

I've used bloodhounds a good deal, and the time that got me interested in them was when a couple of colored subjects broke jail down east
of Coleman at Meridian. Commercial Street here in Coleman runs due
south of the courthouse, a big wide street. Loretta, my wife, and I were
out on the end going south on Commercial just about dark time, and
there was a couple of colored subjects walking along the sidewalk
there. At that time you didn't see a lot of colored people out in that
area, and I run just by 'em and told her, "What are those people doing out here?" I hit my brakes and my tail light come on, and when
I did, they scattered. They broke between two houses and that's when
the chase started.

We run 'em all that night. We never did have much information on
'em then, but the next day we'd get information from people that
they'd seen 'em here and seen 'em there. They were traveling west.
Just the other side of Talpa, they went in on an old man and jumped
him and tied him up and tried to steal his pickup, but they couldn't
get it started. That was just out of Coleman County. To this point we
had been tracing 'em by foot and by tracking, but then we called a
constable from Pyote, Texas, who had some good bloodhounds. This
old man brought his dogs, and it took him a good while to get down
here with 'em. We held off for eight hours. It was real dry and he told
us that them dogs may have trouble, it had been so long since they'd
been here. But he had two good dogs, and they hit that trail and we
started on in daylight and kept on after it got dark on us. These boys
was running just off of the railroad track. They'd stay off of the railroad track some two or three-hundred yards and use it for direction.

One of these dogs played out on us, and after it got nighttime this
old man put a bell on his other one. Then we scattered our cars out
down the highway, which ran in the same direction as the railroad,
and when we'd hear the old dog coming with his bell, we'd leap-frog
the cars on down. This old dog run their track through Ballinger and
right on out the other side. They could hear Old Red a-bellering behind 'em, and they run in a house in this little old town of Rowena.
They was tired and hungry and were sure ready to give up. I drove
up there and, man, I never seen as many officers and guns as there
were around that house. They scared me worse than anything. But
we run them boys two nights, two days, and caught 'em the third night,

and I never slept a wink all that time. That old constable, all he said was, "Just don't let 'em kill my dogs."

We were having a good many jailbreaks around over the country, this, that, and the other, and I decided I wanted to get me a blood-hound. I went to the penitentiary, the Wind Farm, and talked to the dog captain down there, and he give me a dog they called Old Red. He was a real good dog. I made me a dog pen outside the jail there, and I rigged me up a one-horse trailer with a dog box on one side and a grub box and feed box on the other side, and when somebody called me I'd load up my dog and horse and here we'd go. They got to calling me from a good many miles out.

We'd run that old bloodhound at least three times a week to keep him in practice. I'd take the prisoners out and tell 'em to lay me a trail, turn 'em loose out there, and go back and get my dog. That's how I'd keep him trained. He was a mean dog, though, he'd eat their britches up. I wanted him mean. I'd let 'em get a long switch, and whenever he'd tree 'em I'd let 'em fight him and make him mean. My wife bought me one to go with him. She give 50 dollars for the thing, a young dog. One day I took the old dog and the young dog out in the west part of the county, and I had me a prisoner lay me a trail. I turned these dogs loose and I heard 'em a-bellering over there. I went over there, and that young dog had quit the old dog and he was in a bunch of sheep, running in and biting them sheep. Course, there ain't but one thing to do there, and that's to kill that son-of-a-gun, which I did right there. Then I went and talked to the man who owned the sheep. My old dog, he kept a-going and had my man treed when I got over there.

I liked to run 'em, liked to run them dogs. A bloodhound, he's a funny creature. He'll be running a trail and something happen to that trail, and he'll just start going in circles. Directly, he's liable to throw his head right up, not even be on that trail, and start bellering. I've even had old boys, when it was damp and muddy, to walk and make tracks, and then make the same tracks backwards for two and three-hundred yards, and then take off. That old dog, whenever he hit something like that, man, he'd go crazy; but as a rule he'd start circling and he'd pick 'em up. Some of them old boys have even walked fences to try to get away from them hounds. They'd walk down for quite some distance, then step off of it. They can put red pepper in their shoes and that will throw off a dog, sometimes. That red pepper will disturb a dog right smart.

After I had this bloodhound, I got me a German shepard dog. He wouldn't trail nothing like this bloodhound would, though he would trail a colored man. I carried this German shepard in my car with me, and I'd rather have him than I had two or three men. He'd stay right in the back seat of that car. I would open all four doors and tell him to stay there, and wouldn't nobody come and he wouldn't go. If I was hunting somebody and come up to a building, the old dog worked right in front of me in every room. He'd stay in this room until I come in, then I'd motion to him and he'd go on in the next one. And boy, if he run on somebody in there he'd let you know, too. He's the best dog I ever owned. I could pick up a prisoner and put him in the front seat, and this old dog sit back there in the back. I could just talk to him and he'd say, *"GRRRRRR!"* I didn't have to worry about nothing. He's scared a lot of old drunks to death, set 'em right there!

When I got defeated in 1960, I started looking around for a job, 'cause I knew I was going out of office at the end of the year. I went to San Angelo, which is the headquarters of the Sheep and Goat Raisers' Association, and applied for a job as special ranger. They hired me, and I was commissioned as a Special Texas Ranger through the Department of Public Safety in Austin. I left my family in Coleman as my home base and worked all over the state. My main job with the Sheep and Goat Raisers' Association was working thefts of sheep and goats and wool and mohair, and public relations—signing up new members. I worked with the sheriffs. I'd hardly ever go into a county without letting them know that I was there and what was going on. Most of the time, they were the ones that called me to come there. We worked on whatever troubles they had. There were a good many sheep and goats being stolen, and a good many warehouses around the country that were being broken into.

Most of the times I'd just be camped out there on the big ranches trying to catch somebody coming in there stealing. I'd get way out in the middle of 'em with my horse, and ride around at night trying to catch somebody stealing. Lots of these old things will come into a place with dogs and just load up. Some of 'em will run 'em in pens, load 'em from pens, and some of 'em will throw down panels and load up thataway. But I worked nine years, and I'd say I've found more sheep and goats across the fence that was reported stolen than I ever found anywhere else. That's the first place you gotta start, where the crime takes place, then figure it out from there.

There was maybe more goats stolen than sheep. In the wintertime, when the wind is out of the north, you'll find your goats on fencelines at that side. They go in just as far as they can to the wind. These old thugs know that, and they get their places spotted where they can get 'em on that north fence, places where an old road comes down through or anywhere to go in there. They'll be on that north fence when the wind's real hard and blowing. They go into the wind.

I remember one case I worked back when I was with the Association. We had right smart of goat theft going on in the north part of a county next to us. We kept working it and working it, and about daylight one morning we caught the old boy. He had a trailer and his horse and his dog, and had a little loading shute that he'd throw over the fence. All that son-of-a-gun would do is just drive up there and send his dog out. He'd bring 'em in and run 'em up that shute into the trailer. He'd already cut the ear marks off of these goats when we caught him, they was still bleeding. They called him "Slim," just an old cowboy. They sent him to the penitentiary on it.

It was an interesting job, but I resigned from it after nine years. I was traveling everywhere, and to get back home and spend the night with my wife and kids, I might have to drive five-hundred miles. I was averaging three to four-thousand miles a month, and it got tiresome. This chief deputy's job come open here, and I took it and resigned (from the Association). I just didn't want to be away from my family that much.

I was Sheriff Corkey Chapman's chief deputy for five years. In the last year or so there got to be some problems. This wasn't because I'd been sheriff before, I don't guess, but just about things I disagreed with, disagreements on the way things was being handled. And I seen on the wall that Corkey Chapman was fixing to get beat, the way he was handling the sheriff's office. So, in December of ' 75 I took out, resigned. Like I say, the reason I did was because I didn't agree with a number of things that was going on, and I knew the public wasn't satisfied, and I knew that I needed a job. So in January of '76 I come out as candidate for sheriff.

Corkey Chapman was running and three others of us. I wasn't working, and I politicked, I worked. I tried to make every house in the county, and I tried to make every business place in the county. I took me a map of Coleman, and I'd go to town in the morning and I'd make me so many blocks, and I'd go back home that night and take a red pencil and mark out where I'd been, and I done that till I covered that whole town. I worked on that campaign as hard as any campaign I ever worked on, because it was three (others) of 'em running and I sure did want to win it.

We had a good many rallies around over the county, and if a guy wants to be a politician, anywhere there's 10 people, be there. The little old communities would give these rallies, sell pies and ice cream, and they would auction them off. Some of them dad-gum pie auctions and cake auctions got expensive, I paid as high as 30 dollars for them dang pies. That gets rough when you do that. Used to be in some of those communities, not in all of them, you'd have some man there that knew that he could keep jacking these things up. They'd know that you were gonna buy 'em, 'cause you was a candidate and you come there to try to get votes. If you didn't buy these things, them women would get mad at you, and you wouldn't be getting no votes. Back then we had 28 boxes, and nearly all of 'em would have a gathering sometime or another, and you may buy two or three pies, or buy a cake and a pie, and time it was over you had to have a pretty good pocketbook. And then they'd sell ice cream, too. I've enjoyed running, but I've always dreaded them things, too. Finally, all the candidates come to agreement that we'd pay 10 dollars for a pie, not go over 10 dollars.

One night Loretta and I was down here at Trickham at a rally. They called on me to make a speech, but I got up there and I acted like I was feeling awful bad. I told the public that I was sorry, that I felt real bad, but that my wife Loretta was back there and she was gonna make my speech. Course, Loretta didn't know what I was gonna do, didn't know nothing, and she didn't make no speech. Man, she turned every color in the world! I went ahead then with my stump speech, but she give me clean hell after we started home. I pulled another on her one night at one of them candidates' rallies. I told 'em after I got through with all my talking that every man was due three things in this world. I said one of 'em was a good horse, and one of 'em was a good dog, and one of 'em was a good woman. And I looked back at mine and I said, "I'm still . . . ," and I shut up. I didn't say, "I'm still looking."

The people was mighty good, I won it over all of 'em without any runoff. I was mighty happy.

My deputy, Raymond Greaves, lived in the jail there for a while in the early years, but he decided he didn't like the jail. I moved in in '49 and lived there until 1961, then moved back in after I was reelected. My wife, she was a good 'un, she got along good with it. We've raised practically all our kids in that jailhouse there. We have two girls and a boy, and they was practically raised in the jailhouse. I guess we're going on 23 years now that we've lived there.

Back in 1949 we had a bath on the west side, a living room, two bedrooms, and a kitchen. Later on there was a big old junk room there that we redone and made into a kitchen, and then we put a bath over on the east side. Right now we've got three bedrooms, one a little small one, a living room, a big kitchen, and two baths. It's downstairs and the jail is upstairs. It's an old jail, 93 or 94 years old, I believe, but we've been certified in it five times now by the Jail Commission.

That old jailhouse, my wife can probably tell you more about it than I can, but there's one thing I remember about it and her. It's a real old jailhouse, and way back yonder before we got a bathroom on the east side it had one on the west side, and our bedroom was on the east, and there was a hallway, a long hall, running to the west bathroom. Well, at night when she'd have to go to the bathroom she'd wake me up, and I'd have to holler to her all the way till she got back. She said long as she could hear my voice she wasn't scared to go to the bathroom. This hall went right by the stairs, and the door and the stairs led upstairs to where the prisoners are. There was a back door coming in, and one evening there she started across there and I heard her screaming. I was back in the east side, and I didn't know what in the world had happened. I run out there, and a big old bull snake—I don't know how long he was, but he was a long one—he'd crawled in some way or other at the back door and was laying right across that hall. He was long enough that he had that whole hallway covered, and that's what she was screaming about.

Them kids there, they think that old jail's home, that's what they think. They played all around there. I had a prisoner up there one time, stayed a good while, and my oldest little girl, she was just small, he'd take her out in the yard and swing her. She had just got to where she could talk pretty good, and that little snot, if he didn't do just what she wanted him to, she'd call him a name and say, "I'm gonna have my daddy put you back up them stairs!"

We had lots of incidents up there. Like I say, we live below the jail, and them son-of-a-guns will stop up a commode up there and flood the floors, and it will run down in the closets, and down on my wife's clothes, and on the beds. We've had that happen numbers of times. We've had crazy people up there, too. We had a colored man up there, a big son-of-a-gun, one time. Man, he tore up the plumbing, tore up a bunch of plaster off the wall. He was a big, stout, crazy son-of-a-gun. People would start up them stairs, and he had plaster and rock out of that wall that he'd throw at 'em. He'd run 'em back.

In the early days we didn't always have jailers there 24 hours a day like we do now. We was gone one time there for a while and come back in, and when I walked through the front door into our living room I seen plaster and everything all over the floor. A couch over there next to the wall had sheetrock all over it. I walked on in and we had a dad-gum hole in the ceiling right above the couch. What had happened, these doggone boys, we had 'em in a cell up there with a thick—I thought it was a thick cement floor. We'd had a table up there with an iron base on the bottom of it, and these sons-of-guns had got hold of an old knife and a piece of stick and had dug down in this cement. And after they had got started there wasn't but about three or four inches of cement there, the rest of it was just old rock and plaster. Them son-of-a-guns would dig while we was gone, and then scoot this table back over there when we come back. They'd dug a hole through there, and one of them little snots had dropped all the way through that hole down on that couch in the living room. And he went back upstairs and got the key and let two more of 'em out. They took off, but they wasn't out 24 hours.

In the center of this old jail, they've got an attic that goes on up through the top. Then there's a hole up there where you can push a lid off a deal and come out on the roof. We had an old boy out in the runaround up there one time who took our blankets and tied them together and he went on out on top. We had a big elm tree at the back there that run part of the way up the jail, and he made him a rope out of these blankets and slid down this rope to this elm tree and made his getaway. We've had about three of 'em altogether go out through that top. We had a big pecan tree there in the front, and how this one son-of-a-gun ever jumped over from the roof to there I don't know. But he did, he got out that way and come on down.

One time I had a trustee up there that had been in jail for a number of years, had him in the runaround in the middle. I had brought a little old girl up there and put her over on the west side in what we call the tank. And this door (in the tank), a big iron door, had a feeding window going in the west side. It was just big enough to put a platter, a tray, through. Course, I had this door locked. I went up there the next morning and my trustee wasn't there. I walked on over there and looked over inside this feeding window and there he sat, back up next to the bars inside there. I said, "What in the world you doing, boy?" I never will forget the way he looked, he looked like a whipped dog. He looked up at me. He said, "Sheriff, I made it through that hole over there, but I couldn't make it back." That little gal over there says, "Sheriff, we didn't do nothing but sit here on the bunk all night and read the Bible." What was so bad, about nine days later he turned up with the gonorrhea. I had to take him to the doctor to have him treated, and had to turn in expenses on a prisoner with gonorrhea in the jail that had been up there three years!

I've been there 23 years in the jail, and it's more of a problem right now than it's ever been. You got to keep more paperwork, you wouldn't believe it. You got to take care of them prisoners just like they was babies; but if you gonna stay out of trouble, you got to try to get along with 'em. If an old boy hollers he's got a toothache, you better get him over to that doctor. You have to really just baby 'em, is what I call it. Most of them old prisoners have been in and out of jail so much that they know more about that jailhouse law than anybody else does, and if you don't abide by it and take care of 'em like you should, they'll throw a writ on you right quick. Or, they'll be hollering to the Jail Commission, and (then) they'll be down investigating you or be filing federal suits. I've got a federal civil suit for 80,000 dollars on file on me now, filed in federal court in San Angelo. I don't think that it will ever go to trial. That's what my lawyer tells me. Another old boy sued me some years ago and alleged 10 things up there that happened in the jail that he said shouldn't have happened. None of 'em was cruelty or anything like that. He alleged things like he didn't get his mail properly, and that we didn't furnish him with a library, and all such crap as that. And he was in the penitentiary with a record as long as a wellrope on robbery, burglary, you name it; he had that kind of record. We had him in the west side, and then in the east side we had a woman over there. And gosh, it's some 20 steps anyway across from these doors. One of the things he alleged was that we had these little windows open and he didn't have no privacy. And another thing that he alleged was that my son Sean kept pigeons in the top, and pigeon droppings would drop down on his floor. Sean did have pigeons up there all right, but there wasn't no way that any droppings could get where he was at. Another thing he alleged was that my boy Sean was slipping a *Playboy* magazine up to the prisoners. The old judge, after it was over with, ruled that he didn't think his privacy had been hurt by this woman being over there, that the pigeon droppings couldn't get to him if they did fall through, and (that) he definitely didn't think that the *Playboy* magazine could hurt him. But that dadgum Sean had slipped that (magazine) up there to them dang prisoners, and I didn't know nothing about it.

It's as much different now as daylight and dark. You got to keep records on every little thing that happens to that prisoner from the time he goes in to the time he goes out. You got to have everything documented. If he wants you to do about anything, you better do it, because if you don't you gonna be in violation of the Jail Commission somewhere. If they've got medications, you've got to give 'em medications just so. And you got to make certain he swallows it, make him stick his damned old tongue out, put it on his tongue, give him water, and throw his head back, then check his mouth after he's supposed to have swallowed it. If this is prescription dope pills, well, they'll act like they've taken the son-of-a-guns, and won't take 'em, then they'll swap 'em to another prisoner for something or will keep 'em until they get four or five of these things. You give him one at a time like you supposed to and he can't get no charge out of it. If he'll save him up three or four or five of 'em and take 'em all at one time, he will.

It's a pain in the neck to keep it all going. Telephone calls—you got to have a telephone where you can let 'em make telephone calls two or three times a week now. It changes all the time. A federal judge just ruled that you can't strip search a prisoner. Up at Lubbock, the sheriff's office came out with a deal four or five days ago that they'd been having a lot more narcotics and a lot more contraband coming into their jail because this federal judge had ruled you couldn't strip search 'em. Boy, that's gonna mean a lot more trouble. I'm still gonna strip search 'em myself if I think one needs it. If I think that old boy's got something he's carrying with him, I'm gonna strip search 'em.

It was a different ballgame right into the 1960s. It used to be where you could enforce the law. I never in my life intentionally harmed or mistreated a prisoner or anybody, but back when you could enforce the law you could do a lot better job than you can now. Now, they've got officers scared to enforce the law. If one walks up right there and spits in your face, if you do what the law says, you'll turn around and walk off. It didn't used to be that way.

Loretta

After World War II, Coleman was dry and the bootleggers was running wild. We had very little law here in Coleman. H. F. had been overseas, and his old army buddies said, "Fenton, you ought to run for sheriff when you get back to Coleman." They never let him forget it. So, here he came, and can you imagine a boy today, 23 years old, that you would put a badge and a gun on in your community? He was a young kid, and all these thugs thought they was gonna give him a try, every one of them. They'd say, "You can't put me in jail!" He'd have to fight 'em on the street, and he'd usually always win. He said if he didn't win and keep his bluff in that he might as well quit, because they would rule you. Even today, if there's a fight or a confrontation somewhere and they're all having trouble, highway patrol, policemen, and all, and he walks in and says, "This is Fenton," that drunk will know just enough to know who it is. Then he'll say, "Get up those stairs," and that drunk will head for 'em.

We had an air base here that brought a lot of boys into Coleman. When they would have a weekend off they'd want to drink, and there weren't any liquor stores (here), but there were plenty of bootleggers who had it. And there was one drugstore where people was mixing drinks under the table. Well, most of the time during the war our law had just closed their eyes to that. Bootlegging was flying. We had one side of town here that I remember was so bad that my daddy wouldn't even let us go into it. That was "Rat Row," they called it. That was where the thugs hung out and the rats hung out. When H. F. came to town they said, "You won't go over there, the law don't go over there." I remember him with that little hat cocked on his head saying, "I'm H. F. Fenton and I'm gonna go over there." He wasn't gonna let any part of this town rule him. He was gonna protect the innocent and punish the guilty and do his job.

When I married him, he didn't tell me we would be moving into the jail. I guess I didn't care where we went. I was in love with him, and he was my hero, and he could do anything. But I was there to back him up with my short stick, I used to refer to it as my "do-right stick." Back when you could be a sheriff you used those things. They respected you, and they'd say "Yessir" and "Nosir;" and you never heard those words from the bottom of the stairs, "I know my rights, I want a phone call."

Raymond Greaves started off living in the jail, he and his wife, for nearly a year. His wife didn't like it. She had two little girls, and the rats were so bad that one night they were eating on the covers. This is way back when everybody in this country had rats. They didn't have exterminators, and they didn't want to hire it at the old jail. The commissioners thought, "Put an old prisoner in there and treat him like a prisoner. It's not a Holiday Inn!" Since we were on the ground floor of the same building, we had the same conditions at that time, we weren't being prejudiced. And there were bats, there was a hole in that side of the jail that they started going into. Sometimes I'd come in here at night and there would be a bat or two diving around at you, and I'd just take a broom and hit 'em.

That out there was just iron grey bars with the staircase going up. The ceilings were tall. This kitchen was the dump room, piled with old junk. This was the bathroom back here, bars on the windows, high ceilings. His deputy had lived here before us, and it was very cold in the winter, and there was wharf rats up here. We were working with not much money. When H. F. took office here, the sheriff wasn't making but 250 dollars a month, so you know what your county commissioners was gonna spend on the jail. The rats were just running everywhere, and the prisoners were fussing. Finally, H. F. got the commissioners to let us have exterminators, and we put out traps and things. I swore I'd never tell anybody about this! But my husband was sheriff and he was proud of his job, and he thought the sheriff ought to be right here at the jail. If anybody went upstairs, he knew it. If anything happened upstairs, he knew it.

I was the secretary, the jailer, a deputy. We did the whole office, we did it. I went on calls with him to keep him from being by himself, an extra precaution, I thought, for me. I went on calls with him for four years, always, before we had any kids. Ever(y) call he went on, I went. I'd get in the back, and he'd get in the front, and I'd hold my shoe over their (the prisoner's) head! 'Cause, there was no help out there then, you were alone, had no backup. If there was a drunk down at Rock Wood or Santa Anna, he had to go get him. We didn't have two-way radios, didn't have a police station, no dispatchers, just one chief of police and one night watchman. It was just Fenton and Raymond Greaves, his deputy, for that whole county. No highway patrol, no game wardens, nobody.

The first few years he earned every step he made (toward more and better law enforcement for Coleman County). Right before we moved up here he bought me a little old .25 automatic. Every call he went on, I went with him. One night this woman called that her husband was beating up her little boy, beating up on her. Two other drunks, his friends, were there in the house drinking beer. We jumped in the car, and I got my coat and I had my little automatic in my pocket. I was sitting out in the car when he goes to the door, and this guy comes out. H. F. knows enough to get him off of his porch, to talk his way out to the driveway. He followed him out, and when he did H. F. said, "You're under arrest," and the fight was on, 'cause he wasn't gonna be under arrest. Then here came these other two drunks out and pinned H. F. with his hands behind him, and there was his gun. I didn't know what was gonna happen to H. F., so I jumped out of the car and pulled my little .25, and they looked up at me! H. F. told me later, "I didn't know what I was scarder of, those three guys or you with that pistol." Those boys jumped off of him, and they stepped back, and he got up. But then he took my gun away. He didn't let me have my gun anymore.

But when you know that there's no one out there but you and your gun and that billy club and whoever you're apprehending, it's just who's the biggest man. That was the old John Wayne style in law enforcement, and that's why they wanted a fighter for the sheriff. There was a man who had a crooked hand, a deformed hand, and to show his strength he'd get in fights, and naturally he knew H. F. was gonna come and break it up. H. F. would try to put him in jail, and when he did the fight was on. He was just gonna try Fenton, and he knew H. F. wouldn't hurt him. He was a likeable fellow. I'd go along and peel his fingers off the jail staircase while H. F. moved him upstairs. He'd grab those iron bars and I'd peel his fingers off, trying to take care of him. He'd be hanging on to a bar and you couldn't pull him, and I'd help H. F. by peeling his fingers off, and then he'd grab another one like a monkey. But that man was our number one. He'd try H. F. every Saturday night, you could bank on it. He'd get ready and come to town with the idea, "I'll give old Fenton a try." He's come back to Coleman to grow old. The last time we drove by, there was a little shack and he's out in the yard drunk, and I said, "Oh, no! Not again!"

Nearly always when we went out on calls I'd have my do-right stick in my hand, or maybe I'd drive. I'd open the door for him, and I'd watch out for him. I was taking care of H. F., and he was taking care of the guy. Lots of times I'd do the driving. One time this fellow in Santa Anna jumped on the sheriff, Corkey Chapman, and H. F. grabbed him, and he was so mean and hyper and crazy that H. F. handcuffed him and held him in the back seat. That was when I drove, and I drove pretty fast to get here and get him locked up.

After we started having our babies, I had to stay here. But when I'd hear him go on a call, he did have his radio then, I'd hear him get out of his car, and I'd come in here and listen. I'd wait and wait and wait, it would seem like a hundred years until I heard him say, "Ten-eight." That would be his voice and that code meant he was back in the car. I sat in there and waited because I could get somebody to go out there to help him if I had to.

Ginger was the first baby. She was born when I was living here at the jail, and Judy was born four years later. We had both of them, and then we moved out of the jail and I had Sean, and we moved back. Sean got to live in the jail, too, which he thought was a nice thing. They'd call my little daughter "jailbird" at school—call her "jailbird, jailbird!"—but they all loved to spend the night with my kids. And my kids thought this was kind of smart, they could show off. They'd want to go show all their friends the upstairs, first, and then they'd go out and play and whatever. My sister from Houston would come up here to visit, and after they went back home her kids would tell their friends they had slept in the jail, and they'd think they were lying. The Houston jail, well, that was just a different world. They'd say they spent the night in jail and they brought in this drunk—some story like that. One night the kids were sitting in the living room and they brought this drunk Mexican in. Somebody, the highway patrol, had hit him on the head with a billy club, and blood went all over those walls. You know, it was a fight; he was a crazy Mexican and he run right in there where my kids was sitting on the floor.

They didn't know any different. After my little daughter Ginger was about five or six years old, I'd be cooking supper and taking care of the baby, and Dad would get a call and she'd go with him. She was a little girl and she went right with him, every call. When he put somebody in, Ginger would just hop right over into that back seat. We were trained that way; when he put somebody in, they got in the front, you got in the back. One time we got a call on this little drunk, and he was the cutest little drunk you ever saw. Anyway, here she goes with her dad, and they come back in and she says, "Look, Mommy, what we got!"—just like they'd gone fishing. And they had this little drunk. H. F. sat him over there on the wall, and he'd just sli-i-i-ide down, and he'd pull him right up again! And Ginger was jumping up and down,

"See, Mommy, what we got!" Other kids might not have that in their background.

It's kind of hard on a sheriff's kids in a way. Other children get by with things like driving away from the house without a driver's license, but their dad is the law, and they can't do what the other kids do. I know one time Sean was throwing rocks at the train. My little nephew Davis from Houston who didn't get to see trains, when he come up to Coleman at about age 10, he and Sean would go down to the tracks. This time they was skipping these rocks at the train, and the old conductor on the back, he sees 'em. They stopped down at the depot and he notifies the police. Then this policeman calls, says, "There's two boys throwing rocks at the train." H. F. says, "I think I know who the culprits are, just a minute." He hung up the phone, and about that time here come Sean running to the jail right around the dog pen out there. I never seen such a guilty kid; his eyes was big as dollars. Dad was pulling his belt off, and I'm saying, "Don't kill him, Dad, don't kill him!" H. F. says, "I have enough trouble with everybody else's kid in town without my own son giving me more." After he finished whipping on him, he said, "Wait a minute, Son, you're going with me." They went down there to the depot, and Sean had to walk up and tell that conductor that he was the one and he was sorry. Later in the house Sean said, "Mother, when Dad's whipping me you stay out of it. I deserved that."

My son and my daughters and I fixed all the prisoners' plates. We'd be having mashed potatoes, beans, meatloaf, or whatever, and the kids would want some more. I'd say, "There's just not enough for you to have another piece." There's an old saying in my family, "She thinks more of the prisoners than she does of me." I do have to feed those prisoners. The law doesn't say I have to feed my children, but I got to feed them (prisoners). When we had our last inspection, the jail inspector asked 'em, "Are you hungry?" And they said, "Nossir." (He) Said, "They feed you good?" "Yes, they sure do." One fellow says, "I gained 14 pounds since I been here."

In the early days H. F. got 250 dollars a month and we got to live here, and I got 50 cents a day for groceries per prisoner, which was (for) feeding 'em and washing the dishes and everything. We bought our red beans in hundred-pound bags. We did that up until last month. We cook 'em pretty good. Everybody in all our family that ever comes, they know they'll have red beans. How many beans is one hundred-pound bag a month for 30, almost 30 years? It would be a lot of beans, tons of them. We used to really have to make a lot of gravy, you know, but eggs were 10 cents a dozen and bread was cheaper. Then my family had gardens, and everybody in town would have gardens and bring it to our door, give it to Fenton. They'd say, "If you got any peas y'all don't know what to do with, Fenton will take it." I picked a lot of gardens, too. People would say, "I got a turnip patch out here," and I'd go get turnip greens, and all, everything I could salvage, just a lot of times. Then, the game warden would bring in the deer or wild turkeys that somebody had illegally killed. They all knew we could use 'em.

On Mother's Day I would always fix the prisoners a special meal, and on every other day that's a holiday. One Mother's Day the prisoners had 11 red roses delivered to the jail with a card that said, "To our jailhouse mother from her jailbird kids." That Sunday it was a pretty sunny day, and we let 'em eat out in the sunshine. You get kind of to feeling sorry for 'em, and you like 'em, there's not a one of them that isn't likeable. You get smart people in the jail, too, and they're always sending us things from the penitentiary—tools, purses, and things, you know, with our names on them. I've got an ashtray in there now that this guy made out of matches.

The kids loved the trustees, like this Bob Weaver who taught my son to pitch. He'd sit back there and throw it back at him, burn his glove. He had time to do it. Dad was working, I was busy, and he'd work with my son. And, of course, he went to my son's wedding and my son went to his. They're fond of each other now.

We had this old prisoner, Lee Dobbs, who was here a long time. My little daughter, who was just learning to talk, would ride her tricycle around in that big hall in the jail, and she'd run that little tricycle and hit the bottom of that staircase, and she'd say, "Eeee, Eeee! Come out and whing me!" He probably didn't want to all the time, but he'd stand out there in the yard and swing her. In the sunshine, they didn't mind. And he painted all of her little old horses, and he painted her swing set, and she'd make him swing her for a long time. I had a big yard there for my kids, then.

We had one boy stay here four years. He chose to. He had been sentenced to 10 years in the penitentiary for a rape and assault, and had appealed his case; and if you have 10 years, you have the right to stay here or go. If he had more than 10, say 11 years, we could have taken him on down regardless to what he wanted to do. His family was here, and he wanted to stay in Coleman and he liked the jail, so he stayed here for four years. Finally, he got married and was baptized while he was in jail. He got religion, you know, and we let him go out to the church to be baptized. We let him go out and have a part-time job, and he'd come back to the jail every night. He fell in love with the secretary over at his job and they got married, and H. F. was the best man at his wedding and I stood in for his mother. He still idolizes H. F.

He says we're more his family than his real family.

I always think how H. F. would say, "You're in the safest place in the world when you're in jail, don't be afraid." But try to tell a woman that when she's in here all by herself, and those three little kids in there sleeping.

One time H. F. was in the hospital with a heart attack. He was totally disabled, and I'm over here with three babies, Sean, Ginger, and Judy, and I hear this noise upstairs. I had a trustee, and it was a long time ago. Ginger, my oldest, was just 12. I hear this *"BING, BANG, BING, BANG, BONG, BONG, BONG,"* and I just know they're all gonna break out. I go to the phone to call the police, and I dial the number and I can't talk for fear. I can't say a word! Did you ever get that scared? There's my three babies, and I think, "Well, I'd run away, but I can't carry all three of 'em." So, I go all night and get so tired I think, "Well, just let 'em come and get me." I locked the door, put everything I could against it. I had a baseball bat and H. F.'s gun. The next morning I opened the door to feed 'em. I still had to go up there and do that. I was still here alone with my children without having called outside law enforcement, which I didn't want to do. I didn't want 'em to know I was such a coward, and couldn't talk anyway when I got on the phone!

I opened that door and rang the bell and the trustee comes down. I said, trying to act brave, "Harold, did you hear anything going on up there?" He said, "Oh, Mrs. Fenton, did I bother you?" I said, "What did you do?" He said, "Those boys paid me 50 cents to wash their trousers." He was in the shower doing that—*"BOOM, BOOM, BOOM"*—but that cost me a night of horror.

And then, before that, there was the snake. Ginger was just born, we were home from the hospital and I was still kind of weak. H. F. was taking a bath in that old tub down the hall where the bathroom used to be. Bars over those windows, mind you, you were barred in; that's why I cut 'em all off. I went back there, and as I was sitting on the tub talking to him I saw this snake come down that hall right there. He had come in from the back door. Rats, snakes, you know, bats and everything, bugs and roaches came in there. He come around like that, and I went beserk. H. F. jumped out of the tub. Can you imagine a sheriff without his . . . ? And got his boots and chased that snake down the hall and killed it. It was huge, it was tall as that door when he hung it up. I was nervous, too, just having had a baby, and I was having one fit!

When my second daughter was in the hospital and I stayed in there with her for months, on the weekends my husband would go up and stay with her, and I would get out just to get air, you know, to get away from that horrible environment of the hospital. My 80-year-old mother would spend the night with me here at the jail. We were it.

Anyway, one day I came back here and as I drove in I saw water. I could just look at the outside and tell something was wrong. I walked in there and my bathroom was about six inches deep in water. This old drunk lady had shoved a roll of toilet paper down that commode up there. I called the police to circle by and (to) help me go up and check so I wouldn't be by myself, and my mother stayed down there mopping. We went up there and that old girl was laying here, says, "I didn't intend to do that." Here I got my mop, just a-mopping, and she's sitting over there smoking her cigarette. I looks around, and I'm tired and I'm mad, and I said, "Here, you mop that up!" The liquor control man was there with me and heard me, and I said it kind of mean. She got up there and said, "Well I'm not supposed to do that. I'm a prisoner." But she mopped it up. H. F. always said he'd rather have a drunk man any day than a drunk woman in his jail. I hate to say this, 'cause I'm a female, but he's right. They'll cause you a lot more trouble.

One time H. F. went on a call to Odessa, and he called in to see if everything was OK. I says, "Well, this crazy colored man is beginning to get wild. He's throwing rocks down the stairs." He said, "Aw, it'll be all right, don't worry about it. If it gets very bad, call the chief of police over there." He called me back later and said, "How did it go?" I said, "Well, they're big boulders, now." These guys in the next cell had been making fun of him, and he had got angry and started pulling on those bars, then he began digging all these rocks and plaster out of the wall and throwing them down the staircase. I had the chief of police and the night watchman and, finally, Raymond Greaves, the deputy, up here, and every time they'd stick their head up there he'd throw a rock. You couldn't get up there 'cause he was armed like God and he'd throw these boulders. These guys in the maximum security cell next to him were sweating and beginning to shudder, 'cause they didn't know if he was going to get through that wall. I didn't either. I didn't know, and they didn't know, that there was a sheet of steel in that wall. They were saying, "Mrs. Fenton, get us out of here!"

I called the county health officer and got him over there, and he fixed up a concoction that was supposed to knock him out. So this Tony Baker, a colored trustee—been here a hundred years—says, "I'll con him into taking a drink." He got him to drink some of this supposed-to-have-been knockout medication, but he just kept on going. It seemed to give him energy. Then Dr. Jennings said, "I'll fill it up again, but this would probably kill a normal person." So we sent this back up and he drank it again. He was still angry, hitting on that wall trying to get through it, when that medication hit him. He fell the length of that cell, his head touching the commode. Raymond Greaves had a straightjacket, and they slipped it on that old boy and headed to Austin to return him to the mental institution. He was escaped, he'd walked off, and they said he was extremely dangerous— six-foot-three, about 280 pounds, black and raging. Then Dad called again, "How's everything going?" I said, "Aw, honey, you wouldn't believe it." He said, "Now, don't you worry." But my two little babies down here in this jail, and that monster up there . . . !

We've had a number of jailbreaks, and in 1947 we had a guy from Pennsylvania. That was when Raymond Greaves lived here, the first year we were married, (and that was) the nearest H. F. ever did come to killing a prisoner. They picked this fellow up for writing a bad check, it was very minor. They put him in jail, put him on that maximum security side over there. That was back when they could have tin cans in their cells, pork and beans in a can, you know. Well, while he was in there he got this can, and he ripped the soles off of his shoes right there, and he had a sawblade. He had looked at the keys, and he mashed that can flat and sawed out a key, and it opened that door. Then he got out in the middle. It had bars here where I could put the food through, and he took his sawblade and sawed these bars off. He sawed and sawed, and Raymond Greaves could hear this. It was about 10:30 or 11, 'cause a train comes through about 11:20 at night. Every 11:15 or 11:20 you know that train's gonna whistle, and if you're up there (in jail) long enough, you know it, too. He sawed and sawed, and Raymond called H. F., said, "I hear someone sawing. I'm in the jail, and I hear someone sawing out." H. F. said, "I'll be there," and jumped in his car and headed down here.

About then the guy squoze through those bars, and he's out in the runaround. Now he's wondering whether to try to go outside or down the stairs. He was up there, and they knew he was, and they were excited and scared, too. They knew that train was coming, and they waited until it came. (When it) Did, they opened that door and stepped inside, and at the same time this guy came down those stairs. H. F. had his .44 and a flashlight, and he said, "Reach," and he told me later, "If he had done one thing I'd have blown him away." He figured he'd wait until the train come by, and he'd come down those stairs and kick or knock the door open while they slept. That guy was wanted in nine states, and had escaped from the Pennsylvania penitentiary and another state penitentiary. He had a real record.

You don't forget something like that. I can lay in that room and I won't hear that train, but you can make an abnormal noise up there, jump off of a bunk, and I'll hear. I'm the soundest sleeper you ever saw, but I can hear a noise upstairs that's not normal.

They even got a right to escape, now. H. F. told his men, "If you see one of 'em escaping, let him go. It's a new law." The last jailbreak we had wasn't long ago. The night that this guy went out, he broke out on the top, went down the tree, and went in the game warden's office. Then he went across, broke into H. F.'s office, got three of his guns, went back up the tree into the jail, and offered one of these prisoners in the cell this German Luger to shoot 'em when they came back. He said, "Naw, I don't want it." Then he left it on the ledge up in the attic, went back out the top of the jail, down the tree, down the railroad tracks, and hid out under a bridge. Then he had his little brother bring him hamburgers over there, and that's how they caught him. He was mean. He could have got the keys and let the other prisoners out, but he didn't want that. He wanted somebody to get blown away.

I'm a reserve deputy, now, I did pass my shooting test. When I went to my reserve deputy school we had to qualify with firearms, and that was the hardest day of my life. I shot a big .357 magnum, my husband's gun, and these policemen that give the police academy in Abilene, they were our teachers. You had to fire 35 bullets into this little area from 15 to 50 feet. You retreated and kept firing. I fired from 11 to 6 o'clock that night, my hand was blistered from that gun, and I think I wasted all of Abilene Police Department's ammunition. Finally, I got 30 out of 70 in that area. I'm not a gun lady. I'd hit 'em over the head with a skillet if one tried to escape, something close. It was first day of dove season and all of those guys were wanting to go hunting, and I couldn't shoot! I was holding 'em all up. I really did good on my written test. I made sure of that, 'cause I knew how sorry I was gonna be when we got to the firing range.

Now I'm a certified jailer, too; I had to go to a five-day school for that. Just say for instance (that) H. F. and I were here at night and he got a call, if I wasn't certified, we'd have to call in one of these people to be here and sit with me. My husband said, "Why do you want to be a jailer?" I said, "I've lived here all my life and have been running this thing, and you're gonna hire somebody to come babysit with me? No way!" So I went to jailers' school and got my certification. I don't get paid for that. It's just another thing I do for Coleman County.

There was a time when I thought, "If I ever get out of this jail into a house I'll never want to live here again." But now I will hate to leave it, it has so many memories. Our son Sean was in kindergarten when we moved back in here. Whenever Sean found out Dad was going to move back to the jail, he said, "Oh boy, I'll get to live in the jail, too!" And here we come on my anniversary, October 19th. I said, "What a present, I'm going back to live in the jail." But by then it was beginning to grow on me as my homeplace. What do you call a homeplace but where your kids were raised? Where else have I got a homeplace? Each one of 'em will have a picture in the jail up there, and that'll be their homestead. That's the only home they ever knew.

B. RUFUS "RUFE" JORDAN

★

M y father came to Gray County, Texas, in 1908, soon after this county was organized in 1902. My people were all reared in Georgia. My great-grandfather came to Georgia from County Galway, Ireland, a long, long, long time ago. I bear the same name as he had. Everyone in four generations down have the same name, B. Rufus Jordan.

But my father came west in 1908. What was referred to as the Ferno Land and Cattle Company was very active in parts of Wheeler County, Gray County, Donley County, and Carson County. It was an English syndicate, if I understand correctly. My father was employed for quite a while with them. In a couple of years, he went back and married his childhood sweetheart, my mother, and brought her to this country. Her parents were standing at the train when they left, wondering if the Indians would get 'em. They thought there were Indians and outlaws, and (that) that's all there was. I was born in 1912, 23 miles from where we're sitting in the Pampa Courthouse, right due south. I've been here ever since.

The oil boom started in '27. Course, I was just a button in 1927, just a kid of a boy, but it seems to me that the town of Panhandle, 28 miles west of us, the county seat of Carson County, our adjacent county to the west, that's when the boom opened, over there. They was the real boom. They built the city of Borger up from nowhere, with the big false-front buildings. The little old building would be back here somewhere, and they'd be a huge false front at the front of it. Borger, Texas, 28 miles from us, that's where the boom was prior to Pampa, and a much larger boom. Borger, Texas, Ragtown, Oklahoma, and Smackover, Arkansas, were the three largest booms that we know of. In 1929 martial law prevailed in Hutchinson County. There was a young major come and took her over with 75 to a hundred soldiers. And, course, the Texas Rangers were there, they were represented. I was about 14 years old, and my father had told me never to go into Borger. He said, "You stay at home." But I was a vigorous kind of a lad, and did go over with a young uncle of mine one time while it was under martial law. Oh yes, I was very much impressed as I stood there and observed. The soldiers and a few Rangers had a huge pile of slot machines that were being bursted with sledge hammers. The Salvation Army was standing back out here. It was my understanding that the coins from the machines were to go to the Salvation Army. And they were beating the drums and singing rather loud, "Blessed Be the Tie That Binds."

Then, back to this county. We would look up, and here would come trucks going with huge loads of pipe, maybe over here somewhere from over there. After it went under martial law, the ladies of the evening, and all that business, they were ordered out of the community. And sure enough, they were riding out on loads of pipe. Or maybe one would have a vehicle and four or five would get in, and here they'd go. This sheriff had officers standing over by the bus terminal informing everyone of an undesirable character to "Move on, move on."

The boom reached Pampa a year or so later, and there were many changes. People from Kansas, Oklahoma, New Mexico, Colorado, everywhere, all came rushing in. In '28, '29, and '30 it was hard to recognize. The cattle raising community and the wheat farming community that had prevailed 36 months prior was very different. That area along the railroad tracks back in those days had a very rough element. My father was a deputy here by then, and I'd see the officers all come in with anywhere from five to 25 at a time, right to these offices. This jail had the capacity for about 30 people, and I think it was full all the time there for a number of years.

Back in the earlier days of the oil industry coming in here, there was the rig builders, the drillers, the roughnecks, the casers, the pipeliners, and what have you, and they were something else. Back when my father was connected with this office, they were truly a different breed of cats than we have today. I have observed, when I used to sell newspapers here on the street, (that) those guys would be coming in from work, and they went to prepare themselves for the night. They had a hilarious time. At Mike's Emporium Club they'd be fighting up and down those steps and around. But you know, they tell me that all those scoundrels were ready to go to work the next morning, regardless to whether they'd slept one hour or two. I used to sit over there on Foster Street with a stack of papers about that high. They'd come in there five or six in the evening, especially in the summertime. That was back in the bootleg days, and they'd be getting their drinks, I guess, about anywhere they stopped. Then, there'd be disagreements, confusion, and fighting all night long, up and down that street. I used to sit there in the afternoon and just watch 'em. Sheriff Graves told 'em on a number of occasions, "As long as you guys are just fighting, OK, but if I catch a lethal weapon balled up in this, I'm gonna put all of you in jail." He didn't have room in the jail for everybody who got into a fight.

I grew up in the courthouse. My father was a deputy, and I was attending high school right across the street. I would cut my study hall class my senior year, and circle around, and come through the south door of the courthouse up to the third floor and the courtroom. Then I would sit there and listen to those attorneys, and back in those days there were lots of jury trials. That's something else that's different from now. By that time I was determined to have a degree in law, and I would sit there and listen and watch these attorneys. My father was in the sheriff's office, but I didn't care much for law enforcement at all. It never entered my mind. Oh yes, on the point of enforcing statute law, I was very strong for that, I believed in that. But it seemed to me at that time when I thought of law enforcement, that it was at a mad rush. It looked to me like officers maybe throughout the area was looking for someone to arrest. I do not do that even today, 'cause we have enough to arrest without looking for someone. If we need to look for someone after we have that document referred to as a warrant, then we're after him.

I don't know, I certainly wanted a degree in law, but due to circumstances I had to come home. I had a little injured mother and two younger brothers, and I needed to be here. I wound up as the day jailer in the Gray County Jail. I was 19 years and 7 months old, and we had lots of inmates. I worked at that about 14 months, then left and went to work for Danciger Refiners, two-and-a-half miles out of town. I was out there for 13 years until Phillips Oil Company bought them out.

Soon after that, Sheriff G. H. Kyle, they called him "Skinner" Kyle, visited with me two or three times at our home six blocks from here about coming to work for him. Really, truly, my interest was not there, but I eventually did go to work for him, and I worked for him four years. Then in 1950, I tendered my resignation. I had no more idea of running for the office of sheriff than anything, but I say this as humbly as I know how, I had a number of people to ask me if I'd be interested in seeking the office. I said, "I believe not at this time. I have other things in mind." I called on my little mother and we visited. I said, "I can remember making you a promise when I was much younger, that law enforcement was not for me, that I wanted to do something else." She was a very ill person at that time, and spoke very calmly, reservedly, and you couldn't hardly hear her too well. She said, "Son, I've known for a long time that you'd wind up in law enforcement. You've started with Sheriff Kyle, that will probably be exactly what you will be doing the rest of your days." Well, that was kind of news to me! But I entered the race for sheriff, and was elected the twenty-fourth day of July, 1950, and have been in office ever since. 1964 was the last time I was opposed.

In my 36 years in office, many, many things have changed. The law of the land is now very different from when I went into law enforcement. As an example, for years, giving a check that was no good was referred to as "swindling with a worthless check." Well, today, very little change, but it's called "theft by check." That's fine, but if we had some person spending the night in a motel or hotel and got up and ran off and beat his hotel bill, that was "swindling an innkeeper." Well, today, that's "hindering a secured creditor!" I still like very much "swindling an innkeeper."

Many things in the law have changed. The running of an escaped inmate—of the days, so to speak, of the hound chasing you—that's about water under the bridge except in the prison system. I can remember years ago when sheriffs had two or three, most of the time they had three, hounds. Yes, that's surely been a long time ago. Now, I'd say one little nip and you'd be in a lawsuit.

But I have very little derogative comment on anything pertaining to the law of the land. I feel assured that whatever changes that were made in the penal code, they were attempting to make it better.

When I came in to this work, if you had a warrant you went out and arrested a person and said, "Now, this is an order ordering your arrest. We'll take you there and arraign you before the magistrate. If you can, well, you can make a bond. If you cannot, we will arrest and confine you to the jail facility." Well, when you go out with a warrant now, after you hunt around and you find him, you go up to him and the first thing you say is, "My name is officer so-and-so and I have

a warrant for your arrest and I must advise you against saying anything at all. When we get to the office I will give you the Miranda warning, we will get into arraignment . . . ,'' and so on. My point is, if that
is right here in town, that will take you an hour, an hour and 15
minutes, by the time you find him, give him his rights, and arrest him.
That isn't derogatory, it's factual.

There's been a lot of good things that have been surely acquired,
too. Much of our forensic sciences have worked themselves out to
where they are very constructive for the cases that they are needed
to represent. Many cases have been broken in the last five years, as
we've observed, where forensic sciences have prevailed and done
wonders. They sure have. But when something out of the ordinary
happens, and you're working and everybody is doing their utter best
to get the case solved, and some good citizen comes in some evening
and says, "I know who done it, I want to tell you," you know, that's
hard to get away from, too. I feel like that when the people that you
serve feel like contributing the information that they know you need,
that is really good and helpful.

In other words, these advances in scientific law enforcement are
wonderful, but we still need to keep the buggy. Many years ago, when
I was 12 years old, my father drove up to the ranchhouse in a 1923
model Chevrolet touring car. It was black—of course all vehicles were
black in those days. He drove up and surely he was very proud of this
Chevrolet touring car. We all came out to look, and it was black and
shiny and the top seemed to me eight foot tall. As my mother stood
there observing and listening, her children were all having a bunch
to say about the new car, and so was my father. Eventually, it became
time for the evening meal and we sat there, and my father was still
talking about the Chevrolet, the new car. He addressed my mother and
said, "That's the family car, that's your car," and so forth and so on.

We lived probably four miles from Groom, Texas. We were in this
county, but Groom was just into Carson County. I started school in
Groom, Texas. In those days we just attended the closest school. I had
been driving a horse and a buggy to school. I had ridden horseback
until my sister next to me, some two years younger than myself, started school. When she started, she did not care to ride horseback. My
father said, "Rufe, you drive Billy Bob and the buggy, and get your
sister to school yourself." That I did. Of course we had some hard
winters in those days. Snow was rather deep at intervals, but Billy Bob,
the big bay horse that I drove with the buggy, never had any problem
in getting to school. He went right on. I can remember driving up at
the back and picking my sister up at the kitchen door. She'd hurry into
the seat with me, and my mother would put two or three warm bricks

at the bottom and a lap robe over us, and here I went. During certain weather conditions we attended church the same way.

But my mother was listening to my father talk about the new car, and she said, "Frank, I think that's a fine automobile. I feel very honored that we have the car, the family car, and we'll drive it. We know very little about it, but we'll try it and we'll work with it. And we hope it's good, and we feel like it will be. But I want to say this. Billy Bob has taken our kids to school for two or three years in the buggy. Bad Sundays, he's taken our family to church in the surrey. I would suggest, Mr. Jordan, that we do not sell the buggy."

As I apply that to law enforcement, surely I have many things today that are of the old school. Maybe I'm way behind, but I still have my own way of investigating, checking things out, and I think my officers operate in approximately the same way. And I think we get along very well.

The first thing that I want to do upon going out to the scene of a murder, or a crime of that nature, is for everybody just to stand back and observe and look for about five minutes. I like to have three or four there. You know, three or four heads, minds, and sets of eyes will make a difference. Then we rope off our area, and we don't want it left unattended until we get started. We'll be checking for anything that might go with our case. We look, then we put our cordons up around, and then we take a look all around this area and see what we can find. Of course, right after our first observation, we get our magistrate out there to see whether or not he thinks it necessary to have an autopsy. We like to get right down to the basic facts of what is there. We like photography. I liked it then, I like it now. We'll say that it was a murder case, that someone is lying here. We need to know exactly how they were lying when we first observed them. All that.

When you have a crime committed, I think the whole plan is visitation, observation, and interrogation. It takes a lot of visiting, sometimes. You need to think, "I wonder if Joe Jones, one of his friends, Sam Watley or someone else, can tell us something? They used to run together, they used to be friends, I wonder what he knows about this?" That's where I get around to visitation. You've got to visit with people. As you visit with 'em, you ask, "How long has it been since you've seen old Joe?" "Oh, I haven't seen him in seven or eight years." In fact, he may go along and say, "I've just about quit Joe. He went bad," and this and that and the other. And directly, maybe he'll relate to you some little something that happened with Joe that this person remembers, that he wasn't very well pleased with the way it come out. I think visitation with people who are acquainted helps a lot. Then I get around to observation. We want to observe these people that we've talked to. Maybe you'll find one after a while that moves over here a mile or so and talks to another friend, and they visit about Joe. After a while it comes around to where somebody may want to come in here and talk to you about something you're not aware of. When he's served with 'em a long while, an officer knows his people, and they trust him and things surface, occasionally, that he needs to know very badly. Those people will give him the information they have. I've seen that many times. I can think of a number of cases in years gone by where a person just called me and said, "I know who done it." I've said, "Well, that's fine. Do I come to your home or do you come here? I'll be down there in a half hour." But I still think that visitation, observation, and interrogation is three things that needs to be applied when you are, so to speak, stumped. You're looking for something, and you sorely need to find something before you can proceed farther. They're all part of the buggy that we'd better not sell.

My mind reverts back to a man who used to be in Amarillo, Texas, when I was a very young man, by the name of Clark Kane. He was a chief of detectives down there in the Amarillo Police Department. I had the privilege a time or two, when I was a lad 15 or 16 years old, to observe Clark Kane. He was an exceptional fine looking fellow, I thought, maybe 48 or 50 years old. He had a piano in his office. He was a friend of my father's, and I, on occasion, was sitting there when he was interrogating someone. He was a past master when it came to interrogating, maybe the sharpest that I ever saw. They had no Miranda warning in those days. He would introduce himself. "My name's Clark Kane. I am the chief of detectives of the Amarillo Police Department. What is your name, your date of birth? I'd like some information on you." The man would answer, "Well, my name is Joe Jones. I was born and raised in the state of North Carolina. I left that country and I'm here, there, and yonder."

Of course, in those days they referred to a man's past and prior record as a rap sheet. Kane would say, "I observe here that you've had problems, so and so, and so an so, and so an so." And he'd keep on, very cool and collected and right across the board, nothing harsh or ornery. But after they'd visit like that for a while, then he'd become very stern, and while he looked at 'em and started making his speech, he was kind of out of this world.

"I have no doubt about your guilt in this case. If I did have, I wouldn't have you in here," and they'd go from there. And he had a lot of quotations that he used frequently, you know. "We can only realize that there has never been but one perfect man, and he didn't want to be in law enforcement. So, mankind has been making mistakes from time immemorial. You've made yours in the past, and you're making them now. I do not know when the time's coming when you correct your measures and get back and get yourself lined up. But I can assure you that I will get this case worked out one way or the other, because I'm sure that you are guilty of what I'm talking to you about.''

Well, after a while, in a matter of 15 or 20 minutes, you'd see the subject weaken to some degree. And he might even say, ''Well, Mr. Kane, what will a situation of this kind carry, state time, in your state?'' He'd say, ''I could not tell you, sir. That's strictly up to a court of law. I'm a law enforcement officer. You're going to have to pay your debt to society, you're going to have to serve your time.''

There were times after he'd visit and make his speech when he might turn around to his piano and play a bar or two, a tune or two, and smoke a cigar. Then he'd spin around and proceed again, maybe asking questions that had nothing to do with whatever he was interrogating him about. But he'd come up with something else, and after a while, it look to me like he'd gained the confidence of the offender that he was talking to. I know he worked out a lot of cases.

Oh yes, every law enforcement officer has got some little things that he has to say that he thinks might assist a little bit here, there, and yonder when they're interrogating a subject with regard to a case. I've found in my tenure and time (that) I'm not much of a spoofer or a joker when we're talking with one. I want him to know that I respect him to the utmost, and I surely expect to get his respect, and we go from there. You got to visit with one 10 or 15 minutes to find out just exactly how rigid he is, or if there's something that you might say that might soften him a little bit. Then you can tell more about him, and you proceed from there. Anything that he may have to say (that) will help lead you to understand whether he is a rigid individual, or whether there is a place there that you might talk to him about that might tenderize the situation, is helpful. I never have been much on promises. I think that the man or woman you are interrogating must be observed and given the opportunity to make a few remarks, whatever it may be. Take the opportunity to listen to 'em. As a rule, it will give you some kind of little lead or hint as to what their personality is like.

I can remember a case 28 years ago. These boys had been out around Oklahoma somewhere. They were safe burglars, four or five of 'em in two vehicles. We apprehended three of 'em here. The bellweather of the bunch was about a three-eights Choctaw Indian, six-foot-and-an-inch tall, weigh a hundred-and-80 pounds. He was harder than iron, he sure was. He would just laugh when we'd ask him questions. Sheriff Hugh Anderson from Borger—sheriff there for 30 years, we buried him 15 months ago in Lubbock—he took the big Indian over there. Then there was a heavy-set, very fair-complected, kind of tender-looking old boy that I'd say he was 28 or 29 years old. You could tell he'd never worked in his life by looking at his hands. His name was Strum, and I kept him and the other one. They were here in this jail for quite some time. Well, as we visited and interrogated this fellow Strum and went plum on back into his family life, where he was reared and raised, and so forth, I would say that in a matter of hours and maybe the next day he'd given us more information than I'd ever had from any one individual in my life! It covered three or four states.

It was easy that time, but there (are) a lot of cases you don't get worked out maybe for quite sometime. But we have a policy here, we just leave our files intact and open, we never close 'em or write a finish to 'em, we just leave 'em on file. And I'm a great fellow to have everything in that file that we've ever had to do with the case. If there's any writing notes and any doodling around while you're talking to 'em, well, just drop that in the file, too. Things like that I think sometimes mean quite a bit to us. I've known some cases in this county that were years old before you came up with a lead, say, a good solid suspect. Then you got to revert back to that file you got in there. All of that sort of thing is part of the old buggy, too.

In the area, and I'll say in a radius of 25 or 30 miles, we had lots of burglary, and back in those days it was safe burglary. You don't see much of it anymore. Safe burglars were very prevalent, they surely were, and each of 'em had his own way of doing their business, opening a safe, and you could just about tell who it was. Everyone, regardless of what they're doing, has a *modus operandi* of doing it. We definitely believed there was a number of times when we could tell who had pulled this particular safe burglary by the way it was done.

I can remember the Ash brothers, and the one they called "Knob" Ash, they would knock the knob off of a safe. "Knob knockers," they used to refer to 'em. They had a little kit. They always had a little short-handled, three-pound sledge hammer, then they had some old valves out of a car. They did not blow a safe. You had lots of people who had explosives to open safes with, such as nitroglycerine. They'd drill two or three holes in the top of the safe, get the nitro in there, maybe just a few drops, and seal that over with soap. This was right over the door. Then they'd whack that thing a pretty good blow back there on the side or somewhere, and the door would blow off of that safe. But the people we're discussing here, now, they didn't do that. They made their entry and got in there, and the first thing they did, they knocked the knob on the safe. Now, there's a steel plate right back in the combination of that safe, I'd say it's an eighth or a quarter-of-an-inch thick. In would go one of those valves, the top of it about two inches around, and they'd whack that very good with that hammer to drive that plate right on back. Then the parts of the combination would fall, they'd come apart, and the door would open.

I can remember, on the main street of our city here one morning, there was a grocery store right on main street and entry was made into the back in an alley. The safe had been broken into, and as I went over and looked around with two or three other officers, processed the safe and the surroundings for fingerprints and so forth, as I looked and observed, I made mention to Assistant Chief Dumas, "You know, Knob Ash did this. I feel sure he did this, he and some of his cohorts." Sure enough, as we proceeded further in the next two or three weeks, everyone was right regarding to Knob. Knob had come in there, along with one of his brothers and someone else. He had a time limit, he's told me this: 26 minutes. He said, "If I don't have something done in 26 minutes, I want to get out of there. Because there's no use staying there till somebody catches you."

The fingerprint identification has been great for years and years, and always will be, the old Henry system, as they refer to it. Some of the best men that are anywhere are still fingerprint identification men. You could get fingerprints, quite frequently you could, but the old safe cracksman, the old knob knocker, the old lone offender, he'd pull gloves on before he even got to the door.

Today you find so many young folk, 23 or 24 years old, their *modus operandi* is not like that of the old burglar. Today, one of 'em will just about walk up and knock a window light out, and crawl through there, and more likely than not scratch himself up and leave a little blood somewhere. But in they go, and what they take is just what they see.

We had some other kinds of theft peculiar to an oil-field country. Back in the days before I was connected with the office, in the Borger area, every known offender in the country rushed in, and they were highjacking those men out on those rigs and taking their money. Course, that was a long time ago, when I was young. In recent times in our county, pertaining to the oil industry, about the only thing, every once and awhile you'd run into some old boy who'd steal a load of crude oil out of a tank.

We caught some, and some we did not catch. You see, they'd have a battery of tanks, maybe six or seven, five-hundred-barrel tanks that the pump is pumping into. Down 15 inches from the base of the tank and from the ground would be an oil outlet, and these guys would just back up there and load up out of the bottom of that tank. The virgin crude was down at the bottom, and that was what they were wanting. I'll never forget an incident over here in the edge of Carson

County. This old boy pulled up in his truck and filled it with six or seven-hundred barrels of crude oil, but he didn't get his two-inch valve on the back of his truck tank closed off good. Those officers tracked him plum up to his home three miles out of Stinnet! And they went in there and got him, and that oil was still dripping out of that tank. I was over in Borger when they were interrogating him. There were officers from all over the country there, because most of 'em had lost some crude, but he wasn't scared. He'd just die laughing. He'd say, "I'm not gonna have very much to say to you fellows, but if you catch everyone of us that's been stealing some crude oil, well, you're not gonna have a place to put us all." He may have been right.

A lot of things have changed in 36 years, people as well as laws. I was on the program at the sheriffs' conference in Waco two years ago this coming July, and as I was introduced and looked out across the conference floor, I immediately missed 20 men that I'd known for years who were no longer there. You know, Bill Decker, Owen Kilday, J. D. Hamilton, and Wallace Reddell, who was in his thirty-ninth year as sheriff when he died. There's just a lot of the old boys that are gone, they sure are. I can think back to those old scoundrels, and they're all gone. "Big Ed" Darnell died just a few weeks ago.

You know, the old boys that I grew up with and worked with for years, you'd see one with an old hat about like that on his head and his high-heeled boots, and you could nearly tell who he was when you drove into his town and took a look at him. There's still a bunch of those in Texas, even some of the newer ones. And nearly every officer you ever find, as he reverts back, he's putting his copy, so to speak, on some officer that he knew somewhere, sometime, that he was very fond of his operation.

The old breed of Texas Rangers are gone, too. Those boys are all gone. They were truly great men, they surely were. They had a way of doing things that sometimes they might not have pleased everyone. The saying has always been, "I saw my duty and I done it," that's the way they operated. I appreciated a lot of those fellows, and I miss 'em.

Hamer was a great investigator. Bill McDonald, Frank Hamer, Tom Hickman, and the very famous M. T. Gonzaullas. I've heard people say Gonzaullas was the most egotistical man they'd ever seen in their life, but my grandfather used to say, "He is not a bragger, because he can do what he tells you he is going to do." I knew the Captain pretty well, and he was something else. Yes, it must have cost a thousand dollars for him to clothe himself every morning, and he probably changed his whole attire along in the afternoon. He was a great guy to dress up, wore a huge cream color hat turned up on one side, kinda like Buffalo Bill Cody. He was a handsome, debonair kind of a guy, and yes, he was egotistical. I've heard when the radios first started coming in, and before the Texas Rangers and the Highway Patrol had 'em, he had to put two aerials on the back of his car just to have 'em on there—no radio in his car, just the aerials.

Sheriff Jess Sweeten of Henderson County was, I guess, the greatest pistol shot in the Southwest. He had a black boy that had been in a car wreck when he was about 10 years old and lost an arm. He raised that boy around out there, and that's the boy that he shot the apples off of his head and the cigarettes out of his mouth. He'd stand sideways, and (Sweeten would) just pop a cigarette out of his mouth; I've watched him shoot a number of times. He would go off somewhere and take just a little nip about 15 minutes before he shot. He told me he'd been doing that for years. I don't know whether he drank much, or not; I never did know. He said it just steadied his nerves. I don't know anyone who ever defeated him in a pistol match. He was six-foot-four-inches tall and weighed at his best, in his prime, 225 pounds. They always called him the "seven-foot sheriff." He wore a high-crowned hat and bootheels about that high, and I guess he was around seven-feet tall.

Jim Flournoy was another of the tallest sheriffs we ever had in Texas. Jim was six-six. He was one of the finest, cleanest, quietest sheriffs that I ever knew in my life. He wanted to love everybody, but he need never be crossed, if you understand what I mean. He was another fellow, like me, who wanted high-heel boots. His hat was always a large hat, sticking up. He died two or three years ago, and when he retired the *Dallas Morning News* recognized him in a special enclosure in the paper about five pages long. It was fine, it was great, but every time you turned the page you run into the Chicken Ranch. I didn't want him known for the Chicken Ranch, because he was an outstanding sheriff.

North of us 60 miles in Ochiltree County, Sid Talley was sheriff there for 37 years. It just broke my heart, I didn't want him to seek reelection. He was 76 years old, he'd been there always. He was loved by every person in that county, and that's covering a lot of say-so, too. He and I had lunch together in Amarillo, and I said, "Sheriff, why don't you just take out? You been there too long." A tall, slim old fellow, he said, "Why, Rufe, I don't know what I'd do." His wife had gone on several years before him. He said, "I been down there ministering to these people for years and years and years." I said, "Yes, I know, but you got a lot of new people up there now that don't know you like I know you." He got beat in the next election, and it disturbed me to no end. Four years later I was a pallbearer at his funeral. But he was a great old sheriff. He was just a cowboy up there in World

War I. It was a very thinly populated county, and so many of those boys had gone off to the service, the story goes that he had a very light little wagon of some kind with a couple of ponies hooked to it and (he) hauled groceries to all those women and children. Later on, he ran for sheriff and no one even ran against him. He was a great old man. The changing times changes everything. I've known so many changes since I've been in this office. The old school has gone.

Bill Decker was quite a sheriff, a member of that old school. I've known Bill Decker by far the bigger part of my life. He always did things that amazed me. His office was hardly as large as this little old office of mine. It had glass all around it that come up to the ceiling. He wanted to know everything that was going on there, and he knew everything that was going on in the department of Sheriff of Dallas County, which is a large county and a large department. He got to the office at 11 o'clock in the morning and left at one A.M. That was his hours, eleven to one.

He had his own way of doing things. Captain Will Fritz, with the city police department in Dallas for years and years, and Decker were the greatest of friends. And the old saying, always, all my life, was: "Bill Decker knew who they were and Fritz knew where they were." Fritz knew what was going on about as well as any man I'd ever known in my life, and he and Decker together were something else.

Now, when Decker took you out to lunch, he didn't go somewhere downtown to one of the finer restaurants, he took you out to Richardson or somewhere, because if he didn't he couldn't eat. In Dallas, people would be coming up all the time. "Bill, do you remember me?" "Well, yes, I believe I do." "Bill, do you know that Jadie Joe, my daughter, has a son?" "Well, no, I'm not sure." "Well, she named the son for you." That would go on all the time. He could not eat.

Decker had sources of information that were incredible. How he did it, I'll never know. Right up here at Ochiltree County, at Perryton, 63 miles above us, Ray Phagan was the sheriff at that time. Otis Burke had two drugstores there, and he was mayor of the town. A fellow came in there that knew Burke that had something to do with this "Blue Diamond Display" they were showing all over the country. There was in the neighborhood of 850,000 dollars (worth) of stones, they referred to 'em as the Blue Diamonds. This man and the mayor, Otis Burke, had attended college together. They visited quite frequently. Finally, the time came when they went out for a cup of coffee. This man had kept the briefcase with the diamonds handcuffed to his hand, but he left it in Otis' office.

It was in the shank of the evening by the time they had finished with their coffee and conversation and visitation, and the drugstore had closed. This old boy, apparently it slipped his mind or something, because he went up and retired to his hotel. Three or four o'clock in the morning he waked up, and it dawned on him that he didn't have the Blue Diamonds, and he went as wild as he could. Course, he ran to the drugstore knowing it would be locked. When he finally got ahold of Burke, they came down there and the store had been broken into. Someone had gone up on top and come in by the air conditioner. The stones were gone, and three cartons of cigarettes.

Sheriff Phagan was always a very grey-headed fellow, but his hair became snow white. He ran everyone that had any knowledge about this bunch of diamonds on the lie detector, the man that was carrying 'em, Burke, I don't know who else. It didn't do any good. I was talking to Ray in his office one afternoon, and old Ray was just walking the floor. He said, "I don't know what in the world, I don't know where to start." I said, "No one knows, but it looks to me like Bill Decker could do more for you than any man in the Southwest."

The next day he went to Dallas and met with Decker. Bill said, "Ray, you take Mrs. Phagan to the Baker Hotel and stay there, don't come back. You stay there until you hear from me. Enjoy yourself and let's see what we can come up with."

Five days later at 3:30 in the afternoon Decker called. Ray had gone to the lobby to get a paper or something, but he told Mrs. Phagan, "Tell Ray to come down to the office." Well, from the Baker Hotel to the sheriff's office at that time was about five blocks. Ray made no attempt whatever to use his car out there in the garage, he just blared off down there on foot. He got there, and there sat Bill in the corner with an old kid about 20 years old sitting there with him. Ray recognized him through the glass of Decker's office. Bill give him the come-on sign, and he come in. He says, "You know this boy, Sheriff Phagan?" He said, "Why, yessir, I do. He works in the restaurant up there as a dishwasher." Bill said, "He wants to tell you where the Blue Diamonds are."

Well, old Ray like to fainted. He said, "Bill?" The lad was not too strong in his head, you know. Decker said, "Yes, he can tell you all about it." So, the kid did tell him right there in the presence of Decker. He had worked in this restaurant washing dishes, and the fellow that owned it had some hog pens about 350 or 400 yards away. The kid broke into the drugstore, went back in there to get some cigarettes, didn't know what the case contained, just picked it up and left with it. Then he went out to the pig pens, scratched a little hole in the ground, dropped the Blue Diamonds in there, and covered 'em up, but put one of 'em in his pocket. He went to Amarillo and was in the Grand Bar, as the story goes, and said, "Does anybody want to buy a diamond?'' One old boy says, "Let me see it." He showed it to him, and he said, "Well, yes, I'll buy that stone, what do you want for it?" The kid said, "125 dollars," and he said, "I believe I'll take it," and he did. That's the only diamond that never did get found. They got all the other ones out of the hog pen. Ray relaxed for the first time in a coon's age, but his hair still got whiter.

That's just one of the many things that I've known Bill Decker working out. He was something else. He would sit in his office and—I don't know, no one knew—he would get that information somehow at night. He was there at night to one o'clock in the morning, and he'd get ahold of this one and that one and this one and that one, tell 'em something, and they'd pass it on. And after a while, in what was generally referred to as the underworld, it was pretty well known. That's the way he operated. Sheriff Lon Evans, Bill's neighbor over there at Fort Worth, used to say, "If it wasn't for Decker's informers, I wouldn't have an outlaw in my county. They work here and live over there."

There's one thing about the office of sheriff, if something is going on and you're not too well pleased with it, anyway it'll change in a little while, they'll be something else come up. It may not be as good as that was that you didn't want, but they'll be something all the time. There surely will. Of course, the office of sheriff is different than the Texas Ranger, it's different than the police department, because you can see all the civil business we've got laying here on my desk. There are some criminal warrants, but in the last few years we surely have had a lot of civil practice. I mean, just marching and serving citations and getting into executions and writs of sequestration and things of that kind, subpoenas for your courts.

When you have a civil procedure, a divorce procedure, and a child is given to one parent or the other, maybe whoever he gives it to, the other one (currently) has the child. The court gives you an order and says, "Go get him and bring him to me." Well, that is something that is very unpleasant, and you need to be very careful with that. You just have to do the best you can.

Maybe the child's been carried off to another state, and they're very emotionally upset and disturbed. And you get into family feuds, and that's something else that sometimes makes you wish you could go back to section gang, so to speak. But at the same time, I do not have an unlisted telephone in my apartment. My line number is open to the world. I live in the courthouse. Mrs. Jordan and I, she's gone now, we lived in there 36 years.

It's been a long time. I've seen the time, 25 or 30 years ago, when I could sit down and cry, but you couldn't do that. I venture to say that most of it has been very enjoyable, but there's been times I've repeated prior when I could hardly take it. Something would happen, something that we had to get into and do. I don't think there's a sheriff in Texas that hasn't had to put people in jail that didn't disturb him to no end. But you got to do 'er. If the statute law is in violation, you got to act, that's all there is to it. You're expected to. You serve and do the best you can.

And yes, people come in here to see me. On Mondays, they want to talk to the old sheriff. I come down here about 9:30 in the morning, and sometimes I get out by 2:30 or 3:00 in the afternoon. We have 11 field men, capable men, and they do a lot of this work, but at the same time, I don't know why, they want to come in here and tell me their troubles. That's fine, that's fine. And sometimes you can give a sensible answer to what they're seeking, but you do your best.

Elderly people, they want to call, they want to talk a little bit, it means something to them. And yes, I take time to talk with 'em, I surely do. It may be that in a matter of five or seven minutes I can make them feel better about their problem. Oh, I never sit down at my table to eat in my life, I don't believe, especially in the evenings at 6:30 to 7 o'clock, that I don't have a call or two from some very good old people that I love very much.

I can remember a little lady here who lived to be 93 years old. I don't care what was happening, she'd call me, bless her heart. Before she passed away, she called and talked to my wife and said, "I need to talk with Rufe right away." I got out there, it was in the evening, 8 o'clock or 8:30. She was very ill, her daughter was there from the state of Pennsylvania and maybe another relative. But she said, "Rufe." She had one of these little small, slick dogs, I think it was a Mexican Chihuahua. She said, "Rufe, I'm not long for this world, and I'm ready to go home. My people do not live here. Butch, that's the little dog, I want you to be responsible for this little dog. I'm not asking for you to keep him, but you see that he has a good home, somewhere. I want to pass that on to you." I said, "That's fine. That is fine, my dear, and I'll surely do that." Her daughter said as I was leaving, "Sheriff Jordan, you don't have time for that, do you?" I said, "Yes, mam, we'll take time for that. I've known her for 45 years, she's called me on the average from one to 10 times a year to assist her and to help her, and we'll take time." Little things like that.

One day before my wife passed away, when she was gravely ill, she asked me what would happen to her white poodle dog after she was gone. I said, "What do you think? I will keep her with me, always."

I answer calls just like my men do. When I get a call and maybe they're tied up doing something, why I run out and see about it. Surely I do. An', oh yes, there are times I end up driving all over this county and maybe get back here at 3:30 or 4:00 in the morning. That poodle is always along. She wants to go everywhere I go, and she rares up there and looks out that windshield just like she knew what she was looking at. About all she knows is this courthouse and the jail.

TRUMAN
MADDOX

★

After the war, I married and decided to go into business for myself in Sealy, Austin County. I bought a grocery store and meat
market. It was an election year. "Bounce" Reinicke was the sheriff
and Marcus Steck was running against him. After the election was over
with and Marcus won, he came to Sealy and met with quite a few of
the people there. He was looking for a deputy to work that area.

See, that was before communications was as good as they are now,
and Sealy was a long ways off from Bellville. There were no radios,
very little money to work on, and the only communication was strictly by telephone, and the commissioners advised the sheriff not to use
very much of their money for telephone calls unless it was real necessary. He needed a deputy to work in Sealy. Anyhow, this meat market
that I had had a barbecue pit in the back and I was back there. Mostly
on Wednesdays and Saturdays we'd have big barbecue days, fix these
hot links and barbecue, and a lot of people would come to town and
we'd really sell a lot of it. I've sold as high as four to five-hundred
pounds a day back there through that little old pit in the back.

So, I was back at the pit one day when a gentleman by the name of Dallas Hibboldt and Marcus Steck came to see me. Mr. Hibboldt was the owner of the building that I was leasing, and he and Marcus Steck was good friends, so they both came back there and was talking with me. They asked me would I be the deputy with Marcus, since he had won the election. I told 'em in kind of a joking way, "I've been running from the law for 30 years, why should I change and start running with 'em, now?" We laughed on it for a little bit and then they got serious, and I got more serious deciding that I didn't want to take it because I didn't know enough about law. I thought that a man should know more than the average man on the street to become an officer, to tell someone else what to do. I said if they found that it was possible for me to go to some kind of school, then I would consider it. After they left, I talked to various people in Sealy and they encouraged me. I called the Department of Public Safety, and they was putting on a school at that time known as the School for Texas Sheriffs out at Camp Mabry. So, I took the job.

I took over in January of 1949, I was the only full-time deputy that Marcus had. He had a half-time man working in Bellville who was paid 75 dollars a month, and I was paid 150 dollars. The one there in Bellville had to drive a school bus to supplement his salary, and I had the meat market to supplement mine. I was supposed to be a full-time man, but I still run the market.

It was kind of thought of as "the law south of Mill Creek" and "the law north of Mill Creek." That's the creek running through the center of the county. We had part-time deputies in other little old communities, Wallace had one then that I think might have been paid 15 dollars a month, something like that, very little, and then we had one in Industry. About all they did, if they had some kind of argument between a couple of people and if they could settle it, fine. If they didn't, they called us and we went and took over. Sealy had a constable, a gentleman by the name of Mier, and he was well up in his sixties and weighed about three-hundred pounds, and was used mostly as a night watchman. He could hardly get in and out of his car. Those kind of people just held the job 'cause it was there, that's all.

We didn't see each other but maybe every two weeks. We didn't have no radio and couldn't even call much, 'cause it cost 10 or 15 cents to call from Sealy to Bellville, and that run into money and the commissioners didn't like that. We just pretty well run it. The commissioners didn't allow us to do any patroling, either. We furnished our own cars and was paid so much for mileage, up to 25 dollars a month. When that 25 dollars was up, the rest was on you. I stayed down there except on court days, and Marcus would usually stay up here. At that time I was fortunate, I knew the telephone operators real well, they were good friends. Somebody would call the telephone operator, give her the message, and she'd sit there grinding on that phone and find me somewhere. I tried to tell the operators where I thought I was gonna be. Later, I got the city to put in a police phone. It rang at my house and uptown on this corner of Post and Main streets in a beer joint there called "My Place." They had this phone on the outside with a loud bell, and you could hear it all over town. If I was down the street somewhere, and if somebody wanted me and couldn't find me at the market, they'd ring this phone and I'd run all the way up the street up there to answer it. So, that was our communications that we had then. I pretty well took everything down on the south end of the county.

Just a few months after I went in as deputy, I was back at the barbecue pit when I heard a gunshot. Then I heard another one. I ran to the front and looked, and laying in the front door of my market was this gentleman, Dallas Hibboldt. He lay face down, with the screen door open, blood running out of his back. He says, "Forrest Ward shot me, go get him!"

Let me back up just a little bit. The reason why I heard two shots, he shot Mr. Dallas one time, he turned and started to go north from there, and at a cafe next to my market a man opened the door. (The man was one) that some people at that particular time got mixed up with me once and awhile anyhow. He wore a hat about like mine, and usually wore a white shirt like mine, and he was about my size. This guy run to the front door when he heard that shot and swung the door open right quick. Forrest was walking along and he turned, and "POW!"—boy, he shot. He was gonna shoot him right between the eyes, but the man jumped back and the bullet went through the edge of the door facing, through the screen door, through the wall of the cafe into my market, hit the ceiling of my market, glanced over and hit this plaster wall, turned and went through this lattice between the front and the back of my market, and hit a wooden barrel that I used to salt meat down with. Later we found that .45 slug inside that meat barrel.

Anyway, I saw Mr. Dallas was down, and I went out on the sidewalk and looked down toward the City Cafe, which was north on Polk Street, and Forrest Ward was walking down the sidewalk toward the City Cafe, a hangout for a lot of people. Out in front there's an old bench where a lot of the old men used to go sit and shoot the breeze. OK, I started down that way, young and brand-new, knowing that he's got a gun, knowing that he just shot a man, thinking, "I'm going after him, but I don't exactly know what I'm gonna do." That's just about what you got on your mind. You know you got to move on, 'cause that's your job, but he's got a gun, too. If he shot him, he's liable to shoot me! I was heading on that way and he looked back, and when he looked back he saw me coming.

There was a man coming along there by the name of Jim Sailor, a tall, thin, lanky man. When Forrest looked down and saw me, he grabbed this man from the back, turned him around completely in the street, and had the man, Mr. Sailor, between himself and me. He reached into the left back pocket of his overalls and pulled out a .45, and leveled down and fired once at me coming down the street. I saw this in time to make a move, and I jumped in a doorway and pulled my gun. After he fired, Mr. Sailor jerked loose from him and broke to run, and so did all the men on the sidewalk. One other man that I remember was a man named Allen, a gentleman well up in his seventies who must have weighed close to three-hundred pounds. He was very feeble, and was used to people driving him up in front and helping him out of the car and walking him to the bench, and he would sit there and enjoy talking with the rest of the old gentlemen and so forth and so on. It was just a meeting place and he really enjoyed it. He was a fine gentleman, a fine man, but he couldn't walk by himself. But when those bullets started flying, the last thing I remember was seeing him going around that corner down there. He didn't look crippled at all. He was doing real good. The whole street cleared out.

Forrest broke and got behind some cars. He looked through the glass of one of the doors, and I took a shot at him and thought I got him. Looked like that bullet went through the car door right where his nose was. Next time I saw him he had moved down a car or so and was looking through the glass again. He throwed his gun around on the left side with his left hand, he was left-handed, trying to fire around the car. Well, each time I would see him, I had to shoot through a glass of another car, and each time I'd fire I'd say, "Well, that hit him." I shot the glass out of four cars and a pickup. He fired five or six times at me, and I kept getting closer each time. Then, finally, I ran between two cars and he came up behind his car then with both hands up, showing that he didn't have a gun.

Well, I didn't know what had happened to his gun. Then I heard a voice from across the street that I recognized, "Don't shoot my son! Don't shoot my son!" I backed up where I could see this man, too. I might have used some foul language about that time, but I remember I told him that he better get that jacket off of him at once, because I didn't know where his gun is at.

His daddy was the man who asked me not to shoot him. Now, in Sealy his daddy had been known to be a very mean man. He wore a homemade coat, three-quarter-length, his wife would always make these coats. Cold, hot, anything else, he'd have this coat on, and the old story was that he wore that to keep his gun hid. No one ever took the liberty to go and search him to see if he had a gun, but everybody said that he had a gun under there. The old stories was that he had killed three people on the streets of Sealy.

That all flashed back in my mind. I'm standing there with this one over here shooting at me, and him coming there, a man like that. I thought, "Does he have a gun? Is he fixing to shoot? Can I try to finish him off here, or should I wait?" Back and forth in your mind you got to do a lot of thinking.

The old man did exactly what I told him. I told him if he wanted his son he better get that jacket off of him, and he did, he tore his jacket off. He got it off, but he didn't have no gun. Well, a few seconds had gone by by that time. Then a man came from behind me and asked me if I wanted the gun? I said, "Yes, I don't know where it's at." I was standing within two feet of the gun. The last shot that I shot at Ward looking through the car window filled both his eyes with glass. He was having a terrible time seeing and had dropped his gun.

So, I picked the gun up and stuck it in my belt, and marched him up the sidewalk with his daddy. As I went by the market I told my wife, "Call Steck quick, because there's liable to be some more shooting." See, this was an old feud between the Hibboldts and the Wards. Dallas had been carried to the hospital, but Jack, his brother who was a deputy game warden at that time, wasn't there. And neither one of the Hibboldts is no one to play with, nossir, and Mr. Ward is no one to play with, and he's loose on the street. If Jack comes to town and they meet, there could be some more.

At that time I had a little two-cell jail 'cross the track there in Sealy, just a little frame building with windows in it. The cells was in reaching distance of the windows, and there was no bars on the windows. I was taking Forrest to jail, and I knew if I didn't get something done quick there would be another killing, so I told my wife to call Mr. Steck and tell him to get here quick and come to the jail. I headed Forrest for the jail and left his daddy in town. I was thinking that if Jack Hibboldt heard about it, he would come to town with his feathers ruffled; and if Dick Ward was in town and they met, there would be another killing. But if I put Forrest in jail and left to come back to town to take care of that, and if Jack finds out this man is in jail, all he's got to do is go over there and look through the window. And I knew what he would do, he'd kill him right there.

I was torn between what to do, but Steck came and he came in a hurry. He drove up to that old jail over there and that old Plymouth was steaming. I told him, "Get this man in the car quick, and head for Bellville." He said, "Man, this car's hot. I can't now, I got to get . . . ." I said, "I don't give a damn if it burns up, we're fixing to have another killing. Get him and get him out of here, now!"

He put the man in the car and headed for Bellville. He hadn't been gone two blocks when Jack Hibboldt drove up. He was trying to get out of his car, and he had his pistol in his hand. He'd already heard that I had Forrest in jail over there. I talked to Jack for a long time before I even let him know that he wasn't in there. I kept him there, 'cause long as he was there he wasn't going to run into Dick in town, and it was giving Steck more time to get out of town to get to Bellville. He might have to stop for water somewhere, and if I had told him Steck was on the way, he liable to have took off after him.

So, I talked to Jack a long time and finally got him cooled down and back home. Then I went back to town, and they said that old man Dick Ward had already left town. It did cool off there without any further shooting. But, hell, all that happened my first year in the business!

Then, as if that hadn't been enough, Forrest Ward broke jail. We had several breaks down at that old Bellville jail, and this man was one of 'em. He was gone for a few days, and no one knew where he went to. The Wards had a farm down in the Brazos River bottom, way back in the woods, and some people from Freedeck came in and told me that they saw Forrest at that house at just about dark, saw him go in that house and know he's down there. I called Mr. Steck and told him. He says, "OK, I'll be down there in a little bit." He had a man here in town at that time, a part-time deputy, so he brought him along, and I got Dee Brune, who was just a guy that always liked to ride around with me, just a plain citizen. When Mr. Steck got there I told him, I says, "Let's go by and get Mr. (Dick) Ward." Says, "Oh, no, we don't want him!" I said, "Let me explain to you why I think we ought to have Mr. Ward. I believe Mr. Ward can talk him out of that house if he's in there, but if we go down there, we cannot." To be frank with you, I thought Forrest was partly a mental case anyway.

I went by Mr. Dick's house, and Mr. Dick said, "Naw, I'm afraid myself to go down there." I said, "Mr. Dick, let me tell you something. Now, we got to go down there, the people expect us to see if he's there. If we go, he probably won't open the door, we probably gonna have to storm the house. And if he makes any move, the boy may get killed or he may kill some of us." I said, "I'd like you to go along and try to talk him out of that house."

Mr. Dick finally decided he'd go, and I got him in the car with me. On the way down there, there was a narrow road and high bloodweeds on each side. We came to a gate, and it was done dark by this time. Mr. Ward came out with a roll of keys about this big, must have had

30 or 40 on there, and picked one out and handed it to Dee Brune to unlock this gate. Dee jumps out and starts running around in front, and just about the time he stepped out in front he realized, "Now, what am I doing out here in front of this car in the light? We're right at the house, if that man wants to take a shot at somebody, I'm number one!" He got kind of excited trying to unlock that gate. You could hear those keys shaking clean back where we were. Instead of unlocking the lock, I think he shook it open.

Then we went on down to the house. We had three cars, so we kind of surrounded the house so we could light it up good as we could. Mr. Blanchard from Bellville got behind a tree over here, and Dee Brune got out, he had my carbine, and he gets behind this other tree. We was standing around there, and somebody had to go to the house. No one made the move, so I went over and told Steck, "Well, I'll go and see if I can get him out."

At about this time, Dee Brune told me later that he got to thinking, "If that man comes out shooting, this tree that I'm behind doesn't look quite big enough." He looked over to his left, and there was a bigger tree. He made up his mind, thought, "Now, when I start over I'm gonna go in a hurry, so I can get behind this bigger tree." But it just so happened that Blanchard was on the other side about a tree or two over, and his tree got a little too small for him while he was standing there, and he decided he'd get behind this big tree all at once. So both of 'em made a break for the tree at the same time, and they ran into each other there in the dark, and if either one of 'em could have got to their gun, I think they would have had a shooting out there in the dark.

Anyway, about then, I eased up to the house, knocked on the door and no one answered. I shoved it back, still no answer. I searched the house and couldn't find him. We didn't find him that night, but two weeks later we found him in Louisiana. All the time he'd never been in the bottom down there, those people had saw somebody else and thought it was him. But it *felt* like he was there, and he didn't like me too much either. Forrest went to Rusk, and he named five that he was gonna get when he got back. I was one of 'em.

After I run for sheriff, lot of people told me, says, "Man, there's no way of you ever winning sheriff in this county." Says, "There never has been a sheriff in this county that didn't have either a Czech or a German name. There's never been a sheriff in this county that wasn't a native son." And they also said I was too young to be a sheriff. There was a lot of different things that was against me when I run for sheriff. Austin County is an old-time deal, either German or Czech.

I got a little publicity as a deputy down there at Sealy, which helped me get in. Old Highway 90 used to be the hotspot through here, like

Interstate 10 is now. Someone would do a job in Columbus and run off from 'em. I had a 1949 Olds 88, the fastest car on the market at that time, and I used to catch a few of those people from out of the county. They'd call by telephone, "Hey, we got so-and-so coming through there and we after him." On a particular night, Fatty Buller from Columbus was after a guy, and he was running off from him, and I went down there and got after him. I crowded him off right in Sealy, and he went through a fence out in a pasture. He had bought five dollars of gas and run off without paying for it, but when we caught him, come to find out, he had highjacked an old man over close to Luling and left him out in the country. That brand-new Olds 88, it would catch 'em; man, it was the hottest thing on the market. And course, the paper put that out, and different ones heard about it up here in Bellville, and it helped me out.

But I run for sheriff after Steck didn't want to run. He didn't like being sheriff much. He thought he (would like) it a whole lot more than what he did. He'd get worried about things and get upset. He finally just told me, "I've had all of this I want, I'm not gonna run anymore." Says, "I wish you'd stay here and run. I'll help you."

Just to be frank with you, I don't think he liked any of it. I don't think he liked the responsibility. Then he had one little occasion at a dance hall one night where two or three guys jumped on him and overpowered him, didn't hurt him, but they shook him up quite a bit. He had a few bad incidents in his time that kind of discouraged him. And he just didn't like the responsibility, he got nervous over it.

The job used to be a lot worse than what it is now. In a sense of the way, it was worse; and in another way, it was lots better. You had more privilege to kind of do what you wanted to do and do it like you wanted to, but you had better be able to stand your own ground, I promise you that. When you waded in there, it was you or him.

Campaigning then was much different than what it is now. Most all communities would have a kingpin in the community. I'll name some of 'em. In Cat Spring, George Prause. He was a big rancher, he knew everybody over there. Cat Spring is one of the older settlements. The Agricultural Society Hall over there is over 150 years old. In Wallace, Charlie Koekle. He was an old settler, a big cattleman, had lots of land. Old man Budie Mewis here in Bellville, he was another one, and he owned lots of land. Everyone knew Mr. Budie. There was Oscar Voelker up around Shelby and Earnest Bumgard over at New Elm, and then you could go and name others that still had their little domains out there. You mostly went out to them; and if they gave you encouragement, you were in pretty good shape. You still needed to get around and meet all these people, all that stuff, knock on a few doors, so forth and so on like that, but at that particular time one man could control a bunch of votes.

If the man in a community was for you, you kind of did like he said to do as far as meeting the public, and you pretty well had it made. We made all the dance halls, we made all the public gatherings, and Austin County has been known for good-time goers, always. They had 18 public dance halls at that time. These were all country dance halls run by organizations, and all 18 tried to have one dance a month. Just think how many you got! I remember one Saturday night before the election, I went all over handing out cards and buying beer. I remember that night a lot of my friends were in the old Club Rendezvous, a cafe and little dancing place in Sealy, and I come in there about one o'clock. I told 'em, "I believe I just finished my campaign. I've just made five dances and one colored rodeo."

When I first took office as sheriff, most of our crimes was burglaries, and they were light. We had very little major crime back in those days. In the county out here, we hardly knew what an outright armed robbery was, we hardly knew what a real murder case was. We had a few, as we called it, "killings" once in a while, where a couple of people would get over-excited while they were drinking, maybe out at a joint somewhere, and one would pull out a knife and cut the other one. And possibly, ever once and awhile, we had a shotgun killing. We called 'em "killings," we didn't call it murder, and I kind of separate the two, now. Outright murder, I figure, is more or less a planned deal, or someone doing it for hire, or during an armed robbery, or something like that. But if you go out to an old beer joint and get in a fight, and through heated passion or dunkenness (you) pull a knife and kill a person, or if you pull a gun and shoot him, to me that's a plain old killing like we used to have. That's about all we had back in those days.

It was kind of a natural thing to get in fights at dance halls in this county. Years ago, lot of people felt that they hadn't had a good time if they hadn't went out and maybe had a little scrap somewhere at a dance or something like that. Most of the time they didn't amount to much. Many a time at a place like that, I've broken 'em up, separated 'em. If they'd behave, I'd leave 'em alone, if they didn't, I'd send 'em home and never do anything else. Having a little fight and a little extra drinking in this county used to wasn't thought of as a bad crime. All they needed was somebody to control it, you might say about halfway to referee it. Most everybody kind of enjoyed seeing a little scrap once in a while.

When I started, I didn't know too much about how to handle people. One night I was inside this dance hall and they hollered that they was having a fight outside. This was a little old hall called Mixville Hall, out in the country about halfway between Sealy and Wallace. I ran out there and the two guys was scrapping pretty good. I ran in between 'em and shoved 'em apart, caught one of 'em by the collar thisaway and the other one by the collar like this, holding 'em apart. They were swinging at each other, and I'm in the middle and I'm getting a few of 'em ever once and awhile, and I kept hollering at 'em to stop fighting. I thought to myself, "Well, now, as hard as they're wanting together and I'm getting a little tired of holding 'em apart, maybe if I get 'em together real fast and furious I can stop this." So, instead of pushing against them and them pushing against me, I started pulling all at the same time and I brought 'em together and their faces hit, and I brought blood from both of 'em. Their own faces hit just smack as they could, both of 'em. It blooded their noses and I stopped the fight. Then I turned around and put both of 'em in my car and carried 'em in to the old JP at Sealy, whose name was Judge Matekka. He was a fine old man. He smoked a cigarette all the time and he had it in a holster, and he had false teeth and he had a little trouble holding that holster. You could hear it clicking all the time where he was talking. I think he fined 'em five dollars each.

In those days, Austin County was pretty well made up of homefolks. Everybody knew the rest of the people 'round, and most of 'em was either kinfolks or kin to somebody that was kin to somebody else around. At one time in this county, I could almost meet anybody in the whole county, and I might not could call his name but I could tell you what part of the county he lived in. We must have had 25,000 people in the county when I started.

Sealy had had its shootings back before I ever came there. Long time ago we had feuds like in the hillbilly days. One family would be feuding with another, and they'd have a shootout ever once in a while. The Bells and the Schafners, there's a long story to that old feud. We've even had 'em here in the northwest end of the county. I've had occasion to try to settle down families out here, where one family lived on this hill and the other lived on that hill and they'd even fire a few shots at each other. One lady called me one evening and showed me where she had been fixing supper and a bullet came through the window of the kitchen and struck the wall on the back side. Of course, no one ever knew where it came from, but that window did happen to be right in the direction of the neighbor on the next hill.

I've had lot of gang fights, you know, with one family fighting against another. We had one of these Fireman's Frolics, one time, where that kind of a fight between two families broke out. It was equal, at least five on each particular side, and they got into a big squabble out there. That Fireman's Frolic used to draw close to five-thousand people on a Thursday night. It was a dance and a barbecue given to make up money for the volunteer firemen in Sealy.

About that time, I think I was the only officer down there. Someone hollered, "There's a gang fight!" So I ran over and got right in the middle of all those, but by all of the people knowing me as well as they did I was able to control it. I had to separate 'em. I gave one family a chance to go home, and I held the other so they wouldn't meet down the street somewhere and start it over. It all worked fine excepting for one man on one side. He kept coming back and trying to get at one of the others. I shoved him back over, held him for a little bit. Finally, he broke loose and grabbed one of the other guys, and that was one of the very, very few times I've ever used a blackjack. I tapped him a couple of times a little heavy on the head, and I broke up the fight good, then. I held one family in place and made the other go home. I kept them there for maybe 20 or 30 minutes, then I made them go home, too.

I guess about as scarey a situation as I ever got into back in those days . . . . Now, if a man says he doesn't get scared in some cases, I just figure he's doing a little bragging. I got a call from Harris County, one time. A murder had happened out in fifth ward, and they believed that the subject may have come up here. It was a pretty gruesome murder. The guy that did it had caused another man to kneel down and fold his hands and bow his head like he was praying, then shot him in the top of the head with a .45. Then he left, and they thought he came up here.

That was back in the '50s, and my only deputy then was named Ervin Brast. We didn't have any other officers to call in, but there just happened to be one man from the Texas Cattle Raisers Association who was visiting through here, and he said he would drive out there with us. So, we drove out to the house in the country where the man was supposed to be, and I told each one of them, "Now, when we drive up there, one of you go to the right, one to the left, and go far enough so you can cover the back, 'cause the man will probably run if we don't. I'll take the front." I drove up to the house, and they made a run real quick, and I went up to the front and knocked on the door and hollered, and nothing happened, and tried to get through it, but it was locked.

I looked down in the field and I saw a man plowing, so I told 'em to keep the house covered and I went down there to talk to him. Got down there and it was the boy's father, we knew him. I told him the report that I'd had and that they thought that he'd come up here. He said, "Yes, he came up here last night. He's there at the house." I told him, "Now, he's wanted for murder. I've come after him. I'd like for you to go to the house with me and help me talk him out.'' Oooh, he didn't want to, he's scared to! I says, ''I've given you one alternative. You can either go in there with me and help me get him, or else I'm going in there and there may be some shooting. And I'm figuring on coming out, myself, you understand that?'' He said, ''I don't want you shooting my boy.'' I said, ''Well, I'll tell you what, you go with me.''

We got up there and went in the back door, and he went in with me. We covered the kitchen, went to the next room, went to every room, even looked under the beds, didn't find nobody. I noticed in the corner of the wall in one room there was an old-timey chifforobe. A chifforobe is a kind of a closet where you hang your clothes in, and I thought to myself, ''Now, he might be in that thing behind them clothes, but I'm not gonna bother it till I look under this bed.'' I went over and looked under this bed, all that stuff, then turned around and come back to that chifforobe. I told him, I said, ''OK, boy, I know you're in here, you might as well come out.'' I waited a little, and I said, ''I'm fixing to open that door, any move you make is gonna be too bad.'' That was the truth. I had that .45 with the hammer off and my finger on that trigger, and it was getting kind of shaky. I eased one door open and I looked, and it's only clothes hanging there. I eased the other door open, and all it was was clothes hanging there. I think, ''Well, he must be behind them clothes.'' I reached up, and I was gonna slide 'em to the side like that to see if there was something behind 'em; but when I did the damn rail up there broke, and all of 'em dropped on the floor. And I come might near to pulling that trigger, boy! You talk about your heart coming up in your throat, I'll guarantee it did, then. I'm not kidding you.

It was kind of dark in there, I didn't have good light, and it had me stumped. Where the hell could he be? I thought, ''Ain't no way he could be behind it, or is there?'' I looked, and it was kind of off in the corner and not against the wall real good. I said, ''Uh oh, I bet you that's where he's at.'' So I reached over and grabbed this chifforobe, and jerked it as hard as I could, and I hollered. I said, ''You,'' and I used some foul language, ''come out of there, I'm starting to shoot. Come out with your hands first.'' 'Bout that time I saw 10 fingers come around the corner of that wall. I said, ''Now, easy, easy, easy!'' I was really talking to him, and I was nervous; I ain't kidding you, I was nervous. I knew that he had already made that man kneel down and shot him in the head, so he had to be a bloodthirsty dude. I brought him out of there and made him lock his hands behind his head. I didn't even try to put the handcuffs on him or search him or anything inside the house. I made him walk real slow, right behind his daddy, till we got outside, made him lay down on the ground, then I handcuffed him. It was dark in there, and I didn't find his gun the first time I looked. He lied and said he had left it in Houston. But it was there. Later we found it where he'd had it, right behind that chifforobe.

I've rode the old horse a many a mile in the woods chasing people following the bloodhounds. We've had lots of that. We had one, one time, where we chased a guy into a culvert under the railroad and had dogs at both ends of it. They were trying to make those dogs go in and get that old boy out, but they just would not go in that culvert. We finally had to pull the dogs off and let him crawl out before we could get him. Over the years, I've probably joined on 35 to 40 hunts using dogs.

There is a breed of a dog called a bloodhound, but they're too slow. They're a real long-eared old dog and they're so slow, though they're supposed to have a real good nose to smell a cold trail. But the last few years they have bred more into the mixture between the Black and Tan hound and the Walker hound. Black and Tan hound was more or less bred for coon dogs, your Walker hound was bred for fox dogs. Your Walker is much faster than your Black and Tan, your Black and Tan is faster than the old bloodhound. The Black and Tan has a better nose than your Walker hound, yet he would be a little slow, maybe, on some races, so they kinda mix 'em. Then, there's another breed of old dog that they call the Blue Tick hound. He's kind of a blue-speckled dog that makes an awful good bloodhound. They don't have the mean dogs like they used to have. They can't afford to have (them), too many lawsuits. There's some of them old Walker hounds that will nip you pretty good, though you can break 'em from it.

One of the biggest manhunts using dogs was, I believe, in about '76. We had a highway patrol here by the name of Mark Frederick and his partner was Jack Reichardt, a young patrolman just out of school and still on probation. The two patrolmen received a call from our dispatchers that Brookshire had just put out a pickup on an automobile that had left a service station over there and had given a bogus credit card. The patrolmen was in Sealy, and they stopped this vehicle there near the overpass. The car stopped and Mark Frederick got out on the driver's side, approaching the vehicle from the rear. Jack Reichardt got out on the right side, and stood behind the vehicle while Mark walked up to the window on the left side. There wasn't any word passed. The driver of the vehicle just put a gun out of the window, and Mark happened to see it and started backwards. He pulled the trigger, and it went through Mark's left arm, went through his chest cavity, and he immediately fell. Jack Reichardt, being a brand-new man, under pressure from everything else, young and everything, did a marvelous job. As the car took off, he pulled his revolver and fired six rounds. Two of 'em hit this automobile in the back glass, three of 'em in the trunk, and one in the left rear tire. Six shots, and he didn't waste a one, but the car kept on going. Jack Reichardt ran for the patrol car and called for help and stayed there with Mark, and we all got out on the chase. Some minutes later we had a car coming in from Eagle Lake on 3013 south of Sealy, and they spotted the car abandoned out there. I approached the automobile, and come to find out that tire had gone out and begin to wobble so much he couldn't go any further. We kept everybody in the automobiles as much as we could, and didn't bother the vehicle, other than to see that he wasn't in it at that time, and called for the dogs.

We called for two sets of dogs. In a deal like that, I'd rather have too much than not enough. So, we called the Texas Department of Corrections at Sugar Land to get the bloodhounds from there, and called a friend of mine who was constable in Grimes County and who had dogs that they chased with. Whichever one got there first was the one we was gonna use, and the TDC dogs happened to show up just about two minutes before the Grimes County ones got there. We put the TDC dogs out and saved the others. They'd hit a trail every once and awhile and they'd lose it, they'd hit a trail and they'd lose it; they really never did hit anything that night. We made a bad mistake. Somehow or another, we must not have gotten far enough away. Apparently, he came right back down the blacktop toward where he had left Highway 36, 'cause we couldn't really strike. We drug and drug and drug, up and down and back and forth.

Then we began to call for help. This Mark had been killed almost instantly, and of course that set everybody off in the whole country. There's one thing about peace officers in this country, they'll sure come to the aid of a brother. I started calling for help, and within just a matter of minutes we had automobiles from all around this whole county coming in, just like a big net. We hunted him all night. We got out all the news coverage we could, radio and CB, everything else, notifying people that if they saw any movement to let us know. We must have made 10 calls that night on people that would see things, and we'd run 'em out. This went on for two days. The second day, a time or two, there was different ones of the organizations that was wanting to pull out; but I kept insisting that we stay, because I thought we had him pinned down, and I figured he'd starve out soon and would want to come out for help. Some of 'em said he'd already caught a ride out, that they'd been too many freight trains come through, this and that and the other, but I just didn't want to stop, I wanted to keep on going.

I didn't stop or sleep from the day Mark was shot all that night, the next day, the next night, the next day, and the next night. We kept hunting and we kept men up. We kept every road blocked in this whole county, I mean every one of 'em. You had to check through. I was sitting there at the PD in Sealy one night and this guy, they brought him in, and he wanted to know who was in charge. They sent him to me, and he said, "Mister, would you please escort me about two counties over?" He was a sandy-redheaded guy with a beard, about five-foot-seven, who fit the description well. Every time he was picked up, he'd be brought in and checked out and turned loose; and 'fore he'd get out of the county, somebody would pick him up. They wouldn't take his word for it and would bring him back again. He'd been picked up three times and wanted an escort out of the county. Well, I says, "The guys is doing a good job, anyhow." And we did help him, we escorted him out of the county and sent him on his way, and we discussed it on the radio with the people further down toward San Antonio. So, he finally got out of the danger zone.

Anyhow, we kept going and kept going until the third day when they were gonna have Mark's funeral here in Bellville. I did attend the funeral here, but they were gonna take him to Houston to bury him and I didn't take off and go, I wanted to stay here. We didn't pull in near all our men off the road. I wouldn't let 'em come in, I wanted 'em to stay out, because I figured that would be a good time for him to try to make a break.

Anyhow, I left here and was going back towards Sealy when I heard a report that someone down there had called in to the dispatcher. They had seen somebody crossing a road at a certain place. I called in and told 'em, "Send the Grimes County dogs back immediately and I'm going to the scene." I drove down there, and we still had quite a few men out to help. When I got there, there was one of the guys that was wanting to put the dogs on the east side of the road. See, on the west side of 36 there's only minor coverage, wesache and such as that, and there's where they'd seen him go into. They had the helicopter down there, and he'd covered the whole area 'fore the dogs could get there and hadn't seen him. This one man wanted to put the dogs out on the east side, because there's heavy woods there and he was sure that he'd already gone in there, because the helicopter had already covered the other side. They wanted to save time and put 'em out over on the other side and let 'em hunt there to see if they could get a trail.

I disagreed with that. I told him there were two or three reasons why I thought that it was wrong to do that. I said, "In the first place, you don't know what trail you gonna strike over here. You put 'em out right here, and you know this is the trail that he made. The man saw him go in here. They will strike the trail." He said, "Yeah, but they'll lose too much time." I said, "Time ain't what we're after now, we've done lost three-and-a-half days. We can lose some more time. I want those dogs right here." Finally, I told him, "This is my county. We are gonna put 'em here and that's where they gonna be." I told 'em to put the dogs out, and he got huffy and left.

But the dogs did strike. There were only about six acres out there of semi-open woods, but before they came out on the other end they ran him out from under some brush. He had been hiding under that brush out there in that area. That helicopter had been over him several times, but he'd stay on the back side of that brush when it was coming around, and just stay away from it. Those old dogs ran onto him, and you know, he fuzzed up with that little Browning automatic like he was gonna shoot that helicopter. I came in from the south end in my car and ran through a fence to get there, tore that fence down and messed up my car a little bit, but I got there in time. He was fixing to try to shoot that helicopter just when I hit my brakes and stepped out. I had this little old carbine with a scope sight on it, and all at once he just dropped his pistol and throwed his hands out like that and begin to wave. When he quit, I quit. I went on up and apprehended him and brought him in. He got his trail moved from here to Bay City, but ended up with a death sentence. He's still on death row at Huntsville at this time.

Over the years, I've had calls on everything you can imagine, but some of the strangest had to do with dead animals. Fifteen years ago, there was a lot of publicity throughout Texas, Oklahoma, Arizona, and some into Colorado, of the little green men from Mars killing the cattle and using some means of killing 'em that nobody could find out what was going on. Some people even thought they would take out all of the blood of the calf or cow. They had certain things that they did. They would cut the eyes out of the animal, they would remove the sex organs, and they'd do this with an extremely sharp, surgical-type knife. No one was supposed to be able to do a job that good. It spread like wildfire.

The first time I got involved in the thing . . . two deputies from Harris County had been assigned strictly to that job by Sheriff Buster Kern because they'd had so many calls throughout Harris County that these little men from Mars was just mutilating animals all over the whole country, and they wanted something done. And everyday in the TV and the newspapers you'd hear about where they'd struck at another place. Well, being a country boy, I couldn't believe in these people from Mars coming in here and doing anything to us, and I couldn't believe that no type people, even though there is some weird people in the world, could go from place to place and kill these animals. Even though there's a lot of kooks in the country, I didn't think they would fool with an animal, cutting its sex organs out and all that stuff. I couldn't believe it. We had a lot of people in this county reported it, and I went out and checked, and it was true. There were a lot of baby calves that around the rectum would be cut out just as smooth out to the line of hair, and there would be no blood at any time. One vetinary told one of these Houston deputies here that they must have drawn all the blood out of the animal before they performed any of those type of operations—removed the sex organs, the eyes and all that stuff.

Well, I looked at several of those, and it was a pretty smooth job, but I couldn't buy it. I thought that it was some type of animals doing it, and I took it on my own to find out. I went to a diaryman at Sealy and bought a little old baby calf, carried it out to a place, killed it, left it laying out there about 10 o'clock in the morning. Then I backed off with fieldglasses and watched it until dark. And nothing happened. I stayed there up until about 10, 11 o'clock at night, and nothing happened. Then I came back about four o'clock in the morning.

The place where I carried it was equally close to some of the places where they had been found. Some people even had it down to where that it was close to a cemetery any time anything like that would happen. In this county, the ones that was called in always was close to a cemetery. But I got to thinking, there's so many cemeteries in this county, damn near everything that happened could be close to one! There's a lot of little old country cemeteries, that, if you don't know they're there, you won't even believe there's one around. But I even went and put this calf close to one, just in case.

That next morning just at the break of day, we had a visitor. He came in from the sky and lit right on top of the little calf, a big old black buzzard. There's two kinds of buzzards here, the one that my daddy always called a "carrion crow," he's got short stubby wings with white tips and a white head, and another that's called a turkey buzzard, solid black with a red head. Your turkey buzzards eats only animals that's completely dead. The carrion crow, if an old cow gets down and can't help herself, they'll pick on certain parts of her. They will only pick on a place where there is no hair, the animal's rectum; if it's a baby calf, the vagina; if it's a male calf, where its navel cord comes out or where its penis comes out at the bottom; its eyeball or its mouth. And some of these animals that we had found before then, something had taken and cut the tongue off real smooth as far back as it could go. I observed all of that being done on this calf, and it was all being done by the buzzards.

Another thing, some of our baby calves, that had been described throughout the whole state that these notorious people had come in and killed, had their insides taken completely out from only two openings, either from the rectum or from the navel cavity. That was exactly the way the buzzards did it. They would start cutting, and they got a pretty sharp bill, and they'd cut all the way around the animal's rectum, going in there and pulling out the insides. If the baby calf is not old enough to where he's been eating grass and has a lot of other stuff in his stomach, these buzzards will keep cutting and cutting and cutting, and take all the organs out of that calf, but they won't eat in through the hide. And they'll only take the top eye out, because the calf is laying on the other side and they don't get to it. That's another thing, they all wondered why only one eye was taken.

I went back to town to get some proof of this, carried some people back out there and let several people see it. Then I made a tape on this particular deal. It got out through the news, and it stopped most of the stories of the little men from Mars. I was a country boy, and I just couldn't believe it. That's the way that we solved the notorious gang from Mars.

Out of my 36 years of law enforcement, I had 13 years that I had something to think about in federal court. I've had two law suits that each one of 'em lasted over six years. All it is, is aggravation. Neither of 'em, I thought, had a reason to sue, but the federal court will take it and they'll give you a lot of problems over it. You have to go an' answer it, got to get your lawyer to make your answers when they demand 'em, and so forth and so on. Then they just keep on going and putting it off, putting it off. One was for a 150,000-dollar libel suit, and one was for a two-million-dollar suit claiming that I'd violated the civil rights and failed to provide proper medical care for a prisoner. That was after this guy had ended up with two life sentences for murdering two people here in Bellville one night. After we caught him, he broke out of jail, and sliding down the pipe outside he broke his leg. Then, after he ended up with two life terms and a five-year term for that particular thing (the escape attempt), he got down there and sued me and Doctor Harle each for two-million-dollars, and it stayed in court for six years.

They'll sue for anything in the world, that's true. An officer has the legal right to use what force is necessary to protect his own self and his own life, but that doesn't keep 'em from suing you. I guess that's what a court of law is for, to decide if we did have the right to use what force that was necessary and not too much. It may be no case at all, but somehow or another they can keep it in court and cause you to waste a terrible lot of time.

This one man, the convicted double murderer, sued me for two-million dollars and kept it in court for six years before it got thrown out. I'd have to go down to Houston once or twice every year to federal court to testify on this, that, or the other. I was sued by a woman in the west end of the county way before then, way back in the early '50s, for 150,000 dollars. This was over a little old road that had been a road, we traced it back, for over a hundred years. It crossed a piece of land up there, and she wanted the commissioners to close it and they wouldn't let her. One night I was up there at the local dance hall and her uncle, who lived across the road from her, came down there and told me that she had come in from Austin and was blocking that road again. What they'd do, her and her husband would drive all the way down for the weekend, and they'd put one car on one end of the road and one car on the other, so no one could cut through. It wasn't far around, but the people in that town didn't want to do that. So, I went up there, and sure enough, there were the cars.

I went around everywhere trying to find 'em and couldn't, so I got a ticket book out and was just gonna put some kind of ticket on there and ask her to come in to the judge and get the thing straight. I didn't know there was (as) big a feud as there was over it. But before I'd got through writing the ticket out, her and her husband and her mother came out, and boy, boy, boy, the foul language that started going on, as if I was the cause of the whole thing!

You need to feel these things out a long time before you start with something, so I listened to this a long time, and finally, in a sense of the way, they physically attacked me first. She grabbed this ticket book out of my hand, wasn't gonna let me write no ticket. I tried to explain to her that they hadn't been in sight, I didn't know where they were, and I wanted them to know that I'd been there, for them to come in and get with the judge, and that whatever the judge ruled on this situation would be it. But they wouldn't listen. She grabbed my ticket book and took it away from me, and he grabbed my pencil, and that just happened to make me a little bit mad. I grabbed him up and was gonna put him in jail then, and went to take him to the car. I had a model of a Ford that the back windows wouldn't roll all the way down. On account of the curve in the door, it wouldn't roll all the way down, it would just go halfway down. Well, while I was on the way dragging him to the door to physically put him in there, she jumped up on my back and began to beat on me, pulling on my coat, almost tore it off. Her mother run around in front of me trying to keep me from putting him in there. I just kept walking, and finally opened the door and shoved him in, and when I turned back she grabbed one of my hands and bit my finger that you just wouldn't know, boy! Then is whenever I lost my temper. I popped her a good one. Whooh, I popped her a good one! I got her loose from my finger.

I threw her in the car then, too, but while this was all happening her husband had opened the door on the other side—I didn't have a cage like we have now—and had jumped out. I put her in there and slammed the door on her, and ran around and tried to catch him as he ran for the house. Then I looked back, and the poor lady didn't know how to open the door. All she had to do was just raise the handle up and open the door and she could have got out, but instead of that, the window was rolled down and she was trying to crawl out through the window. She had one leg hanging out and her arms were hanging out and part of her body, and about that time she got overbalanced and fell flat out on the ground. She jumped up and ran. Wasn't nobody left there but the poor old lady, so I just shook my head and drove off.

I called for my deputy here in Bellville. I told him, "Get a warrant for the two and come on up there and we'll pick 'em up." But when we got there, they physically put themselves in the house and barred all the doors and we couldn't get in, and I wasn't gonna break in a house for a misdemeanor. So I came back and sent this warrant to Austin, and had 'em picked up in Austin. I had filed on her for something. They had to make bond, it went to trial, she hired a big lawyer and he got a change of venue to Colorado County, and they had the case in court. She lost, and they fined her 25 dollars and cost of court. I remember that her lawyer and the county attorney was standing in the hall talking when it was over with when she came a-roaring out there and told her attorney she wanted to appeal that. He told her, naw, they didn't have anything that he thought he could appeal the case on. He thought everything was in pretty good shape. She demanded that he appeal it. He said, "Well, it will cost this five-thousand dollars to appeal this case, and you've only got a 25 dollar fine." She says she didn't care, and stood right there and wrote him a check for five-thousand dollars.

So, they appealed it. And in the meantime, then, she got another lawyer and sued me for 150,000 dollars damages. She went to a photographer and literally pulled her clothes off, and they took pictures of her leg, which was bruised up, and said I bruised her leg! Her leg was all messed up, clean up to the top, from trying to scramble out of that window. That was another one that stayed in federal court in Houston for over six years and finally got throwed out. That's just part of the life that a man has gotta take when he's in this business.

Sometimes you can go on family problems and help, and sometimes you can't. Sometimes you can get in there and get in trouble. You have to play it pretty cool when you go out on these domestic problems.

You have such little protection, you know. You go to another man's house without a warrant, or without anything in writing, and the woman naturally is extremely mad at the husband or she wouldn't have called, or visa versa. If you go there and the one that is violent attempts to do something, and you have to use extreme force, nine times out of ten the other one will change their mind right quick and want to blame you for the whole thing. And you've ended up there without anything in writing as to why you were at that house.

So, you've got such a little bit of help, you definitely should have someone with you for a witness when you go, another officer or whatever. However, we still make the calls and we don't have two-man units all the time. We still make 'em, but we're awful cautious. I've made 'em for all these years and been awful lucky. There's a lot of people go on these domestic calls that only make one or two, they get in trouble right away.

I think all officers can aid in his own trouble. I don't mean to say that an officer is the cause of his own trouble ever' time, but sometimes he is. For instance, don't ever tell a drunk that he's drunk, 'cause that drunk knows he isn't, and resents you telling him he's drunk. And if you go out to a house and go in and try to bully people into doing something, that alone, lot of times, will cause the opposite person to turn against you, even the one that calls you out there. You have to use a little diplomacy when you enter into something like that. Brute strength is really not the answer anymore. I believe that left when they outlawed everybody from wearing a .45 on his belt.

I'll have to say, though, that you have got to be strong enough to stand up to whatever you start. You better be that, because you gonna be tested a lot of times. If he's already in an uproar, however, you might have to take it a lot easier and take a lot longer, and I've found out that it's a whole lot easier to spend 15 or 20 minutes talking a man into something than it is to spend five minutes forcing him into it. One time, about 25 years ago, I was traveling down farm market road 949 out here and a guy like to ran me off the road. I pulled around and chased him, had to drive a long ways to get him stopped, and course I'd done got heated up pretty good. It excited me when he ran me off the road, I figured he was drunk, and then he kept going and wouldn't stop. Finally, after I did get him stopped and I got out of the car and started up to his car, you know, I was kinda huffy. I opened the door and this old boy started to getting out, and I started to looking up and up and up! I thought he never was gonna quit going up. He was about six-seven when he finally got straightened up, weighed about 270 pounds, and no fat man. I thought to myself, "You know, just in case he doesn't cooperate, I don't know exactly what I'm gonna do, here."

And he was kinda huffy, too. He was drunk enough that he didn't want to cooperate, he didn't even want to get in the car with me. So I figured right then that it was gonna be a lot better for me to do a lot of smooth talking. I must have spent five minutes or more talking to him 'fore I even got him to sit down in the front seat of my car. Then I took a lot of information down to try to spend as much time as I could to help get him to cooperate. And I didn't tell him, "Now, you're drunk, I'm gonna take you to jail," I shore never did tell him that. I just told him that we needed to run uptown, here, and do a little further talking, and so forth and so on. Finally, then, he agreed to go, but on the way to town all at once he decided that all lawmen was bad, bad folks, and there were things that he wanted to do to 'em, and was going to do to 'em. I thought to myself, "If he ever breaks loose and starts working on me while I'm driving this car, I'm gonna be in bad shape." I knew good and well that if I called for help on the radio, I was gonna need help 'fore they got there, so I decided to take it on my own. I took it as easy as I could. It must have taken me 45 minutes and possibly an hour from the time I first stopped him to the time I finally got him upstairs in the old jail, and I did it all by talking. That man, I do believe until this day, that if I had used any type force on him, I would have had to call for more than one for help, and it would have been after the battle.

If a man is drunk, handle him careful, 'cause you don't know what he'll do. A man under dope is actually worse than a drunk. A man under any kind of critical condition, like if he's being charged with a felony and he knows he is, sometimes he will do things that he wouldn't normally do. And mental cases, that's another kind that you got to play each one of those separate. Talk to 'em as long as you can. Sometimes you got to take holt and force 'em to do things, but be careful, 'cause those people will hurt you. And they're not all the same, they're like drunks in a way. One man, if he's drunk, thinks everything is funny and just wants to have fun and loves everybody, and the next man that's drunk wants to fight everybody and nobody's any good. One drunk will go out here and want to take an automobile and drive a hundred miles an hour; next drunk you see is driving so slow you can't get around him. There's no two of 'em alike, they're unpredictable, and mental patients are exactly the same thing. One mental patient, he wants to love you to death, just do anything for you, just so calm and easy and everything, yet his mind is completely warped. Then again, another mental patient can kill you. These schizophrenics or people with split personalities, that's the ones that's dangerous. They'll go out here and do something awhile that's real bad, and the next minute they'll turn around and be just as cunning and pleasing and meet you with a smile. They hardly realize they've done those other things their ownself. They're terrible dangerous.

You better not get used to anything in this job. All that does is cause us to get lax and get killed. A good friend of mine down at Hallettsville picked up the town drunk several times and went to the jail with him. Then this time he and his deputy picked him up again, a young punk, and throwed him in the back seat and started to jail with him, didn't handcuff him or anything. And this dude reached around the side and got the deputy's gun and killed the sheriff and shot the jailer. That's how routine stuff will get you in trouble in a hurry. We should not ever get used to doing anything. We should not do anything routine, we should do it in a manner that every man is a criminal. Course, you get talked about, you get cussed, you get everything in the world when you start treating everybody as a criminal, but you'll live a lot longer if you do that. I don't mean that an officer should be abusive when he goes to arrest someone, I just mean that he should treat every man very, very careful.

An officer should weigh out the whole thing before he walks in. You don't want to let no one ever think you're a sissy. You want to keep the general public to respecting you. You do that by . . . if you say to a man, "I'm gonna put you in jail," put him in jail. Don't tell him you gonna put him in jail and then get soft-soaped and back out. Once I start to deal with him and tell him he's going to jail, he's going. But don't say it if you don't mean it, and wait a long time before you say it. Try everything that you can before you decide to do that.

I don't think that every man that messes up a little bit needs to go to jail. All rules are made to be distributed to the people as the person sees fit. Start with speeding. The law out here says 55 miles an hour. There's no one that would agree to give a man a ticket for 56, but that is more than the law says he is allowed to do. There's a law against a man using abusive language, but a man can do that up to a certain point. He might raise a little cain and cuss and cut up a little bit, but go give that man a chance to go on home. If he's got too much to drink, give him a chance, let him go on home. Study all that out before you make up your mind you're going to do something. But once he goes far enough so that you have to threaten him with something, go through (with) it and don't back down.

I know some officers abused the privilege, but I liked it a lot better in the old days because my motto is "To free the man if he's innocent, prosecute him if he's guilty." I'd just as soon help a man prove his innocence as I had the other way, and I'd a whole lot rather see a guilty man go free than an innocent man go to jail. I don't want that, under no circumstances. I sure hope that I never have that on my conscience. In the old days, I'd pick a man up and tell him, "If you've got a reason to show me that you're not guilty, you've got a chance to do it right now. I'll do this, I'll go with you anywhere and we'll check your story out. We'll check it from one end to the other, and I'll not be prejudiced in any way. If you can prove to me that you're not guilty, that's what I want to do. I'm gonna do my best to prove that you are guilty, long as I think you are, but if you're not guilty and you've got a way of proving it, let's get in my car and take out and we'll go do this and do that and lets find out you're not guilty." I've cut a many a man loose thataway. He never had nothing on his history, never did have a charge. The record does not show that he's been to jail or anything else.

On the other side, there's no doubt in my mind that I've sent a many a one down to the penitentiary that if I'd have had to do all this Miranda stuff before I did that, I wouldn't have been able to do it. If you keep an old guilty guy there very long, he's gonna begin to trip himself up, and the more you can talk to him and the more you can remember, the better off you are. And the minute he makes a slip, you better be able to jump right in on him. Then you get him excited and then he says, "Well, I meant this or I meant that," and he'll get to stuttering. Then the first thing you know he'll throw up his hands and say, "Hell, I'm guilty, lemme go!" That happens time and time and time again. There's an old saying: "Tell the truth and you won't have to remember what you said."

But now, you've got to treat 'em like kings. You have to first go get the papers and you got to file on him. Well, OK, he's got it on his name right then that he's been filed on for burglary. And then you've got to bring him in and just almost beg him not to tell you nothing. You got to prove it all your ownself, and if you don't have much to go on, without his help, sometimes it's hard to prove a case. The scientific investigation is a help, but when there's not a thing in the world to go on, when there's nothing, when you can't even see a thing that tells he's been there, the scientific way ain't worth a damn! Nothing is worth anything, then.

We have to have informants to help us break cases. There's no way I can walk down the street and buy dope from somebody, they all know me. In fact, most of these thugs can smell a cop when he walks in the front door. I guess they look at us and think of us like we look at most of them. I used to think I could almost tell an old thief whenever I saw him, just by his looks and actions, by observing him for a little while, and I ain't sure that I can't get 90 percent of 'em, now. And I know they can probably do us the same way. There is some under-cover officers that practice that kind of talk, that kind of way—in fact, they just almost get right down in there and live with 'em—and they

make awful good officers, but they're few and scattered and far between. So we have to use snitches.

There's many ways of using informants. You have to have somebody out there that's kind of on their level to really be of much good.
In this county, I'm not big enough to have money to pay undercover
men to work all the time. And I'm not big enough a county that I could
use the same undercover men all the time, either. We'd burn him too
easy. In a big city, they can work the south side for six months or a
year until they get burnt there, then move to the north side and work,
but we can't do that. We depend on the help, what little help we can
get, from the state undercover men. The state Alcohol Beverage Commission, they have some undercover men, and if it pertains to alcohol
beverage or dope on licensed premises, they occasionally help us some.
Then, sometimes, we borrow a man from another county or use some
local nonprofessional officers to help us, and then we just have some
old outright common snitches. They'll be people kind of on the same
level as the thugs, but kind of burnt out with them. They like to get
some in trouble and they want to help, and so they'll just go around
and follow up these dudes and get with 'em and then come snitch on
'em. They give us information. You get by with that for a while until
you get into a tight where you have to insist that the snitch testify,
then you got him burnt. The poor devil, he's in bad shape then, 'cause
when he goes back out on the street they're liable to get him. And if
he stays in here, we ain't got no place for him but the jail. It's a tight
bind with a short stick, sometimes!

There's a whole lot of ways to get a snitch going. Maybe you pick
an old boy up, some of 'em are pretty easy to get to, and maybe you
don't have a real good case on him and you're gonna have to turn him
loose anyhow. You might just get to talking to him and tell him, "Now,
we gonna cut you loose and let you hit the ground, but you need to
help us a little bit." And a lot of times they'll do that. I don't mean
that I would turn a person out footloose that's done a crime (in order)
to get him to squeal on another, but sometimes, when you don't really have a case anyhow, when you turn him loose he wants to help
you. A lot of times you do help people, and then they help you.

There's all kind of ways of getting somebody to work for you.
Sheriffs don't do all this stuff alike, everybody's got his own thing.
And you can't expect all these people to sit up here and tell you all
their ins and outs on how they do these things, because if they did,
sometimes it would get out and that would mess up their way of operation. Some will and some won't. Another thing, it's sometimes just
not easy to actually tell you. I've had several occasions where we'd
be working some people and the other man be questioning somebody

for hours on hours, and I'd come in and take 'em away from him, and move down the hall and talk to 'em five minutes and they'd tell their whole story. And visa versa, I've had times that I'd do my best to get something out of somebody and I couldn't do any good, and maybe some other good officer would take him in there and start talking to him, and he'd end up telling him the whole story. It's something that you can't tell someone, sometimes, as to how you go about it.

There used to be a saying that if you want to check a man's history, go into the county where he was raised and ask the sheriff about him. If he doesn't know him, you know damn well he's all right, because he would know him if he wasn't. At one time, most of the people throughout the whole county was related, or living with people in places where they had grown up. The county was full of people living out in the country. But it's not that way anymore, there's some guys in here that I guarantee you that I don't know, now. This county has had so many outsiders move in here the last several years, and I don't know near all of 'em.

But, see, nothing happened back in that old day! Like I said, somebody might steal a trace chain from somebody once in a while, steal a little gas out of a car, steal some beer ever once in a while, but we didn't have the crime we have today. I can remember back when the county was close enough knitted here that you could almost just sit around and think about who has probably done the crime, but not now. Not in the last 15 or 20 years, anyhow.

Since the county has got so busy, we're having to go more to a scientific way of solving cases now than we used to. We solved one murder and rape case in Sealy just a short time back with nothing but the scientific way. We found a shirt there at the scene of the crime, and we ended up with a suspect. The laboratory checked the sweat in that shirt, typing the blood to him. We found some hair on the shirt and hair on the bed, compared them. We found semen on the victim, and compared it back with the man. We had several different things that we carried to the lab and used as evidence. The judge checked all the possibilities. A human hair out of a head, if it matches, they can't say that it's one-hundred-percent sure, but it's one out of a very large number that it wouldn't be the man. Then we had some pubic hair, checked those, and they compared, and it was one out of some other large number that that wasn't him. The sweat we had was one out of so many chances. The way the judge figured this up, when he got through all the things we produced as evidence, the possibility that he didn't do it was like one in twenty-five billion. And we got a conviction of life sentence. So, the last years, we have had to go to a later model of investigation than the kind we used when we first started.

In the old days we never did have any real murders, we didn't have any rapes. Occasionally there might be a little argument between a male and female as how the act took place, but I didn't consider those real rapes like we have now. We had one here where a girl was going to work in Houston at five o'clock in the morning, got out of her car and started to the office where she worked, and was abducted by a man who caught her from behind and made her go back to her car and unlock it. He got in her car and drove her out to San Felipe, got out of the car and raped her and beat her up pretty good. He got in her car and was fixing to leave and found her own pistol in the car, a double-barreled derringer, and he went back to where she was lying face down and shot her through the back chest part into the ground. He thought she was dead, but after he left she got up and walked out on the road, and someone came by and brought her in, and, luck would have it, with the aid of information she gave us while she was still conscious at the hospital, we went out and in less than two hours had him picked up. Now, that's what I call kidnapping, attempted murder, rape, all those kind of things that we didn't have back in the other days.

The Ranger that we have now, I was working on a murder case the day that he came in. They told me that the new Ranger was here at the office, and I said, "Well, send him out here, I got a job for him." I was looking over a bridge into water about four-feet deep with a body in it. We pulled this body out and it had been stabbed 42 times. There was no identification or nothing as to where he came from, but in less than three months we had the man that killed this one picked up, and went to trial, and got a conviction on him.

We're having lots of murders, now. We've had elderly people killed. We had one in Sealy that was raped and murdered, and we caught him and sent him to the penitentiary. We had three elderly ladies at Wallis that was raped and two of 'em murdered, and we caught that one and sent him. Then we had this 70-year-old woman in the west part of the county. This black man came in her back window and raped her and killed her and left her laying there on the bed, just blood everywhere. We were lucky enough that we caught him and sent him to the penitentiary.

And drugs—when I first started I myself didn't even know what marihuana was, I didn't know what coke was, I didn't know what heroin was. Just a few days ago we made a buy off a man of four ounces of cocaine and seized a Mercedes automobile he was in, and two days later we made another buy off of another man with 10 ounces of coke and seized his money and his automobile. Well, that's the difference in the type crime that (there) was whenever I started here and what we're having now.

We've sent a lot of these old boys to the pen. And when they're drunk and they're desperate, they may think they have been treated bad by somebody up and down the line, and they think everybody is treating 'em bad, and they've made threats on me. I've had several that we sent to the pen that promised me that when they got out they'd even the score up. Luckily they haven't tried it yet, I hope they don't. Ten years ago I would have thought that I'd probably be able to recognize just about everybody that I'd sent down there, but (the) last six or eight years we've sent so darned many until I ain't sure I'd recognize all of 'em. Most of 'em forget about it, but there's some of 'em that holds a grudge, you know. They say an elephant never forgets anything, maybe some of these dudes might not.

The job of being sheriff today depends on which county you're in. You take your drifting people, your shipwork people that work from place to place and don't settle down, they go through life and don't even know who a sheriff in a county is. They get a lot of publicity down in Harris County, but I bet the sheriff could walk in a place that he's not used to going and there wouldn't be one out of two-hundred people recognize him. It's not that way in a little county. Most of the time I can go almost anywhere in this county and everybody knows me. It's according to the class of people.

In the big counties, you can call the sheriff's office, but you'll never get the sheriff. Ain't no way of getting him, unless you're a special friend of him. Johnie Klevenhagen, Jr., is a good friend of mine, a very good man, I've known him ever since he went to work in law enforcement, but when a call comes in from one of those cheaper sections of town out there, Johnie is not going to go out there hisself. He's got 1,500 other men he can send 'fore he gets to him. He don't go out and make personal calls hisself, he just don't do that. Being sheriff there is a different life completely. Buster Kern worked some cases, I went to work when he did, but even then he just worked big cases. I go out on calls all the time.

I just love to be around people. I love to be near whatever excitement is going on, I like to be near it. But I've told all my deputies, used to, when we worked accidents, they've got to be ready to pay the price. I hired a man one time who was retired, a 55-year-old man hired to be deputy in Sealy. I told him, his name was Pop, "Pop, when you go to work here, let me tell you something you gonna run into. You gonna run into some wrecks where people is torn all to pieces. You gonna go out there and you gonna find one with an arm tore off, another with a leg tore off. You'll go to another where his insides be scattered all over the ground, maybe brains knocked out on the ground." I says, "Now, if that's gonna bother you, you better not take this job, because part of our job is going out and investigating these things."

Well, he thought he could take it and had probably run into two or three, but one night we got a call down on the San Felipe railroad crossing. Somebody had run into a train on a motorcycle, and when he got down there it happened to be a good friend of Pop, a boy about 18 years old. He had been riding a motorcycle that night and the train had already crossed the road and it was a blind crossing, no lights, no nothing, and he came down there with dim lights and he didn't see the train going across until he got right on it. And he just flat run into the train, and it a-going. Well, it tore that boy up something bad, just all to pieces. He must of got up under the wheels or something, I don't know. That almost ran that man crazy. He was paining real bad, though he finally got over it.

There's a lot of those things that is real bad. This first chief deputy of mine made a wreck out south of Bellville here, one night. A flatbed trailer pulled by a pickup had been whipping behind it, and another car with five or six people in it had came along there and the trailer went out like this and caught the car as it went by. It killed two or three of 'em, and my deputy was out there helping work the wreck, and when they rolled one over to try to identify her—she'd been killed instantly—that was his daughter. He didn't even know she was out there. Now, that set him back, that set him way back.

I've never had anything as bad as either one of those happen to me, but I've had lots of wrecks, lots of fists, and lots of cuttings, and shootings with their heads blowed off and all over the ceiling, and wrecks where the body is tore up everywhere. When I first started, it kind of followed me home. Once in a while I'd be laying there on that pillow when I'd want to go to sleep. But I made my mind up that somebody has to do this work. I like to be in on the excitement, I might as well harden myself down to where I can take it. And I did. I have to say that now it just doesn't bother me a bit.

Sometimes it gets pretty rough. For instance, it is amazing how many people that commits suicide use a shotgun on their own head, and that's a nasty thing; it don't leave much to go by. I guess there wouldn't be much thrill in it if a man took an overdose and went to the funeral home and lay down with it.

Less than 30 days ago I went down to San Felipe on a day we had two people drowned in the river, and while we was working on that we had a call about a suicide. Went over there and this guy was sitting in a chair just like this, and he'd put a 12-gauge shotgun down in front of him, put that barrel right here between his eyes, and pulled the trigger. And it blowed everything off the top of his head from his ears up, and scattered it all over the ceiling for 20 feet on each side. The biggest piece of bone was slightly over the size of a silver dollar. A couple of 'em went in there and got sick real quick, but it doesn't make me sick. Someone has to do this work, why not build myself up until it doesn't make me that way? I don't want to see it, I don't want it to happen, but if it does happen, I don't mind being somebody that helps work it.

We had those two black men drowned in the river down here at San Felipe that day, and we've been looking for 'em ever since. I guess over the years I've been sheriff there has been a hundred or more people drown in the Brazos. I'd be very safe in saying a hundred. I've drug in boats using these old hooks, run up and down the river, and got out in the river without any clothes and searched around in brush piles with a rope tied around my body. I've done everything that can be done to try to rescue them out of there, and we've never lost a body up till now. We had five at one time drowned when a bridge under construction fell in over here between Bellville and Hempstead on the Brazos River. We found four of 'em within two days and the fifth one in about 30 days, he'd done drifted three or four miles down the river. The bodies don't do exactly the same thing, hardly ever there's been two of 'em alike, but most of the time they'll float off to the side and get hung in a drift and just stay there.

But this has been over six weeks and both of these is still gone. I believe, due to the fact that the river was high, real swift, lots of trash . . . . This old river here has got a lot of suckholes in it. It'll eat a hole out in the sand in the bottom 50-foot deep. If bodies are floating and come along there while they're still cold, they'll go to the lowest place, they'll go to the bottom. If they went down one of those holes, they went all the way to the bottom. Very possibly, they could have clinched each other and went in one of those deep holes and got hung under the brush. And if they did and then the river goes down . . . the lower the river gets, the more these holes fill back in. They fill up with silt and the bodies may be 10, 15 foot under the mud. They won't ever show up.

We had a big excitement about that last night at the peace officers' banquet. Just as I got my plate I got a telephone call. The dispatcher says, "They found one of the bodies down in San Felipe." I said "Oh, boy!" and went and told the JP, got to have a JP for the inquest. I ended up with four phone calls on that while I was trying to eat, and the fourth was to tell me that they'd already went down there and when they pulled it out it was a calf instead of one of the men. That sort of thing comes with the job.

I.R. "NIG" HOSKINS

★

I was born in Red Rock, Texas, on April 17, 1908. My uncle John Wainscott came over about two days after I was born, and this black woman was holding me. (Her arm) From her elbow out was bigger than I was. My uncle asked her, "Higgie, what you got there?" And she said, "This is my little man." And my uncle picked me up and looked at me and said, "Come here, little nigger." And from that day to this one, I go by the name of "Nigger."

I plowed in the field when I was eight years old with a mule, the sweep-stock handle held right outside my head. I had eight brothers and one sister, but in 1918 I did all the fieldwork. Everyone was in bed sick with the flu but me and my daddy. My family never owned anything, we were sharecroppers. My first job was tying hay on the Eagleston farm east of Smithville for $3.50 a week, and I carried my own lunch.

My granddaddy got killed there in Red Rock. It was over one of his granddaughters that he'd taken and raised. Her daddy come over there one morning to get her, to make her go home and go to picking cotton. She was 12 years old, and she didn't want to go. My granddaddy told him, "Let her alone. I'll bring her on home after a while." Her father was drunk, and he said, "She's going now." Granddaddy says, "No, you're not gonna take her now, you're not just gonna whip her and make her go now. I'll bring her on home after a while." Then he cussed my granddaddy, and went out to the woodpile and got an axe, and started back to the house. My granddaddy told him, "Don't you come on the porch with that axe in your hand. What are you gonna do with that axe?" And he cussed my granddaddy and said, "I'll show you when I get there." He come up the steps of the porch and my granddaddy shot him off the porch backwards with a shotgun. Then my first cousin, who was two year old when that happened, he was taught from two year old till he got up to 16 years old about that, and he killed my granddaddy in Red Rock one day. He was mean, he was a mean son-of-a-gun; wasn't no question about it.

In the 1920s I had a friend down there near Sugar Land that was guarding prisoners at the prison farm, and I taken a notion I wanted to do that. It paid big money, 50 dollars a month. You worked from daylight to dark, and that was big salary back there then. I decided I wanted to do it, so I come over here to the old sheriff here in Bastrop, Woody Townsend, asked him for a letter of recommendation, and he gave it to me. I went down there to the farm and give it to the captain, and he read the letter and put me to work. The old sheriff told me to go down there and keep my eyes open and my mouth shut. That's the advice I got.

The camp then was just an old wooden building with bars over the windows. The building was double, with a picket between the two wings, and a kitchen there for the guards. We didn't have much to eat. If we got eggs, we had to take our own eggs to the camp and the trustees would cook 'em for us.

This was Harlem Number One, at Raymondville, Texas, and it was a work camp, it was penitentiary. It wasn't a recreation center like it is now, it was penitentiary. The prisoners did regular farm work, just regular farm work. They had dairies there, hogs, such as that. It was just a regular farm. We had a barn with mules and cultivators. Didn't have no tractors or nothing, it was mules. When we planted corn, we dropped it by hand, didn't have no planters. A guard would take about 10 men, and he'd drop corn. Another guard would have a bunch of plows out there with mules. He'd be going ahead and opening furrows with 10 plows, and then this man come along with his crew of 10 and they'd drop the corn. The same man that had the front plows had the back ones, too, and then he had 10 with cultivators. They would come along and cover the corn.

That got 10 rows at a whack, 20 rows at a round. I've forgotten how many thousand acres we had, but it was a big farm, a big farm. We had a hundred acres in garden. We raised our own garden and had the milk and butter and pork and chickens, all that.

The captain would turn us out about 20 men apiece, and them 20 men was his, you see. He carried 'em to the work, a-hoeing or a-cleaning out ditches, whatever he was doing, and just kept 'em right together. He'd get on the danger side, where one might run or something, and he'd try to sit on that side as close as he could to keep 'em from running.

Many a one did run. After a while I run the dogs, I had a bunch of dogs that I trained to run a man when they escaped. It's kindly hard to say why I got the job. I guess I made 'em a good guard, I guess, a good hand with the men in the working part and all. I just got the job. I was called in one day by the captain. He says, "How would you like to have the dog job?" Well, I've hunted all my life, far as that was. Us kids had hunted at night. I said, "I'd like it." "Well," he said, "I'm gonna put you on it. I don't want you to lose nary a man; if one runs, I want him caught." I said, "I'll do my best." So, I wound up as the dog man at Harlem Number One.

They had a pack of 36 hounds, 'cause lots of times we'd have one to run. Say, there'd be an old trustee that was up at the hog pen, or somewhere, and we didn't check him every hour, well, he'd take off. A lot of people don't understand why a pack of dogs can't catch a man right quick. First place is, a pack of dogs can't run a man like they do a varmint. You can get on a horse and follow a pack of dogs running a man all day long, and keep up with 'em. But I've got some wolf dogs now, and if you go up and get on a horse and try to follow 'em through the woods running a wolf, you can't do it. A dog can't run a man like they can a varmint. And if you put a man in middle-buster beds, where the land is fresh-plowed, throwed up in beds, and as he crosses that field he steps down in the middle of the beds, it just takes 'em a long time to walk him across there. The best thing to do is just take your dogs, pull 'em off and loop around to the other side, and just drag up a-side of that field, pick him up where he went out at. 'Cause, you can't hardly run a man in plowed ground at all.

You see, a man just don't leave the scent a varmint does. The scent from a man comes from under his arms and between his legs, and lots of 'em, when you caught 'em, they wouldn't have on a thing in the world but their shorts. They were hard to run, then. If he kept his britches on, a shirt on, when the scent came out it would settle on the brush or weeds and go to the ground, and you could run him pretty good. But if he pulled that shirt and britches off, nothing but his shorts on, you had trouble. They knew that. They told each other,

"If you ever run, pull your clothes off as quick as you can." If it was cold, they wouldn't hardly pull 'em off, but in the summertime they'd get out of 'em fast.

If I wanted to tell you how to get away from dogs, the first thing I'd tell you to do is to pull all your clothes off, right down to your shorts. That would be the first thing, and then the next thing is not to go very far at a time straight, just go a short ways and take a sharp turn. They'll be running, and when you make a sharp turn yonder, they'll overrun it for a piece, and thataway, then, they're losing time. They got to come back and find where you went. And stay in clean ground, if you can, out of grass and weeds. Stay on just clean a ground as you can get on. A plowed field would be the hardest of all. Getting in a creek wouldn't help you too much, they'll still work it. If you touch anything, a stick, a rock, the creek bank or anything else, they'll work it out. They'll work you out of a creek, out of water.

Even in deep water, they can still smell you. They can locate you, 'cause I had 'em to do it, once. One was hid in some water, and he'd come up just so often to get his breath. He was in under the water and he'd just come up there with just his nose, just where he could breath, and then he'd go back under and come up and breath again. My other dogs had gone on and I whipped one of my old dogs twice to make her come on and follow me. But she wouldn't leave that place to follow me, she kept going back to it. So, I went back there and searched it and watched it real close, and directly he stuck his nose up. Then I got down in the water, and when he stuck his nose up there again, I hit him with a whip right in his face, and he got up. But this old dog wouldn't leave him. She was the only one. She was one of the old ones that went through it all.

We just used dogs to run men, just a common dog. A lot of people holler, "bloodhound, bloodhound," but a full-blood bloodhound is too slow. They'd never catch 'em, never catch 'em. I used Bluetick and Redbone, mostly. We didn't use Walker dogs because they was too fast, and you'd have trouble follering 'em, you see. I've been a dog man all my life. I hunted at home when I was just a kid 10 or 12 year old, on up like that. We had hunting dogs that we hunted varmints with—coons, possums, skunks. And my older brother had some wolf dogs that we run wolves with back there then. My brother had some good ones.

I've got 18 wolf dogs now. They're all kinds of dogs, different breeds. July and Walker hounds is best for wolves, and the Hudspeth. The Hudspeth and the July are old lines of dogs, they're not no new-comers, they're old line dogs. The Hudspeth is a big, white dog, with some light lemon spots on 'em, and pretty long hair. They're a longer-haired dog than a July or a Walker. A July is a light grey, smoky-colored dog, just a dog only a little different than the rest of 'em. Some of 'em that you get will kill a wolf when they catch it, and some of 'em won't even bite it. That runs in all dogs.

Now, I just put 'em in a truck and take 'em out to where I want to hunt and turn 'em a-loose. You just turn 'em loose and they light out through the woods and find a wolf, and then you just sit there and listen at 'em running. You catch one wolf out of every 10, maybe, that you run. You don't catch many wolves. A wolf is just about the fastest thing on four legs, but they can't last as long as a dog. A dog will just out-last 'em, that's the only reason they catch 'em. I have sat and listened at it all night long.

A wolf is bigger than a little old coyote. A coyote is just a little old thing, and you can catch them pretty good, but you jump one of them wolves that's got some coyote and some wolf in him, the timber wolf part in him, or crossed with dogs, and they're hard to catch. These Game and Fish boys that say there ain't no wolves is wrong. I can get you a boy that lives in Buda, Texas, that was out here with me in my pasture deer hunting, and there was four come across right by his stand. He said they were as big or bigger than any German shepards he'd ever seen. I was feeding the wolves down there in my pasture so I'd be able to run 'em, I got 1,140 acres, but he said, "I hope you ain't a-feeding *them*!"

The Walker, the July, the Hudspeth, them are wolf hounds. They're too fast to use in running a man. Now, you might breed 'em down a little, say, to a half or a third, and then they'd be all right. We had Redbone, and Black and Tan, and some Bluetick, something that's not so fast. And bloodhound, they had some bloodhound mixed in. If you get a full-blooded bloodhound, they're too slow. There's a slow dog, but have a cold nose; they can smell a track where other dogs can't smell it.

To train one to run a wolf, all you have to do is use your old dogs there. When your younger dogs gets big enough to keep up, just take 'em with the older dogs and let 'em run. You don't train 'em by just looking at a varmint, or something, you just train 'em with older dogs. That's the natural way, and it works fine with varmints. Running a man is not natural at all for a dog. You couldn't take a year or a year-and-a-half old dog and make him run a man at all, because it just ain't in 'em to do it. They've got to be trained from a puppy up. But on a varmint, you can take one a year-and-a-half old, turn him a-loose with some old dogs out yonder, and he'd train naturally. It's altogether different.

At the camp when we had a good one, maybe a Bluetick bitch that really worked a track good, we'd breed her with a male that was also a good dog. Baby pups, when they got to where you walk in a pen and the little old puppies will run to you and rare up on your britches leg and such as that, well, that's when you start training 'em. You didn't train 'em with older dogs, you trained 'em from a puppy up. You'd put 'em in a bushel basket and pack 'em out yonder in the field somewhere and let 'em out, and they'd start walking, and you'd just let 'em foller you. They're trained from little bitty puppies, just from the time you can walk along and wait for 'em to hop over a clod of dirt or a clump of grass. Maybe one of 'em would give out and couldn't go, and you'd pick it up and put it in that basket and pack it for a piece, let it rest. The bigger they got, just the little faster you got ahead of 'em. At first you'd just walk along slow while they're playing around your feet, but the bigger they got, just the little faster you got. When they get to where they could keep up with you in a good walk, well, you just get a little faster, just a little faster all the time. When they got to where they were really follering you good, you'd go somewhere to where there'd be a little grass or something so they couldn't actually see you, and you'd stay 50 or 60 feet in front of 'em so that the trail would be really hot, to where they could really smell you.

The bigger they got, the faster you'd get, until it got to where you couldn't outrun 'em. Then it would take two men. One of 'em would go out there and walk on maybe three or four-hundred yards ahead of 'em, and then the other one would take 'em and mess around with where he went, and then they'd pick up his track and just light out to running him. He'd stay about that far ahead of 'em just about as long as they could run, till they were just about give out, then he'd climb up in a tree or on a fencepost or something, let 'em come on up to him to where they'd tree him. A trustee, a dog boy, would usually do that.

You had to run your pack all the time. On weekends, I'd send my dog boys off. I let two go off Sundays, that was a big day. The picket boss would let 'em out about three o'clock in the morning, and they'd take off. I'd take my dogs and pick their trail up at about seven, and I'd run 'em till two, three o'clock that evening and catch 'em. I'd know in general which a-way they were going. We'd run 'em all over that country down there, on the free labor farms and private farms and everything, but they'd always go down the fence lines till they come to a gap, a gate, that I could get in on my horse. Then, maybe, they'd take off across that pasture, come on around and hit that other fence until they found another gate that I could get through again. I'd run 'em six or seven hours and catch 'em. They'd usually go and tree pretty close back to the camp. Whenever we caught him, if it was just one dog boy, we'd neck all the dogs in twos and maybe he'd get up behind me on my horse, and the dogs would follow us and we'd go on to the camp.

The dog boys laid trail and kept the dog pen clean and fed the dogs and took care of my horses, such as that. I'd have three or four of 'em. One of 'em would stay at the dog pen all through the day and do the cleaning up, and I'd have two or three that would go with the hoe squads and plow squads. All they'd do is just go out there and sit in the shade with the dogs. Each of 'em would have part of the pack. When they carried them a-foot thataway, they usually took five or six dogs each. One of 'em that would mind good, they wouldn't neck him to nothing, but the others that they'd have a little trouble with sometimes—making 'em mind—they'd neck two of 'em together with a little lead about nine inches long. They'd have collars on 'em with snaps and rings, and they'd neck two together. They'd just take their dogs in the shade down there somewhere and wait.

See, some of those fields is a mile and a half from the camp. Maybe they'd be cutting wood down in the woods, well, they'd be three, four, five miles from the building. There were thousands and thousands of acres in those 21 farms, and 1,700 men. Over here there's a bunch of 'em working on this side of the farm, well, you'd have a pack of dogs with them. And if there's a bunch working over here, you'd have a pack with them, too. So, if one would run or something another, all you had to do, then, is get there on your horse. A pack of dogs was already close. They would shoot a gun twice when something happened, and I'd go to it. The dog boy wouldn't go when I run a man, he'd go to the water wagon. They had the water boy there with the wagon, you know, and two or three barrels on it with water. He'd just sit up there on the water wagon so that nobody would get him confused with somebody out of another squad. Maybe when the squads would come by the water wagon to get water he might just help the water boy. Or, they had a bucket for the guards, and he might just take that bucket and go to that guard with it to give him a drink of water. Oh, it was penitentiary back in the '20s and '30s. It was penitentiary, it wasn't recreation.

Lots of times two or three would run at once. If you got to where you were working up close to brush or a creek or something, two or three might run at one time. And more so where there was a plow squad team, you know. They'd drive right up to a corn patch right over the fence on a free labor farm, or something, and when they turned around, maybe they stopped the mules and maybe they didn't, but just over that fence they'd go into that corn. The guard didn't have much chance to stop 'em. We'd average about three runs a week. Yessir, I was on the road pretty muchly. Course, if nary (not one) didn't run today, I'd just sit up under a shade tree out there in the field and wait for one to do it. If he didn't run, I didn't have to do nothing.

All the tracks that I run was all about the same. You could run some better than you could others, it's according to how close you was getting to him. He would go a mile or so, and after you got up to within 15 or 20 minutes of him, you had trouble follering those dogs, because they'd run him, they'd run him hard.

At first, you just had to take your time and let 'em work it out. You would ride your horse and just lope down here a little piece and stop, just sit there and wait on 'em, till they work him away from a certain spot where he'd been at. Maybe he went 'cross a creek in some water or went down that creek in that water, such as that, and come out down yonder somewhere. It took time for them to find him.

You just don't want it too hot, 'cause no dog can stay there too long when it's too hot. But cold, (or) water, they don't make no difference with a dog. I've run men 'cross rice fields where the dogs just jumped to get through it, they couldn't run. They'd smell the scent on the tops of the rice and then see that there's where he went, there's where he mashed the rice down. A dog would look at that, too.

They'd get up a tree before the dogs got to 'em, because those dogs would fight 'em. Course, he had to fight 'em anyhow. When I got to him, he had to come down. He wasn't gonna stay up there and me chain them dogs up and not let them get to him. Naw, he had to come down from there and fight 'em. I'd cut him some switches and he'd come down. I'd cut some switches myself and give 'em to him and tell him what to do. Most times he'd jump down out of that tree, then back up to the tree like this, you see. Then he'd just fight from each side of him out in front to keep the dogs away from him. I'd let him fight 'em for two or three minutes, then I'd pop my whip, and when I popped that whip he'd drop his switches and the dogs would just run up to him, and that's all. They wouldn't bite him.

I had some dogs down there, six particularly, that was my picks. I could have rode through the streets in Austin, and if anybody run over one of them dogs they'd have to run into that horse. They would just be right under his feet, just far enough away from his feet that the horse wouldn't step on 'em. They wouldn't get in front of you, they'd be right agin his hind legs. If a car hit one of them dogs, they'd have to hit that horse. They was that close. I could run a man right through town with 'em. It'd take 'em time to do it, 'cause so many different tracks, it would take 'em time to work 'em out, but they'd never bother somebody else. Once they run one track a couple of hundred yards, that's the track they was gonna run, they ain't gonna switch off on somebody else.

If they got in a bunch of other tracks like that, usually they'd swing out and get out yonder away from it. I trained 'em to do that. I would run the dogs right through the field work on purpose, right through those that's in the field working. They learned pretty quick that whenever they come up to that, not to fool there too much, but go out yonder and look for the trail, swing off out yonder and look around. One would find it out there, and he'd open up and the rest would go to him.

One chase that I remember, I had one run off that went through Sugar Land trying to go to Houston. Sugar Land wasn't too far from Richmond. I had one little Black and Tan female and she worked that by herself through Sugar Land. I helt the other dogs behind me and just let her work it. I could hold my whip in my hand, and you couldn't make one of them dogs get in front of me. She worked it through Sugar Land and out the other side, then I turned the rest a-loose and we caught him just before he got to Houston.

Another time we had an old trustee to run off. Every hour the trustees had to answer the call, and we had one that wasn't there at five o'clock. He'd answered it at four o'clock, and by five o'clock he had an hours start, you see. He didn't answer it at five, and by the time I got started he'd done gone two-and-a-half hours. I run him all night till eight o'clock the next morning. I run him from there into Richmond, Texas, over to Katy, Texas, plumb across there, I guess 20-something miles. They could lay a pretty good track. Them that's out in the weather, used to it, hard, and working, they could just start in a little trot and go a long ways in an hours time.

I was short down there one morning of a dog boy, a trustee, and had one there in the field that just had six months to go. The captain give him to me. When he put him on the dog job, he had two days for one, or maybe three, and that's all he'd have to had done. Well, the second morning he was out, he saddled my horse and carried him down to the dog pen, and he got on him and run off. He rode him across to Richmond to the railroad river bridge and tied my horse there, then he got up and went on through Richmond and on down to a big hay barn and got in it. But I caught him. I had some that would run a horse, a bunch of just-half-grown pups. Man, they'd eat a horse or a mule track up. I run him to the river bridge with them, and then taken the old dogs that had been helt behind me and they picked up his track and run him through Richmond on out to that hay barn. He lost all of his good time and everything then, you see, and had to go back into the field. You don't never know what one's gonna do, that's one reason you can seldom ever trust a man.

I run two that I had to fire some shots. Nothing smart about it, if I had it to do over I figure I'd run a little bit 'fore I would do it. I had to shoot one and would've shot the other if he hadn't of stopped. They was coming at me just straight as they could come. I'm not proud of it. I didn't do nothing smart, didn't put no feathers in my hat. But it was on the twenty-seventh day of July, my horse was stumbling he was so hot, and I couldn't have got away on foot from 'em. I just had it to do, but I'm not proud of it.

I went out on call with my dogs lots of times. I got deputized under the Texas Rangers by them calling me, wanting to use me, and the sheriff of Fort Bend County deputized me, T. R. Roane. I went all over the state of Texas. I remember one chase particularly, they had called me down to Jackson County, to Edna. There was an ex-convict who had shot a black woman with a shotgun. You ain't gonna believe this, but it went right under one breast on this side and come out on this other one, just followed the bones around. They called me down there. I went on out to a little old place they called Sandy Point, and picked up this black man's track about 1:20 that morning. There was 11 deputies there and two sheriffs, they just had one horse for me to ride. Wasn't none of 'em on horse with me, I was by myself. I picked up his trail with my number one pack of six dogs, and run him through a big old bottom in the moonlight. They'd be a big black shadow here, and over here between these two trees just light as it could be. Well, you went right out of a shadow into a light, and you couldn't look back in that shadow and see nothing. But I run him, anyhow, until just at daybreak the next morning when I found where he'd went into a house. I told 'em, "He's in this house here, now. We've got to set on it." And nobody wouldn't go up to the house till one of the sheriffs, a little bitty old sheriff, "Buckshot" Lane—weighed 130 pounds soaking wet—he run up to the back window and busted some tear gas in there. They still wouldn't go up and open the front door, and I said, "Well, somebody's got to. I'll tell all of you, I'm gonna go to that door and kick it open, and I'm gonna jump out of the front of it." And I did, but I didn't jump quick enough till tear gas hit me in the eyes. That was my first experience of tear gas. And, why, he could have come out of there and done whatever he wanted to do to me, I couldn't have seen him! I couldn't even open my eyes.

So, then the back door slammed. Ever one of 'em was at the front door to see what was gonna happen, and I heard the back door slam. I hollered, "He's gone out the back door!" And how that man stayed in that tear gas and then run like he did, I don't know. I came out of there and got my eyesight cleared up to where I could see at all, and I taken the dogs and went around to the back and picked up his track. I mean, they was running him just like they was looking at him! It was just at the break of day, and you could get down this-a-way, and just skylight through there. I had a red dog that jumped about that high, and I told 'em, "There he is, fellers, right there." We heard a shot. I says, "He's killed hisself or he's warning us not to come to him." Well, somebody had to go. I told 'em, says, "Now, if I holler that I'm gonna get up, y'all wait, but if somebody gets up without hollering, y'all protect me." They said they would. We was in broomweeds about this high. I got down on my elbows and stomach and just drug myself through them weeds. When I got to him, I could see he was lying there dead. He'd shot himself right under the chin with a .38-40 pistol. I hollered to 'em, "I'm gonna get up. He's killed hisself, here."

And that old sheriff at Richmond, Texas, if he was living today he'd still tell you I killed that black man. He killed himself with a .38-40 six-shooter, and I was wearing a .38-40 six-shooter. I went through Richmond and he said, "Well, did you catch him?" I said, "Yes, he killed hisself right in front of us." And the words he said to me—so help me God, if he lets me live to open that door and walk out of here—he says, "I knowed that nigger was gonna kill hisself with a .38-40 six-shooter 'fore you went down there." He's accusing me of killing the man. I said, "I didn't kill him." "Aw," he says, "I know you didn't. But how come that nigger was wearing a .38-40 six-shooter and you was wearing a .38-40 six-shooter, now, tell me that?" I said, "I couldn't tell you. All I can tell you is I can prove where I was at by 11 other men."

Course, he was just hurrahing me. He didn't care about that man. He didn't care.

I was down there 16 years. After 16 years of it, I got enough and come home on the fifth of June, 1942. I worked on the railroad from then till '52 when I run for the sheriff's office here. I got it, I taken the sheriff's office in '53 for eight years and got beat. I was out 16 years, and then people got after me to run again, and I run again and was elected again. I was in for four years, I got beat, and after that four years was up, they hollered for me to run again. And I run again and I was elected again. I been in three times in three different decades.

Wasn't no speeches to be made, you just went and seen everybody that you could and give 'em a card. You had to see a whole lot of 'em or you wouldn't get no votes. You'd go to town on Saturdays, they'd be a lot of people in town in those days, and then maybe you'd send out a lot of cards. I lived down yonder in the country, out in the woods. There was a policeman in Smithville and then one of the deputies here under Mr. Cartwright that run that first time, but I lucked out. We got three big towns in the county, Elgin, Smithville, and Bastrop, and it was hard for a man to carry all three. If he can carry two of the big towns he can pretty well be elected.

Politics is dirty, it's just dirty as dirty can be. And it's 10 times worse now than it was in the '50s. The old saying is, "If you've ever done anything in your life, you can bet it'll come out on you if you get in politics." They'll do anything in any way to try to beat you. Now, my granddaddy was killed in Red Rock in 1916. When I run for the office back here in '52, they brought that out against me, about my granddaddy getting killed in 1916, about how rough I was, and all such as that. My daddy got mad about it. He went to Red Rock and he told 'em, says, "I don't want to find out who said it. I just don't want nobody to let me know who brought my daddy into this. He's been killed in 1916, he's not here and got nothing to do with it. Don't let me find out who's talking it." And he never did find out, either.

The old story was, way back there the law wouldn't go to Red Rock. They just wouldn't go out there. So, when I was elected back in '53, I got a call from Red Rock and I went out there. Course, I was raised in Red Rock, I run around there as a young kid, I married there in Red Rock, and all, and I knowed everybody there. But I didn't go out there no "bully of the woods," either. I went out there as a man and talked to this feller and told him the complaint I had. He was running a beer joint and selling beer to kids, and then they were gambling in the back of it. I just told him, "If you don't quit it, now, I'm gonna have to come out here and catch you." And he quit it. He wasn't no bully of the woods, either.

My wife and I and my kids all lived downstairs in the old jail in those days, right over here. It had three bedrooms and a living room and a kitchen. Back in the early '50s, the population of this county was only 10 or 12,000, now it's over 35,000. Back in '52, '53, along in there, I had give the kids here in Bastrop the keys of the jail. Many a day they played in the old jail. They had the keys, and these kids here on Saturday and Sundays, let me tell you, they'd have a time locking them others up in the jail! We didn't have nobody in jail. Many, a many a day we went and didn't have nobody in jail. We had no dope, not a whole lot of drunks, and when you got 'em you could do something with 'em. The laws is all built for the crook and for the criminal, now.

I had a deputy and a secretary after two or three years, and they paid her a big salary of 25 dollars per month. And back there then, I got 350 dollars and the deputy got 275 dollars. The deputy was just a man out here that you knowed was a pretty good feller, and had been all his life. You just hired a man that you pretty well knowed. There wasn't no training, we never even thought about it. But we knew every house in the county, every road. You knowed where you was going 'fore you left here, and you knowed who you was gonna see.

Now then, man, you don't know where you're going or where they live. Most people that had telephones, if they called in to you then, you might near remembered their phone numbers. Just didn't have no whole lot of phones.

We just went on calls. And when we'd get a call at 12 midnight or one or two o'clock in the morning, we didn't think about calling the other one for two of us to go and get it together. Just one man went off by hisself, 'cause there just wasn't a whole lot of danger to go. You never thought of danger. We'd have some burglary cases, not too many. Then we'd have some family arguments and some cow stealing, such as that. It just wasn't a whole lot of nothing.

Now, you name it, and they ask us to do it, you just might near name it. Two of the boys here just now, I heard 'em call in on the radio. You didn't pay no attention, but I did. Out at a cemetery here, a woman had called that takes care of the cemetery that somebody had run through it with a car and run through the fence at the back gate. And there's a little car standing out there. They went out there and checked it, and there it is. It's got damage all over it and all; that's the car that done it. Then, a man was jogging the other day and his dog was follering him, and another man's dog come out and jumped on it. He was trying to get him off of him, and the dog bit him. Another one said, "A man has killed one of my chickens that got over out of the pen awhile ago and got over in his yard, and he shot it." You name it and we get the calls on it. "There's a polecat under my house!" or "There's a snake in my house, come out here and get him out!" You just name it and we get them calls. It don't make no difference.

On some of 'em, they just imagine these things, but you still have to go on 'em. Down at Smithville, out on Rocky Hill, they's a woman called for someone to come out there, says, "There's somebody here in the brush watching my house." She just insisted on it, and the deputy went out there and couldn't find nobody. Called again, and he went out there. Called a third time, and he went out there. She said, "Don't you see him yonder? Right yonder, look, right under that cedar tree!" Well, he said wasn't a thing in the world there. He tried to convince her of that, but he said he couldn't. Then, the other night, one of the deputies up here at Elgin, a woman called him, she's about 90 years old, and told him, says, "There's a light right down below my house here, by that barn." He went down there and wasn't no light. He told her, says, "There ain't no light down there." He just kept talking, talking. It was about 12 miles from his house to hers, and finally she says, "You just don't want to come down here, that's all! I know it is a big light down there, I can see it!" And he says he couldn't see a sign of a light. But you've got to answer it, because next time it might be a light down there. We have lots of that.

A lot of our trouble is these people that are common-law husbands and wives, which I call "dog marriage." They're not married people, they're just living like dogs. And they'll bust up, then they'll go to court, and the judge will give 'em this and that and one thing and another. Before they go to court, she'll say, "I want to go out there and get some of my clothes and he won't let me," and want us to go and protect her to go get her clothes. Well, I won't do that. I don't have any rights to do that. She goes to pick up something, and he says, "That's mine," and she says, "It's not, it's mine," and there's an argument. I'm no judge, then, how am I gonna settle that? I don't like it, I don't like it at all.

But I'm a peacemaker wherever I can be. Many a family has trouble in the house—mothers and fathers, sons fighting their daddies. There isn't one of these I go to settle that I don't think of my own family. I've got enough trouble on my hands. I don't want more of it, I'm dragging now.

The job has changed a whole lot, just a whole lot. You've got a lot more people, and you've got ten-to-one crimes right now over what we had back in the '50s. I'll be frank with you, back there then, I'd go out here and just grab one, far as that goes, and just work him over. Everybody expected it, and they respected the sheriff and that was all. But nowadays you can't do that. He's got to jump on you now, and then you got to prove that he jumped on you. I got one lawsuit against me in all my days, all my time, and it's pending now—one-hundred-thousand dollars. The district attorney is trying to get that dropped. The man can't win it, I don't see how in the world he can, because he hit a deputy and was down on him, on top of him, and knocked four teeth a-loose in his mouth when he hit him. I couldn't get him off of him, and I hit him with my billy club. But, anyway, he filed on me for it. You don't know what's gonna happen, now. This was a prisoner in jail, and we went in there to make him clean up his cell. He just told me, says, "Don't you goddamn _____ come in here!" I said, "You get down here and get to work and clean that cell up, 'cause the federals require a prisoner to keep his cell clean." And he give me that kind of look, again. He was a black man and this was a black deputy that he hit. The deputy run in front of me and when he did, he cold-cocked him, knocked him down. The old boy was dazed. I grabbed him to pull him off of him, but he just kept a-beating him with his fist, and I rared back with that nightstick and hit him. I'd do that again if I had to, I won't lie about it.

And, oh yes, I've had threats. I've got letters that have a heart drawed on it, then an arrow sticking through it, and then look like blood dropping from it, all such as that. I've had my life threatened many, a many a time, just a many a one. They call me, daring me to be at such and such a place, saying, "There's a 30-30 waiting for you." But I've went to 'em and I never could find a 30-30. That's another of them things wasn't nothing smart about it. It could've been, I could've got killed, but it was just one of them threats that didn't mean nothing. I didn't have no better sense, is all I could tell you.

Nine of 'em out of ten won't mount to nothing. We had one in here the other day that we turned out. He said he had a 30-06, and when he got out and got ahold of that, he was gonna kill the highway patrols that brought him in here and all the deputies and everybody else. Just talk, talk.

Right now I don't think I'll run in '88; I'd be 80 years old then. Ain't none of this job a pleasure, it's a worry and a headache. Right now, I say, "No," but I've had a bunch of 'em tell me, "Well, if you don't run, we're gonna write you in." I don't know what they're gonna do. If they want to run me, they can run me. And if they write me in and I win the election, if I'm able I will serve.

Course, I donate most of my money back—to churches, fire stations, fire departments, cemeteries, and all such as that. In 1979 my salary was 14,000 dollars and I spent nine-thousand dollars of that back. I had five-thousand dollars that I lived on out of my salary. I give some more money back at the auction fund raisers. I bought a chicken for two-thousand dollars at the Smithville FFA Livestock Auction in 1984, and paid 750 dollars for a watermelon one summer at McDade. It was outrageous, there's no question. I guess it'll go down in history.

I lucked out, I'm lucky. I don't say I'm smart, I just say I'm lucky. I'm the only man that has ever been elected three different times in three different decades, and right now I am the oldest sheriff in Texas.

I'm proud of myself for this reason, that the people think that much of me. I just think I stand pretty good in our county. I have to be, or they wouldn't support me like they do. When the people have stood with a man like the county has stood with me, well, I think there's something wrong with him if he wouldn't be proud of himself.

But this six-shooter on my hip hasn't made no fool of me. I'm just Nig Hoskins, and that's all, till today. I'm proud of it, but it hadn't made no fool out of me. I'm just what I am, and that's it.

JIM
SCARBOROUGH, III

★

I t's interesting, all my people were either law enforcement officers, Baptist preachers, or horse thieves; there is no in-between.

My grandfather, Jim Scarborough, I, was first elected sheriff in Lee County—Giddings, Texas—back in the 1880s. He was a farmer when he was elected sheriff, and was put up by a bunch of friends. There were some brothers who were really terrorizing that country from College Station to La Grange. He had never been an officer before, but they wanted him for sheriff. He was sheriff there two different times for a total of 16 years.

The way I remember him telling it, the day he was elected sheriff he was plowing behind an oxen out on the family farm. He was single, then. He didn't marry till after he was 40-some-odd-years old and had been sheriff a little while. But the way he told it, this particular day he was in his shirttails with his pants hanging on a tree at the other end of the field. It was customary in those days to follow the oxen barefooted with your pants off, so you could be cool. A bunch of the citizens that were his supporters, after counting the votes were over, all rode out to his place in buggies and on horseback and came running up shooting and making noise and hollering and whooping. They rode up and caught him there without any pants on, barefooted, to tell him that he'd been elected sheriff.

He became a well-known sheriff up there, and was known to be mean. He usually got his man. He chased one man all the way to Chicago on the train, and had a shoot-out with him in the train station. That's a long, long, long story. And then he had a shoot-out with a guy who shot his moustache off in Lee County. He was a bank robber named Coleman, and he was trying to waylay the old man just about dark. As Granddad passed by, Coleman shot his long-handled moustache off. It left a little scar that made it hard to shave. We have the gun Coleman used. It was the first Bisley Colt, a revolver. I can hear my granddad telling the story to this day from when I was a little boy. He'd say, "It was getting dark, and I seen the flash of his gun, and I shot him twix the eyes."

I've got a picture of him with this guy Coleman that he killed. Coleman is sitting in a chair with my granddad holding his head up by the hair of his head. And he's dead, and his eyes are about half-open, you know. Granddad's holding him and he's got a pistol out like this, all rared back. They put that in the *Houston Chronicle* and said, "Scarborough gets his man."

He carried a single-action Colt, a .45 thumb-buster, same gun he shot Coleman with. Finally, he had it nickle-plated, with mother-of-pearl handles, and he had honed down the sear till you didn't know when that trigger was being pulled. I have shot the gun. I shot it as a kid, and after the war I took it out there again, shooting prickly pear, stuff like that, with it, and I had forgotten how smooth the action is. I've never had a smoother-actioned weapon in my hand in my life. It was just like pulling butter, almost. Quite a gun. And the old 30-30 Winchester that he killed a lot of people with, my son still has that, that was his saddle gun. Somewhere I've got a picture of him on his horse after he came down here. The horse was named Prince, and was given to him by the King Ranch. He's reared back, he's got his saddle gun butt sticking up where you can see it, he's got his pistol up in the air, and his horse is standing at the alert.

He was 10-feet tall in a lot of ways, actually six-one or six-two, something like that, and a heavy boned man. He may have killed 30 men in the line of duty, and he didn't count everybody. But I know for a fact that he didn't kill anybody after he came to Kleberg County, all of that was done in Lee County.

Lee County had a tradition of colorful sheriffs. Jim Brown, one of the earlier sheriffs there, had racehorses and raced against Sam Bass. Later, Jim Brown turned outlaw and went to Chicago and was killed by the Chicago Police Department out at the race track in a shoot-out. He was really shooting 'em up, and a friend thought he was gonna shoot at him and hollered, "Jim, you're not gonna shoot me, are you?" He said, "No," and he pulled the trigger and shot a policeman. Says, "I'm shooting that skunk behind you." He died full of holes. He went from sheriff of Lee County to bandit and race horse owner in Chicago. My grandfather was no Jim Brown, but he was almost as bad a desperado as the guys he chased.

Most of the sheriffs in that area, when my granddad used to tell these stories, they sounded pretty rough. I guess they needed to be. This gang of brothers called the Yegua Notch Gang was terrorizing the whole area. They were the main reason my granddad was elected in the first place. They were desperados and were wanted for murder, bank robbery, rape, you name it, and they had been getting away with their crimes in an area that included all those counties. They'd just range around and kind of terrorize everybody. The sheriffs of Caldwell and Bastrop counties, and my grandfather, and a Texas Ranger got after 'em, and didn't give up until they had 'em all. Then the court ordered them hung and they were hung in Bastrop, and all those sheriffs that had been chasing 'em, which included my grandfather, were present at the hanging. After that, what remained of the outlaw family put out a reward, not only for my grandfather but for the two sheriffs and, very likely, the Texas Ranger. It was, "Bring me his head in a towsack and I'll give you one-thousand dollars." So, he carried that to the grave with him, and he was always very cautious.

Sheriffs worked together in those days, worked into each other's counties pretty regularly without any problem, 'cause they were dear friends, and they had to team up. He'd go to visit the other towns, maybe his friend the sheriff in La Grange, or Bastrop, or Caldwell. If he was going to Lexington, Texas, which is about 22 miles from Giddings, he'd save his horse, rest his horse, before he went on into town. He'd loosen the girth and let his horse get all its wind back and everything, he was a big man. And then he'd gird all up and he'd come running into town! He'd usually do that on a Saturday when everybody was down at the town square trading mules and stuff, and he'd shoot off his pistol a couple of times, and everybody would holler, "Here comes the sheriff!"

Humble was not his middle name. Humble was my father's first name and second name, but not my granddad. He'd do things like that. He had a single-footing horse, one time, that they put up a lot of money on, and, in a two-hundred-yard race, he outran a racehorse that was running while he made his horse singlefoot all the way. Now, if that's true, that's a pretty high-stepping saddle horse, don't you think? He was known for getting his man, like that picture of him with Coleman, "Scarborough gets his man," that kind of stuff. He enjoyed the publicity that went with it; but he hustled, too, and he actually did some great detective work.

I think I told you about one desperado that he chased to Chicago on the train. He started out several trains behind, chasing this boy to Chicago. He had got word through Pinkertons. The old-time sheriffs evidently did a lot of business with the Pinkertons all over the country. Through his friend in Houston, who had charge of the Texas Pinkerton Association, he got word that this guy was gonna go to a certain address in Chicago. The old man was told by Western Union and caught another train, several trains behind him, and tried to chase this guy down. He got on and off, changing trains, and finally go to where he was just one train behind the fellow. They pulled into the yards in Chicago, where, even in the 1880s, there must have been a lot of trains coming in. A lot of the trains made up there and started there, and after they came in, they'd go to the yards. Then they'd be put out of action there until the cars were refurbished and all that sort of stuff. That's what happened to these two trains, and he traced this guy through the railyard. Someone said that they saw a man fitting that description get out on the opposite side of the stairs and start running. So then he just took off and left his grip, as they called it, there and everything. He took off by himself to see if he couldn't locate him, he knew what the guy looked like, and so they had a shoot-out down there and he killed him.

There's some newspaper clippings on this, headlines, front page of the *Chicago Tribune,* about this. He demonstrated at the inquest of this guy he'd killed how he had fanned his .45. It was a single-action, and he told how he hit the hammer with his thumb in order to shoot fast enough to out-shoot the guy. Whoever the JP was, or whomever it was that was the head of the inquest, asked him how it was that he was able to fire so quickly. He said, "Well, I'll demonstrate," and he got up and started fanning his .45, and the newspaper article said, "They all hit the floor. They didn't know that his gun was unloaded."

He did a lot of work that took him to Houston, a lot of his cases took him there. And he dealt with sheriffs and police departments, whoever else that they dealt with in those days, law enforcement agencies, and he was well respected. That's how come he was asked to come down here. Mr. Robert Kleberg, Sr., who was the president of the King Ranch in those days after Captain King's death, asked him. He was Captain King's son-in-law, and may or may not have ever known my grandfather before. He could have met him in Austin. Anyway, he contacted him and they met someplace, and he asked him if he would resign the sheriff position of Lee County and come down to the King Ranch. Kingsville was formed in 1904. I guess we had a little town and the railroad here then, but we were still in Nueces County. He told him, "We're gonna form our own county in the south part of Nueces County, 'cause it's just too far to do business having to go all the way to Corpus Christi all the time." He said, "When we do, we'd like for you to come down and be our sheriff."

He didn't do it immediately. I guess they must have met several times. This country was known as "the jumping-off place" in those days, and there were bandit problems down here. That must have intrigued him, he felt like he could get back in action down here. You got to remember, when he came here he was 66 years old, so he wasn't a spring chicken, and he wasn't jumping without groaning when he stepped up into the saddle. Model T's were in vogue by then, but there wasn't a lot of places you could drive one, especially down here.

He didn't bring the family right away. When he brought the family, they moved everything in a cattle car—the family cow, their buggies, and everything else. They drove down in a Model T, and it took them from nearly in the morning to way into the dark to get from Giddings to Kingsville. My great-grandmother had been living with my grandfather at that time, I guess he was the oldest living son, and she refused to come down here at all. She was 104 when she died, still in Lee County. She had come out of Georgia with my grandfather's oldest sister in a wagon train, riding a horse sidesaddle with her daughter behind her. They had settled in the Lee County area before Texas was a republic.

My grandfather came down here and sold real estate, and brought a lot of Rockdale, Bastrop, La Grange, and Lee County farmers down here later on. Those families are mostly still here, and all the Germans who bought farms north of here, most of 'em came from Lee County. So, it was a cinch for him to be elected sheriff when they finally made him run.

He was off selling a ranch to some Scotsmen over in Duval County, and you didn't get over there, way deep in that brush country, and come back in one day. They were over there a week, 'cause those people wanted to see all the ranch from one corner to another. And he had left word that he did not want to be appointed sheriff by the governor. All of the original officers of this county, when it was formed by the Legislature, were appointed by the governor, then they had an election immediately. Mr. Kleberg filed for my granddad, and when he came back to town he discovered he'd been elected sheriff. Course, he accepted it; it was his life's work. He was 66 when he came down here, and several years older than that when he took office.

Banditos were raiding all the ranches, stealing their cattle, shooting up their headquarters—not only here, but all over south and southwest Texas. They were making raids across the border stealing and pilfering and robbing and killing, and then running back and hiding across the border. It was kind of a common thing, and it was a problem. But my granddad hired two or three deputies, and he was just a tough guy. One time he caught a Mexican general down here by disguising himself and going into the bakery, where the guy worked, with a hidden gun. The man was supposedly just a tortilla maker, but was really a famous general. His people were supposed to infiltrate, maybe two thousand or so in the entire area, and then when he had enough people in place there was gonna be an uprising. They thought all the Hispanic people that were living here then would join 'em, but the *Kineños* in the King Ranch would not.

The *Kineños* are still here, still part of Kleberg County and the King Ranch. They came out of Mexico with Captain King. He brought a whole village out of Mexico up here to the Santa Gertrudis to populate this area, and those are the men who are the ranchhands out there right now, six generations of 'em. *Kineños,* it means "King's men." He went down there and bought a whole *puebla.* He bought all their cattle, all their chickens, all their donkeys, all their mules, all their horses, all their pigs, everything. And then the mayor came up to him and says, "Captain, where are you going with all these? You bought everything we have, and we don't have anything to do." He says, "You all go load, come on with me, and we'll go up to the big ranch in Texas and you can all go to work for me." So, he brought all these citizens with him out of this little town.

An interesting thing about the *Kineños,* the Captain learned to speak Spanish down on the border running a riverboat, and he mispronounced a lot of names. So, out of courtesy, the *Kineños* would all pronounce the words the same as he did. And to this day, there are some terms and words used out on the ranch that are not used anywhere else.

Anyway, the bandit raids went on for a time, and they had a real shoot-out at the Norris Ranch. My granddad had a bunch of sworn deputies, a posse, down there on that. He got there after the battle was over, after the ranch had fought 'em off, but there was still some sniping and shooting. They had a hearing in Austin, and my granddad had to go. So did the foreman of the King Ranch and a bunch of people who were in on that thing. It was a hearing in Austin called by the Legislature, because they had worked the dead bandits on horseback, roping their feet and dragging 'em on 30-foot ropes up the ramp onto the railroad loading dock, where they were loaded into boxcars to be brought back to Kingsville for burial. There were quite a few dead ones.

When they had my granddad up before this committee, they said to him, "You tell us, sheriff, why you roped those dead bodies of those bandits and drug 'em through all that sand and brush up to that loading dock." He gave the best answer. He said, "Did you ever smell a dead bandit that has been laying out in the sun two days?" That was his answer that they quoted in the Austin paper. He said, "We wished our ropes were 60 foot long."

Cattle rustling was a problem from the bandit days right down through my father's time. I've got families here that my grandfather dealt with their ancestors, my father dealt with 'em, and I'm dealing with 'em and sending 'em to Huntsville. They've changed from cattle stealing to dope running, but it's the same bunch.

My grandfather, and my father, too, could go out to where a cow or a steer or a calf had been slaughtered and look at the way they'd cut the legs off, and the way it had been butchered, and the way the hide had been cut if the hide and the head were left—they always used to take just what they were going to use and leave the rest to the coyotes—could look at it and tell you who did it. Each rustler had his own way of butchering. Some of 'em would take a heart and some of 'em wouldn't. Some would take the kidneys, 'cause they liked kidneys, too, and others wouldn't touch things like that—the organs, the liver and the kidneys and the heart. They'd know the difference, who did and who didn't. They could actually look at the butchering and say, "Well, old Juan Domingo did that," and then they'd go get Juan. Back in those days civil rights didn't amount to a whole lot. They'd stop the Model A, and get him out under a mesquite tree; and when they were through, Juan was telling 'em what he did. Things didn't get drug out even in my daddy's days until the '60s and '70s, far as the courts were concerned, and they weren't too careful about how they got a confession.

An interesting thing he (Jim Scarborough, I) did, long after he was defeated here and retired, was to clear up an unsolved crime back in Lee County. He was a Texas Ranger. It was customary in the '20s and '30s, and I guess in the '40s, for all former sheriffs that left office or retired to be made special Texas Rangers so they could carry their guns and be able to defend themselves. No one was gonna take his away from him, anyway, but they did that for him. This bank president hired him to come back to Giddings to try to solve an old bank robbery that took place up there some 12 years back. The Texas Rangers had given up, and whoever the detectives were that served the bank had given up, and this old man went up there in the '30s when I was a teenager.

He went up there in the '30s and decided that he knew who was involved in this thing. One of the persons that he thought was involved in it owned a filling station in Giddings, Texas. And here he was, an old man in his seventies, a guy that hardly went to school, a self-educated man, putting a Dictaphone up in the attic with a hidden mike to make his case. He did it, and those guys went to the penitentiary. The old man, he was considered a smooth detective.

I never heard my grandfather in his life call God's name in vain, or call somebody a son-of-a-bitch. He may have, but I didn't hear it. His choice word when he was really hot was "gosh-a-mighty," that was his way of saying "God-a-mighty." But he'd shout, he'd lose his temper, and man, when he did, he lost it!

In fact, my grandfather had the shortest temper of any man I ever knew. I think I told you I was afraid of him. Even when he was in his seventies and eighties, if somebody made him mad, he'd kick a goddamn chair all the way across the room in his own home and just raise hell. He didn't cuss, he just said "Gosh-a-mighty!" But when he said "gosh-a-mighty," he meant something else and he was plum hostile.

He always wore a big, unblocked, white Stetson hat. That was his trademark, his hat never had a crease in it, he wore it just like the old Indians. There were some other strange things about my granddad like that. He drove a Model T for a long, long time, way into the early '30s. It was a coupe, and he tied back the doors with a rope across the hood so that air would circulate. He always had the doors tied back, I guess except in the wintertime. And he never sat in a cafe with his back exposed. He always sat against the side wall—always. In church he was very uncomfortable, and would sit all the way to the back. Most of the time he would sit in the back in a folding chair, and not in the pews, where he could see this door, that door, that door, that door. He always carried his spittoon to church with him, and he'd sit back there and chew tobacco. He never smoked in his life, but he always chewed. He was the only person I knew that chewed tobacco in church. Nobody would say anything to Sheriff Jim.

That family in Lee County had one-thousand dollars offered for his head in a towsack, and maybe he thought there were some other people after him, too. Like I said, he wouldn't even go in a cafe unless he could sit with his back against the wall and see the front door. Even right before he died he was that way. He dressed always with a coat on, I don't know why. I never saw my grandfather in his coat-sleeves except in the house. He always wore a big hat and a gun, I'll guarantee you he dressed with a gun. And he was probably the kind of guy that would have a little one hid in his saddle or in his boot or something.

I'll tell you another thing about him. About 1935, when I was 15 years old, my younger brother and I sent in to Charles Atlas for his literature on this "dynamic bodybuilding." He sent this full portrait of him in a pair of jockey shorts in a pose, and all his dimensions— how big his biceps were, how big his everything was, his calves, waist, chest natural and chest expanded. All of that stuff was on this chart. I'd give a million dollars if I still had that, I'd have it hanging right here. Anyway, my granddad came in our little old room where we two boys stayed and looked at that, and he took it and pinned it up in his bedroom at the back of the house. He got a tape measure and measured himself against Charles Atlas, and he wrote it all out. He called us all in after he got it measured and said, "I want to tell you boys something." He says, "I've got Charles Atlas beat all the way 'round. I've got an inch more bicep," and on and on and on and finished up, "I'm taller, I'm heavier, and course I've got him 'bout 14 inches in the waist."

He was way in his seventies, and he really was strong as an ox. He had a dumbbell made out of concrete built on a Model-T axle. And I'd wake up in the morning, and I'm talking about just at the crack of dawn or still dark, and he'd be using that thing out there. I'm talking about a man in his late seventies. He'd roll it up on end, and he'd beat himself in the stomach with it.

And it was amazing the way he could still shoot, too. I remember taking him hunting. We used to have a Packard two-door touring car, a '28 model, and it had a jump seat that instead of folding down into the trunk folded up, and the seat set high, like they do now when they rig up a hunting car. He could sit back there in that jump seat and see over the canvas top. I'd take him out to the Canales ranches, the King Ranch. He could hunt anywhere he wanted to, always did. He would shoot a buck on the run, he felt like that was the sporting thing to do, and even in the year before he died, when he was 83, he killed his two deer, killed his turkey, killed his two javalina, with one shot. I was a teenager and I couldn't do that, not with one shot. He'd get 'em running and make me stop the car, and he'd lead 'em with a 30-30 saddle gun and end 'em over. It was just amazing.

After he got his moustache shot off, he never wore one again, and he had a little faint scar on his upper lip that gave him trouble when he shaved. It was so funny to watch him shave, I can remember that as a kid. He shaved with a ten-gallon hat on, and he was completely bald-headed. He had (on) I don't mean a ten-gallon hat, but a hundred-gallon hat, if there is such a thing. And he never creased 'em, he wore 'em like the Indians did, blocked, the way you'd buy 'em in a store. He'd be sitting in his long-handled underwear in the bathroom in a chair with the mirror down on the lavatory, with his old razor-strop razor, shaving. And it was the funniest sight, it was all that my brother and I could do to keep from giggling. He'd have that damn hat on while he was shaving! And he had to work so hard to get around that scar. He was the only man I ever saw that did everything with his hat. He'd have slept in the hat if he could have done it without messing it up.

Watching him get ready for bed was another funny sight. My grandmother passed away in 1930 and he passed away in 1936. I remember him in the late '20s and early '30s sitting in a chair in front of a gas stove with his house shoes off, just getting ready to go to bed. He always slept either in his BVDs or his long johns, winter wear, and never owned a pair of pajamas in his life. He'd be sitting in front of the gas stove all mad about something, saying, "Gosh-a-mighty! I wish to hell I was back in Lee County in a log cabin with a dirt floor!" And here he was soaking up the comforts of the gas, with hot water in the house and all. We used to snicker about that, my brother and I. Then, when he'd go to bed, he'd always hang his pistol belt on the bedstead. He had an old, high, four-poster bed, and right next to his big old pillow, that's where the pistol would go, with the butt toward him so he could reach and get it. He could shoot with his left hand just as well as his right hand. And the last thing to go off of his head was his felt hat, the very last thing, and it went up on top of the same bedstead. And then he'd go to sleep and he'd dream, and I'd hear him calling the hogs back in Lee County, "WHOOOEEE." It's something I remember pleasantly, like hearing the steam engine whistles blow early in the morning, to hear my granddad calling the hogs in his sleep. Then, when he got up in the morning, he'd get up on the side of the bed and before he put his house shoes on, he'd reach up and get that damn hat and put it on his head.

He was a tough old guy, too tough for his own time. When he was defeated, his type of sheriff was already going by the way of the old-time Rangers that finally faded out. He was a tough man, and he believed in an eye for an eye and a tooth for a tooth. Like Vail Ennis, don't take anybody to the hospital, take 'em all to the morgue.

Vail Ennis was a sheriff in Bee County, Beeville. He became a master shooter, that's how good he was. He was better than an expert. He just loved to shoot, and he'd do trick shooting. You could flip a quarter up and he'd pull his pistol out and shoot a hole in it. I found out how to do that from a friend one time. You wait till it comes to an apex, and for one second it's not going anywhere—it's not going up and it's not falling—that's when you shoot it. I got to where I could do that with a .22 pistol, usually with four-bit pieces. But Vail Ennis was that kind of a guy, and Vail Ennis could put up a sheet of copper and punch the outline of an Indian, shooting from the hip. He was a sniper in World War I, a very successful one. He believed in the gun, and that's the way he ran Bee County.

Back in the 30s, he got ahold of a civilian model Thompson submachine gun and had it mounted by a blacksmith on the hood of his car over the little emblem in front. The thing had the old Mafiosa Chicago drum, a round drum, and he had it raised up so that drum would clear the hood. He had a strong wire, stainless steel or something, that attached to the trigger and then came on back into the hood and into the car, and he had a ring and he could pull that ring and the damn thing would shoot. It wouldn't move, it was just like a fighter plane. He aimed it with the whole car. I guess if he hit a bump he was gonna shoot a duck, or something.

One time he caught my daddy coming back from San Antonio or somewhere, and insisted that he stop to see him. He wanted to show him something. So, he got him in this new souped-up Ford automobile where he had that machine gun mounted and they took off, going right down a country road driving like hell. He drove like he shot, just everywhere. Dad said that when they went over the railroad tracks they were airborne, and he said, "Good God a'mighty, Vail! You gonna kill us. I don't give a goddamn about this machine gun." But Vail said, "I got to show you this, Jim." He knew Daddy didn't carry a gun and didn't use a gun. And so he leveled off and they were heading toward a creek and he opened that mother up! *"BRRRRRRT, BRRRT, BRRRRRRRRT!"* Bursts and all that. He said, "See, when you get to chasing a goddamn bank robber, you can keep both hands on the wheel and keep this car going, and you can run up behind those mothers and blow 'em away!"

That was Vail Ennis. Years later, Vail was in the hospital dying of lung cancer. My dad was in the hospital at the same time for a cataract operation. He knew I had just run for sheriff here and been elected, but hadn't taken office yet. Vail's wife came around to my dad's room and told me he wanted to talk to me. I went around to his room. He couldn't talk, he had to force a whisper. He pulled me right down into his face, had me lean over, and said, "Jim, I'm gonna give you the best advice that you ever had in your whole life. I want you to remember it." His voice was raspy and everything else. It took him forever to say it. All this time he had a death grip on my hand.

He said, "Now, your dad won't agree with this at all, but I'm telling you, don't never get caught without your gun. When you go after a man, you get him and you kill him. Don't bring him back to the hospital. When you bring him in, bring him in dead. Take him to the morgue. Now, that's the best advice I can give you." I said, "Mr. Vail, coming from you, I appreciate it from the bottom of my heart. Thank you very very much,'' and I shook his hand. That's the last time I spoke to him. He was dead a few days later.

Looking at it now, I would think that because of the type of law officer my grandfather was, my dad decided that if it ever fell his lot to be an officer—I don't think he ever intended to be one—he was gonna do it differently. My dad's uncle on my grandmother's side, Pink Barnhill, was a Texas Ranger down here and a gun slinger when they used to run the Mexicans down and shoot 'em. It's sad but true, that's the history of the Texas Rangers, I think you know that. My dad was aware of all that, and was aware of all the gunfights that my grandfather and his deputies had been involved in. My dad was a very different kind of man. He had two things going, he was compassionate to a fault and he was humble to a fault. There ain't no way you'd be doing with him what you're doing with me. No way at all, no way at all.

My dad learned to type in school at an early age, so back in his early teens he was typing correspondence for my grandfather and typing confessions and things like that. Then, later on, when my granddad had to use a Model T, especially for out of town, he relied on Daddy to chauffeur for him. Until my dad had to go to World War I, except when he was working at the bank, when you'd see my granddad in his Model T, my dad was behind the wheel.

In 1916, when he was working at the Kleberg Bank, he was a special Texas Ranger, underage. Because of the bandits, all boys his age was sworn in as special Texas Rangers and issued pistols and 30-30s by the King Ranch, so if any problems arose where they needed a bunch of people, they could be called out. They all had Model Ts in those days, and some had horses, and if they needed a bunch of people somewhere, they'd put out the alarm. The alarm was a special whistle of the shop whistle down at the railroad yard. The way they did it meant "emergency," so people would meet someplace or something to find out what they needed. They might need to get on a railroad flat car and go down to a ranch that was being raided.

Dad's first job was bookkeeper for the Kleberg Bank, a private bank. It was 1909, I think, when he went into the bank after he finished his business college in Waco. He stayed there till he left for France with the Expeditionary Force in 1917. He saw 18 months of combat with the field artillery. They were back shooting the 75s, but were overrun two or three different times to where they were actually fighting in the foxholes.

Then he came back. He had made up his mind that bank officers died too slow, especially the president, so he didn't want to go back in the bank. He could see himself staying a bookkeeper or maybe a teller, and at the end of a million years probably become a cashier, something like that. He was asked to join the general office at the railroad, 'cause he had a business education, and so he went to work in the cost accounting department.

Then in 1922 my grandfather was defeated by Tom Moseley. Tom was a young man, and my grandfather was an old man by then. As my grandfather went out, the mayor and a bunch of people from the town came to my dad and said, "We're gonna change the city marshall's job to chief of police, and let him have a night man and a day man. Would you please take that job?" He did and he liked it. Until about 1928 he worked half-a-day on horseback and half-a-day on a motorcycle.

Part of his job as chief of police was to catch stray cattle and put 'em in what was called the Pond Pen. It was a jail for loose horses, donkeys, and milk cows. Even in those days it cost you a dollar to get your cow out of there. That was his job up to '37, when you could have no more cows or chickens in the city limits of Kingsville. And boy was I glad, I was milking two cows twice a day when they changed the city ordinance.

In 1926, my dad rode a horse that was named Chief—a big cutting horse—when he was chief of police. His own nickname among the Mexicans was "Jefe." What he'd do, half the day he'd ride his horse, 'cause stray cattle was part of the chief's job, you know, and the other half of the day he'd ride a Harley Davidson motorcycle. He had a hard time with it, so he had to keep the side car attached to the thing. It was funny, you'd see him get on his motorcycle and take his great big old Stetson off and put it up underneath the front, and come out with a little dinky policeman's hat. He looked so funny in it. I remember one time downtown, he'd taken his horse around to the pen on the Mexican side of town, the motorcycle was parked in front of the White Kitchen Cafe, and when he started to get on it he still had his spurs on, an' they got hung up in the chain! He was cussing and raising hell about that. But he was six-foot-three and a bean pole, and he looked so funny on a motorcycle. He continued to use a horse and a motorcycle until the Model As came out, then he got rid of both of 'em.

This yellow horse, Chief, that my dad rode all those years, did about five or six good tricks. The 101 Ranch bought that horse and he ended up in Hollywood with Hoot Gibson. Hoot was down here with Will Rogers, Tim McCoy, and Jack Hoxie, all cowboy movie stars. They were guests of Mr. Ceasar Kleberg, Bob's cousin, down at the Ranch. Coming into town with 'em, my dad was doing something on his horse, and some music was playing in the bandstand where we used to have Saturday afternoon band concerts. The band struck up, and the horse quit walking and started doing the cake walk. He'd been taught to dance, a little thing he did with his hips. And Hoot Gibson like to had a fit over that horse. Will Rogers thought it was funny, and they called Dad over there. He had him to kneel down while he stepped off, then told him, "Go lie down over there, Chief." And Chief went over and laid down and played dead. This guy that owned the 101 Ranch had an interest in Republic Films, and he bought this horse for Hoot. I used to go to the movies with all my friends to watch Chief and Hoot Gibson. All the little neighborhood kids knew Chief, and we'd all go to the picture show just to see Chief. We didn't give a damn about Hoot Gibson.

Mr. Tom Moseley resigned and went back with the Cattlemen's Association as a special ranger, the job that he held prior to his becoming sheriff. Later on, he got murdered. But he resigned, and the people that had the say-so down here then, practically the same ones with say-so now, the King Ranch and all that bunch, the city fathers and the county fathers, just told Dad that they wanted him as sheriff. So, they appointed him in July of 1935 and he remained sheriff for 38 years.

My dad was just the opposite of my granddad as sheriff, just the other way. He never owned a badge in his life, and he never carried a gun except in France in World War I. He said that he made a little pledge to himself that if he ever got out of there alive, he'd never raise a gun against a man as long as he lived. He never did. He took guns away from people while they were shooting at him, and he wouldn't have a gun on. There was an incident out on a farm, a murderer had come to visit his parents. People like that always go home, you know, sooner or later. If you want a crook, you just go to his home and wait and be patient. This man was wanted for murder and he came home to see his mom and dad. Dad and his chief deputy, Bob Stevenson, drove out and started to go in the gate to walk up to the house. Course, he knew who they were, and he started shooting at 'em with a 30-30. Bob Stevenson had a gun, and they ran back to the car and got behind it to where he could get ahold of his 30-30. He asked Dad, "What do you want me to do?" Dad said, "Just stay right here and put your gun down." Then he just walked up to the front door of that house with that guy shooting at him. He took the 30-30 away from him, and got him by the hand and led him out and put him in his car and drove to town.

That happened around 1941 or '42. Not long before I retired and came home, there was a black man over here in the black neighborhood that was pinning down a bunch of people. The city police had him surrounded and were trying to get him, but every time somebody would act like they were gonna come get him, he'd shoot at 'em. Somebody told the chief of police, said, "Look, why don't you go get Sheriff Scarborough. He can get him out of there and there won't be anybody get hurt." So they did. He walked up wearing his standard uniform of khaki pants, khaki shirt, bow tie, and a vest—a khaki vest that was made for him out at the King Ranch—no badge and no gun. Everybody knew him in that. He got there and just asked everybody to put their guns down and get back away from the fence. Then he walked in and got the guy and brought him out, brought him out with the man's pistol in one hand and his arm around him. He got his only badge when he retired. They put it in a shadow box and gave it to him with his name engraved on it. But they knew him, I don't care if he was in Houston or where he was, everybody knew him.

A newspaper article quoted him as saying, "If I had a gun, I probably would have killed somebody. A six-shooter never solved a problem." He was sued once in federal court for pistol-whipping a man. One of our former governors was the federal judge then, Jimmy Allred. Dad went over there, went to the courtroom, and they had just got started—I don't think they had even picked a jury or anything—when Jimmy Allred said, "I have known Sheriff Scarborough for many years, when I was governor of the state and before, and I have never seen him with a gun in my life. Case dismissed."

It wasn't that my dad couldn't shoot. Even as a retired man, when he'd go to Lee County, he'd get a .22 and go squirrel hunting. That's what he did as a kid and that made him a good shot. One year when he was chief of police, back in the '20s or early '30s, he won a matched pistol set-up for (being) the top shooter of the chiefs of police in the state of Texas at their convention. It was a mahogany box with felt lining and two .38s, one with a four-inch barrel and one with a long, long barrel; they were target pistols. I remember that so well, and I was impressed with it, 'cause my dad never wore a gun but yet he was a good shot.

The only weapon he carried, in the back pocket of his pants, inside of his handkerchief, was a pair of knucks. That was in case he got ahold of some big guy he couldn't handle. I remember one time we were having a high school dance in what was called the Mopac Booster Auditorium. It was a recreational dance hall built by the railroad for everybody to use. We had high school proms there and we were having this dance my junior or senior year, and we had a live band playing and all that, and we were all having a good time when these college football boys crashed our dance. They were tapping us on the shoulder and taking our dates away from us, walking out the front door with 'em and stuff like that. The chaperones finally realized what the problem was and called Dad. He went through the hall and tapped 'em on the shoulder and said, "Y'all meet me outside." There were two of 'em that I guess had had something to drink. These were big boys, too. He told 'em, "I want you to get out of here. This is a little high school dance. You boys are not gonna mess here, you're gonna have to go back out to the school or go somewhere else." Then, two of 'em said something to him that made him mad, and he just reached up and grabbed 'em by the back of the neck and banged their heads together, and they both fell to the floor. Then he had some kids help drag 'em out the door. I saw the dragging out the door, I didn't get to see the bumping of the heads. But they told me, "Man, he just grabbed 'em and swooshed those heads together!" He just did what he had to do, he wasn't a violent man.

My dad was considered a personal sheriff. Everybody in this county felt like he was their sheriff. He earned that. He'd throw great barbecues, Thanksgiving dinners. We still do that; just last year they served three-thousand Thanksgiving dinners with a dance following it. He'd dance with the little three-year-old girls, then he'd dance with the 80-year-old grandmas, and all the women in between—things like that. He knew every child and grandchild in sight by name. He knew everybody in this county; and he made it his business, if a new person came to town, to know about him. Even after we got as big as we are now, he'd make it his business to find out who new people were. Especially out in the country, he'd personally drive out and tell 'em who he was, give 'em his phone number, tell 'em, "If you ever need anything done for you, if you're in trouble, if you leave on vacation and want us to watch your house, you let us know." He introduced himself and then he remembered 'em. Of course, he'd go to these annual dances, he'd go to family reunions. He was invited to every reunion that ever took place within three counties of here, and that's where he refreshed himself with the new kids coming up. Even before he died, when I'd been sheriff awhile, he could recognize kids walking the streets, teenagers, that I didn't know, 'cause I'd been gone so long, you see, before I came back. He could just tell who the child was and it was amazing.

He knew everybody's secrets, too. He used to chuckle and tell me a story. Every time he'd see this lady, she was very prominent and her husband was very prominent, probably a college professor at A & I, he'd always tip his hat and smile. And she'd always smile back, and when they were alone she'd wink at him. This lady, way back before, back in the teens, used to work at the Chicken Ranch in La Grange. Then she'd retired to be a respectable upper-class leading citizen of Kingsville, and it was their little secret. Dad never, ever, divulged who that lady was. He carried a lot of secrets like that, family secrets, to his grave.

They used to run two years at a time. He had as high as five run against him one time when he hadn't been sheriff too long. It was his second or third term, before World War II, and he didn't even get in a runoff. Can you imagine that? If there're three of 'em with me, I end up in a runoff. In those campaigns there would be some mudslinging going on, but after it was all over with, everybody just shook hands and forgot it.

After a while, though, George Parr tried to take over Kleberg County like he was trying to take over Nueces County, to go with Jim Wells and Duval, and that was a little different. They called themselves the Good Government League, and a lot of people didn't know that George Parr's money was behind all those candidates; they just didn't know it. He'd run candidates for office in those counties and give 'em all the money they needed. They tried to get my dad after the war, and (they) wiped out everybody in the courthouse except one justice of the peace and the sheriff. And in the city, they wiped out the entire city, George Parr's people did. There was some pretty hot politics going on. Course, the King Ranch was fighting George Parr, but Parr's people would pay 'em five dollars a vote, and those Mexicans would drink the free beer, take the five dollars, and walk in and still vote for my dad! They just couldn't vote against him, they just couldn't do it. They'd take the beer and food and money, and vote for my dad. Parr got what he paid for with the other candidates, but because he didn't get the JP and my dad, he immediately turned around and lost Kleberg County. It's strange how politics works down here.

It was bad, sometimes, being the son of the sheriff. When the guys was going out watermelon stealing, they wouldn't let me go—you know, things like that. It was kind of like being a preacher's son, a bad spot to be in in a lot of ways. But I'll tell you the good part, when a carnival came to town I always got free tickets, and I never paid to go into a picture show in my life till I grew up and found out that the automatic pass didn't go with me. That stayed here in Kingsville.

The sheriff's family was anything but rich. He was paid by a fee system. Dad had to keep 13 or 14 docket books. I remember one year I went to Austin with Mother and Dad with the back end of that damn Model A just stacked up with these giant heavy docket books. Can you imagine that, now? Every sheriff in the state of Texas had to take his docket books, all his financial records, to Austin where the comptroller audited 'em while he stayed for two or three days. They'd audit those books, then they'd cut a check for Kleberg County, and Dad would bring it back. The county, then, would deposit (it), and they'd cut him a 3,500-dollar check, which was his salary. Everything over that (that) they had collected in fees went into the county general fund. I've got a brand book in my office. Every bovine that was slaughtered in Kleberg County had to be inspected by the sheriff or by his deputy, and the fee was 10 cents a head. Those were the kind of things he had to do to make a living. Until 1955, all the sheriffs lived on fees and borrowed money. They could go to their local bank and borrow enough money to live, to pay the grocery man and all that, then they got their money once a year.

By 1939 I didn't know what I wanted to do. I had flunked out of Texas A & I with five Fs, and two friends of mine did the same. We were at T-Jacks, which was a place where we had coffee and ice cream and stuff across from the campus. Davy Jones, Jimmy Nicholson, and myself all compared our report cards, and we all three had worked real hard and got five Fs. You don't have the slightest idea how hard I worked to get those five Fs! David had a car, and I said, "Let's go join the cavalry." They said, "Fine, Hitler's gonna start a war, you know he's gonna start a war and we're gonna be in it, so let's just go on." I said, "I know if I go home there is gonna be a war." So, we took off right from there, and three days later the old colonel at Fort Sam Houston said, "Boys, there's not gonna be a horse cavalry, anymore." I said, "Well, what in the world are they gonna do?" He said, "They're gonna drive tanks, jeeps and trucks, and weapons carriers." He was telling us all these things, and it sounded like we were talking about the space shuttle. I said, "Well, we're country boys from south Texas, we grew up on horses. We don't know what to do." He said, "You've got your high school diplomas, you can go in the Army Air Corps." I called Dad on the phone three days later and I said, "Dad, would you call Mr. Jones and Mr. Nicholson and tell 'em that David and Jimmy are with me and we're all in the Army Air Corps." His comment was, "Thank God!" He was greatly relieved.

I ended up a provost marshal. I was only selected because I was my father's son. S. J. Malakus picked me out. His job between World War I and World War II was to be the military liaison officer in the police station and the sheriff's department of San Antonio, Texas. S. J. Malakus was a Greek, and everybody was "Doc" to him, even the commanding general was "OK, Doc." That was his way of talking. He was a splendid man and a dear friend of my dad's. Anyway, S. J. Malakus was talking to Dad one day, and Dad said, "By the way, Jim's up there at Brooks Field. He joined the service. He and two other boys figured the war was gonna come up."

That was in 1940, and I already had gotten two stripes. Malakus called me one day and said, "I'm gonna transfer you downtown." I went to work with him down there, and six months later they formed the Eighth Service Command Composite Military Police Detail from all the bases close around there. We were one-hundred MPs, and we lived in an old hotel at 510 South Main and worked in town. So, I started law enforcement in 1940 walking a beat in San Antonio. By 1943 I was a warrant officer and a provost marshal at Brooks Field, Texas, they said the youngest provost marshal in the service, 23 years old.

I was downtown in San Antonio 24 hours a day, and I really grew up in a hurry. The Eighth Service Composite Military Police Detachment was made up of a hundred selectees from all the units in the area—Army Air Corps, Field Artillery, Kelly Field, Normal Field, Stinson Field, Brooks Field, Randolph Field, Fort Sam Houston, and Camp Bullis. Master sergeant Malakus selected each of the hundred, including his first sergeant, and then we set up downtown at 510 South Main. We were a proud outfit. Course, we were "chicken shit MPs" to the troops, you could never shake that. We had an investigative team, we solved burglaries, lots of things like that. It wasn't all just walking the beat downtown. We'd get word through the mail about an AWOL coming from somewhere whose hometown was San Antonio. For a while I was on the desertion detail, and then they'd rotate me around. What we did was stake out a place and watch it. We didn't wear civilian clothes, we couldn't do that. We'd watch his parents or his wife until finally we'd catch this poor son-of-a-bitch. He'd go home. Guys that were wanted for robbery, burglary, anything, AWOL on top of it, they always go home. That's something we know about our criminals here; sooner or later they're going home and we catch them.

But we walked a beat a lot, and certain areas were really rough. My partner was six-feet-three, and I weighed 140 pounds and had a 28-inch waist. I could run and was agile, but that was all. Well, Tiny Atkinson was my hand-picked partner, and when we got (assigned to) Rattlesnake Hill above the main gate out of Sam Houston on payday weekend, we'd just go to the order room and tell the first sergeant or the clerk to put us on sick call, because we got the Hill tonight. There wasn't any way you could work a tour on Rattlesnake Hill outside of the gates of Fort Sam Houston without getting hurt. You would have to get stitches or you would have to get something, 'cause we just got into it with those Ninth Infantry guys. The Second Division was still there, and in '41 the 81st Airborne came in temporarily before they went on to Europe. And you know, it was just like the Nazis fighting the Second Division! We really had a mess. Goddamn, we almost had to have six cops, MPs, for every block. It was a mess. The Second Division, the Ninth Infantry, and the 38th Field Artillery, that was their home, Fort Sam belonged to them. So, when the 81st came in there, my God, it was just like sending the Nazis in. They fought at every opportunity, stole from each other, did everything.

Those 81st Airborne guys just didn't give a damn. One time, Tiny and I were at the first bar outside the gate at Fort Sam and there was a little melee going on in there, but no real hard fighting yet. Tiny and I walked in and Tiny said, "I think you guys from the 81st ought to go on down, there's hardly anyone in the bar on down, and leave these Second Division guys alone." They all wore their patches. Second Division was the American Indian, you know, with the feathers. You could spot them, they had to be in uniform. Anyway, we suggested they leave. Well, one little old kid, he could have been five-feet-four—he'd have been a jockey in civilian life, but he was a paratrooper—he didn't want to leave. By God, he was gonna stay there and all by himself whip the whole Second Division if they could get in the bar. We finally got him by the arm and kind of forced the little bastard out on the sidewalk trying to reason with him. Old Tiny was doing that and I was standing back, kind of backing him up. Our staff car was right out in front of that bar. We usually walked, but we used the car to bring prisoners in or take hurt people to the infirmary. So, this little shitass got out there and started to arguing with Tiny, and Tiny says, "I'll tell you what, I'll fix you up. I'll stuff you in that car. We'll take you out there to your barracks and we'll turn you over to the CQ, and your payday holiday is all over. Do you understand that?" I remember so clearly, he said, "Yes, I understand that." Then he leaped about three-and-a-half feet up on the fender, that made him eyeball with Tiny—I guess Tiny was 220 pounds. And that little devil went back to the hood and cold-cocked Tiny and knocked him out, knocked him back against the building and he slid down knocked out. Then he jumped down and faced me like this, "Do you want some?" I said, "I don't think so." He said, "Can I go back in there?" I said, "Go on and get your ass killed, I don't give a goddamn." Then I had to slap old Tiny awake and take him down there, and they put smelling salts under his nose and found out his jaw was OK. But that little shit weighed 120 pounds and knocked out a 220-pound MP. That told me something about paratroopers, I'll tell you right away!

Later on, after Pearl Harbor, there was a curfew. All military people had to leave town after a certain time. There were a hundred of us and we'd run 'em off, the busses would come from all those posts, camps, and stations, from everywhere, and we'd see to it that they all got out of town. Some would hide out in the hotel, but they were off the street. And if we caught a guy down in "Whoretown," on Matamoras Street, in that area, or if we caught him up on East Commerce, which was the other prostitution area, he had to take a pro. Those women got health certificates every week and all that, so it was a controlled environment. All the fences, all the crooks, all the whores, and everything, were in these certain areas. We knew it and had our pro kits down there at stations. A green light indicated them. When you were walking down the street and saw a green light, that's where you went in to take your carbolic acid pro that damn near killed you. If we caught a guy down there trying to come out, he'd say, "Oh, all I did was go down there and drink a beer," well, he had to go in and take a pro. That was our orders, you know.

We worked hand and glove with the civilian cops. Weekends, we used to ride with 'em, and I ended up finally working for Bexar County Sheriff's Department because I was a sheriff's son. I worked with a little deputy sheriff called Billy Cristolph, and Billy Cristolph believed everybody he talked to had to get hit in the head with the barrel of his pistol first. It didn't matter whether it was a military, civilian, or what, and I didn't like working with Billy, because he was hitting military. I'd say, "You can't do that, that guy is gonna go over and give his life for you." "Jim," he said, "I just like to get their attention. I don't want anybody to give me any bullshit." He always did it. First thing he said to anybody was, "Come here, boy! Come here, boy! Come here, boy! Who do you think you are?" See, Billy was little, and that pistol made him nine-feet tall. Then he'd pull that guy out and say, "Now, you listen to me," or he'd say, "I want you to get out of here and don't come back." And then, "Who the hell you think your talking to," and *"BAM!"*—he'd knock him across the top of the head. Then he'd say, "Now you know who you're talking to, get your ass out of here." I didn't like working with Billy.

I spent 32 years in the Air Force, and I had a rule that anytime a pilot was willing to take a plane up, I was willing to go with him. I probably came close to being killed a number of times, but my closest call in law enforcement came while I was a MP in San Antonio. There was a Negro nightclub that was out of town run by a guy named Leroy. The black cavalry troopers would come about once a month from the fort at Brackettville. This was horseback cavalry, they hadn't converted to tanks, then. They would come into town, and course there was segregation in those days and they'd have to go down on East Commerce to the "Froggy Bottom" nightclub, or out to this Leroy's big nightclub, a bunch of 'em.

One night we were closing it because curfew time had rolled around. By then I was a buck sergeant, the major was with me, and I had a corporal along who is now a Baptist minister. We had about a six-man detail, and what we had to do, usually either me or the major would walk up, get the mike, stop the band, and say, "This is it. You gotta drink up, eat up, whatever you're doing. We'll give you 15 minutes to clear the club. You gotta get off the street and out of the public." Course, we'd always get a rash of crap, 'cause the club was way out alone and it wouldn't have hurt if it ran all night, 24 hours a day, but we had our duty to do.

So, this night we were clearing the place out, and there was this drunk buck sergeant that just looked like a giant, and he had a .45 automatic and he pulled it and shoved it and stuck it in my gut, just like that. I was the one who told him . . . I says, "You get your boys and tell 'em to get in that damn bus." They had a big old bus they'd come in. I said, "This is all over with. Y'all go get you a hotel room, whatever you gonna do. Everything is closed, you can't be in public." And he was just drunk enough that from somewhere he just reached in and pulled out this automatic and stuck it in my gut and says, "I ain't going nowhere. My boys is not going nowhere. We came to town, we hadn't been to town in a month, we came to town to have us a good time, and we gonna have it. And if you don't like it, we just gonna blow you away, baby."

The major just nudged me with his elbow, like to tell me, "Say when." Well, I ain't gonna say "when" with a loaded .45 stuck in my nose! I think that's what made this corporal become a Baptist minister. I don't know what came over me, but I looked up at this old boy and I said, "Sergeant, are you ashamed of that uniform that you're wearing?" Somehow or other that rattled him a little bit. He said, "What do you mean?" I said, "Are you ashamed of being an American cavalryman and being sergeant?" He was a buck sergeant then, but of course he'd been in all during the Depression, he wasn't a kid. He said, "Of course I'm not, I'm proud to be an American, I'm proud to be a sergeant." And I said, "Well, save those bullets for the enemy." Then he gave me a real funny look—like, "What am I doing here?"—and he let the hammer down and gave me the gun.

The black cavalrymen came to town only once a month, and when they did, they really let their hair down. One time Tiny and I went in the Froggy Bottom, a nightclub in a basement on East Commerce Street, down close to downtown. It was a black nightclub and had a little combo that wouldn't quit. I loved jazz music and still do, and I loved working at East Commerce 'cause it was good music all the time. What we'd do, we'd walk through all these places just to see that the military were all OK, that nobody was gonna roll 'em, and so on. We were looking out for them as well as running 'em out of town on curfew.

This one night we went down there and the military and the civilians were all dancing in a circle, and after the music quit, you know, while they set up another three or four tunes, they'd be three or four minutes before they'd start again. Usually they'd go back to their tables and get after their beer, and they wouldn't stand around the floor, but these people wouldn't budge. We stayed just off the bottom of the stairs where we could see out over their heads and everything. Tiny says, "Well, everything looks peaceful here. Man, they're crowded tonight, aren't they?" And they were, there wasn't room for anybody. We started to go and Tiny said, "Just a minute, let's stay here just a minute longer." So we sat through that next set, and when the band stopped long enough to set up another three or four tunes they all stayed right there, just all bunched up on the dance floor. Tiny said, "Something's up. Let's go, let's walk through there." We walked through there, and there was a civilian laying there dead with a butcher knife stuck out of his back. There'd been a murder in that nightclub, and they were all dancing to cover up, hoping the guy could get him and drag him somewhere. But there was only one way in, and there wasn't any stairs going up. They were trying to figure out how they were going to get that body out. We contained the thing, wouldn't let anybody leave until the civilian cops, the city police department, got there.

My date of rank when I made E-8 was November, 1942, and I made warrant officer in '43. I had damn near one of the oldest dates of rank as master sergeant in the Air Force. Whenever I went to a new base I was the senior non-com, so I was automatically the president of the NCO Club Council, all that junk. That was the job of the senior non-com, he was chairman of this, the chairman of that; it went with the date of rank. I never had a boss, hardly. From the time I was first sergeant, even before I was a warrant officer, I ran things for the officer who was supposed to be my boss, and saw to it that he never got in trouble. Because of that, every time I walked up to the bulletin board I had a promotion. And I was one of the regular guys. I shot dice and played poker with 'em, and all that kind of stuff, but I just took care of my men first and my bosses next. I made that really my career. And I tried to use what influence I had to do things that made where I was a better place. I was the instigator of consolidating guardhouses in the '50s, things like that. I really enjoyed it. I had a beautiful career in the service.

In my travels in the Air Force I worked in 16 foreign countries, and I found officers to be identical. They don't take care of their damn cars or equipment, and they're the sorriest report writers in the world. I don't care if they're French gendarmes, or the Gestapo, or English bobbies, or who they are, the son-of-a-bitches cannot write a report, and they will not take care of their equipment. That's universal. They're none of 'em paid enough, and payday, worldwide, is when they successfully make a case. They get the same euphoria that we do.

They all operate different, of course. Gendarmes can grab you out of your car and beat the shit out of you on the streets of Paris, and you don't have a thing to say about it. The French people think that if they turn their lights on they're wasting electricity. Even the physicists think that, it's a national disease. So they'll be running along in their cars long after it's dark and they won't turn their lights on, 'cause they don't want to waste electricity. Can you believe that? I used to drive into Paris, and you just had to have guts to do it, that's all. You'd get in these big circles, and it was just who gets there first has got it, and if I can squeeze in ahead of you and cause you to have a wreck, that's too bad, baby, I'm gone!

In Germany, if you're convicted of DWI one time, for the rest of your life on this world you don't get a driver's license. How about that? There's no speed limit over there, so you don't get stopped for speeding, you get caught DWI because you're running people off the road. And the Turks, they got strange laws there. Long as you're honking your horn you can kill your mother-in-law with your car, and you're clean. All the GIs are told, "The minute you leave the base, you keep one hand on your goddamn horn. And then if a guy on a donkey is there or some woman throws her baby under your car . . . ." Standard pay for a child in Turkey in the '60s was six-hundred dollars. In Viet Nam, it was eight-hundred dollars. We had to be careful. There were no sidewalks in those villages in Viet Nam, and we'd be going through with convoys bringing stuff back to the base from the port. The doors would open up right on the little roads, and they're tight little roads, and you'd come through there at 25 miles an hour and they'd throw a kid at you. And if you hit the kid, there'd be all this crying and screaming, but eight-hundred dollars would solve it all.

When I'd leave a headquarters, I'd make personnel send me back somewhere where I'd end up being the top cop on the base. I'd not only have security under me, but law enforcement, too, with all those problems. Elmendorf Air Force Base had 29,000 people living on it. That was as big a city as I've got right here, and I was the provost sergeant of the base. My boss, the lieutenant colonel, didn't get involved in anything except golf and fishing, I did the damn work. The junior officers we had couldn't hardly find the back door, so us old non-coms, we were it. I had an eight-hundred man outfit up there at Elmendorf in the '50s. We had Strategic Air Command tenant on our base with B-47s, and we had to provide a hell of a lot of security for them. I had the Air Defense Command fighters, too. Then I had a law enforcement problem, too, requiring a town patrol of 38 people. It was just Air Force in the town patrol, but I had Army, Navy, and Air Force, and there wasn't any law enforcement in Anchorage, Alaska. There was a few deputy marshals up there that we worked closely with and some FBI people, but Anchorage had about a 12-man police department that didn't give a good goddamn about military people. They had their own problems. So, we actually ended up helping to enforce civilian law up there, was what it amounted to. We just forgot about *posse comitatus* and all worked together.

In the military, from the mid '50s on, my nickname was "Uncle Jim." I was a fixer in the Minuteman business, a trouble-shooter. I didn't go out with the IG teams except on rare occasions and run the check list, but when they got into problems that had to be solved, they always asked for me. The wing commander at Malmstrom Air Force Base, Great Falls, Montana, would call and say, "I want Uncle Jim down here, I've got something that's got to be solved." And I'd get on a commercial airplane and fly up there, maybe be there two days, three days, sometimes a week. We had ADT alarms, naturally. These Minuteman missiles, nuclear weapons, are out by themselves. The whole state of Montana is covered with Minuteman missiles. That's a nuclear weapon, ready to go. You strike a match or push a button, and it's gone. We had over a thousand of 'em. At one time we had four-thousand kids on TDY, that's temporary duty away from your base, from all over the United States in SAC (Strategic Air Command) up there guarding those damn missiles in Montana, North Dakota, and all.

Minuteman was a different game. Your command module, where the operational crew was, was 125-feet underground, floating on hydraulics, 60 or 70 miles from their furtherist missile. They were in all kind of patterns, and it was interesting. Boy, I stayed over six years in the Minuteman program without even realizing it. At that time I was based at 15th Air Force Headquarters, but I was gone all the time. I kept clothes with friends at all these different bases. The 15th Air Force was the major command of SAC, we had all the ballistic missiles in the world. That's the way General LeMay wanted it.

The security equipment finally got to where it worked. We had beams that if you broke 'em would set an alarm off. If you touched a door or a light, ADT would set an alarm off. And we had ground movement detectors, that's what the Border Patrol uses now to catch wetbacks. If you walked up within 30 yards of that it would pick you up and set off the alarm. Then we had underground movement detectors on the outside of the silos so that you couldn't tunnel in to a Minuteman missile from a half-a-mile away and blow it up. We even had those underground sensors, and we had to pay the ranchers to keep their Whiteface and Angus cattle away, because 15 or 20 Angus cows would come within three-hundred yards and set off the damn underground alarm. We could almost bet our life that Russia wasn't digging a hole down there, but we didn't know it. It was really interesting. I wouldn't trade that part of my service career for anything.

That was my life. I was in the Air Force for 32 years, three months, and five days. But I would come back to Kleberg County and visit when I had vacations. And when I changed bases, as a rule, as time permitted, we'd always swing down and visit two or three days, a week at the most.

After I retired from the Air Force I started buying up quarter horses, and my wife and I were gonna raise quarter horses and that was all. We were just coming back here to be with Mother and Dad. I had spent a generation away from home except for short visits. We were a close family, and we'd call and write and visit when we could. I kept seeing Dad slip a little bit, and he wanted to retire long, long before I came on the scene. But the King Ranch wouldn't let him do it, and they wouldn't let anybody run against him. From 1922 to 1973 Dad's whole life was being a peace officer here in Kingsville. The last 28 years as sheriff he didn't even have an opponent. There's a bunch of 'em thought about running, but they never did.

I hadn't even thought about being sheriff, not in 40 years. I've got a picture of me at 10 years old in chaps, vest, cowboy shirt, cowboy hat, and the old .41 Bisley that shot my grandfather's moustache off in a holster, with me standing posing for the camera drawing my gun. But that was just little boy stuff, you know. I knew better than to want to be anything like this. It's like being a schoolteacher, you work your butt off and don't get any money for it.

Dad talked me into it. He said, talking about Bob Kleberg, president of the Ranch, "Bob doesn't want me to retire, but he'll consider it if you'll take my place." I got to thinking about it and talked to Kathy. She said, "I don't know, at least make him happy by telling him, 'yes.' " It was really to make my dad satisfied. I hadn't been returned home but for a couple of months when I thought, "Well, if I'm gonna do that, I need to get a degree in criminal justice." So, I went to Sam Houston State University, which was the best in the state of Texas in law enforcement, and studied under Doctor Killinger.

While I was at Sam Houston, Dad came to see me and said, "Bob wants a brochure or resume, or something, on everything you done since you left town to join the service." I said, "My God, you're talking about 1939." He said, "That's right." I'm not really a humble pie sort of guy, my dad was, bless his heart, but I couldn't see sitting down and bragging on myself in a damn resume for all those years to a man that gave me my first horse when I was a boy.

I sent my resume to Dad. I said, "You look that over and see if that's what Mr. Bob wants. I can't bring myself to sit down and talk about a bunch of junk. This is all I did, shows all my responsibilities, my rank, the whole damn nine yards, and exactly what I was doing." It was pretty complete. Well, Mr. Bob thought it was the greatest thing he ever saw in his life. Dad said that he read it four times before he ever put it down, then he passed it out to friends in Kentucky who wouldn't even know me from Adam. He said, "Read that and tell me what you think about that son-of-a-bitch. What do you think, you think that guy will make a good sheriff?"

And then I had to go see Bob. Bob Kleberg called my dad up and said, "Jim, can you bring Little Jim on out here to meet me at 6:30 in my living room, and I can spend about 30 or 40 minutes with y'all." So, I went out there, and he poured me a shot of whiskey over the rocks, Running W Whiskey made for him at 35 dollars a fifth. It was just like drinking sweet milk. He visited for a while and said, "I enjoyed that brochure very much, Jim. I liked that. It was detailed and went right on back. You almost took it to where I gave you your first horse." I said, "Pretty damn close, Mr. Bob." He said, "Well, son, I don't have any objection to you being sheriff here in Kleberg County. If your dad is dead set on retiring, then I'm for you taking office. I don't want any of these other SBs (sic) I been hearing about to get in here."

Then he turned to Dad, who was the same age as he was, only a month apart. They had helled around the King Ranch together as teenagers. He said, "But boy," and those were his very words, "boy, I don't see what the hell you want to retire for." Here's my dad on a walking cane, lost a lot of weight, he's stooped and can't see, he can't hear! It was all right for me to take his place, but by God, he didn't understand why it had to be so soon. So I didn't come in here and say I'm gonna run for sheriff. I knew better than that.

I went back to Sam Houston and was in my last class in November of 1971. I was on the dean's list, taking 22 hours a semester and just having a ball, you know, going to school, when my dad called and told me that I had to physically live in Kleberg County six months prior to filing for sheriff. He said, "You been gone for a while, you best quit what you're doing and come back down here." I said, "Dad, I'm in my last semester for my degree." He said, "Son, it's been so long since anybody's run, and a lot of people don't know you because you been away all that time. You better come home right now." That was November and I would have graduated in December, but I quit and come down here, the hardest thing I ever did in my life.

It turned out there were five guys in the race, and I had my work cut out for me. I grew up watching Kleberg County politics, all that malarky, but I had no idea what it meant to get out and actually do it. My mother, bless her heart, who was the fire behind my dad, she said, "Wherever three people gather, you got to be there, just like Jesus and his disciples.'' And Lord, I met myself coming and going! It was something else. I had been a politician in the service, all right, but not like this. That was an individual type thing. What I was going through now was like a medicine show. I had to out-lie my opponents, or out-promise 'em, or something. I'd go everywhere and I had a field day. Debating was just something that came natural to me.

Mr. Bob had already felt around among the leadership here in the county, and the businessmen and the doctors. But I didn't get a landslide, I got in a runoff. They were all younger than me by a whole lot. They had televised campaign ads that said, ''We like Jim Scarborough. We know he's well qualified and all that, but don't you think it's time that we had a Jones or a Smith or a Kelly for sheriff?'' Then they were saying on the street corners, ''Well, he's spent his life in the military, he's gonna be knocking heads around here. It's gonna be an army platoon, not a sheriff's department.'' They were all second-guessing. I won easily in the runoff.

I told you, my dad was a personal sheriff, and he (still) was right up through the end of 1972. The commissioners court were reluctant to swear in a new sheriff, to tell you the truth. I was looking forward to working New Years Eve, but I didn't get that opportunity.

My dad didn't have an awful lot of advice to give me about being sheriff of Kleberg County, but he did suggest that I visit some neighboring sheriffs that were friends of his. Bob Gladney was one, from Brazoria County. Then there was Gus Kruse in Brownsville and Porfirio Flores in Laredo. He just said, ''You ought to go spend a day with 'em and visit, and see how they run their outfits, and talk to 'em. They're all more modern sheriffs than I am.'' Then he smiled and said, ''I made time sort of stand still with me in Kleberg County.'' So I did, and I got some good ideas from them and I enjoyed the visits.

Another thing Dad told me was, ''Take care of the courts. Whatever the judges want, the district judge down to the JP, be sure you serve the courts in any way they want you.'' He said, ''Don't send a deputy out with a warrant or civil citation to go knock on somebody's door with a gun and a badge and a marked car. You call 'em on the phone and tell 'em you got it, so they can come in.'' I do that. People I don't know, I write 'em letters and give 'em seven days to come in, and it works, too. I serve a good 85 percent of my warrants and civil citations just that way. We serve over four-thousand papers a year here in Kleberg County.

When I took office, my dad said I had to take care of old man Walker, a black man, with 30 or 40 dollars a month. Maria Rendon, a Mexican lady, had to have 25 or 30, or her water bill paid or something, every month. Then there was Jim Barnes, a shine man. Tuesdays and

Saturdays he shines shoes. He's been shining my boots since I was six years old. He shined my grandfather's boots and my dad's boots. He's in his eighties and we all pay him five dollars a shine now, though it used to be a dime. But I inherited him and about four or five old folks in the county, some way out down there.

Dad just said, "You gonna have to take care of Jim Barnes and Laura, that's his wife." He said, "They're in their seventies right now. They can't crawl up on the bus. They don't have enough money to go to Edna to the reunion every year, so you gotta have a deputy or you drive 'em up there and bring 'em back." I've done it. This is my fourteenth year and I'll be taking 'em for the fourteenth time on the Fourth of July. Old Jim is just as black as the ace of spades and has been a shoe-shine man here shining my boots since I was a little boy in 1926. Years ago, for a dollar you could get a shine and a quart of tequila. He was a bootlegger at the barbershop down there. Now then, he's a deacon of the church and doesn't drink, and everybody loves Jim. My dad started something, that's giving him five dollars a shine. They're always teasing me about that, "You're the SOB that spoiled Jim Barnes." I say, "Naw, I didn't, my dad spoiled him." Jim was teasing me about a year ago, said, "You know, I made my living and raised my family right here in Kingsville all these years just for 10 cents a shine." I didn't say a word, and when I got down from his chair I said, "Jim, here's your dime. You done so damn well with a dime, here you are." And you could hear him squalling for a half block! Course, then I gave him a five dollar bill. He just shined my boots this morning.

There were some other things I inherited. I'll tell you something about my little department here. I'm into my fourteenth year as sheriff and I have never had to file a case against anyone for assault against a police officer. That's a felony charge, as you know. Unfortunately, another agency here in town files 'em every week. It's all in how you approach the problem, whether you make it worse or whether you make it better. We've got one guy, Jesse "Man Mountain" Dean, that when a city policeman or a DPS trooper tries to take him, they have just bought the farm. He's a great beer drinker and he likes to tear things up, and if he gets in an argument with you he'll whip you and your four buddies. That's no joke. But he has never laid a finger against a deputy sheriff, just because he has respect for the sheriff's department. I inherited him from my dad. He knows we're not gonna handcuff him and then beat him with a billy club or something to try to get even. They used to be having him upstairs trying to book him for DWI and he'd be tearing my jail up. I'd get a phone call and it would be (about) Jesse, and they'd say, "He told us to call you, Sheriff." I'd say, "Put him on." I'd say, "Jesse, now you stop that. You're up there in my jail and you don't want to hurt any of those kids. You just behave and sleep it off, and I'll have one of my deputies take you home as soon as you're sober, in four hours." And he'd say, "Yessir," and for no damn reason whatsoever. I never ever had a confrontation with Jesse, I just inherited from my dad the ability to make him calm down. It's still that way to this day.

Then I had three brothers, the Dowlearns, that were all roughnecks. They were big bruisers who lived out near Layola Beach, and if they couldn't find someone else to fight—like sailors, they love to jump sailors—they'd fight among themselves. They'd break chairs, break tables, break windows, just literally tear things up. If they'd get a call from down at the Green Frog or De La Rosa's Barn, which is a dance hall, wherever, that "the Dowlearn boys are at it," the next phone call was to me. I'd jump up and get my clothes on and go down there, and I could just walk in the door, and if they were still fighting, they'd stop. Their wives would be there egging 'em on. But they'd stop and apologize to everybody and find out what it cost to patch 'em up at the hospital. Then they'd reach in their pockets, and they were tool pushers and things like that, they made good money, they'd just ask the bartender, "Well, how much damage did we do? How many of these chairs and tables is broken and all that?" And the guy would rattle it off, and they'd pay him 250, 300 dollars, whatever it was. Then they'd put their arm around me. I'd say, "Now, you guys are gonna have to go home for the night," and they'd say, "OK, Jim, we're going." I'd go outside and talk to 'em for a while and then they'd leave. Well, I inherited them, too.

They got mad at a new bartender down in Riviera about nine or 10 years ago. The Dowlearn brothers didn't take anything off anybody, and this new bartender had a bad habit. It's all right for a bar to have a gun at the cash register, but he was always showing this .38 around and waving it at people. He waved it at the wrong guy when Ray and Bud Dowlearn were in there, just the two of 'em. He said, "You either calm down and turn that jukebox down or I'm gonna run you out of here," and he showed 'em the pistol.

Well, Bud walked over there and said, "Let me see that again." The bartender showed it to him and Bud grabbed it, jerked it out of his hand, pulled him over the top of the counter, and then Ray got into it. Ray got behind him and pinned him down, and he kicked him in the shins and they fell over to the floor. Then, with Ray holding him, Bud took his pistol and stuck it right in the middle of his forehead and pulled the trigger. There were 12 witnesses in there that saw that, though the ones that had had any sense had gone out of the front door when they saw the Dowlearns making their move. But they shot that SOB.

I got out of bed, got my people. My people were out on 24-hour patrol and had it all laid out by the time I got there. The ambulance was picking up this mother. It took him to the local hospital and they saw a hole in the front of his head and a hole in the back, so they rushed him to Corpus Memorial Hospital where they found out that that bullet went in, traveled around the skull, and came out through the skin back there. The guy didn't even get a headache. They reamed it out with iodine, or something like that, as best they could, gave him a massive tetanus shot, put a Band Aid on the front and a Band Aid on the back, and released that sucker from the hospital.

Of course we filed attempted murder charges on 'em, both of 'em, tried to get 'em together. I had the gun, I had the slug that fell out on the floor, we had eyewitnesses, we had everything. But also, the defense attorney had the doctors that had treated him here and the ones that treated him there, and people that testified that the guy was back down walking around the next day at Riviera. Soon, the good citizens ran his butt completely out of Kleberg County for me. And do you know that the defense attorney got Ray, who had held him, acquitted—acquitted, for attempted murder! And then he got Bud, who pulled the trigger, and argued that it was self-defense because the guy had threatened to kill him, and got him out on 10 years probation! Ten years for that sort of attempted murder. Now that's what I call Kleberg County justice.

Isn't that amazing, 10 years probation for that? We do send people up to the penitentiary, but we've never sent anybody up for a capital case out of Kleberg County, to my knowledge. If a guy's daughter gets raped, the grand jury is gonna no bill it. We've taken 'em before the grand jury as a precaution to keep 'em from being sued. If a guy shoots his wife's lover, even to this day, the grand jury here will no bill him.

I'm still a personal sheriff, just like my dad. They know that they can call, and we've got a 1-800 number for our out-of-the-city calls, a long distance line. A lot of people just want personal service, and they get it, there's no argument about it. If they ask for help, I give it to 'em. Sometimes that takes a trip to Houston and wherever it takes. I've had to go to Aspen, Colorado, to bring back a person who went berserk and had a mental problem on an airplane. That was a public service, that's all it was.

The latest call was about a 16-year-old girl whose family lives out in the county. This man says, "My daughter didn't come back last night." I say, "Well, I'm sure she's all right." He said, "I'm afraid something happened to her, she went out on a date." I said, "Who'd she go with?" He says, "That's another thing, I don't like this boy. Now, I didn't call your office 'cause I want anybody else to know this, I just want you to know. I don't want the police department to be looking for her or your department to be looking for her, or anything." So, I'll get out there and go to every motel in town in person and describe this boy, and find out if they are or if they are not in Kleberg County. If they are, I'll call him back, say, "She's out here at the Sage Motel, unit four." And then I'll leave it, I won't bother with it anymore.

I have found runaway girls in motels out of the county with the help of other sheriff's departments. One case, the guy said, "I want you to get her and bring her home, but I don't want to see that boy. I'm afraid I'll kill him. I don't even want to know who he is." This was a case where the father knew she was out seeing a boy, but didn't know his name. We've done that, we've found girls out of the county. They'll bring 'em as far as our county line, and I go get her and take her home, and even my deputies don't know about it. I do that; I don't do it every week, but it happens pretty regularly. They don't want the embarrassment of any knowledge, you see.

Some of these personal calls are worse than that, especially about doper kids, pregnant girls that have to get sent off, things like that. They've come to me and said, "Where is a good place for my daughter to go to have this child?" I don't even tell my wife. My wife doesn't know what we've been doing down here till she reads it in the paper. I've been that way, my father was that way, my grandfather was that way. Some of those people now resent me because they know I know their family secrets, and I feel uncomfortable about it, because when I say hello to 'em they give me that jaundiced look, like, "I wonder who he's told?" Yet they call me knowing that I won't tell anybody. They know that whatever the problem is, it's gonna stay with me.

And then, I get calls about marital squabbles. I had a couple that lived down at Layola Beach on the bay who fought all the time. There are a lot of nice homes down there facing the water, private piers and everything. He was a retired Navy pilot and they fought all the time, but they wouldn't fight if I was out of town. They'd find out, and they wouldn't fight if I was, 'cause they didn't want anybody there but me. They'd call me and I'd get out of bed and drive down there. What I'd do in these husband and wife fights was to get in and calm things down, and then let the wife talk and make the husband keep his damn mouth shut and just sit there. She'd get the whole problem off her chest, tell me what happened, what brought it on again, what she expects from him, and blah, blah, blah, blah, blah, blah. When she's finished, she's run down and gotten it out of her system and is usually a lot calmer. Then I let him talk, and he usually starts out in a tirade and wants to wring her damn neck. Finally, when it's all over with and he's got his part said, I get into the conversation a little bit then and ask one of them, "Well, if so-and-so does this, won't that make a difference?"—

whatever the problem is. If they're people I've known a long time I try to think of something pleasant where we were all together at a social function, or something about the family where the boy won a track meet, anything that's pleasant for 'em. I bring all that up and try to reminisce as much as I can. Then after a little while I say, "Look, you guys are wasting my time. Why don't you kiss and make up?" Well, they do, and then they want me to get the hell out of there, 'cause they're all made up now and I've done my thing. I used to do a lot more of that than I do now, but I have some of 'em that I know their secrets and (they) are resentful of it. When they look at me, they always look like, "Well, that son-of-a-bitch remembers all of that."

Another thing that goes way back in this sheriff department is our relationship to the King Ranch. I had a sheriff approach me in Las Vegas in '73. The National Association of Sheriffs meeting was over, and this group was sitting there at the bar having a drink and swapping lies and all that kind of stuff. This sheriff from Missouri named Williams walked over and introduced himself. He said, "Aren't you the sheriff from Kleberg County?" I said, "Yessir." He said, "The King Ranch is in your county?" I said, "Nossir, it's sure not." He looked kind of bewildered. I said, "My county is in the King Ranch. There are nine others besides me." He's since been down here to visit me, and I took him all over the King Ranch, and he still just couldn't believe it.

My dad loved peacock and learned to eat 'em in Lee County. From time to time, someone would come in the King Ranch drive going fast and run over two or three of their peacocks. If Bob Kleberg or somebody else run over one and it wasn't ruined, it had to be cleaned up, dressed, and sent in to my dad. That was just the tradition. If any of 'em accidentally got killed, it went to the "Jefe." Dad always had a peacock or two in the freezer.

There's a bunch of 'em out there to this day, and you know, they're curious old things and kind of get in the way. They're left over from Captain King's daughter, Mrs. Kleberg. Those were her things, and she had every duck and goose that you could think of out in a big pond out behind that house while I was a little boy. Mrs. King died in 1926, and Mrs. Kleberg, her daughter, died in 1943. I was a warrant officer in the war when Dad called and told me, and I came home for her funeral. I remember Mrs. King. I remember going out to the King Ranch with my dad and granddad to say hello to old man Kleberg, Senior, and she would be there. She always wore high-collared dresses and hooked shoes, those ladies' shoes that came up over the ankle, even in the summertime. The thing I remember, when the families went in and visited, it was cool out on the porch and the drink was always buttermilk, that's what they served. Course, the men may have been sniffing something else 'round at the side, but everybody drank their buttermilk.

The King Ranch brought the college here. Dad and everybody else worked campaigning by train and Model T all over the Valley with everybody else fighting for it, too. The King Ranch gave all the land and built the first buildings. This has been a King Ranch town up until just right now. No one does anything, unless they do it deliberately, to offend the King Ranch, I've seen 'em do too much in my lifetime for the people. When the Depression was on, they sent Percheron horses with wagons loaded with fresh slaughtered beef and beans and Irish potatoes going down all the streets of Kingsville. All you had to do was come out with your own utensils and fill 'em up. You got beans, you got flour, you got Irish potatoes, you got fresh-killed meat, and you got milk, because they had a big dairy products plant here. I saw that with my own eyes as a kid. They've been benefactors. There's not a church in South Texas that didn't get their land given to 'em, free, for their church building.

There are nine King Ranch deputies on the ranch payroll. They're all my deputies and are certified Texas police officers, but they don't wear guns and badges. They have King-Ranch-bought radio equipment and we dispatch for 'em, the whole nine yards. They handle trespass, poaching, illegal hunters, stuff like that. And whenever I've got a civil paper, I just call security out there and tell 'em, "Hey, I got a paper for a Placio Maldenado," and they say, "Come on out, send your man out, Jim, and we'll find out where he is." Or they may serve it themselves. They're Kleberg County deputy sheriffs.

It's a unique arrangement. Up around Victorio there's the Honor Ranch, there's the Welder Ranch, they've all got their security people, but Sheriff Dutch Myer, he wouldn't dream of deputizing one of those guys. They're private and can't arrest anybody on the roads. But the King Ranch can catch an old boy trespassing, and if he jumps the fence and hops in his car, they can run him down the state highway and still arrest him, 'cause they're deputy sheriffs. The Ranch really appreciates this.

We don't have much cattle rustling anymore. Before '72 they did, they had a bunch of cattle rustling cases. My father and his good friend, Texas Ranger Joe Briggs, were a real cattle rustling team. Once, my dad threw a barbecue for Company D of the Texas Rangers that lasted a whole week. Dad and Joe Briggs were renowned for breaking up cattle rustling down here in Kleberg County and in other counties in South Texas. Dad played the good guy and Joe played the bad guy when they'd get a suspect in. They didn't run off cattle in a herd like the old movies show, that only happened on the cattle trail, way back beyond my people's time. The cattle rustling that was common down here all this time has been for a cattle rustler to go get a calf for you and butcher and sell it to you. It was just like you order dope right now, or like you order a certain kind of TV set for burglars to go out and get what you order. Rustlers would slaughter meat for their own families, too, but it was mostly commercial. They'd actually go out and slaughter beef and deliver it and sell it, and it had to be close by, you know, (because) there was no refrigeration. It wasn't possible to get away with 10 at once, then.

OK, but now as trailers came into vogue after World War II, and as these little local sales barns came into vogue, rustling changed again. When I grew up down here, and even just after the war, my dad and all these little ranchers down here had to ship their cattle all the way to San Antonio. That was the nearest market to auction off live cattle. But then these local sales barns came in at Alice, Hebronville, Beeville, and so on, and you didn't have to go over 40 miles to sell a trailerload of cattle, or 10 trailerloads for that matter. Then rustlers started using these big cattle trucks where they could let down the gates, and the gates then became the walkways, and then you could steal a whole load of cattle again, like in the old days.

In 1972 a man named Woelfel lost a bunch to a goose-necked trailer. He was getting ready to ship, and overnight they just walked in there, ran 'em through his chute into their gooseneck, and that was the end of those 12 or 14 head. I've only had four instances of cattle being rustled that were for real, four in 14 years, when it used to be 10 or 12 a year. The difference is my 24-hour patrols. The cattle raisers' ranger who works out of Kingsville doesn't even hang around Kleberg County, hardly. He said, "Jim, when you went into 24-hour patrol you knocked it in the head, 'cause they never know when one of your cars is gonna ride up on 'em." We really put an end to it, and I'm real proud of that. But the criminals have remained criminals. The same families that were cattle rustlers have gone into dope dealing and auto theft.

We have a 24-hour patrol. We check all the school buildings, we check all the public buildings. If you're gone on vacation, we check your farm. I have got 29 sworn deputies, and that includes my dispatchers, 'cause they're sworn deputies, they're not just clerks. I've got 29 sworn deputies, nine more deputies on the King Ranch, and myself, and a cook. My cook is the only person in my department that is not a certified police officer, and also my jailers are all certified jailers.

It takes a minimum of three years to make a man a really effective patrolman. We rotate so they get familiar with all the nooks and crannies in the south part of the county and also do the same thing for the north. The city handles most of Kingsville, and we don't patrol in the city limits of the town, but if we get a call on a burglary, a fight, a disturbance, or something, we respond, and there's no problem with the police department. Quite often the police department has got a guy tied up with something, say they're answering a fight call from a family or at one of these bars. Well, our night patrol will swing in behind the city policeman and be back up. We'll go in there with him. And if we're close to the city limits, like a quarter of a mile, we'll ask the city to come out there with us to back us up. And the city police, highway patrolmen, National Seashore cops, game wardens—all these guys are on my radio frequency, and it pays off in a thousand ways.

I've got 36 reserve deputies in the county, too, and these are farmers, pharmacists, college professors, retired military and Exxon people, unemployed people, housewives. They're all in our reserves, and they're required to help us eight hours a month. They help patrol Padre Island in the summertime, and work with the constable whose main job is to take care of that seven miles of the beach that is not part of the Seashore, just to find lost dogs and children and to keep the sand dune rats from stealing watches and cameras and stuff like that. Every weekend, starting in the spring, we send a patrol of two old-time reserves over there to work Padre Island. My reserves live out in the county and people know it. They all have my radio in their pickup trucks, and all it takes to go on duty is to radio in and say, "There's a problem out here. This is so-and-so, call sign number, put me on the duty roster and log me in, and ask the lieutenant if he wants me to handle this."

DPS is on my frequency and the Texas Ranger's office is right there next door to me. By doing all that, those guys are mine, too. One thing my dad told me was, "Be sure to take care of the Department of Public Safety men and the game wardens, 'cause they're gonna take care of you." And I do that. They all have my radio frequency, we do all the dispatching for 'em, and it pays off like a charm when we get on a manhunt, and we've had some lulus down here. Sometimes people will run that King Ranch check point and get out on the Ranch. There have been times when we've been down here with bloodhounds, helicopters, light airplanes, deputies on foot, Border Patrol on foot— I've just had a little army working out there. And it's fun, long as nobody gets hurt or killed or shot.

There were four guys that had escaped from my jail, and two of 'em were seen getting out of a truck and running into the Ranch six or seven miles northwest of Kingsville on the road to Alice. T. O. Kleberg, the young manager of the Ranch, used that as an occasion to burn off 70,000 acres of the Santa Gertrudis Ranch. Every spring they burn off,

especially over here at Lometta. Man, do they burn it, it just looks like
the world is on fire over there! Occasionally the wind turns, and then
they get sued by Corpus Christi. But he burned it off this time, and
thanked me later and said, "I tell you what, you let three of 'em go
again next year and we'll run 'em out here and I won't let 'em get
away." One of these two went to Bishop and we caught him later,
but the fire flushed one of 'em out. Lee Duckworth, my chief of security at that time, was in an unmarked car and was working Highway
141 in the flames and smoke and everything. Then here was this kid
running out in the road. He wasn't even thumbing, he was waving him
down. Lee stopped, threw the door open, said, "Get in, son!" He
jumped in. Then Lee said, "You're under arrest, you little son-of-
a-bitch."

Padre Island National Seashore is a special problem for us. I can't
get to Padre Island without driving 60 miles out of my county. I have
to leave Kleberg County, drive 60 miles through Nueces County, down
on their part of Padre Island, until I come to the county line. That's
60 miles from this courthouse. So, when we've got a murder or a rape
or a suicide or a drowning, we've got that kind of a trip to take.

It's a problem. I never understood why they didn't give the National Seashore the whole damn thing, then all I would have to do is
respond to felony situations. As it stands now, the National Seashore
takes care of misdemeanors. On aggravated assaults, rapes, murders,
attempted murders and attempted rapes, and expensive burglaries, we
have joint jurisdiction. If it's on the Seashore, it's the FBI or us. We
don't get a lot of support out of the feds anymore. There's only three
FBI people now in Corpus where there used to be eight, two DEA
agents for this seven-county area where they used to be 17, and four
customs agents where there used to be 10. Those are all Reagan's cuts.
The feds rely on us more and more. If a crime happens on our part
of the Island, from the northern boundary of the Seashore to Nueces
County, it's all ours, and we have a constable there all the time. And
on weekends, like Fourth of July and Labor Day, and all, I might have
four reserve deputies over there and two patrol cars in addition to the
constable and deputy constable.

I had a demographic study done by Professor Richard Davis of the
sociology department at Texas A & I in 1975. On our seven miles of
Padre Island at one time there were 45,000 on the beach—13,000 more
than my county, which had a population of 33,000. They're all
together, a hodge-podge of people: Yankees, Canadians, Kleberg
County people, Houston people, Dallas people, Oklahoma, Kentucky,
Colorado people. And runaway girls, runaway girls, you could use a
bus just to handle the runaway girls!

We couldn't even hope to stay up with our law enforcement

problems here without the help of modern technology. My granddad had to get all his law enforcement checks on IDs and such through the U.S. Mails, and when my dad was police chief they had a signal for him and they had a signal for the sheriff. There was a water tower down by the old city hall with a red light that they could turn on when there was an emergency. If it was a straight, solid beam, without blinking, it was for the sheriff, and if it blinked off and on, it was for the chief of police. People in town knew that, and when they saw the signal they'd go in the house and pick up the phone and tell the operator to call Dad, that his light was blinking. Those were very peaceful days, I suppose.

Corpus had the first mobile police radios in Texas. My dad then got convinced, and in 1935 we got two-way Motorola radios and a dispatcher, and the King Ranch bought and paid for all of it. That was right after my dad became sheriff. I'll tell you another first. The Kingsville Police Department and the Kleberg County Sheriff's Department were the first to get these new high-band radios in 1973, first in the state of Texas. The DPS didn't get them till three years later. I was letting the DPS officers use my radios. With these high-band radios there's reduced interference.

For criminal records, as well as for drivers' licenses, license plates, drivers' records and so forth, we're linked into the DPS system, the TCIC, the Texas Crime Information Center. Every sheriff's department and police department in the state of Texas has the same identical Teletype, and we converge on Austin through the TCIC. These are high speed, too. I can have that information so fast it would make your head swim. And we're tied right in to NCIC, that's the FBI's network, the National Crime Information Center. And I can go direct to any state on my Teletype. I can go straight to a sheriff in New Mexico or Arizona, and I do. They have state Teletype systems just like ours. Nearly every town in the United States with over 2,500 population has one of these Teletypes in its police station, and I can go directly to any of 'em, or they to me. All they have to have is my access code, and there's a big index that lists 'em all. We use the damn telex all day long, all the time. We do a lot of welfare work, helping people get emergency messages from home and locate missing persons and stuff like that. It's a beautiful network. I don't know how they survived without it in the past. Then, like my grandfather, all they had was the U.S. Mails.

The FBI gets any Interpol information for us, and they act as our contact. Interpol is a world-wide international police organization. It has different functions in different countries, but it has to do with international fugitives, and it's a busy damn place.

Of course, the real intelligence is still transferred direct, person-to-person. I deal real closely with Customs because of my friend down there. The leading officer, the agent in charge, of Corpus worked his way through college as my dispatcher. I have personal friends at the two nearest Customs offices to here, and they keep me informed and I do the same for them. They come in here and ride around where no one can eavesdrop, and I update 'em on what I know and they tell me things.

I was instrumental in starting what we call a multi-county task force. We ended up calling it the Coastal Bend Major Crimes Task Force. It's made up of investigators from all of our police departments, sheriff departments, DPS, Rangers, some constables. We pool our resources and the intelligence flows back and forth. Really, most of our intelligence is where we keep in touch with each other and pass it on to each other. We have a Coastal Bend Peace Officers Association that is 14 counties. It's made up of all federal officers in our area, the DPS officers, sheriff's deputies, constables, even campus security here at A & I, and all police departments. We have a barbecue every 90 days and get together socially to eat barbecue and drink beer and swap lies, and at the same time we're passing information and helping each other out.

We have to, because it's unbelievable now on drugs. What Commissioner Van Rabb told the Senate or the Congressional Committee on Dangerous Drugs about de la Madrid (Miguel de la Madrid Hurtado) and his damn henchmen and Mexican authorities in the drug trade is absolutely true. Lord, yes! It hasn't been 10 years since at Rockport they caught the chief of police of Matamoros in a stolen Cadillac.

Down here the drug-running and the gun-running are all tied in together. We're working on boats through the Cut, we're working several drugs and gun-running cases that I can't talk about. I've got one boat that is taking in cocaine from Mexico. It's a Gulf shrimper, come up through the Cut, goes all the way out to Rockport. It unloads some stuff here, goes to Corpus and unloads for the Victorio–Corpus area, goes on up to Rockport and lets some little stuff out there. Then that's where the main load goes into automobiles and trucks and heads straight to the panhandle of Florida. Would you believe that the feds and the locals and the snitches have gotten Florida so saturated that they can't get it in there by airplane or boat anymore, they're doing it by driving from Texas all the way to the Florida Panhandle to supply cocaine? I've been working with Customs on that. We've confirmed that some of our dopers got in a 16-foot boat and went out when it was too choppy for anybody in their right mind, and were gone six-and-a-half hours. Then, when we made a call to Nueces County and they ran a paper on these people, they found about two hundred ki- los of marihuana, and you could just run your fingers down the pack- ages and lick 'em and taste the salt. That was the stuff that was unloaded in that choppy water. So, we're just beginning to lock that one up, we're busy.

The United States has special drug task forces. The first one was in Florida, but now they've got one in the New York area, they've got one in the Chicago area, one in the Los Angeles area, and they're work- ing like dogs. But the trouble is, they've just made people like us more vulnerable. It's all coming in this bay now, up that Cut, coming out of Mexico, when before, Florida handled at least all the hard stuff. And have you seen the Cable News Network? What is it, a third of the Mia- mi police have been indicted for dealing in drugs?

And it's coming up our damn highways, grandmothers are bringing it. I don't know what to tell you there! Everybody but you and I are selling narcotics, and I don't know about you. That's the way it is, we're overrun, and so is every little spot, I suppose, in the United States. Those of us on the border are on the main route, and we're just catching tons of it down here at our check point through the Bor- der Patrol. We're just overrun with dope, and we can't do any under- cover work in our own goddamn county. They know us like they know their school teachers. The feds can't furnish us undercover operators like they once did, so there we are. Narcotics are our biggest problem. Hell, I'm no different than anybody else. Every little sheriff in South Texas has got several things going. We'd give a million dollars if we had a lot of buy-money, and if I could call Houston or Austin and get me five goddamn undercover people in here—you know, do it right. We can't. We're flat ass doing it the hard, hard, hard way, and it's frustrating.

We have Customs intelligence and we've got our own snitches. We've got dopers that are jealous of each other. They'll tell just to get their competition caught. They have fallings out with each other. If we get any intelligence here, we see that it goes to the sheriff or chief of police that needs it, and visa versa. We're always meeting in little places and calling each other on the telephone, passing on infor- mation. It's like a damn war.

We caught an empty 18-wheeler going north with 18-hundred pounds of marihuana on board. For them it was worth the risk. That's what all this stuff is, worth the risk. And these kids with a hundred pounds caught all the time, two-hundred pounds at a check point, they're just mules. They're being paid to run the stuff. They're told, "You go to the Holiday Inn. There's gonna be a grey Chevrolet there with license number such-and-such. The keys are gonna be on the floor under the front seat. You get in and you drive it to the Ramada Inn on Highway 59 in the south end of Houston, and you park it in front of door number so-and-so, get out and leave. And this thousand dollars is yours, and we'll use you again.'' And we're busting 'em, we're fining the shit out of 'em, they're paying their fines, and they're putting 'em on probation. For a while on the small cases, Prosecutor Berg was just taking the illicit drug and letting 'em go, not even writing their names down or their license plate numbers. There ain't no way that the prosecutor can file all those damn little cases. You're talking about 40 or 50 a month.

We're just now getting crack in our area and into Corpus, and we're getting the black tar heroin from Mexico, which is deadly. That has just now hit Kleberg County. It was on the streets just this last week. We've got about 250 known heroin addicts in Kingsville. Only 15 of those are going to Corpus for methadone every week, then we've got about 12 on Trexan in treatment by the doctor that dispenses it here. So, all the rest of 'em, then, are taking heroin. Our roughest estimate— and you got to appreciate what I'm saying, that this is just an estimate—is that the town of Kingsville is being burglarized and armed robbery and muggings and so forth to the extent of 21 to 23-million dollars a year, just from our heroin addicts. When you look at it that way in a little town, it gives you an idea what it's doing to our nation. I happen to agree wholeheartedly that we're at war, and it's gonna take this nation down if we don't do something about it.

The drug problem is the root of nearly all our armed robberies, thefts, burglaries. We've always had auto theft, but it sure has increased since the drug problem has increased in the '80s. I would guess that 90 percent of our crime is drug-related, even the rapes. A guy gets spaced out on speed or something like that and he'll commit rape.

I've got to say something in favor of what de la Madrid said. De la Madrid said, ''If you son-of-a-bitches weren't such a wonderful market, we wouldn't be sending you narcotics.'' So, it comes back to us, that we are the market. The United States has become the world market for all illicit drugs.

My dad, bless his heart, was old-fashioned, but he believed in the methadone program. He believed in it wholeheartedly. He said, ''Whatever they're on, the government should provide it with tax money, so that they don't stick a dirty needle in their arm, and keep 'em high. If they want to be high, that's a offense against themselves.'' He said, ''I think if we provide it, if we put a certain percentage of marihuana in cigarettes so that you could walk up to a drugstore and say, 'I want Winston ten-percent,' that would knock the hell out of marihuana and the price of drugs, if you gave it freely to every addict." It would wipe out the crime, it would kill the Mafia; it really would, he was absolutely right. He said, "They ought to be able to smoke the damn stuff. I got kids upstairs going to jail that should be going to college." I don't disagree with that, but a lot of my colleagues would. I remember Prohibition, and legalizing booze at the end of it didn't change our ethics or our morals one way or the other, 'cause the people that wanted it, got it. Course, they got bathtub gin, crap like that.

I've known Chief Mason down in Brownsville personally for 15 years. He was a policeman here in Kingsville. Ed and I have always helped each other. He sent a guy up here to do some undercover work, a few years ago, on a bodyshop that was building all kinds of little hidden compartments to stash guns to go across the bridge into Mexico. Off and on he'd tell me, "Hey, there's some stuff coming through your county," or about a boat or something like that. Hell, I've spent many a night myself in the past out there with ticks and fleas biting me, cold, wet, tired, and nothing happened. Once it took three days and three nights, and nothing. That's the way a lot of that work is.

Anyway, he called and then he came in to see me and sit down with Dick Mosley. He said, "Look, we got this airplane and he's making little triangle flights out of El Salvador, Panama, different places down there. He goes from Salvador to California, where he sells the cocaine. Then he brings the cash to Florida, and he has to stop here." They'd made three runs down here. Once before they'd refueled at Kleberg County, the other two times they'd refueled at Alice, Texas. He said, "I've talked to Sheriff Lopez over in Alice and I'm talking to you. He's gonna refuel somewhere here in Kleberg County or Jim Wells County. What they do, they file their flight plan to go on to Florida, but when they get airborne they gonna change their flight plan to El Salvador, get out across the Gulf, and go down there with all that money and buy more cocaine. They're doing all this to finance the rebels in El Salvador. This is not Reagan's people. We're supporting Duarte's government down there. This is the other side."

He said, "The other two times they just made little token runs to see if they could do it. Their last biggie was when they had exactly one-million dollars out of Panama, to California, to here. Then it was supposed to be Florida, but they ended up going to Honduras or someplace else." He said, "The co-pilot is a U.S. Customs man. Jim, we're not gonna be giving you much notice. You're gonna be getting a call from Agent Alexander, who will be in an airplane tailing them out of sight." They never did tell me, but I had the idea that there was a beacon put on somewhere around the tail assembly of that plane where you could follow him five miles back, and just follow him like you were looking at him.

Anyway, here's how much notice we got. The telephone rang and it was Alexander calling us, saying, "We got a call from the airplane and they're on the ground at the county airport in Kleberg County refueling right now. Hold the plane and its occupants and whatever's aboard for Customs." We dispatched a man right out of the office and a state trooper with him. They got to the airport, which is 10 miles away, in 12 minutes. Those guys were already walking out of operations, the plane was refueled, parked out on the front ready to roll, when we pulled up and stopped everybody.

I got to hand it to my boys, there were 14 suitcases in that airplane and two people, and that's a few too damn many suitcases, but they controlled themselves. I was so glad that Al Gutierrez was out there, he had a lot of experience. I'd taught my people to never rush, because when you rush you don't know what in the hell you're doing. We just sat there. We didn't get Customs there for 10 hours. We even rotated another group out there to guard the men and the airplane. God, they wanted to open those suitcases! We called in Border Patrol to run an immigration check on the individuals in the airplane, and tried to see if we could find any amount of illegal drug on the floor, under the seat, or anywhere. You could smell it and you could see little pieces of powder, but not anything you could put your fingers on. So, anyway, INS, they're capable of doing this, they picked up the suitcases and put 'em under the wing, but didn't pop one of 'em open. One of their guys started to do it, and Al Gutierrez said, "They're ain't no aliens in there," so he put it down. A good thing, 'cause that would have blown our case. Finally, Customs came on the scene and we got Bob Berg, our U.S. assistant prosecutor, over here with some more Customs men, and we got the most beautiful legal search you ever saw.

Soon after that, we had 'em all in my jail and we were interrogating 'em. The federal government has got a little form, you know, that they fill out on everybody. At three o'clock in the morning we cut the co-pilot, the government agent, loose there in Kingsville. Everybody said, "I don't understand, what happened to that one guy?" He was cut loose and the others were taken, and 5,963,000 dollars and some goddamn cents went to Nueces County! And of course, they held it as evidence until they got in federal court.

I didn't know I was even entitled to any of that money, Customs told me. The President signed a bill in 1984 where federal agencies could share with state and local officials that assist in drug busts. Well, this wasn't a drug bust, this was a money bust, they were taking United States currency, without reporting it, out of the country. But anyway, I got in on it and I plan to use that one-million dollars to help build Kleberg County a new jail. I'm the first agency in the United States to get a million dollars cash. They've shared in equipment, they've shared in boats, busses. They've shared in all that under this law, but I'm the first one to get in on a million dollars. I'm also the first one to hand them nearly six million, too!

But what really burned me up is that they gave them back the airplane, and had them sign a release that they had no damn claim on the money. I knew that airplane is worth five-million dollars, and I raised hell. "What's the idea of giving that son-of-a-bitch back that goddamn airplane? We can double our take on this thing." They said, "All we can tell you, Sheriff, is there was a reason, and we asked the prosecutor and the judge to make a deal and give those guys probated sentences and pay a fine and forfeit the money, and let 'em have their airplane. That's all I can tell you." Well, six weeks later the same plane, same guy that owned it, same pilot, was caught in Puerto Rico with eight-million dollars worth of coke. Shit! This time they got the airplane. They were trying to make up that six-million-dollar loss.

It could be that the last Scarborough hasn't been sheriff yet. My son became a science teacher, teaching chemistry and biology; but in '67 he called me on the phone and said, "I just resigned. I can't stand it anymore. I'm gonna be a cop," and boy, I went through the ceiling. I said, "Dan, I didn't send you to college to be a goddamn cop." I cut myself a leave and got down to Sinton as fast as I could. I said, "Let's go talk to the superintendent and get all this straightened out." He said, "I can't. I burned my bridges real well. I told both of those guys where they could go and what they could do."

He insisted that he was gonna be in law enforcement. I made him promise that he'd either go to the federal government or the state, that he wouldn't be a deputy sheriff or a city policeman someplace. He did. He put in for the Fish and Game school and they snapped him up, and I don't think anyone has graduated with higher academic honors than he since he graduated 14 years ago. They assigned him to Dallas, but the King Ranch wanted him, and Dad wanted him down here; so without telling me about it, they got him transferred to Raymondsville, which is just 54 miles below us. He remained a game warden for over 12 years, then they offered him the chief deputy's job in Kenedy County. Kenedy County has six-hundred people and 200,000 head of cattle.

He lives in a double-wide trailer out on the Garcia Ranch in the southern part of the county. He's got it and 19 acres that they rent (to) him for a whole dollar a year. He speaks Spanish with a "you all" accent. The Mexicans love to talk to him, because he talks so slowly.

My granddad was called "Sheriff Jim," my dad was called "Mr. Jim" or "Jefe," and I was called "Baby Jim." They had to distinguish between us somehow. While I was in my first year in office, or maybe the second year, my dad was still alive and getting around pretty well. Old Jim Barnes, the shine man, the only one left in the county, was shining my boots one day when he said, "Sheriff, Mrs. Lily needs to see you. She's got a problem, she's got a grandson from Chicago that's down here forcing her to write checks. He's stealing things and hocking 'em, and he's got a motorcycle, and he has parties. He's abusing her." He was talking about Lily Caraway, the widow of a railroad brakeman that lived next door to him. I said, "OK, Jim, if you see her when you get home, tell her I'll be down after work for sure today."

So I drove up to her house and got out. Jim Barnes was sitting on the porch waiting, and he looked over and saw me and joined me. He took me to the door and knocked. He hollered, "Mrs. Lily, Mrs. Lily, I got the sheriff here. He's come to see you." She said, "Y'all come in." She stayed seated, and I walked in and she looked up and said, "Baby Jim. I didn't send for you, Baby Jim. If I'd have wanted Baby Jim, I'd have asked for Baby Jim. I want the sheriff!"

I said, "OK, Miss Lily, I'll take care of that." So I walked out to my car and got on the radio and told 'em to call home and tell my dad to be sure he was ready to roll. I was coming to pick him up and I needed him for an emergency. So I took Dad in there, and she explained about all the abuse this boy was doing. She said, "I want him run back to Chicago." And Dad says, "Well, Lily, we're gonna do that, but I'm gonna have to let Jim do it." Says, "He's the sheriff now, he took my place. I'm retired, I don't do anything anymore." She said, "Well, I knew if I told you I'd get it done." He said, "I'm gonna tell Jim, and Jim's gonna do it, then we'll let you know." She says, "OK, Sheriff."

I got ahold of the guy and gave him the old-time treatment and he left. I don't know if he went to Chicago, but he left and he has not come back. Baby Jim was the nickname that I had, because there was my grandfather, and my dad, and then me. I didn't like it as a child, naturally, but it tickles me now. When I see the elderly ladies in the post office they still call me "Baby Jim," and I kiss 'em all. But Lily wasn't having any part of Baby Jim, she wanted the sheriff.

BIOGRAPHICAL
NOTES

★

Tom Brown. Born: October 17, 1903. Died: April 24, 1979. Birthplace: Caldwell County, Texas. Law enforcement career: chief deputy sheriff of Caldwell County, 1933–1940; sheriff of Caldwell County, 1941–1946. Interviewed by Jim Lutz, January 19/February 16/March 10, 1977. Tapes at Barker Texas History Center, the University of Texas at Austin (hereafter BTHC).

Jess Sweeten. Born: May 7, 1905. Died: November 16, 1980. Birthplace: Enterprise community, Indian Territory. Law enforcement career: constable of Trinidad, Henderson County, 1929–1931; deputy sheriff of Henderson County, 1931–1932; sheriff of Henderson County, 1933–1955; special investigator for Mobile Oil Company, 1955–1970. Interviewed by James G. Dickson, 1979. Tapes in possession of James G. Dickson, Political Science Department, Stephen F. Austin State University, Nacogdoches, Texas.

Corbett Akins. Born: October 21, 1892. Birthplace: Fairplay community, Panola County, Texas. Law enforcement career: constable of

Athens, Panola County, 1938–1939; sheriff of Panola County, 1942–1952. Interviewed by students from *Loblolly* magazine, 1972–1985, and by Thad Sitton, May 4, 1986. Tapes at BTHC.

Gaston Boykin. Born: May 20, 1906. Birthplace: Sipe Springs, Comanche County, Texas. Law enforcement career: deputy sheriff of Comanche County, 1928; sheriff of Comanche County, 1947–1953, 1965–1977. Interviewed by Thad Sitton, February 10/February 26, 1986. Tapes at BTHC.

T. W. "Buckshot" Lane. Born: October 7, 1903. Birthplace: Matagorda, Matagorda County, Texas. Law enforcement career: constable, precinct one, Wharton County, 1932–1940; sheriff of Wharton County, 1941–1952. Interviewed by Thad Sitton, November 3/December 15, 1986. Tapes at BTHC.

Frank Brunt. Born: July 24, 1913. Birthplace: Alto, Cherokee County, Texas. Law enforcement career: special officer for Southern Pacific Railroad, 1936–1939; deputy sheriff of Cherokee County, 1939–1940; sheriff of Cherokee County, 1941–1954; special agent for Humble Oil Company, 1954–1975; sheriff of Smith County, 1983–1984. Interviewed by Thad Sitton, February 20–21, 1986. Tapes at BTHC.

H. F. Fenton. Born: July 29, 1922. Birthplace: New Central community, Coleman County, Texas. Law enforcement career: Pampa Police, 1946; sheriff of Coleman County, 1947–1960; field representative (special Texas Ranger) for Texas Sheep and Goat Raisers Association, 1961–1969; chief deputy sheriff of Coleman County, 1969–1975; sheriff of Coleman County, 1977–present. Interviewed by Thad Sitton, March 13–14, 1986. (Loretta Fenton interviewed by Thad Sitton, June 2, 1986.) Tapes at BTHC.

B. Rufus "Rufe" Jordan. Born: October 8, 1912. Birthplace: Grandview community, Gray County, Texas. Law enforcement career: correctional officer, Gray County Jail, 1931–1932; deputy sheriff of Gray County, 1946–1949; sheriff of Gray County, 1951–present. Interviewed by Thad Sitton, April 18–19, 1986. Tapes at BTHC.

Truman Maddox. Born: September 30, 1917. Birthplace: Oak Grove community, Madison County, Texas. Law enforcement career: chief deputy sheriff of Austin County, 1949–1952; sheriff of Austin County, 1953–present. Interviewed by Thad Sitton, March25/April 2, 1986. Tapes at BTHC.

I. R. "Nig" Hoskins. Born: April 17, 1908. Died: December 27, 1987. Birthplace: Red Rock, Bastrop County, Texas. Law enforcement career: correctional officer, Texas Department of Corrections, Harlem #1, Raymondville, Texas, 1927–1942; deputy sheriff of Bastrop County, 1952; sheriff of Bastrop County, 1953–1960, 1977–1980, 1985–1987. Interviewed by Thad Sitton, March 27/July 21, 1986. Tapes at BTHC.

Jim Scarborough, III. Born: September 15, 1920. Birthplace: Kingsville, Kleberg County, Texas. Law enforcement career: provost marshal, USAF, 1939–1971; sheriff of Kleberg County, 1972–present. Interviewed by Thad Sitton, April 28/June 25, 1986. Tapes at BTHC.